Adam and Eve in Scripture, Theology, and Literature

Adam and Eve in Scripture, Theology, and Literature

Sin, Compassion, and Forgiveness

Peter B. Ely

LEXINGTON BOOKS
Lanham • Boulder • New York • London

Published by Lexington Books
An imprint of The Rowman & Littlefield Publishing Group, Inc.
4501 Forbes Boulevard, Suite 200, Lanham, Maryland 20706
www.rowman.com

Unit A, Whitacre Mews, 26-34 Stannary Street, London SE11 4AB

Chapter one was previously published as "Paul Ricoeur on the Symbolism of Evil: A Theological Retrieval," in *Ultimate Reality and Meaning: Interdisciplinary Studies in the Philosophy of Understanding*, University of Toronto Press, vol. 24, no. 1, 2001.

Part of chapter three was previously published as "The Adamic Myth in the Christian Idea of Salvation," *Ultimate Reality and Meaning Journal*, vol. 28, no. 2, 2005.

Part of chapter four was previously published as "Forgiveness in Christianity," *Ultimate Reality and Meaning Journal*, vol. 27, no. 2, 2004.

Part of chapter five was previously published as "Chrysostom and Augustine on the Ultimate Meaning of Human Freedom," *Ultimate Reality and Meaning Journal*, vol. 29, no. 3, 2006.

Chapter eleven was previously published as "Detective and Priest: The Paradoxes of Simenon's Maigret," *Christianity & Literature*, vol. 59, issue 3, June 2010, 453-477.

British Library Cataloguing in Publication Information Available

Library of Congress Cataloging-in-Publication Data

Names: Ely, Peter B., author.
Title: Adam and Eve in scripture, theology, and literature : sin, compassion, and forgiveness / Peter B. Ely.
Description: Lanham : Lexington Books, 2018. | Includes bibliographical references and index.
Identifiers: LCCN 2017058247 (print) | LCCN 2017054680 (ebook) | ISBN 9781498573900 (Electronic) | ISBN 9781498573894 (cloth : alk. paper) | ISBN 9781498573917 (paperback)
Subjects: LCSH: Adam (Biblical figure) | Eve (Biblical figure)
Classification: LCC BS580.A4 (print) | LCC BS580.A4 E49 2018 (ebook) | DDC 222/.1106—dc23
LC record available at https://lccn.loc.gov/2017058247

To my brother, John, and our mother, Janet, who first taught us compassion, and to my sister in law, Kathy, who embodies it.

Contents

Preface

In a notebook written prior to his monumental novel, *In Search of Lost Time*, Marcel Proust observed, "The work [of writing] makes us a little like mothers"; he wondered if he would ever be able to bring what was in him to light (Proust 1988, xix). I now understand his use of this similie. The gestation of my study has been long indeed. The seeds of my interest in the connection between the story of Adam and Eve and forgiveness were planted when I first read Paul Ricoeur's magisterial 1967 work, *The Symbolism of Evil.* Ricoeur compares four *myths* relating to the origin and end of evil, one of them being the Adamic myth. I concluded from Ricoeur's study that only the Adamic myth—a good God, a good creation, and a disobedient humanity—opened up any possibility of forgiveness. But what was the connection between the Adamic myth—along with its offspring, the doctrine of original sin—and forgiveness? I wrestled with this question, and it is the question this book attempts to answer.

The crucial moment of awakening came during a month-long retreat at the Trappist Abbey of Our Lady of Guadalupe in Lafayette, Oregon. In the contemplative atmosphere of the monastery, thinking about the book I was about to begin, but had not yet begun to write, I came across an article from *Theological Studies*: Boyd Coolman's "Hugh of St. Victor on 'Jesus Wept': Compassion as Ideal *Humanitas*." Coolman's article explores the contents of Hugh of St Victor's (1096–1141) brief work, *On the Four Wills of Christ.* In this text, Hugh "offers a carefully nuanced depiction of Jesus' human nature that showcases his human capacity for compassion" (Coolman, 528). But, as Coolman points out, Hugh is eager not only to underscore Jesus' compassion, "but also to identify such fellow-feeling as the signature attribute of ideal human nature" (Ibid). Hugh of St Victor's moving treatment, as interpreted by Coolman, worked in my unconscious mind, what Proust calls the "involuntary imagination," until, in an unguarded moment, the notion of compassion pushed its way into my consciousness with a startling impact, as if it were an idea I had never before thought of. Here, at last, was my answer to the question I feared people would ask, "So what *is* the connection between sin—the disobedience of Adam and Eve, its consequences for their descendants, and the individual actual sins of human beings—and forgiveness?"

Coolman's article and Hugh's *The Four Wills of Christ* opened for me a pathway to explore possible connections between sin and forgiveness. In the light of my newly heightened awareness about the centrality of compassion, I reread texts beginning with the Old and New Testaments and saw with new clarity the pervasiveness of mercy. With the help of Peter Brown, author of the compelling biography, *Augustine of Hippo,* I came to see at the heart of Augustine's elaboration of original sin a movement toward compassion. Recognizing the universal tendency to sin disposed Augustine toward forgiveness of sins that were committed, not out of pride, but out of ignorance and weakness, "and often done by persons weeping and groaning" (Augustine *On Nature and Grace,* 29.33). I had found the theme of my book.

Compassion became a heuristic concept that influenced my re-interpretation of familiar texts, but also works I discovered in the course of writing this book. Such a book was Julian of Norwich's *Revelations of Divine Love.* Julian's visions showed her a troubling possibility that neither she nor anyone else could have derived from Church teaching, the possibility that God's compassion would mysteriously extend to universal salvation. Julian's *Revelations of Love* is the subject matter of chapter nine. Frederick Bauerschmidt's excellent work, *Julian of Norwich and the Mystical Body Politic of Christ,* finds in Julian's visions a way of imagining political life. "Julian should be read as *one who theologically imagines the political"* (Bauerschmidt, 3). And Julian's imagining of the political, according to Bauerschmidt, consists in seeing a society grounded in the compassionate image of Christ rather than the image of an omnipotent God. After I had finished my own manuscript, I discovered the compelling work of Cardinal Walter Kasper, *Mercy: The Essence of the Gospel and the Key to Christian Life.* And, of course, the writings of Pope Francis and, indeed, the tenor of his papacy, have confirmed the insights central to my work. Francis' work, *The Name of God is Mercy, A Conversation with Andrea Tornielli,* beautifully sets out what is most central to my own work. James Voiss' 2015 study, *Rethinking Christian Forgiveness: Theological, Philosophical, and Psychological Explorations*, a carefully developed account of how Christian forgiveness differs from other types of forgiveness, offers an important contribution to the field of forgiveness studies. Though Voiss does not explore an explicit connection between forgiveness and compassion, his conclusion about the distinctiveness of Christian forgiveness points in this direction. God forgives even before we repent, says Voiss, and opens a space for repentance. We might argue that the open space is precisely compassion. When my manuscript was already with the publisher, I discovered another book germane to my subject matter, Stephen Greenblatt's *The Rise and Fall of Adam and Eve*. Greenblatt's exploration of the origins of the Adam and Eve story, its varied interpretations, and its recurrence as a literary theme attests to the continuing inspirational power of this small but unforgettable narrative from the beginnings of the Judeo-Christian tradition.

I have come to see that compassion stands in a dialectical relationship with justice. Justice and compassion are two possible responses to sin—I am referring here to actual sin. Justice responds rationally to an injury done through sin by weighing the appropriate punishment, given the seriousness of the event, the intention of the one who did wrong, etc. Justice represents an advance over a more primitive response to wrong done through another's action, namely, vengeance. Vengeance rises up in the injured person as an immediate, irrational, quasi-physical response to the one who inflicted the injury. So the first dialectic is between vengeance and justice, but once justice has triumphed over vengeance, a new dialectic comes to the fore between justice and compassion. Whereas justice punishes in a rational, balanced, and appropriate way, compassion responds to the suffering that lies at the root of sins committed. Compassion opens up a new horizon within which to assess the harm done. Without excusing the evil done me, I am able to see that the one who offended me and I are not utterly different beings. The offender is not just evil, and I am not just good. In this book we will discover the dialectic of justice and compassion played out in a variety of settings; Julian of Norwich will push compassion, God's compassion in Christ, to its most extreme limit, such that God does not even blame the sinner. Other authors, as will become evident in the "Introduction," will explore this dialectic in a variety of ways.

Acknowledgments

I am grateful to Seattle University for granting me academic leave from the University in 2008–2009 to pursue this project and also to Santa Clara University for welcoming me and supporting my work with a Bannan Fellowship. Both the welcome and the fellowship provided a favorable environment for writing. I am particularly grateful to Sonny Manuel, Kevin Quinn, Jerry McKevitt, David John Pleins, Michael McCarthy, and all of Santa Clara, who supported my project in a variety of ways.

Four Seattle University professors—David Leigh, Valerie Lesniak, Cynthia Moe-Lobeda, and Jason Wirth read the first version of the manuscript and offered valuable advice and support. Other readers and scholars have helped with all or parts of the manuscript: John Topel, Jim Tracy, Karen and Dan Quinn-Shea, John Ely, Kathy Ely, Monica Horsman, Mike Herzog, and Matthew Whitlock. I am particularly grateful to Catherine Smith who read and edited the entire manuscript. Even more valuable than her editing was Catherine's enthusiastic support. Finally I acknowledge and thank the editors of *Christianity and Literature* for allowing me to reprint chapter eleven of *Ultimate Reality and Meaning*, and for permission to reprint portions of chapters one, three, four, and five. I am, of course, also most grateful to Sarah Craig, Julia Torres, and Meaghan Menzel of Lexington Books, for their assistance in bringing the manuscript to publication.

Introduction

Adam and Eve, Original Sin, Compassion, and Forgiveness

When he saw the crowds, he had compassion on them, because they were
harassed and helpless, like sheep without a shepherd.

—Matthew 9:36, NRSV[1]

This book considers the story of Adam and Eve, the history of its interpretations—especially the doctrine of original sin—and forgiveness. The Jahwist
editor who introduced the story of Adam and Eve into the Pentateuch was
giving an account of how hardship and difficulty and contradiction entered
into human life. More important, he was setting out the remedy, a way of
overcoming the consequences of the first couple's disobedience. The remedy
that emerges in the Hebrew Testament's description of God's relation to his
people is compassion. A tiny gesture on God's part offers an indication of the
response that would characterize God's relations with sinful humanity. Seeing their nakedness, God made leather garments for the couple (Gen 3:21).
Admittedly, the gesture is ambiguous. God could have just been providing
a better version of the fig leaves Adam and Eve had sewed together. David
Clines, as we will see in chapter two, notes this gesture as one of several
"mitigations" God devised to soften his punishments. Full forgiveness does
not take place in the Genesis account of Adam and Eve, but compassion does
emerge as a defining characteristic of God's dealing with his people in the
Hebrew Testament.

The mediating role of compassion between sin and forgiveness forms the
subject matter of this book. I will argue that compassion performs a crucial
mediating role, enabling people, once offended, to move toward forgiveness.
This position addresses a fundamental challenge both for human conceptions of God and for human self-understanding. A natural human tendency,

1

attributed even to God in our anthropomorphic representations, is to hold on to a hurt rather than let it go, and to contemplate vengeance rather than forgiveness. How, then, do individuals and groups move toward forgiveness? Through compassion. This, at least, is the argument the book advances.

This general proposition, however, applies differently to God and human beings. Compassion as a response to sin comes from the convergence of justice and mercy in God, who is by nature, as the reluctant prophet Jonah confessed, "a gracious and merciful God, slow to anger, rich in clemency, loathe to punish" (Jn. 4:2b). Or as Hosea puts it when describing God's intention to put an end to Israel's Exile: "My heart is overwhelmed, my pity is stirred. I will not give vent to my blazing anger, I will not destroy Ephraim again; For I am God not man, the Holy One present among you . . ." (Hos. 11:8–9). But the convergence of justice and mercy natural to God occurs in human beings only as the result of long effort sustained by grace. Some people seem by nature more disposed to compassion than others, but generally human beings struggle to be compassionate and thus must follow a different path than the one indicated by natural inclination. The general theory about the role of compassion as mediator between sin and forgiveness requires further elaboration, a kind of special theory.

If God moves through compassion toward forgiveness by the perfect blending of justice and mercy, what moves human beings? Original sin—not the doctrine, but the awareness of original sin in oneself—I will argue, acts as a powerful motive toward compassion and forgiveness. The consciousness that I personally participate, not only in the possibilities that belong to humanity, but also in a general vulnerability of the human will that frustrates those possibilities and leads to sin, helps me to be compassionate toward other sinners. Compassion means entering into the weakness, or suffering, or distress of the other person and seeing it as my own. If I cannot see that the sinner who did this or that horrible deed against me (or against us) shares a common human weakness that afflicts all human beings—including me, the offended—and if I cannot feel that weakness and find myself *at home* in it as a fellow traveler who could have done the same thing, or worse, then it is hard to be forgiving. Or, to put it positively, if I can feel this kind of compassion for the sinner, I have at least opened a path to forgiveness. If we all participate in what Alan Jacob calls the "democracy of sin" where no one is simply and without qualification *just* and no one completely wicked, we are more likely to be open to forgiveness. John Paul II has said that there is no peace without justice and no justice without forgiveness.

Two examples will illustrate the thesis. Everett Worthington, a psychologist who has written extensively on the dynamics of forgiveness, found himself in a position that seemed at first to give the lie to his own commitment to empathy as an opening to forgiveness. His mother was brutally murdered in her home by a young man who broke in to burglarize. Worthington found himself filled with rage and thoughts of vengeance toward the young man. "I'd like to have that murderer alone in a room with just a baseball bat. I'd beat his brains out" (Worthington 1999b; Schimmel, 100). This desire made Worthington wonder if he really believed what he had written about forgiveness, namely "that empathy was a key to forgiving." So imagining the scene of the crime, Worthington reconstructed what he thought must have happened. The young man, he suspected, had broken in to rob without any intention of harming anyone, thinking that the occupant of the house was away. Then, confronted with Worthington's mother in the doorway, the intruder panicked and killed her. This reconstruction was already an act of compassion. It meant being willing to put a more favorable interpretation on a terrible act. "Through empathy, I understood that he had lashed out in fear, surprise, guilt, and anger." Not only did Worthington experience empathy, he was humbled to recognize that his own wanting to beat the young man's brains out was equivalent to the crime committed against his mother; he was like the killer. This combination of empathy and humility allowed Worthington to commit himself to forgiveness.[2]

A second example comes from a survivor of the Rwandan genocide. In her book, *Left to Tell,* Immaculée Ilibagiza vividly describes her three-month confinement in a tiny bathroom with seven other women, barricaded from the adjoining room by a wardrobe put in place to cover the door. The eight women could hear the Hutu soldiers chanting on the other side of the wall: "Kill the Tutsis big and small . . . kill them one and kill them all. *Kill them!"* (Ilibagiza 2006, 92). For hours Immaculée struggled in prayer to move from thoughts of vengeance to forgiveness. Finally she heard God's answer "as clearly as if we'd been sitting in the same room chatting: *You are all My children*" (Ibid., 94). This simple answer from God opened Ilibagiza's heart to forgiveness. "Yes, they were barbaric creatures who would have to be punished severely for their actions, but they were still children. . . . For the first time, I pitied the killers. I asked God to forgive their sins and turn their souls to His beautiful light" (Ibid., 94).

The movement toward forgiveness does not always display the mediating role of compassion in such a clear light. Forgiveness comes as a gift and comes mysteriously. Sometimes it happens spontaneously without manifesting the clear stages I have described. In some people, compassion becomes so habitual that they move toward forgiveness without noticing the process. Perhaps we can consider the thesis negatively: without compassion, it is difficult to forgive. And without a sense that we are, as Ilibagiza came to realize, all God's children, all capable of evil, and still all loved infinitely, it is difficult to forgive.

APOLOGIA

Having briefly laid out the subject matter and theme of the book, I now offer a kind of *apologia,* a rationale for the writing of this book on original sin, compassion, and forgiveness and an account of how my thinking has progressed to the point of moving me to write. I use the Latin word *apologia* as John Henry Newman used it in his famous, *Apologia Pro Vita Sua* where he describes a very personal account of the process that led him from the Anglican form of Christianity to the Roman Catholic. He was reluctant to give this account until he was confronted with a very public challenge stating that he had no respect for the truth in itself. Newman felt obliged to respond, not only to defend his own reputation but out of respect for his brothers in the Catholic priesthood whose reputations were also impugned. The response was his *Apologia Pro Vita Sua: Being a History of His Religious Opinions* (Newman 1924, v–xiii).

Though I use the term *apologia* in the sense used by Newman, I do not begin with his same provocation. I am motivated rather by an uncomfortable tension in me between two opposed views, one my own conviction that the teaching on original sin makes profound sense and is, in fact, hard to escape if one looks around at human behavior, and, another view that believes the teaching about original sin makes no sense and is demeaning to God and human beings. My *apologia* then, describes why I think the book might be important, states what I hope to accomplish, and details how the subject matter has developed in my thinking for a long time. I will also articulate the hermeneutic principles that will be at work as I describe my view, and give a brief account about how each chapter contributes to the whole.

RESISTANCE TO THE NOTION OF ORIGINAL SIN

This book claims for the doctrine of original sin or, more precisely, the personal awareness of original sin in oneself and in groups, a liberating function. Yet anyone deciding to write about original sin must be aware of the widespread resistance to the idea. The resistance itself makes the study important. For if, as I maintain, the consciousness of original sin has a liberating function, as motive for forgiveness, then the denial of original sin eliminates an opportunity for liberation. A closer look at the resistance will help clarify the scope of this study.

Many have found, and many still find, the doctrine of an inherited *original sin* unworthy of a loving God. Alan Jacobs of Wheaton College, opens his 2008 book, *Original Sin: A Cultural History,* with the comment: "All religious beliefs prompt rejection. . . . But of all the religious teachings I know, none—not even the belief that some people are eternally damned—generates as much hostility as the Christian doctrine we call 'original sin'" (Jacobs 2008, ix). And James Alison, author of *The Joy of Being Wrong,* says that "original sin is capable of arousing a huge depth of feeling: some blame it, and the stage-villain Augustine, its senior brandisher, for the most spectacular crimes against humanity" (Alison, 1).

I have encountered, even in devoted Christians, this kind of adverse reaction, most recently as I was preparing to write this book. When people would ask what I was writing about, I noticed a tendency in myself, as self-protection, to avoid beginning with the topic of original sin. When I said that the subject was forgiveness, questioners would look interested and say, "I would like to read that when you are finished." When, in my braver moments, I came right out and admitted I was writing a book on original sin, people tended to be more reserved, even puzzled, as if on the verge of asking, "Does anyone believe in that anymore?" Sometimes I would say that I was writing a book on the connection between original sin and forgiveness. People's quizzical looks seemed to say, "That could be interesting," and I was immediately anxious that they might ask, "So what *is* the connection?" My answer to that question has evolved gradually, as I will show.

Adam and Eve's story, the foundation of the doctrine of original sin in the Christian tradition, did not lead to the same belief among the Jewish people, even though the Hebrew Scriptures do, as we will see in chapter one, recognize the universality of sin. The Hebrew Bible does not trace the origin of universal sin to Adam and Eve. Their story does not even recur in the Hebrew Testament after its appearance at the beginning of Genesis. Thus, this story of a couple at the beginning of history disobeying a command of God with disastrous consequences, does not, as Paul Ricoeur says, form a cornerstone of Israel's faith, or even of the Chosen People's sense of sin. In the Hebrew Bible, sin is infidelity to God's covenant, turning away from worship of the true God to idolatry, reliance on one's own strength rather than God's protective love. The disobedience of Adam and Eve is rooted in these same defects, but the writers of the Hebrew scriptures do not look back to the Adamic Myth for an understanding of sin. They look to the exodus from Egypt, the conduct of life in the Promised Land under the judges and kings, the abominations that brought about the Babylonian exile. The Hebrew scriptures rarely speak of a condition that could be called original sin. Psalm 50's "In sin my mother conceived me," offers a rare exception.

The prophetic books of the Hebrew Bible explicitly and forcefully reject the earlier doctrine of Exodus that teaches a kind of inherited sin: "For I, the Lord your God, am a jealous God, inflicting punishment for their fathers' wickedness on the children of those who hate me, down to the third and fourth generation" (Exod. 20:5). The prophets Ezekiel and Jeremiah teach the responsibility of each person for sins committed. The children's teeth are not set on edge just because the father has eaten sour grapes: ". . . only the one who sins shall die" (Ezek. 18:4). Jeremiah repeats the same saying and comes to the same conclusion: ". . . but through his own fault only shall anyone die: the teeth of him who eats the unripe grapes shall be set on edge" (Jer. 31:29–30). We do not hold the German people of today responsible for the horrors inflicted by the Nazis on the Jewish people, homosexuals, gypsies, and anyone who opposed their practices.

Many who object to the doctrine of original sin, however, imagine it in just the terms rejected by Israel's prophets and see in it the same unfairness the prophets saw. The possibility remains, of course, that the Christian doctrine of original sin means something quite different from what Exodus taught about the passing of guilt from one generation to the next, from blaming present-day Germans, for instance, for the Nazis' sins.

Understanding the Christian doctrine of original sin is one of the aims of this study. For the moment, it is probably sufficient to say that the passing down of guilt connected with *actual* sins, such as those committed by the Nazis, is *not* part of the teaching on original sin. The sin that Christians call *original* or *originating* is a tendency toward sin rather than any particular sin in itself. Contemporary medical science offers a helpful analogy in the theory of the immune system. A healthy immune system enables a person to ward off diseases. When the immune system breaks down, opportunistic diseases invade the body. Original sin, like a compromised immune system, disposes us to a variety of actual sins.

Some object even to the idea of a *tendency* toward sin. Paradoxically, Pelagius and his tenacious follower Julian of Eclanum, helped define the doctrine of original sin through their protracted struggle with Augustine of Hippo. For both Pelagius and Julian, the idea that the human will is somehow wounded or compromised from the moment of birth, and thus incapable of consistently choosing the good without the aid of a special help from God called *grace* was unfair to human beings and unworthy of God. They believed that we are equally inclined toward good and evil, and it is up to us to choose the good and reject the evil. After all, we have the example of Jesus and the law, and for Pelagius and Julian of Eclanum these are enough.

Many outside the Christian tradition, most contemporary Jews for instance, and many Christians too, find the doctrine of original sin abhorrent. To see young children, to cite one aspect of the doctrine, as being afflicted with some kind of sin before they are even capable of committing moral faults or taking responsibility for their lives, goes against our spontaneous inclination to see children as innocent. Jesus' setting children as models for those who want to enter the kingdom of God appears to go against the notion that they might be contaminated by a disordered inclination prior to any actual sin on their part that sets them up inevitably for future sins unless they are rescued by the help of God. It seems to make more sense to see children as heading into life with an even chance of choosing the good as of choosing the bad. Thinking of the scales as somehow tilted against them from the start chills the optimism of our pedagogical efforts, including moral example, enlightened discipline, and parental love.

Rabbi Michael Lerner, editor of the liberal journal *Tikkun*, in a beautiful article on the opening of the Jewish feast of Yom Kippur, puts this position persuasively when he says that at the beginning of life we are "born pure and with the best of spiritual intentions to be the highest spiritual being we can be, as though we were an arrow being shot straight toward God to connect more fully, yet at various points in our lives the arrow gets slightly off track and misses the mark. Repentance is really about a mid-course adjustment to get back on trace [sic]." How different this is from the doctrine of original sin that says we *begin* life off track and need God's grace to get back on the right path.

But, James Alison, whose forceful statement of resistance to the idea of original sin is cited above, is also conscious of a more positive evaluation of original sin: ". . . others," he says, "see it as a vital control on the self-defeating idealism of those who restructure the world as though humans might one day be good" (Alison, 1). Human beings, Alison suggests, will never be simply, and without qualification, good. An Old Testament author, affirming the universality of sin, said the same thing, "Surely there is no one on earth so righteous as to do good without ever sinning" (Ecclesiastes 7:20). And if the doctrine of original sin can control naïve idealism, it can also mitigate the self-righteousness of those who think of the world as divided into the good and the bad; that is, themselves, the good, and their opponents, the bad. Desmond Tutu, champion of the struggle against Apartheid in his own South Africa, understood in the midst of his outrage against the injustice of racial oppression, that the black majority was not uniquely good, or free of fault, purely victimized, never victimizing; nor were the agents of apartheid simply evil. When he and Nelson Mandela set up the famous Truth and Reconciliation Commission, they began with the conviction that both sides had committed atrocities against the other and were subject to the radical disorder Christians call original sin.

The conviction that a radical wounding of the will afflicts every person coming into the world, a wounding that can be healed only through the redemptive grace of Christ, remains a fundamental teaching of the Christian churches. To borrow a description from Julian of Norwich's visions, we are all the servant who has fallen into a slough and cannot get out through our own efforts.

In this book I propose to show how the logic of the Adamic Myth, mentioned earlier, runs through Christianity's history, discussing how it helps make sense of the Christian story of salvation and is, in fact, necessary for understanding that story. I will argue that the teaching of a solidarity in sin shared by all humans, once appropriated as a personal conviction, is a primary motive for the forgiveness at the heart of Christianity. We have all received forgiveness and so we must all forgive. In a brief essay in Simon Wiesenthal's' *The Sunflower: The Possibilities and Limits of Forgiveness,* Dennis Prager argues that no doctrine, except the divinity of Jesus itself, distinguishes Jewish theology from Christian more than the teaching about forgiveness (Wiesenthal 1997, 216). Perhaps Christianity's deeper sense of the democracy of sin helps explain why Christians are more prodigal in forgiving. Christians repeat every day the Lord's Prayer with its plea to "forgive us our trespasses as we forgive those who trespass against us."

THE BASIC AIMS OF THIS STUDY

My approach to the subject of original sin is fourfold: To illustrate the proposition that compassion opens the path to forgiveness. The connection might seem obvious until we reflect on how often we find ourselves trying to forgive someone for whom we have no sympathy, in whom we see nothing that would provide grounds for our mercy, someone who does not deserve our forgiveness, and wondering why we cannot overcome our reluctance to forgive. And we see others, individuals and nations, who regard their enemies across a chasm without any bridge to the other side, filled with outrage at injuries experienced over tens or hundreds of years. Compassion, I will argue, is the bridge. The second aim is to explore the story of Adam and Eve, its various interpretations—especially the doctrine of original sin—and some of the guises under which it has appeared in the history of Christianity. I wish to show how this story and these interpretations open the way to a liberating vision of human life. These first two aims converge in the movement toward compassion implicit in a consciousness of original sin in oneself.

Aim three, implied in what has already been said, is to awaken this consciousness of original sin, not just as a doctrine to be believed, but as a reality to be confronted by individuals and groups. Unconsciousness of original sin at work in individuals and groups leads to the phenomenon of excusing oneself or one's group and blaming others. The recognition of a universally shared condition that is not sin itself but leads to sin, opens us to recognize fault in ourselves and mitigates our tendency to blame others. The same suffering in others—for the condition I am describing is something we *suffer*—that disposes them to sin, also disposes me to sin. Recognizing the affliction in myself, allows me to enter into the suffering of others. This ability to enter into the suffering of others we call compassion. Compassion is a precondition for authentic forgiveness.

Aim four is meant to clarify the abstract notion of original sin by looking at its various names. We recognize certain tendencies in ourselves without connecting them to the notion of original sin; I will make those connections. For instance, René Girard interprets original sin under its biblical name, "covetousness," which he calls "mimetic rivalry," or desiring what the other has because the other has it. Such rivalry, when it becomes epidemic, leads to "the war of all against all." Girard's thought is examined in chapter six. Another name comes from the contemporary awareness of "addiction." Gerald May, in his book *Addiction and Grace,* has explored not only the prevalence of chemical addiction, but also the universality of addictive behavior in human beings. According to May, to be human is to be addicted. "We all suffer from both repression and addiction. Of the two, repression is by far the milder one" (May, 1991, 2). Reading May's book helped me understand the various addictive behaviors that Augustine refers to in his *Confessions.* Julian of Norwich, as we will see in chapter eight, names blindness to God's love as the structural sin at the root of other sins. The title of Marcel Proust's monumental novel, *In Search of Lost Time (À la Recherche du Temps Perdu),* suggests another possible name for original sin. The lost time to which Proust refers in this title is in fact the loss of contact with the creative self amid the distractions of the social self that plagues the story's narrator until the very end of the novel. The lost sheep, the lost coin, the lost son (Lk. 15), lost time, the lost self—all can be taken as metaphors for a lost paradise. "The true paradises," says Proust, "are the paradises one has lost" (Proust 1989, 177). Loss of contact with the true self names what Adam and Eve experienced along with shame at their nakedness after eating the forbidden fruit.

The Belgian novelist, Georges Simenon, who began life as a devout Catholic but renounced his faith at age fifteen, developed a profoundly sympathetic character in the person of inspector Maigret. In one case, while trying to get to sleep after a difficult day, in the space between waking and sleep, Maigret experiences an insight into the mystery of a suspect he is struggling to comprehend. The insight enables him to understand not only the suspect in this case, but the irrational behavior of human beings in general. In his waking hours, he had often discussed this idea with his good friend, Dr. Pardon—this name itself is suggestive. Without claiming to name original sin, Maigret reflects on a universal human weakness that does in fact identify the root of much irrational behavior in human beings, fear. "At the base was fear," says Maigret. For Maigret images of fear change form through the various stages of a human life; we experience fear of water, of fire, of darkness, fear of making bad life choices, of failing to take hold of our life. For Maigret these became "the notes of a muffled and tragic symphony: the hidden fears that one drags behind one, sharp fears that make one cry out in pain, fears that one dismisses once they have passed, fear of accidents, of sickness, of the police, of people, what they will say and the looks they give you as they pass" (*La Patience de Maigret,* 128). It would be hard to find a more concrete characterization of original sin. During the course of this study, we will see other names for the sin that gives rise to sins.

SEVEN HERMENEUTICAL PRINCIPLES

Hermeneutical principles name the processes by which thought develops. Six such principles inform the development of this study, with different principles coming into play in different places. The first principle consists in a combination of truths that early Christian writers used to guide their search into the reality of Christ. Only God can forgive sin, and God can heal only if he takes on what he heals. From the mouth of the Scribes we have the first half of the principle. In response to Jesus' healing of a paralytic they say to themselves—with Jesus reading their hearts—"Who can forgive sins but God alone?" (Mk. 2:7b). The second half of the principle arose in the controversy between Gregory of Nazianzen and Apollinarius, who maintained that Jesus had a human body but not a human mind. Gregory maintained that Jesus must be human in body and mind, everything that makes us human, "For that which he has not assumed he has not healed" (Gregory of Nazianzen, 1978, 441, col 2). The whole of our human nature fell in Adam so the whole of it has to be taken on by the divine Christ who alone can heal us. Christ did not just "take on" our nature as something external to him; he entered into it, experienced it in its heights and depths, even death itself. What does this mean for the doctrine of forgiveness? It means first that to forgive is divine. When we forgive we participate in the divine. It means also that we can only forgive what we take on, what we enter into, what we become, what we suffer with. In other words, we forgive through compassion. This combination of the divine and the human in forgiving will appear powerfully in the character of Georges Simenon's Maigret, which will be treated in chapter eleven. Martha Nussbaum writes about a parallel process in the ancient world in which judges—divine figures in a way—enter into the lives of those they are judging to produce a merciful judgment.[3]

The second principle is contained in the famous definition of theology, articulated by both Augustine and Anselm of Canterbury: "faith seeking understanding."

Augustine's version of the principle, "faith seeking understanding," is circular: "I believe in order to understand; I understand in order to believe more fully" (Augustine *Sermons,* 43, 7, 9, *Patrologia Latina,* 38, 257–58). Anselm writes his *Proslogion,* the work in which he lays out his controversial ontological proof, "in the person of one who strives to lift up his mind to the contemplation of God and seeks to understand what he believes" (Anselm "Preface," *Proslogion,* 102). In another place Anselm accuses of laziness those who do not strive to understand their faith. The force of the principle depends on one's understanding of "faith." If by *faith* one means an act by which the mind fastens on some truth it does not understand, but feels obliged to accept, then it makes little sense to speak of faith seeking understanding. But if by *faith* one means the dynamism of the spirit by which it is receptive to truths it does not fully understand wherever it discovers them and however they are expressed, the formula "faith seeking understanding" is profoundly useful. This dynamism is what the Canadian theologian, Bernard Lonergan, calls "the pure desire to know," Hegel calls it "the concept" (*der Begriff),* and Bergson names it the *elan vital.*" Understood in this way, faith naturally seeks understanding, is, in fact, a dynamism toward understanding and, as such, the beginning of all science, philosophy, and human wisdom.

The third principle, that liberating truths are revealed to the heart through conversion, is suggested, if not explicitly formulated, by Paul's prayer in Ephesians: "May the eyes of your hearts be enlightened, that you may know what is the hope that belongs to the call . . . " (Eph. 1:18). Paul's own conversion was an instance of such enlightenment, as was Augustine's. A less likely source for illustrating this principle, since he does not claim to be religious at all, is Marcel Proust who speaks of aesthetic rather than religious enlightenment. At stake for the narrator of Proust's novel was the reality of his own literary gifts, even the reality of literature itself as a human project. Deep moods of discouragement led him to doubt both. But periodically during his adult life, the narrator experiences profoundly liberating moments that restore his confidence in his own gifts and his belief in literature itself. In the context of this study, the principle of conversion means that the truth about sin is revealed only through grace. Sometime grace comes through the dramatic conversion of a Paul or an Augustine. More often it comes through the small conversions that mark the daily turning from sin to the source of healing.

Awakening the consciousness of original sin can be dangerous. Julian of Norwich realized that we can face sin in ourselves without being overwhelmed only if God reveals our sin through the gift of grace. Fundamental to the argument of this book is the conviction that only through God's healing grace can we recognize the existence of original sin in ourselves and begin to contend with its effects. And the deepest work of grace is to show us the fundamental goodness in ourselves that original sin obscures. We are not worse than we think, but better. Paul Ricoeur calls this goodness of human beings "primordial." He calls the evil in us "radical," which means that for him evil is rooted in our existential condition but not the deepest level of our being. Julian of Norwich, in her medieval retelling of the fall, which she calls "the parable of the Lord and the Servant," tells us that when the servant (Adam) falls, he is blinded and "he neither sees clearly his loving lord, who is so meek and mild to him, nor does he truly see what he himself is in the sight of his loving lord" (*Revelations* Long Text, 51, par. 8).

A fourth hermeneutical principle is that truth is revealed historically. Bernard Lonergan refers to this as historical consciousness which looks for the truth of things in their gradual unfolding over time. For Lonergan, historical consciousness is opposed to classical consciousness, which sees truths as extra-temporal and absolute, existing in a realm above the changes of human history. Hegel saw the revelation of truth in history as a dialectical process in which one-sided truths give rise to their opposites and then to a reconciling process in which the opposing claims yield to a higher reconciling truth. Proust, a novelist rather than a theologian or philosopher, describes a process in which first impressions give way to deeper insight, thereby gradually revealing the truth of his characters. In Proust's monumental novel, *In Search of Lost Time,* character development unfolds in over three thousand pages. I will be briefer, but I do invite the readers of this book to regard its principal characters, not as fixed doctrines, but as ideas whose truth has been revealed only over time in the various manifestations cited as well as many more that this study does not encompass.

The fifth, sixth, and seventh principles underlie the structure of the entire book. The fifth principle is that the truth is first articulated in myths and symbols before it is expressed in thought. The story of Adam and Eve, for instance, is *mythical*, by which I do not mean that it is false or merely imaginary, but that it expresses the truth in a symbolic narrative. This principle forms the basis of Paul Ricoeur's, *The Symbolism of Evil,* which we will examine in detail in the next chapter. This principle underlies the first part of the present study. The sixth principle also comes from Ricoeur, "the symbol gives rise to thought" (*"le symbole donne à penser"* (Ricoeur *The Symbolism of Evil,* 347–357). The myth of Adam and Eve has given rise to a vast quantity of speculation that will provide much of the content of this book. When Jesus says, "I am the vine and you are the branches," he is using symbol, image, and metaphor. Such language is suggestive; it makes us think, gives rise to thought. The movement from symbol to thought provides the underlying aim of the second part of this study. The seventh principle, which undergirds the third part of the present study, completes a circle that begins in symbol, moves to thought, and then returns from thought into symbol and narrative. Archetypal symbols give rise to thought, thought seeks to clothe its cold abstractness in literature, poetry, and narrative.

The challenge in applying these principles is to keep the integrity of each phase of the circle without submerging it in that to which it gives rise. The Adamic Myth, for instance, has given rise to thought in a variety of forms in the Christian tradition. The danger is that one or other of the theoretical frameworks into which the myth gets sublimated takes away the generative power of the myth itself. The dogmatic structure that has formed around the Adamic Myth has kept people from looking at the biblical narrative itself and allowing it to give rise to new thoughts that might break through the theoretical frameworks that dogma has imposed. One of the purposes of this study is to examine how the generative power of the myth of Adam and Eve has given rise both to thought and to literary forms.

The appropriateness of the three divisions of this study—symbol giving rise to thought, thought returning to metaphor and narrative—receives confirmation from an unlikely source, a study of the brain's division into unequal but related hemispheres, right brain and left brain, by Iain McGilchrist in his magisterial work, *The Master and His Emissaries: The Divided Brain and the Making of Western Culture.* McGilchrist's work, twenty years in the making, affirms a circular character to conscious activity. The right brain provides the imprecise, implicit, originating insights that give rise to the left brain's work of conceptualizing, explicitizing, and elaborating. For thinking to be in contact with the real world, the work of the left brain must yield to the source at its origin. McGilchrist expresses the idea succinctly in his Yale University e-book summary of the larger work: "So the meaning of the utterance begins in the right hemisphere, is made explicit (literally folded out or unfolded) in the left, and then the whole utterance needs to be 'returned to the right hemisphere, where it is reintegrated with all that is implicit—tone, irony, metaphor, humour, and so on, as a feel of the context in which the utterance is to be understood" ("The Divided Brain and the Search for Meaning," Loc 350 of 476).

A PREVIEW OF WHAT IS TO COME

Proust uses a striking image that can serve as an introduction to my preview of the chapters that follow. The image occurs in Proust's response to a critic of *Swann's Way,* the first published volume of the seven that would become *In Search of Lost Time.* Too many characters appear in this volume, said the critic, and none of them has a developed profile. Proust responds that the full development of his characters will require the passage of time in which the various dimensions of the personalities introduced in his first volume will appear (Proust 1988, 458–459). In his first volume Proust has, he says, lined them up "like horses at the gate" about to run their course. Only the running of the course will tell us who the horses are. It is not only works of art that need to "mature slowly" through the course of time but all ideas (460).

Because of the variety of texts, and even genres of text included in this book—like so many horses at the gate—one may ask why I have chosen the writings I have, how the horses have qualified to run the race. I can best answer this question first by restating the fundamental aims of my study, then by exploring the historical development of the Adamic Myth, and finally by relating the texts to the three parts into which I have divided the material of the book .

My fundamental aim, through all the texts I have chosen, is to seek the truth of the Adamic Myth. This truth, something more than doctrinal definitions, reveals itself only to those willing to sort through a mixture of true and false interpretations, following some leads, rejecting others, like a detective. I find myself, in fact, learning from Georges Simenon's famous police inspector, Maigret (see chapter eleven) who says of himself at the beginning of a case where the witnesses refuse to cooperate," "My profession (*mon métier)* is to look for the truth, and I am looking for it" (*M. and the Recalcitrant Witnesses, 50).* The texts examined in my study are my witnesses to the truth of the Adamic Myth. After questioning all these witnesses and sifting through the results of others' investigations, I have concluded that the truth of the Adamic Myth lies in the common vulnerability, darkness, confusion, and helplessness in which all human beings participate and which have, from the beginning, evoked the grace of divine compassion and forgiveness. This compassion and forgiveness in God we call Redemption.

Julian of Norwich dramatically illustrated the intimate connection between human sin and divine redemption in her retelling of the story of Adam's fall. Adam, out of inadvertence rather than as an act of disobedience, fell into a hole from which he could not get out by himself. Adam's fall, says Julian was identical with the *fall* of the Word of God into the womb of Mary and the beginning of our redemption. Julian simply disregards the temporal lapse between the event of the fall and the event of the Incarnation. No sooner had Adam fallen, we might say, than God set about with a plan for getting him out of the hole (chapter nine on Julian of Norwich). Even the account of Genesis 3 seems to proclaim this intimate connection between fall and redemption when God, in cursing the serpent, promises to "put enmity between your offspring and hers; he will strike at your head while you strike at his heel" (Gen 3: 15).

The last book of the Bible, Revelation, recalls this divine promise in its account of the woman and the dragon (Rev. 12—see chapter three of this study).

In human beings the connection between our fallen state—being in a hole—takes a circuitous path. The study I am introducing here is my attempt to trace that journey. The consciousness of original sin in oneself *ought* to lead to compassion for others similarly afflicted—everyone that is—and through compassion to forgiveness. You would think it would. We would expect, for instance, that Angelo in Shakespeare's *Measure for* Measure, having felt the dark stirrings of lust in himself, would be sympathetic to his subject Claudio against whom he has initiated a process for improper sexual activity. Not so (see chapter ten). We cannot assume that all are conscious of original sin at work in themselves. Original sin for many hangs over their conscience as a dark, abstract, and incomprehensible doctrine. And not all those who are conscious of original sin as something real in themselves move toward compassion and forgiveness. To become conscious of original sin in oneself in such a way as to move toward compassion requires a conversion. This study invites its readers to a meditation rooted in symbol, theory, and literature intended to awaken such consciousness—leaving conversion to the Holy Spirit.

My argument in favor of a connection between original sin and compassion will probably surprise some readers. Many people, as I have already noted, even committed Christians who have grown up in the tradition that proclaims original sin as a fundamental doctrine, find in the Adamic Myth and in the doctrine it has spawned only an incentive for self-loathing. For them the doctrine of original sin means that all of us are fundamentally bad. Such a conclusion, I will argue, comes from going down a false path in the investigation. The Adamic Myth in fact teaches that we humans are fundamentally good, that we have strayed from our original goodness, and that the way back is through compassion and forgiveness. The medieval mystic Walter Hilton describes accurately the path of true self knowledge. ". . . There is one useful and deserving task on which to labor, and (as I think) a plain highway to contemplation . . . and that is for a person to go into himself to know his own soul and its powers, its fairness and its foulness. Through looking inward you will be able to see the honor and dignity it ought to have from the nature of its first makings: and you will see too the wretchedness and misery into which you have fallen through sin . . . ." (Hilton, *The Scale of Perfection,* par 41, 112). Our first beginning—historically and existentially—is the honor and dignity of paradise. But paradise is lost through sin and regained by compassion and forgiveness. This inner logic of the Adamic Myth, its truth, will thread its way through the chapters of this book and the writings they investigate.

I can also find the warrant for the texts I have chosen in the history of the Adamic Myth. The Adamic Myth has a history that extends far beyond the story in Genesis 3. The full truth of the myth lies in this history. Each of the texts I have chosen is a turning point, or a moment, or a stage in that history. The history begins even before the account of Adam and Eve in the Hebrew Bible, but for our purpose the story of Genesis 3 is the beginning. From the point of view of Christian theology we are dealing with the development of doctrine. The culmination of that development comes in the doctrinal definitions of the church councils from Orange to Trent. But if I had to rest my case for the *truth* of the Adamic Myth on those definitions, I would be in trouble. Those very definitions, in fact, with their dry formulations, their anathemas against those who hold other views, and their categorical quality provide fuel for those who find this teaching inhuman. The definitions, of course, have their own validity. I am not arguing against them. Their clarity about the fact of original sin and the necessity of redemption by Christ and the ongoing need for God's grace opens a sure path for those who accept them. But definitions do not aim to touch the heart. The history of the myth of Adam and Eve is deeper, longer, and richer than the formal definitions. Though in one sense the definitions clarify the history, in another sense, they obscure it and, by their very incompleteness, impel us to find other richer expressions. This book aims to do that by exploring a variety of types of expression, symbolic, theoretical, and literary that extends from the story in Genesis to modern literature.

These three types of expression in which the history has unfolded, symbolic, theoretical, and literary, provide the basis for three divisions in the text under which I have gathered the various texts and arguments that mark the progress of my study. These divisions mark both a historical progression and a circular development between different modes of expression. In general, the major division of the book and the chapters follow one another chronologically. After setting the stage with Paul Ricoeur's comparison of four ancient myths of the origin and end of evil, I turn to the symbolic narrative of Adam and Eve in the Pentateuch and Paul's transformation of the myth in Romans and I Corinthians. These first three chapters belong to a symbolic, narrative mode of expression. The next four chapters, which begin with Augustine and move chronologically through various doctrinal and theological formulations of original sin, constitute a second, theoretical mode of expression. This second part of the study illustrates Paul Ricoeur's hermeneutical principle, "the symbol gives rise to thought," which I have mentioned above. The third part of the study, moves from theory back into the realm of literature and consists of four chapters exploring, in chronological order, different literary genres.

These three phases of the book consist of different ways of speaking about the truth, interpreting the truth, and appropriating it. They represent a range of expressions that together provide evidence of the truth of the Adamic Myth that I have taken as the aim of this study. My claim is that the Adamic Myth is true, not principally because its implications have been defined doctrinally but because those implications prove to be inescapable. They keep recurring, expressed in a wide variety of linguistic modes over a long period of time, continuing up to the present. And the different modes of expression invite readers to confront the evidence of their own consciousness where the real truth of the Adamic Myth, the reality of human weakness and the promise of divine grace are revealed. Ultimately readers of this book must verify, in the courtroom of their own consciousness, the claims I make.

Finally, I conclude this preliminary exposition of the logic that lies under the development that will follow by relating the individual chapters to the three major divisions of the book in which they occur. Part One, Adam and Eve: Symbol, Myth, and Biblical Narrative includes chapters one, two, and three. These chapters follow a historical sequence and also introduce the reader into the symbolic mode of expression. I begin Part One with Paul Ricoeur's *Symbolism of Evil* because this text first awakened my interest in the connection between Adam and Eve and forgiveness, and even more important for my study, because Ricoeur here explores the role of symbol and myth in the articulation of human consciousness. Ricoeur begins his study by examining the symbols in which human beings, before they develop any philosophy or theology of evil, first articulate the dark impulses they find in themselves and in nature. The aspect of Ricoeur's analysis that interests me most in the study I have undertaken is his comparison of the myth of Adam and Eve to three other ancient mythical accounts of the origin and end of evil, Ricoeur shows how the Adamic Myth alone opens the door to forgiveness.

Following my treatment of Ricoeur's situation of the Adamic Myth in the cycle of myths of the origin and end of evil, I turn to Adam and Eve in the context within the Old Testament where their story occurs in its completeness in a form available to us today, namely, the Pentateuch. The elements that make up the subject matter of this book—the disobedience of Adam and Eve, its consequences, and the reversal of those consequences through God's compassion and forgiveness—occur in a fundamentally important way in this first part of the Hebrew Bible. But the story does not become thematic in the Old Testament the way the Exodus narrative does. The Old Testament contains few references to Adam and Eve. Adam and Eve enter the biblical narrative again only in the New Testament with Paul's comparison of Christ and Adam. Paul's treatment forms the core of chapter three, "The Adamic Myth in the New Testament." In Paul's treatment of Christ as the second Adam, we have already begun the ascent from a symbolical, mythical form of expression into the realm of thought. Paul still works with symbols but in tying symbols together begins to speculate and to elaborate a biblical theology.

Paul's move into speculation brings us to Part Two of this study, The Symbol Gives Rise to Thought: From Biblical Narrative to Autobiography, Theory, and Doctrine. Part Two includes chapters four through seven. Chapter four, "Augustine: Original Sin and Compassion," traces Augustine's development of St. Paul's theology into a full doctrine of Original Sin. Chapter five, "Classical Formulations and Modern Developments," shows how Augustine's formulations gave rise to the doctrines of the Christian churches, and a variety of speculative interpretations from the middle ages, the time of the Reformation, and modern times. Chapter six, "Compassion as Prelude to Forgiveness," contains my own elaboration of the central thesis of the book that compassion is an integral ingredient of forgiveness. Chapter seven, "René Girard: Original Sin as Covetousness," explores the contribution of René Girard to the theory of original sin.

The chapter on Augustine, then, initiates the movement of Part Two from symbol to thought. I begin this chapter, not with Augustine's elaboration of the doctrine of original sin, which comes in the last period of his life in his controversy with Pelagius, but with his autobiographical exploration of original sin in his own experience. Augustine's best-known, most-loved, and most often read work, *The Confessions*, probes, in the author's own life, the evidence of St. Paul's famous lament, "The things I want to do, I do not do and the things I do not want to do, I do" (Romans 7). This autobiographical step is crucial and grounds in Augustine's own life, his later theoretical development of original sin. Augustine does not, in other words, leap from biblical narrative to theory but rather passes from biblical narrative through interiority into theory. Or, more precisely, the biblical narrative helps Augustine make sense of his own life story.

If we can discern the elements of Augustine's theology of original sin in his *Confessions,* we must wait for the writings that came out of his controversy with Pelagius for the fully developed teaching. Augustine's connection with the doctrine of original sin is well known, a doctrine that has earned him friends and enemies. Less well recognized is the connection Augustine makes between original sin and compassion. Since this connection lies at the heart of my argument in this book, the chapter on Augustine is crucial. A reader will find the argument of the whole book compactly summarized in the pages of the chapter on Augustine. Compassion is, of course, the work of grace, God's grace working in the sinner first to forgive and heal, and then working in the healed sinner to forgive others. For this reason an understanding of Augustine's teaching must include both his consciousness of sin and his deep awareness of the absolute necessity of grace. For Augustine, grace was primary.

Chapter five presents an exposition of successive steps in the doctrinal and theoretical interpretation of the myth of Adam and Eve. Doctrine expresses the Church's definitive teaching about the meaning of original sin for the Christian. Early councils following Augustine set down the basic framework that successive definitions would follow. Theoretical interpretation reformulates the doctrine in the light of philosophical or other systematic frameworks. Thomas Aquinas provides a striking example of such speculation in his application of Aristotle's four causes to the subject of original sin. Original sin will, in Aquinas analysis, have a material cause, a formal cause, an efficient cause, and a final cause. I lay this out in chapter five. This chapter also contains an account of the dispute between Catholics and Lutherans over how deeply sin enters into the nature of human beings. I look, too, at attempts since the 1960s to reconcile the notion of original sin with evolutionary theory and feminist perspectives.

Chapter six contains my own best effort to express systematically the elements of this study. Of particular importance for the subsequent development of my investigation is what I call "the wounding of the four intimacies," intimacy with self, with God, with the neighbor, and with nature. These four wounds correspond with indications in the text of Genesis 3 itself. The shame Adam and Eve felt at their nakedness after disobeying God's command, correlates with the loss of intimacy with the self. Their hiding from God when he walked in the Garden indicates the wound in our relation with God. The desire of the woman for man and his lording it over her express a fundamental disorder in human relations, beginning with the fundamental relation between the sexes. And the woman's difficulty in childbearing and the man's frustrating labor in cultivating the earth for crops signal the loss of intimacy with nature.

Chapter seven explores the thought of René Girard as a contribution to the theory of original sin. First, it is important to note that the trajectory of Girard's own thought led him from literature to anthropological theory. So his work recapitulates within the scope of one author's work, the whole movement of Part Two of the present study. Girard first discovered the fundamental themes of his lifework in his study of literature. His first work, *Deceit, Desire, and the Novel* (English translation, 1966), revealed the pervasiveness of the phenomenon of mimetic desire. Later works in the area of anthropology would lead Girard to the discovery of the scapegoat mechanism and his study of the Bible led him to the final stage of his development, the realization that myth disguises the reality of scapegoating in human life whereas the Bible reveals it.

Several other elements in Girard's work support the fundamental aims of my study. First, Girard provides an impressive version of the inner dynamic structure of original sin. He calls the original sin "mimetic rivalry" or, to use the biblical term, "covetousness." People desire what belongs to another;

the desire becomes universalized and turns into the war of all against all. The resolution of the war of all against all takes place through the scapegoat mechanism. Myth disguises this mechanism, scripture reveals it. Girard's exploration of the dynamics of original sin gets at the heart of what I am trying to do in this book. Girard also explores other themes central to my work. Most important, he finds that the only way to reverse the cycle of violence is forgiveness, a central theme of my argument. Moreover, making the disposition to forgiveness habitual requires a conversion through which one recognizes the operation of original sin—in Girard's language, "mimetic rivalry"—in oneself before one can forgive it in others. One of the six hermeneutical principles I present above is that "liberating truths are revealed to the heart through conversion" (18).

At the same time, the account of Girard's development in this chapter serves as a transition into Part Three, in which I show how thought, once developed out of symbol into the form of theory, returns once again to metaphor and symbol in the form of literature, poetry, and other symbolic and narrative forms. Having begun in the study of the modern novel where he discovered the patterns of covetousness or "mimetic rivalry," Girard later returns to the literature of Greek myth and biblical narrative to rediscover those patterns again. Girard has helped me see a kind of hermeneutic circle in which symbol gives rise to thought, and thought returns to an intentional use of symbol and narrative by authors who have already become familiar with theory and doctrines, a circle expressed, as we have seen above, in Iain McGilchrist's study of the divided brain.

So Girard's work provides a pivot by which I turn from the more theoretical treatments of Part Two to the analysis of literature and autobiography that makes up Part Three, The Word Becomes Flesh: From Theory and Doctrine to Literature and Autobiography. Part Three consists of four chapters: chapter eight, "Perceval: Compassion Awakened through Conversion," chapter nine, "Julian of Norwich: From Blindness to the Vision of Love;" chapter ten, "Shakespeare's *Measure for Measure*: Compassion in the State;" and chapter eleven, "Detective and Priest: Georges Simenon's Compassionate Commissioner Maigret."

So, from the medieval period I have chosen two literary-mystical works. The epic poem *Perceval* by Chrétien de Troyes (chapter eight) tells the story of a young aspiring knight who, without even knowing it, breaks his mother's heart as he is leaving home. Perceval's failure of compassion, we find out later, causes the young knight who has begun a strikingly successful career, to miss the opportunity to heal the wounded Fisher King and restore his kingdom. The opportunity was stunningly simple; if Perceval has just asked certain questions at a crucial point, the king would have been healed. A failure of compassion, Perceval shows us, can block the ability to ask a liberating question. If Perceval is about the consequences of a defect of compassion, the fifteenth century mystic, Julian of Norwich (chapter nine), pushes the possibility of compassion to its limits. Julian recounts the sixteen visions given to her as a personal revelation in which the compassion of God reaches well beyond anything taught by the Church. When Julian repeats her often-quoted refrain, "All will be will, and all manner of things will be well," she means it quite literally. Even the most egregious sinners will ultimately find divine forgiveness. Julian begins the account of her revelations with a dramatic retelling of the story of Adam and Eve that fuses the "fall" of the servant (Adam) with the "fall" of God's Word into the womb of the Virgin Mary.

Shakespeare's *Measure for Measure* (chapter ten), from the period of the Renaissance, dramatizes the conflict between legalism and compassion in the politics of the state. The play ends in a kind of truth and reconciliation procedure in which a just ruler metes out appropriate healing remedies for those who have sinned against compassion. I then move into modern literature with Simenon's Inspector Maigret (chapter eleven), a man who like his inventor had lost his Catholic faith but retained a profound sense of original sin and a deeply moving compassion that led him to ambition being a "mender of destinies."

I can say in summary that I have chosen these works because I have found in them lively illustrations of the fundamental themes of my study. My criterion for choosing them has been simply their power to illuminate. I trust that my choices will call to readers' minds other works that exemplify, perhaps even better than the ones I have chosen, the themes I am presenting. They might even ask, "Why did he not choose this or that work of literature that makes the very points the author wants to make?" I would be happy to know that others find the basic themes I have developed present in a wide variety of texts.

I invite the reader to think of this work as an extended meditation, in a variety of settings, on the mystery of iniquity and grace. The chapters do not have to be read in order. Each illustrates the basic thesis in a way that can stand on its own. That original sin provides the ground of grace is paradoxical. And the notion that grace is more abundant than sin stretches our understanding even further. The superabundance of grace enables the Church in its Easter liturgy to call Adam's sin "a happy fault." The Adamic Myth is more than a simple story. It can illuminate our experience if we allow it into our consciousness. The dynamism of its logic flows through the Christian tradition, finding expression in the Gospels, the letters of Paul, and in Christian and non-Christian writers from the Fathers of the Church, with their various interpretations, to contemporary writers and thinkers who interpret it in diverse ways, dismissing it as insignificant, rejecting it as harmful, embracing it, or even manifesting its logic in their works without acknowledging the doctrine formally. I do not presume to give a comprehensive account of interpretations of the Adamic Myth. I do aim to illuminate this rich story through an examination of some of its interpreters and, most of all to illustrate the workings of compassion in the divine and human project of forgiveness.

NOTES

1. This scriptural quotation is from the New Revised Standard Version Bible: Catholic Edition, copyright © 1989, 1993 National Council of the Churches of Christ in the United States of America. Used by permission. All rights reserved worldwide.

2. I discovered Worthington's theory about forgiveness as I was completing the manuscript for this book. His approach from the perspective of psychology confirms the theological position I have presented. Worthington talks about the "primacy of emotion in forgiveness." Rational conviction is not enough, he says. The model Worthington develops in his writings consists of three steps, empathy, humility, and commitment. Worthington's treatment of empathy coincides with the role I assign to compassion; these are two words for the same thing. Worthington assigns to humility the same role I assign to awareness of original sin in oneself. Commitment in his thought adds the step of actually choosing to forgive. Worthington's own brief summary of his position shows how closely it parallels my own: "I see my offender's motivation and understand his or her point of view. I feel what he or she might have been feeling. Further, I have similar feelings. I see that I have done things or wanted to do things as wicked as the other person. In those instances of weakness, I would like to have forgiveness extended to me" (Worthington 1998, 63).

3. In her excellent article, "Equity and Mercy," Martha Nussbaum explores the development of a doctrine of mercy in the ancient world from the strict Greek notion of justice (*dike*), through the Aristotle's treatment of equity (epikeia) to Seneca's appeal to mercy (*clementia*) as an antidote to retributive justice. The exercise of mercy entails entering into the life of the accused: "The merciful judge will not fail to judge the guilt of the offender, but she will also see the many obstacles this offerder faced as a member of culture, a gender, a city or country, and, above all, as a member of the human species, facing the obstacles characteristic of human life in a world of scarcity and accident" (Nussbaum 1993, 103).

Part I

SYMBOL, MYTH,
AND BIBLICAL NARRATIVE

Chapter One

Paul Ricoeur

A Wider Context for the Adamic Myth

The presupposition of my undertaking is that the place where one can best listen to, hear, and understand what all the myths together have to teach us is the place where the pre-eminence of one of those myths is proclaimed still today—namely, the Adamic Myth.

—Paul Ricoeur, *Symbolism of Evil*

In his 1967 work, *The Symbolism of Evil,* the French phenomenologist Paul Ricoeur compares the myth of Adam and Eve with three other ancient mythical accounts of the origin and end of evil. Ricoeur's comparison not only helps us see what is most characteristic in this story that has become foundational for the Christian tradition and to appreciate its inner logic, but also how aspects of the other myths can complement the logic of the Adamic Myth. Christians, like followers of any received tradition, are likely to lose a critical sense of the value as well as of the limitations of their own founding myths. A study like Ricoeur's helps us re-gain perspective. In particular, Ricoeur illuminates the inner logic of this dynamic narrative—a logic that has deeply influenced the Christian tradition and continues to affect the way Christians view sin and salvation—and compares it with the logic of other myths. Comparison provides a basis for interpretation and moves us one step from the naiveté by which we are likely to look at our tradition. Consideration of Ricoeur's work is a first and foundational step in the interpretation of the Adamic Myth. Interpretation is everything. Wrongly interpreted, the logic of the founding myth becomes perverse. Interpreted with insight, it becomes liberating.

A word about language is in order. I have, following Paul Ricoeur, been speaking of Adam and Eve's story as *myth*. Some contemporary scriptural scholars call it folklore. The crucial point is to free ourselves from the notion that the story describes a historical event situated at a certain point in time continuous with our time and in a place locatable on a map. Interpreting the story as a historical event introduces a distorting ingredient and precisely opens the text to the objections that have occurred over the centuries. The notion of a deed carried out one afternoon at some point in time continuous with our own time is hard to distinguish from the early Jewish doctrine found in Exodus that the sins of the fathers are visited on the children to the thousandth generation. As we saw above, the later prophetic writers of Israel, Jeremiah (31), and Ezekiel (18), rejected this doctrine as unworthy of God. Even if we say that it is only a sinful *condition* and not the guilt attached to actual sinful deeds that is passed down, the question of divine injustice still rears its head. But if we look for the truth of myth rather than the truth of history, then we find that we are looking at the existential origin of sin and its metaphysical structure rather than its historical origins. Adam and Eve's distrust of God and their consequent disobedience names the origin of all sin, and it is fair to say that we do not know a time when this original sin was not at work among human beings. Certainly, the Jewish scripture writers recognized the universal presence of sin even though they did not speak of original sin or refer to the story of Adam and Eve.

Ricoeur also insists that his project is pre-philosophical and pre-theological. Ricoeur believes that philosophy begins, not in some kind of intellectual vacuum but in the relations expressed by symbolic and mythical narratives, such as the story of Adam and Eve. My aim in this chapter is to retrieve for theology the essential insights of Ricoeur's study by transposing his pre-philosophical and pre-theological reflection into a theological framework on which I can base the development of this study. In particular, I offer a theological justification of Ricoeur's choice of the Adamic Myth as the privileged standpoint from which to view the other myths. This procedure helps to show how the Adamic Myth, even though it was never a cornerstone of Israel's faith, has become such a foundation for Christianity. The symbols and myths that Ricoeur studies constitute a complex language already articulated before philosophy and theology come on the scene, a language that is available for systematic reflection.

A third key point is that the myths Ricoeur treats represent *mythical types*. Mythical accounts about the origin of religious traditions abound, but each does not represent a different type. Ricoeur himself addresses the problems presented by the multiplicity of the myths to be studied. The solution to the problem, he says, lies in the notion of typology. The types that Ricoeur proposes give him a key to deciphering multiple myths, while leaving him open to expand his typology (Ricoeur 1967, 171–172).

Ricoeur's *Symbolism of Evil* is divided into two parts. The first part, "The Primary Symbols: Defilement, Sin, and Guilt," concludes with a "Recapitulation of the Symbolism of Evil in the Concept of the Servile Will," a key notion to which I will return at the end of this chapter. In the second part Ricoeur treats "The 'Myths' of the Beginning and the End," concluding with a chapter on the hermeneutical principle, "The Symbol Gives Rise to Thought." This principle means that theology and philosophy begin, not in some speculative vacuum, but out of the rich system of relations embodied in symbolic narratives.

This chapter focuses on the second part of *The Symbolism of Evil*, Ricoeur's treatment of the myths of the beginning and the end. Ricoeur calls these accounts "myths," not because he considers them false, but because their truth lies in the realm of the meanings that ground human activity rather than in historically verifiable narratives. "Myth," says Ricoeur, "will here be taken to mean what the history of religions now finds in it: not a false explanation by means of images and fables, but a traditional narration which relates to events that happened at the beginning of time and which has the purpose of providing grounds for the ritual actions of people of today and, in a general manner, establishing all the forms of action and thought by which people understand themselves in their world" (Ricoeur 1967, 5). Below the myths, at a still more basic level, are the symbols of defilement, sin, and guilt, already mentioned, in which the religious consciousness first expresses fault. Myth takes up these symbols into a narrative form that accounts for or *explains* the origin and end of evil. Ricoeur treats four myths, which he names: "The Creation Myth," "The Tragic Myth," "The Adamic Myth," and "The Orphic Myth."

Each of these myths contains an image and conception of the divine being, God, the gods, fate; and an account of the origin of things, including both man and woman. More specifically, each myth tells us something about how the divine Being or beings are related to evil: whether they are subject to evil or above it, whether they in any way cause evil or stand utterly opposed to it, whether we can look to them for help in our struggle against evil. The myths also answer the question about how the human being is related to evil, as cause, as victim, or both and whether human beings need divine help in the struggle against evil, or can save themselves by their own efforts. The answers to these questions lie in the account that each myth gives of the origin of evil, not just this or that specific evil, but evil itself, and in the idea of salvation or redemption each proposes. Also, the idea of salvation expressed in each myth is congruent with its account of the origin of evil; so, for instance, the Orphic myth accounts for evil by describing the process through which the spiritual gets trapped in matter and presents salvation as the reverse process by which the true spiritual self gets liberated from matter. Let us look at Ricoeur's treatment of these four myths.

THE FOUR MYTHS

The Creation Myth

Sometimes Ricoeur calls this the "Theogonic" myth because it begins, not with the account of how the world and human beings came to be, but with the story of the divine coming to be. This is a key point for Ricoeur and will distinguish this type of myth particularly from the "Adamic Myth." Instead of affirming the existence of a good God at the origin of all things, as the Adamic account does, the creation myth begins with the struggle by which the "younger" supreme god emerges as triumphant over the "older" gods. Only after describing the origin of the gods does the creation myth turn to the world and humanity. The coming to be of the world and human beings is, as Ricoeur says, "the last act of a drama that concerns the generation of the gods."

That the coming-to-be of the gods is described at all is significant. The way in which the gods come to be is also significant. The supreme god emerges through a kind of domestic violence. Thus, chaos, disorder, and evil are prior to the gods themselves and even enter into their very being and their way of acting. Human beings do not originate evil, but only continue it. Evil is not only prior to the beginnings of the human being, it even predates the divine being. Ricoeur uses the Babylonian myth *Enuma Elish* to illustrate this type of myth. Tiamat is the primordial mother, Apsu the primordial father. Together they represent the "initial commingling of the vastness of the marine waters with the fresh waters" (Ricoeur 1967, 177). The younger gods, led by Marduk, plot against Tiamat and Apsu. When Apsu discovers the plot, he develops a plan to destroy the younger gods. Before he can carry out his plan, Apsu is killed. Enraged, Tiamat gives birth to monstrous creatures.

The creation of the world follows upon the violent struggle through which Marduk, the younger god, emerges triumphant over the older Tiamat. Marduk has saved the gods from the evil power of Tiamat. So creation follows the salvation of the gods by Marduk, who has imposed order on chaos. Not only does the creation of the world follow on the violent victory of Marduk, but it emerges from that violence. Marduk cuts the body of Tiamat in two and the distinct parts of the cosmos are formed from her divided body. "Thus," says Ricoeur, "the creative act, which distinguishes, separates, measures, and puts in order, is inseparable from the criminal act that puts an end to the life of the oldest gods, inseparable from a deicide inherent in the divine" (Ricoeur 1967, 180).

And the human being is born from a new crime. The chief of the rebel gods is slain and from his blood Marduk advised Ea to create the human being. Humanity takes its origin from the life of a god, but from a rebel god "ravished by murder" (Ricoeur 1967, 180). And so, just as violence is at the heart of the coming-to-be of the gods, it is at the heart of the creation of the cosmos and the creation of the human being. "Thus violence," says Ricoeur, "is inscribed in the origin of things, in the principle that establishes while it destroys" (Ricoeur 1967, 182–83).

Where does salvation lie in the Creation myth? Because creation itself comes about through the struggle against evil, salvation is not distinct from creation. "If evil is coextensive with the origin of things, as primeval chaos and theogonic strife, then the elimination of evil and of the wicked must belong to the creative act itself. In this 'type' there is no problem of salvation distinct from the problem of creation; there is no history of salvation distinct from the drama of creation" (Ricoeur 1967, 191).

Human participation in this drama of creation takes place in two ways, in the sphere of ritual in which the people re-enact the cosmic drama that gave birth to creation, and in the sphere of politics where the king wards off the enemies of the state and of the gods. Human beings, according to this myth were created for the service of the gods, and this service "calls for the real re-enactment of the drama of creation" (Ricoeur 1967, 192). "By the celebration of the festival," says Ricoeur, "the people place their whole existence under the sign of the drama of creation" (Ricoeur 1967, 192). The king plays a crucial mediating role, standing as he does between the people and the god, mirroring the god to his people, representing his people before the god. It is through "the role of the king in the festival that the transition from cosmic drama to history is affected" (Ricoeur 1967, 193). In fact, the king is divine, although "by investiture and adoption rather than by actual filiation" (Ricoeur 1967, 194).

As the recognized representative of the gods of cosmic order, the king is charged to see that the political order, mirror image of cosmic order, prevails in his kingdom. This particular idea of kingship, specifically the relation of the king to the gods who imposed order on the original chaos, has implications for the "conception of violence and its role in history" (Ricoeur 1967, 194). The king's position as ruler is precarious, just as was the position of the triumphant gods in the cosmic order. It is important that the king control his enemies by whatever means necessary. The king's control of his empire is not just a political necessity, but a mandate from the god he represents. In fact, it is an easy step, says Ricoeur, to identify the king's enemies as representing the forces of chaos overcome in the original cosmic battle between the gods.

This view of political reality as reflecting the divine struggle through which the creation itself took place is the ultimate justification, says Ricoeur, of any holy war theology. Though he does not find that the Assyro-Babylonian culture (which gave rise to the epic of *Enuma Elish* which Ricoeur uses as an example of the first type of myth) explicitly developed this theology of war, Ricoeur maintains that "any coherent theology of the holy war is founded on the first mythological 'type' of Evil" (Ricoeur 1967, 198).

The main features of Ricoeur's account of the Creation Myth can be summarized in a series of propositions: "Before recounting the genesis of the
world it recounts the genesis of the divine" (Ricoeur 1967, 175–76); Chaos
is anterior to order, and evil is primordial. ". . . If the divine came into being,
then chaos is anterior to order and the principle of evil is primordial, coextensive with the generation of the divine" (Ricoeur 1967, 177); The coming to be
of the gods involves a kind of domestic violence through which the younger
gods triumph over the older gods; Human beings do not originate evil but
only continue it; Humanity itself comes into being through an act of violence
between the gods; Since creation itself is the overcoming of evil, salvation is
not distinct from creation; Salvation takes place through a twofold participation in the drama of creation: first in the sphere of ritual where the people
put themselves "under the sign of the drama of creation," and second in the
political sphere where the king carries on a holy war to overcome the enemies
of the state and of the gods.

The Tragic Myth

The Greek tragedies of the fifth century BC express this myth in its classic
form. Ricoeur gives three reasons why, in his opinion, we must begin with
Greek tragedy. First, Greek tragedy is not just one example among others.
It is "the sudden and complete manifestation of the essence of the tragic; to
understand the tragic is to relive in oneself the Greek experience of the tragic,
not as a particular case of tragedy, but as the origin of tragedy—that is to say,
both its beginning and its authentic emergence" (Ricoeur 1967, 211). In addition, the Greek version of tragedy shows the connection of the tragic with
theology, i.e., with ideas of the divine (Ricoeur 1977, 212). Greek tragedy
carries "all at once to its utmost limits" the theme of people blinded and led
to their destruction by the gods. The third reason for beginning with the Greek
example of tragedy is that it is particularly well suited to demonstrate "that
the tragic vision of the world is tied to a spectacle and not to a speculation"
(Ricoeur 1967, 212). The dramatic form of presentation is necessary because
the idea of predestination to evil by a god is "unthinkable" and thus cannot be
translated into philosophy. It can only be represented in the form of dramatic
action without the benefit of philosophical justification.

For Ricoeur "the crux of the tragic," the specific characteristic that makes
tragedy tragic, is the combination of two themes, divine predestination to
evil and heroic greatness. It was Aeschylus, says Ricoeur, who tied together
the tragic themes of "blindness" sent by the gods, fate, jealousy on the part
of the gods, and immoderation on the part of humans and added this specific
element that defines tragedy, the conjunction of divine predestination and

heroic greatness. The tragic emotion of fear (*phobos*) arises when fate or destiny, confronted by the resistance of the hero, finally crushes him or her. Ricoeur takes the figures of Zeus and Prometheus in Aeschylus' *Prometheus Bound* as the representatives of the divine and human poles of the tragic vision. The figure of Zeus sums up in a personal way the "diffused Satanism of the *daimones*," the impersonal fates. Opposite Zeus, facing him, is the figure of Prometheus who represents the hubris or excess of the hero "treated as authentic greatness and not as unwarranted exaltation" (Ricoeur 1967, 220).

This crucial element of the conjunction of divine predestination and heroic greatness produces what Ricoeur calls "the dialectics of fate and freedom" (Ricoeur 1967, 220). Without this dialectic there would be no tragedy. Tragedy requires both the hostile divine transcendence, the "pitiless god," and the freedom of the "hero that *delays* the fulfillment of fate, causes it to hesitate and to appear contingent at the height of the crisis" (Ricoeur 1967, 220). It is this hesitation and delayed realization of what has been determined by fate that gives tragedy its dramatic quality. The spectator knows that fate will win out in the end, but waits in terror (*phobos*) through the delaying action of the hero until the predestined future arrives as something new. Ricoeur cites the example of *Oedipus the King*. Oedipus has been predestined to kill his father and marry his mother. When the play begins Oedipus has already carried out his fate and the audience knows it, but Oedipus does not. Through the painful process of recognition, what was already true historically becomes true *for Oedipus*.

Ricoeur points out that *hubris*, the immoderation or excess of the hero, is not of itself tragic. Before the rise of tragedy in Aeschylus, Greek writers like Solon treated *hubris* as a moral defect and denounced it as something to be avoided because it *could* be avoided. In tragedy *hubris* cannot be avoided because the hero is a victim of divine possession. "This malignancy of good fortune, which is turned into misfortune by greed and pride, does not become tragic until it is brought into conjunction with the mystery of iniquity of the wicked god" (Ricoeur 1967, 222). Yet, in spite of the divine possession in tragedy, we can discern the emerging shape of responsibility in the form of immoderation or excess.

> In return, the immoderation introduces a human movement, a contrast, a tension into the heart of the mystery. 'Man's share' must at least begin to be discerned if the ethical moment in evil is to appear; there must be at least an indication of a dawn of responsibility, of avoidable fault, and guilt must begin to be distinguished from finiteness. But this distinction tends to be muted, annulled by predestination; the indistinctness of divine and human guilt is an incipient and annulled distinction (Ricoeur 1967, 222).

The failure of this "dawn of responsibility" to emerge into the full day of an ethical vision of life is precisely what distinguishes the logic of the tragic myth from that of the Adamic.

If the hero carries out evil deeds under the necessary decree of Fate, what meaning can we give to the notion of salvation? In the creation-drama, as we have seen, salvation was identical with creation itself, since creation was the overcoming of evil. And the original act of creation "was re-enacted in the battles of the king and in every conflict where the eye of faith could make out, behind the face of the enemy, the ancient adversary vanquished at the beginning by the deeds of the gods" (Ricoeur 1967, 227). To the question "What can the end of evil be like in the tragic vision?" Ricoeur answers that "when it remains true to its type" it can only offer deliverance through sympathy, tragic pity, "an impotent emotion of participation in the misfortunes of the hero, a sort of weeping with him and purifying the tears by the beauty of song" (Ricoeur 1967, 227). This answer seems to apply to spectators of the tragic drama. But Ricoeur's discussion of salvation—he uses the term "deliverance"—takes in both the spectator and the hero of the dramatic presentation.

The hero of the tragic drama experiences deliverance through the passage of time: " . . . the passage of time in the Greek tragedies suggests the thought of a redemption by time, which wears out the claws and teeth of the wrath of gods and men" (Ricoeur 1967, 227). In *The Eumenides*, the last play of the trilogy, *Oresteia*, Aeschylus moves away from tragic type of myth to a logic more typical of the creation-drama, namely the transformation of the gods themselves from malevolent to benevolent characters; "holiness wins out over primordial badness" (Ricoeur 1967, 228). But this movement away from the tragic does not, for Ricoeur, constitute a real deliverance for the hero. It shifts the action to a conversation among the gods and a new constructive role assigned to the Furies.

In Sophocles this movement away from tragedy does not take place "and in this sense Sophocles is more purely tragic than Aeschylus" (Ricoeur 1967, 228). Sophocles' *Antigone* "which is a tragedy of insoluble contradiction, begins precisely at the point where Aeschylus, in the *Eumenides,* saw a way out of the tragic; the city is no longer the place of reconciliation; it is the closed city which drives Antigone into defiance and the invocation of laws incompatible with the historic existence of the city" (Ricoeur 1967, 229). Though Ricoeur qualifies his interpretation of Sophocles by pointing to the end of the tragic in *Oedipus at Colonus*, he maintains that Oedipus' transformation "is a suspension of the human condition rather than its cure" (Ricoeur 1967, 228). Salvation within the tragic vision takes place through what Aeschylus in the *Agamemnon* calls "suffering for the sake of understanding."

Ricoeur does not believe that Greek religion ever offered "a genuine end for the tragic." It offers the possibility of divine possession, "the penetration of the divine into the human," and of divine ecstasy, "escape from the human into the divine." Apollo accomplishes this descent of the divine into the human as "counselor" and "guarantor of legislative activity of the great founders of laws" (Ricoeur 1967, 230). But Apollo does not heal the tragic soul. His role as "master of ritual purifications" indicates the continuing necessity for the tragic hero to return to the old purifications to wash away the stains of defilement. And Dionysus, the god of ecstasy, "seeks even less to make the wounded soul whole again" (Ricoeur 1967, 230). Rather than offering human beings a way of being reconciled with themselves, Dionysus offers "exaltation, a sort of sacred immoderation, by which one escapes from oneself rather than becoming reconciled with oneself" (Ricoeur 1967, 230).

Thus, we come to a key point of Ricoeur's interpretation of salvation in the tragic vision: ". . . the tragic vision of the world excludes forgiveness of sins" (Ricoeur 1967, 230). The lack of forgiveness in the tragic account of salvation is congruent with the lack of full responsibility that we saw earlier in the tragic account of the origin of evil. These two parallel features of the tragic vision of existence, the absence of full responsibility and of genuine forgiveness, distinguish it from the "Adamic" myth and the "eschatological" vision, which we will take up next.

The above summary refers to Ricoeur's treatment of salvation for the hero who is the subject of the tragic drama. Ricoeur also considers, as we saw earlier, a kind of salvation for the spectator, the ordinary person who, entering the spectacle from the outside, shares in some sense the destiny of the tragic hero. How does the dramatization of the tragic vision provide deliverance for the spectator? The tragic spectacle, says Ricoeur, offers the spectator a way of entering into the "place of tragic reconciliation," the chorus. "One must become a member of the chorus in order to yield oneself to the feelings which are specifically those of the tragic reconciliation" (Ricoeur 1967, 231). Those feelings are "the specific sort of fear (*phobos*) which comes over us when we are suddenly faced with the conjunction of freedom and empirical ruin" and pity (*eleos*), "that merciful gaze which no longer condemns but shows pity" (Ricoeur 1967, 231). "Such is the deliverance which is not outside the tragic, but within it: an aesthetic transposition of fear and pity by virtue of a tragic myth turned into poetry and by the grace of an ecstasy born of a spectacle" (Ricoeur 1967, 231).

We can summarize Ricoeur's account of the tragic type of myths in a series of propositions. First, and most important, Ricoeur finds the crux of the tragic in the convergence of the theme of divine predestination to evil and the theme of heroic greatness. Ricoeur calls this the "dialectics of fate and freedom"

(Ricoeur 1967, 220). On the side of the hero's freedom, and this is the second point, the ethical dimension of human responsibility emerges but never comes to fullness because of divine predestination. In the third place, though human freedom cannot prevail against the predetermined will of the gods, human beings can resist their fate, as is seen most clearly in the case of Prometheus, who says no while submitting to his fate. A fourth point concerns salvation in the tragic myth. It takes place in two ways. For the hero, deliverance takes place through the passage of time and entails the understanding that comes through suffering. For the ordinary people who participate in the tragedy as spectators, deliverance takes place through fear and pity aroused by the poetic presentation of the tragic myth. Finally, though a kind of deliverance occurs within tragedy, "the tragic vision of the world excludes the forgiveness of sin" (Ricoeur 1967, 230). Forgiveness is at the heart of the Adamic Myth to which we now turn.

The Adamic Myth and the Eschatological Vision of History

From the beginning, Ricoeur gives us an orienting compass to keep us from getting lost. "The 'Adamic' myth is the anthropological myth *par excellence*; Adam means the human being" (Ricoeur 1967, 232). This myth is anthropological because in it the human being, not some form of divine being, is the origin of evil. For Ricoeur, this entails three characteristics. First, Adam, the ancestor of the human race, is human like us, not some kind of supernatural being. For this reason Ricoeur avoids the language of the "fall." The Adamic Myth is "a myth of 'deviation' or 'going astray' rather than a myth of the 'fall'" (Ricoeur 1967, 233). Second, this myth is "the most extreme attempt to separate the origin of evil from the origin of good" (Ricoeur 1967, 233). Here Ricoeur makes a distinction that is crucial to his thinking. In the Adamic Myth the origin of evil is "radical," the origin of good is "primordial." Though evil, symbolized in Adam's turning away from God, lies at the root of human existence, it is not the deepest or primordial level. The goodness of the original creation lies deeper than evil. The third characteristic of the Adamic Myth is that the role of the central figure, Adam, is balanced by the subordinate figures of Eve and the Serpent who represent the presence of temptation, indicating a prior existence of evil that mitigates in some way the responsibility of Adam. This already-existing character of evil in the form of temptation suggests a resonance with the other myths of evil that I will explore later.

Ricoeur's presentation unfolds in four sections. The first section, "The Penitential Motivation of the 'Adamic' Myth," shows how the myth functions within the penitential consciousness of the Jewish people. In the second section, "The Structure of he Myth: The 'Instant' of the Fall," Ricoeur shows how the *intention* of the myth is "to concentrate all the evil of history in a single man, in a single act—in short, in a unique event" (Ricoeur 1967, 243). The third section, "The 'Lapse of Time' of the Drama of Temptation," shows how the "unique event" is spread out in a drama "which takes time, introduces a succession of incidents, and brings several characters into the action" (Ricoeur 1967, 243). The final section, "Justification and Eschatological Symbols," shows the orientation of the myth toward the future in which some kind of deliverance or salvation will lie, as they did in the Creation Myth and the Tragic Myth, each of which entailed some kind of "way out" of evil. Broadly speaking, then, Ricoeur's treatment of the Adamic Myth falls into two phases. The first is an investigation of the myth in its function of symbolizing the *beginning* of sin, the second an exploration of Jewish history and theology to see if they contain corresponding symbols of the *end*, symbols which would entail deliverance from sin. What follows are the essential elements of each of these phases.

Ricoeur begins his treatment of the first phase with a question: "What does it mean to 'understand' the Adamic Myth" (Ricoeur 1967, 235)? First, answers Ricoeur, we have to understand that it is a myth, not a historical account of events that occurred in a certain place at a certain time. "It must be well understood that the question, Where and when did Adam eat the forbidden fruit? no longer has meaning for us" (Ricoeur 1967, 235). Abandoning a historical interpretation of the story opens up the possibility of interpreting it as myth. "But then we should not say, 'The story of the "fall" is *only* a myth'—that is to say, something less than history, but 'The story of the fall has the greatness of myth'—that is to say, has more meaning than a true history" (Ricoeur 1967, 236). That meaning "resides in the power of the myth to evoke *speculation* on the power of defection that freedom has" (Ricoeur 1967, 235). By "power of defection" Ricoeur means the will's ability to deviate from what is good for the person choosing, and to *freely* choose situations that constitute a form of slavery.

The second point of Ricoeur's answer to the question of how we are to understand the Adamic Myth is that this myth is not a "point of departure" for Israel's experience of sin but actually "presupposes that experience and marks its maturity" (Ricoeur 1967, 237). The myth is itself an interpretation of earlier symbols of sin that had arisen out of Israel's experience, symbols such as "deviation, revolt, going astray, perdition, captivity." The question for Ricoeur will be to find what the Adamic Myth adds to these prior symbols. Whatever it adds must be recognized as a later and non-essential addition. As Ricoeur remarks, the figure of Adam is not important in the Hebrew Testament. Nor does Jesus refer to Adam in the New Testament. "It was St.

Paul who roused the Adamic theme from its lethargy; by means of the *contrast* between the 'old man' and the 'new man,' he set up the figure of Adam as the inverse of that of Christ, called the second Adam [I Cor. 15:21–22, 45–49; Rom. 5:12–21]" (Ricoeur 1967, 238). For Ricoeur, then, it is simply not true that "the Adamic Myth is the keystone of the Judeo-Christian edifice; it is only a flying buttress. . . ." (Ricoeur 1967, 239).

The answer to Ricoeur's question about what the Adamic Myth adds to Israel's consciousness of sin lies in his understanding of how myth functions. All myths, according to Ricoeur, have a threefold function; (1) they universalize experience, (2) they establish a tension between a beginning and an end, and (3) they investigate the relations between the primordial and the historical. The Adamic Myth illustrates each of these three functions. It takes the universalizing tendency already present in Jewish consciousness of sin and concretizes it in the figure of Adam, the original and universal human being. It establishes a tension between the beginning and the end by projecting Israel's historical experience of the dialectic of "judgement and mercy" into a myth of the beginning and the end. Human beings experience the judgment of God in the form of exile from the garden, the tower of Babel, and the flood. They experience God's mercy in the rescue of Noah from the destructive powers of the flood, in God's promises to Abraham, and through the transformation of those promises in a series of figures leading up to Christ, "the second Adam." Finally, the Adamic Myth investigates "the relations between the primordial and the historical" by distinguishing a "primordial" divine act of creation that is completely good and a "radical" historical act of the original human beings falling away from God. "Thus," says Ricoeur, "the myth appears at a high point of tension in the penitential experience; its function is to posit a 'beginning' (an existential not a historical beginning) of evil distinct from the 'beginning' of creation, to posit an event by which sin entered into the world and, by sin, death" (Ricoeur 1967, 243).

Having shown how the Adamic Myth fits into Israel's consciousness of sin, Ricoeur turns to the meaning of the narrative itself. First, we look at the central instant of Adam's sin. What happened? Underneath his elaborate and nuanced analysis, Ricoeur's answer to this question—what we need in order to show the direction of his thought—is simple and clear. When Adam ate of the forbidden fruit, he altered the relation of trust between himself and God (Ricoeur 1967, 249). More precisely, he took upon himself a prerogative that belongs to God alone, the determination of what is good and evil. The specific content of the prohibition, eating of the fruit of the tree of the knowledge of good and evil, was insignificant in itself, especially if you compare it with the sin of murder subsequently committed by Cain. What is significant is that the act was *prohibited*.

The consequence of the rupture between God and Adam is that something *ends* and something else *begins*. What ends is a "time of innocence," what begins is a "time of malediction" (Ricoeur 1967, 244). It is significant, says Ricoeur, that the story of the fall is inserted into a story of creation. The creation story designates the beginning of something good, the fall indicates the beginning of evil. Human life, then, from its beginning, shows the ambiguity of having been created good and having become evil. The goodness always remains as the primordial condition on which is superimposed a condition of evil which, though "radical," does not reach deeply enough into humanity to eradicate the "primordial" good. "Sin does not define what it means to be human; beyond our becoming sinners, there is our being created" (Ricoeur 1967, 251). Nevertheless, the ambiguity, "created good and become evil, pervades all the registers of human life" (Ricoeur 1967, 246). Human life "after" the fall is subject to hardship.

Ricoeur has answered the question "what happened in the 'instant' of the fall?" Now he turns to the question "how did it happen?" How did the drama that led to the rupture between God and man unfold over time? "The same myth that focuses the 'event' of the fall in one man, one act, one instant, also spreads it out among several characters—Adam, Eve, the serpent—and several episodes—the seduction of the woman and the fall of the man" (Ricoeur 1967, 252). The serpent's seduction of Eve, for that is where the drama begins, expresses the "transition" from innocence to sin. The transition leads from the innocence in which Adam first accepted God's prohibition against eating the fruit to a doubt about God's intentions. What had first appeared as a "creative limit," a limit that allowed human beings to develop within the finite status of creatures, came to appear as something negative. The serpent's question: "Has God truly said . . . ?" initiates the transition. "It is," says Ricoeur, "a question that seizes upon the interdiction and transforms it into an occasion for falling. . . ." (Ricoeur 1967, 253). The limit which had formerly provided an orientation now appeared as a "hostile negativity." The serpent denies the consequence that God had predicted if Adam were to eat the fruit and opens up a new possibility, which will follow on breaking God's command: "You will not die; for God knows that when you eat of it your eyes will be opened and you will be like God, knowing good and evil" (Gen. 3:4–5).

In striving to "be like God" by breaking the commandment, Adam, in effect, chooses to become his own creator. From this rejection of creature status follows what Ricoeur calls "the evil infinite of human desire—always something else, always something more—which animates the movement of civilization, the appetite for pleasure, or possessions, for power, for knowledge . . ." (Ricoeur 1967, 254). As we will see later, René Girard finds what Ricoeur calls "the evil infinite of human desire" at the heart of the notion of original sin. But for Girard it is a "mimetic" desire, wanting what the other has precisely because the other has it, not because it is good in itself. The scriptures call this *covetousness*. For Ricoeur, Eve represents the point of vulnerability in human beings, men and women alike, to this kind of temptation. The serpent represents the phenomenon that the temptation to evil always seems somehow external to human beings, that evil seems to be "already there" before individuals add their own sinful contribution, and that evil even takes on a kind of cosmic structure. "Thus the serpent symbolizes something of man *and* something of the world, a side of the microcosm and a side of the macrocosm, the chaos *in* me, *among* us, and *outside*" (Ricoeur 1967, 258). The temptation represented by the serpent exists in me, even before I have sinned, and it exists in the world—a world of fallen angels—luring me toward deeds that contradict my desire for happiness. For Ricoeur the serpent "represents the aspect of evil that could not be absorbed into the responsible freedom of man . . ." (Ricoeur 1967, 258). The serpent is a kind of residue of the tragic vision that cannot be entirely expunged from the Adamic Myth and its emphasis on human freedom as the origin of evil.

Ricoeur now moves to a consideration of salvation, what he calls "Justification and Eschatological Symbols." The question here is whether we can find a set of symbols of the "end" of human existence that are "homogeneous" with the symbols of the beginning. We have already seen this sort of correspondence in considering the other myths, each of which offered its own version of salvation. It is clear that for Ricoeur, the Adamic Myth has a kind of "career"—the word is mine, but it corresponds to Ricoeur's treatment of the myth from its fixed point at the beginning of Genesis to its reawakening in the writings of Paul in the New Testament. As we have seen, the Adamic Myth does not come at the beginning of Israel's experience of evil, but sums up and universalizes that experience. The story of Adam and Eve in Genesis was most probably written after the account of God's saving acts in history. To answer the question about the symbols of the end corresponding to the symbol of the beginning, Ricoeur will trace the development of symbols of promise and redemption first found in the Hebrew Testament and fulfilled in the New Testament. Two figures from late Judaism, the Gospels, and the Pauline epistles express the culmination of this development, the symbols of the Son of Man and the Second Adam. Ricoeur works his way up to these later symbols phenomenologically by tracing "the progressive enrichment of the figures or images that answer from the beginning to that of Adam in order to overtake the symbols of the Son of Man and the Second Adam" (Ricoeur 1967, 261).

"The figure of Abraham may be said to be the first answer to the figure of Adam" (Ricoeur 1967, 262). In him Israel represents its development as "a history directed by a 'promise' and moving toward a 'fulfillment'" (Ricoeur 1967, 262). At this point in history the promise refers to land and blood: a promised land and a posterity as innumerable as the sands on the seashore. This original promise, delayed as Israel's fortunes waxed and waned in the course of its history, was transformed into eschatology, the focus on a future world that will follow on the destruction of this present world. The figure of the king is an example of this evolution of the promise. The oracle in II Samuel (7:12–16) concerning the permanence of David's line speaks of "earthly and political hopes." "Your house and your kingdom shall be made sure forever before me; your throne shall be established forever" (II Sam. 7:16). But in Jeremiah, Ezekiel, and Isaiah "The King, the Anointed One . . . begins to be 'eschatologized' . . ." (Ricoeur 1967, 264). Ricoeur cites the words of Isaiah 9:1–6: "For unto us a child is born, unto us a son is given: and the government shall be upon his shoulder: and his name shall be called Wonderful Counselor, The mighty God, The everlasting Father, the Prince of Peace."

Here Ricoeur makes a point that is crucial not only to this passage from Isaiah, but to his whole interpretation of the Adamic Myth, and in particular his refusal to call it a myth of the fall. "The important thing for us is that the representation of a reconciled cosmos which accompanies this image of the coming Reign expresses not at all the regret for a lost golden age, but the expectation of a perfection the like of which will not have been seen before" (Ricoeur 1967, 265). The promise of a harmonious and peaceful future is not the restoration of a state of innocence lost through the disobedience of Adam, a state not expressed or implied in the story told in Genesis, but something new.

Ricoeur refers to two other figures that emerge during this same period when the image of the messianic king is evolving into that of a future Prince of Peace. The first is the Servant of Yahweh found in II Isaiah (42:1–9; 49: 1–6; 50:1–11; 52:13–53:12), the second is The Son of Man found in the books of Daniel, Ezra, and Enoch. The Servant Songs of Isaiah introduce something new, the image of a mysterious figure—we do not know whether this is an individual or the people of Israel or a remnant—who will restore Israel and be a light to the nations through his sufferings, through "the voluntary 'gift' of a suffering taken on himself and offered to others" (Ricoeur 1967, 266). This is a very different image from that of the king: "we need a new ear to understand the song of the suffering servant who gives himself for the remission of sins" (Ricoeur 1967, 266). "Surely he has borne our infirmities, and carried our diseases; yet we accounted him stricken, struck down by God and afflicted. But he was wounded for our transgressions, crushed for our iniquities; upon him was the punishment that has made us whole, and by his bruises we are healed" (Is 53:4–5). In this figure of the Suffering Servant Ricoeur finds the first manifestation of the idea of pardon, the central theme of the symbols of the end that correspond to the symbol of the beginning of sin. "It is through an enigmatic personage who substitutes his suffering for our sins that pardon is announced" (Ricoeur 1967, 266). Ricoeur is not thinking of just the passive carrying away of sin by the scapegoat. A scapegoat does not choose to carry the burden of sin. The Suffering Servant does choose and in doing so becomes a source of salvation for others. "Expiation through the voluntary suffering of another, however mysterious the *Ebed Yahweh* [the loving kindness of God] may be is an essential key to the idea of pardon. We may not understand how a loving God can allow one he loves to suffer," yet, says Ricoeur, the suffering of the innocent is crucial to redemption. René Girard, as we will see in a later chapter, explores the willingness of Christ to suffer rather than to inflict suffering on others.

The other, very different, figure is that of the Son of Man: "I watched during my visions in the night, and behold, on the clouds of heaven there came one like a son of man; he advanced toward the Ancient of Days, and they brought him near to him. And there was given him dominion, glory, and kingship; and all peoples, nations, and people of every language served him. His eternal dominion will never pass away, and his kingship will never be destroyed" (Dan. 7:13–14). This figure, the man of the end, corresponds to Adam, the man of the beginning. The son of man will be both Judge of the world and the King to come.

Both of these figures enter into the earliest Christology; Ricoeur calls it that of Jesus himself. In Mark, Jesus refers to himself as the Son of Man: "Again the high priest asked him, 'Are you the Messiah, the Son of the Blessed One?' Jesus said, 'I am; and you will see the Son of Man seated at the right hand of the Power and coming with the clouds of heaven'"(Mk. 14:61–62). "[A]fterwards," says Ricoeur, "Jesus for the first time unites the idea of suffering and death, which had previously pertained to the theme of the suffering servant of Yahweh, with the figure of the son of man; . . ." (Ricoeur 1967, 269). The son of man is precisely "man." And the suffering servant contributed "the idea of substitutive suffering that is voluntary in character" (Ricoeur 1967, 270). The result of the combination of these two figures is shown in the story of the last judgment of the sheep and goats; the judge (the Son of Man) is identified with the oppressed (the Suffering Servant). Jesus identifies himself both as judge and as victim. "As often as you did it to one of these, you did it to me" (Matt. 25:40). "The Judge of human beings is identical with them insofar as they come face to face in action and insofar as they are crushed by the 'greater' ones" (Ricoeur 1967, 270). The notion that "The Son of Man came not to be ministered to but to minister, and to give his life as a ransom for many" (Mk.

10:45) "expresses completely the fusion of the two figures—the Servant of the Eternal and the Son of Man" (Ibid., 271).

Ricoeur now introduces Paul's figure of the Second Adam, which, he says, "adds a decisive trait" to the figures Son of Man and Suffering Servant. St. Paul establishes a comparison between the first Adam and the second: "For if the many died through the one man's trespass, much more surely have the grace of God and the free gift in the grace of the one man, Jesus Christ abounded for the many" (Rom. 5:15). The "much more surely" is important. It indicates that the gift is not just a restoration of what had been lost through sin but a new creation that is better than what was lost. Ricoeur clarifies his point by referring to two phases in Paul's treatment of the drama of sin and salvation, the first contrasting disobedience and obedience, the second contrasting sin and grace. "For just as by the one man's disobedience the many were made sinners, so by the one man's obedience the many will be made righteous" (Rom. 5:19) And not only did Adam disobey, but after Adam's disobedience, "the law came in, with the result that the trespass multiplied; . . ." (Rom. 5:20).

Even though the contrast between Adam's disobedience and Christ's obedience is crucial, it is in the contrast of sin and grace, that the "decisive trait" of the figure of the second Adam comes to light: " . . . but where sin increased, grace abounded all the more . . . "(Rom. 5:20b–21). This abounding "all the more" of grace is the fullest expression of the work of restoration entailed in the Adamic Myth as Ricoeur interprets it, extending from the first Adam of Genesis to the second Adam of Paul's Letter to the Romans. Ricoeur notes that Paul even gives a certain finality, i.e., intentionality, to the disobedience of Adam and its results, a finality that points to the merciful intentions of God toward all people: "For God has imprisoned all in disobedience so that he may be merciful to all" (Rom. 11:32). Adam's sin was the "happy fault"—to use the Church's words—that "merited such and so great a redeemer."

Before leaving this recapitulation of Ricoeur's account of the Adamic Myth, a final point needs to be treated. In ending this section on the Adamic Myth, Ricoeur returns to the notion of pardon. "This detour through the 'images of the End' permits us to give the notion of 'pardon' all its richness" (Ricoeur 1967, 274). Clearly the notion of pardon is central to Ricoeur's version of the Adamic Myth. The key point is that pardon is not primarily a psychological, i.e., individual, event but the participation of the believer in the "types" of the first and second Adam. Ricoeur cites St. Paul who says that the individual is "transformed" [*metamorphousthai*] (2 Cor. 3:18) or "conformed" [*summorphos*] (Rom. 8:29) to the image of the Son, and that "Just as we have borne the image of the man of dust, we will also bear the image of the man of heaven" (1 Cor. 15:49). Ricoeur insists on the point: "It is not that individuals undergo a certain experience and then project it into a world of images; on the contrary, it is because they are incorporated into that which those 'images' signify that individuals attain the experience of forgiveness (*pardon*)" (Ricoeur 1967, 275). Again,

> in order to arrive at the experience [of forgiveness] one must have come from the symbolic universe constituted by the accumulation of figures stretching from the Adam of the Yahwist editor to the two Adams of the Pauline epistles and including the figures of the Messiah-King, the Shepherd-King, the Prince of Peace, the Servant of Yahweh, and the Son of Man, to say nothing of the Lord and the Logos of the apostolic Church. Pardon, as something experienced, gets its meaning from the participation of the individual in the 'type' of the fundamental human being (Ricoeur 1967, 274).

As we have already seen, Ricoeur begins his treatment of the Adamic Myth with the affirmation that "The Adamic Myth is the anthropological myth *par excellence*: Adam means Man" (Ricoeur 1967, 232). The myth puts a human being at the beginning of sin, the First Adam, and at the end, the Second Adam, who is also the incarnate God. It is time to summarize the stages through which Ricoeur has traced the "career" of the myth.

The first point is that in the Adamic Myth God simply is, without history and without competition; no account is given of the coming to be of God. Second, God creates the universe in all its parts, physical and spiritual, the world of nature and the human world, and God's creation is good. The third point is that evil entered the world when Adam went against God's prohibition and ate of the fruit of the tree of the knowledge of good and evil. The deeper meaning of Adam's deed was the intention to become like God, determining what is good and evil. Fourth, the consequence of Adam's deed was the introduction of *hardship* into human affairs. The fifth point is that, although human beings are responsible for evil, their responsibility is mitigated by the figure of the serpent who, in tempting them, represents an "already-there" presence of evil. Finally, God's response to the "turning aside" of human sin is to promise a restored state of humanity that is better than the state lost through sin. The promise is fulfilled definitively in Jesus Christ, the second Adam. "Where sin abounded, grace abounded all the more" (Romans 5:20). This abounding of grace over sin is an expression of the infinite compassion of God.

The Myth of the Exiled Soul and Salvation Through Knowledge

We move now to the fourth type of myth about the origin and end of evil, "The Myth of the Exiled Soul and Salvation Through Knowledge" (Ricoeur 1967, 279). This type, says Ricoeur, is at the base of all expressions of "anthropological dualism." "What distinguishes it from all the other types is that it divides the human being into 'soul' and 'body'; it is on the basis of this myth that man understands himself as the *same* as his 'soul' and *other* than his 'body'" (Ricoeur 1967, 279). This type is well illustrated by ancient Orphism, which is accessible to us now principally through the Platonic tradition. Ricoeur comments that some authorities "identify the myth of the exiled soul purely and simply with the Orphic myth." But studying the Orphic myth presents difficulties because we no longer have it in a pure form. Platonic and neo-Platonic philosophy is nourished by this myth and presupposes it, but we do not know what the original myth was like before Plato transformed it philosophically.

The essential lines of this mythical type, what Ricoeur calls "The mythical schema of the exiled soul," become evident in a comparison with the other types.

> . . . This myth is the only one which is, in the proper sense of the word, a myth of the 'soul' and at the same time a myth of the 'body.' It tells how the 'soul,' divine in its origin, became human—how the 'body,' a stranger to the soul and bad in many ways, falls to the lot of the soul—how the mixture of the soul and the body is the event that inaugurates the humanity of man and makes man the place of forgetting, the place where the primordial difference between soul and body is abolished. Divine as to his soul, earthly as to his body, man is the forgetting of the difference; and the myth tells how that happened (Ricoeur 1967, 280).

Ricoeur distinguishes between a "myth of situation" which describes the present human situation and a "myth of origin" which explains how that situation came about. Though we do not have it in its original form, the myth is well known. The "cunning and cruel Titans" assassinate the infant god Dionysos, then boil and eat his members. Zeus punishes the Titans by incinerating them with lightning. From their ashes Zeus creates the human being who thus participates in "the evil nature of the Titans and the divine nature of Dionysos, whom the Titans had assimilated in the course of the horrible feast" (Ricoeur 1967, 282). Because this "myth of origin" is known to us, not in its primitive form but only through the Neo-Platonists, Ricoeur turns first to the "myth of situation" which we can reconstruct "on the sole basis of the documents of the archaic and classical epoch . . ." (Ricoeur 1967. 282).

Ricoeur finds the nucleus of the situational myth in Plato's *Cratylus* in which Plato traces the etymology of the word "body" defined in distinction from the soul.

> It was the Orphics in particular, I think, who imposed that name [body], in the belief that the soul atones for the faults for which it is punished, and that for its safekeeping [*hina sozetai*], it has round about it, the body in the likeness of a prison; hence, that it is, as its name implies, the *soma* [the jail] of the soul, until the soul has paid its debt, and there is no need to change a single letter. (*Cratylus*, 400c)

The soul seems to bring with it some kind of previous fault for which it is atoning by its sojourn in the body. Interestingly, Origen, one of the most creative of the Church Fathers, held this theory of a fault committed before beginning of the individual's life on earth. In the Orphic myth, the body, though not the origin of evil itself, becomes a place of exile for the soul, a prison in fact. The prison of the body is also "a place of temptation and contamination," "a degrading sanction" (Ricoeur 1967, 284). Prison life itself, which is first a place of punishment for a previous evil, becomes in its own turn a source of new evil: ". . . the soul in prison becomes a secondary delinquent, continually subject to the hardening effect of the regime of the penitentiary" (Ricoeur 1967, 284). But the myth of the exiled soul goes even further. Not only does the soul dwell in the body as a kind of prison, but the soul's life in the body alternates with its life in Hades where it atones for evils committed in the body. So the soul is caught between two forms of punishment, one during life, the other after death. It is indeed a vicious circle. "The circularity of life and death is without doubt the more profound myth that underpins [*soustend*] the two myths of punishment in the body and punishment in Hades. To be born is to ascend from death to life, and to die is to descend from life to death" (Ricoeur 1967, 285).

It is a pessimistic vision. In fact, to use Ricoeur's words, "This mixture of condemnation and reiteration is the very face [*figure meme*] of despair" (Ricoeur 1967, 287). In reaction to this despairing interpretation of the body "as an instrument of reiterated punishment," the Orphics developed the notion of the soul as divine, "not from here . . . from elsewhere" (Ricoeur 1967, 287). " . . . [I]n its present body it leads an occult existence, the existence of an exiled being that longs for liberation" (Ricoeur 1967, 287). This notion of the soul as something divine led the Orphics to a different interpretation of altered states of consciousness. Other Greek cults spoke of "enthusiasm," literally, possession of the soul by a god. But for the Orphics altered states of consciousness were "ecstasy," a standing forth or excursion of the soul from the body. "Ecstasy is now seen as manifesting the true nature of the soul which daily existence hides" (Ricoeur 1967, 287). Only the Orphics among the ancient Greeks "attained the revolutionary intuition that the human being is no longer a mortal but a god" (Ricoeur 1967, 288). The crucial dividing line in Orphism is not between the gods who have kept immortality for themselves and human beings who are subject to the law of repeated alternations between the two prisons, Hades and the body. The division is between the soul which is in itself divine and the body its prison.

"The important thing now," says Ricoeur, "is to escape from the alternation of life and death, from reiteration; the 'divine soul' is a soul that can be delivered from this reciprocal generation of contrary states, from the 'wheel of birth and rebirth'" (Ricoeur 1967, 288–89). This leads us to a "new understanding of the self." This Orphic idea of a divine soul independent of the body inspired philosophy's efforts to "conceive the soul's identity with itself" (Ricoeur 1967, 289). .

This, then, is the "myth of situation," which proclaims the duality of a divine soul imprisoned in a body. Now an essential ingredient of the Orphic view leads to the necessity of a "myth of origin." For human beings in their present state have "forgotten" the true nature of their existence. "The question raised by the myth, then, is this: Why is that duality forgotten? Why is that twofold nature experienced as a confused existence?" (Ricoeur 1967, 298). The myth of origin explains how the two natures came to be confused in our present state as human beings, a state that "makes necessary a constant effort to regain the vision of duality." This myth of origin is the story we have already seen of how the human race came from the ashes of the Titans who had eaten the divine infant Dionysos. And just as the Adamic Myth was formulated by the Jahwist after Israel had already articulated its consciousness of sin, so the Orphic myth of origin is an evolution of the myth of situation.

Having considered the "myth of situation" which lays out the fundamental human dilemma of being a divine soul in an imprisoning body and the "myth of origin" which "explains" how this confused situation came about, let us turn now to Ricoeur's account of the "type of 'salvation' that goes with this type of "evil" (Ricoeur 1967, 300). The essential ingredient of salvation in the Orphic myth is knowledge. The tragic myth with its "not-to-be-avowed theology of the wicked god excludes philosophy and finds fulfillment in the spectacle" (Ricoeur 1967, 300). This was a key point in Ricoeur's treatment of tragic vision: the idea of predestination to evil by a god is "unthinkable." But "the myth of the exiled soul is *par excellence* the principle and promise of "knowledge," or *gnosis* (Ricoeur 1967, 300). And knowledge is precisely this act "in which man sees himself as soul, or better, makes himself the same as his soul and other than his body—other than the alternation of life and death . . ." (Ricoeur 1967, 300). This "awakening to itself of the exiled soul" is, says Ricoeur, the basis of all Platonic and Neo-Platonic philosophy. The body is "desire and passion," the soul is the principle of all attempts to put a distance between the reason (*logos*) and passion. "All knowledge of anything, every science, whatever its object, is rooted in the knowledge of the body as desire and of oneself as thought in contrast to desire" (Ricoeur 1967, 300–301).

We can now summarize this myth. First, this is the only one of Ricoeur's four mythical types that separates the human being into a soul and a body, the soul being the divine self, the body a prison. Second the true situation of the real divine self imprisoned in a body has been forgotten by human beings in their natural state. The myth of origin that tells the story of Dionysus and the Titans serves as a reminder of the real human situation. Third, the soul is subject to a cycle of dying and rebirth that entails punishment both for sins committed by individuals and for the evil that is inherited. Finally, liberation from the cycle of death and rebirth is *gnosis*, the knowledge that the soul is the real self and the body its prison.

THE CYCLE OF THE MYTHS

The Primacy of the Adamic Myth

Having explored each of the four myths, Ricoeur takes his stand in one of them, the Adamic, and situates the other three in relation to it, like planets revolving around a star. This cycle of the myths, as Ricoeur calls it is, in my view, the boldest, most interesting, and most provocative feature of Ricoeur's treatment of the myths concerning the origin and end of evil. First, Ricoeur says we cannot equally relate to all the myths even though each of them speaks to us in some fashion. Not wanting to be the Don Juan of myths, we need a vantage point from which to view these four symbolic narratives of the origin and end of evil. For Ricoeur, that vantage point is the Adamic Myth, "the place where the pre-eminence of one of those myths is proclaimed today . . ." (Ricoeur 1967, 306).

Resonances between the Adamic Myth and the Other Myths

Having chosen the Adamic Myth as standpoint, Ricoeur now shows how each of the other myths is related to it. Within the concentric structure set up by the gravitational space around the Adamic Myth in the center, the tragic myth is closest to the Adamic, the Creation myth next, and the Orphic myth farthest away. From the standpoint of the Adamic Myth, Ricoeur reaffirms the tragic. Even though the Adamic Myth is anti-tragic, it manifests several tragic aspects. Ricoeur's essential point is that although the Adamic Myth presents human beings as the initiators of evil through the act of disobedience, it also reveals evil as already there in the figure of the Serpent who tempts Eve. In more universal terms, it is already there in the ineluctable reverse side of sin implied in the very act of freedom. The exercise of freedom inevitably involves potentially negative consequences not intended by the one acting. We might aim, for instance, to acquire enough wealth to live a dignified life only to find ourselves trapped in the very possessions that are meant to liberate us. Developing certain possibilities necessarily excludes the development of others. "Who," Ricoeur asks, "can join the intensity of friendship and love to the breadth of universal solidarity?" (Ricoeur 1967, 312). Ricoeur says that the fateful aspects are experienced as fault, not in an ethical sense but in an existential sense. "Because fate belongs to freedom as the non-chosen portion of all our choices, it must be experienced as fault" (Ricoeur 1967, 313).

We have been discussing the tragic aspect of human freedom. The tragic aspect also appears in the divine side. Conceiving of God as ethical, rewarding the good, punishing the evil, was a great achievement of Jewish theology. But even within Jewish thought this vision "ran aground" (*echouer*) over the contemplation on the suffering of the innocent. The story of Job, the classical expression of the Jewish challenge to the ethical vision, presents us with a phenomenon Ricoeur calls "unverified faith." God shows Job the grandeur of creation and, in effect, asks Job to surrender his claim for an explanation that will justify God's actions. The figure of Adam and the figure of Job represent two poles of the Hebrew vision. The evil Adam commits leads to a just exile. But the evil suffered by Job is an unjust deprivation. The figure of Adam calls for the figure of Job, which acts as a corrective in that it helps us come to terms with the evil that happens to the innocent. Only a third figure, says Ricoeur, "could announce the transcending of the contradiction between a suffering justly deserved and a suffering for which the victim is not at fault. That figure would be the 'Suffering Servant'" (Ricoeur 1967, 324). Isaiah develops this idea of the suffering freely accepted by the innocent one. By accepting unmerited suffering, the innocent one turns it into "an *action* capable of redeeming the evil that is committed" (324). The action of accepting the suffering makes of it a "gift that expiates the sins of the people" (324). "The suffering that is a gift takes up into itself the suffering that is a scandal (Job), and thus inverts the relation of guilt to suffering" (Ricoeur 1967, 325). Now, rather than being caused by guilt, as in the case of Adam and Eve, the suffering of Isaiah's Servant takes away guilt. This in brief is Ricoeur's notion of the "reaffirmation of the tragic." As we have seen earlier, this image of the Suffering Servant along with the image of the Son of Man appears in the New Testament as an explanation of Christ's redemptive mission. As we will see later, Japanese author Shusaku Endo, in his last novel, *Deep River,* powerfully portrays this notion of redemption through innocent suffering.

From the perspective of the Adamic Myth we can, Ricoeur contends, also affirm the Creation myth, but only "up to a certain point" because the myth of chaos is further removed from the Adamic Myth than is the tragic. The key to the connection is that the Creation myth allows us to "think" the presence of evil at the heart of being. The tragic myth with its idea of predestination to evil by the gods is "unthinkable" in Ricoeur's view. But the notion of an evil at the heart of things, before the creation of the world or of human beings seems to have survived into modern times even though its symbolic form in the myth of creation has been superceded by ethical monotheism of the Hebrew Testament. ". . . Although the naïve theogony of Babylonia and archaic Greece is dead, more refined onto-theologies have not ceased to appear, according to which evil is an original element of being" (Ricoeur 1967, 327). Ricoeur points to the cosmological fragments of Heraclitus, the German mysticism of the fourteenth century, and German idealism, all of which "propose philosophical and learned equivalents of theogony: evil has its roots in the pain of being, in a tragedy that is the tragedy of being itself" (Ricoeur 1967, 327). This means that if being-as-evil is equally primordial as being-as-good, neither having final power over the other, then all we can hope for from life is an endless struggle between good and evil. No hope of final redemption is possible. We can never say, as Julian of Norwich did, that "all will be well." But if evil comes into the world only through free choice, angelic first, then human, then, perhaps, redemption is possible. If the free choice of evil, that is, of deviating from the good, is committed against a good and loving God, then that God can forgive and restore what has been damaged. This is, in fact, the logic of the Adamic Myth which differs essentially from the logic of tragedy.

In this "dynamics of the myths," standing in the place of the Adamic Myth, we have "reaffirmed" the tragic, and to a lesser extent the theogonic. But, says Ricoeur, the Adamic Myth struggles with the Orphic myth. This myth of the soul exiled in the body, precisely because it is the only myth that separates the human person into soul and body, is furthest removed "typologically" from the Adamic. Yet, it too has persisted in Christianity, principally through the influence of Platonism and neo-Platonism. The basis of the connection between the myth of exile and the Adamic Myth is, as with tragic and theogonic myths, "the experience of evil as already there" (Ricoeur 1967, 331). This is the "other side" of the Adamic Myth that first sees human beings as the origin of evil and then sees the evil that is already there. "But, while the tragic myth interprets passivity and seduction in terms of *divine* blinding and the theogonic myth interprets them in terms of a resurgence of the *primordial* chaos, the Orphic myth develops the aspect of the apparent externality of the seduction and tries to make it coincide with the 'body,' understood as the unique root of all that is involuntary" (Ricoeur 1967, 331).

Even though this Orphic myth is far from the Adamic, still Ricoeur finds related themes in the Hebrew understanding of sin. The captivity in, and Exodus from, Egypt, the Babylonian captivity and the return to Israel are all related to the notion of exile. The mythical expression of these historical experiences is found in the notion of banishment integral to the story of the fall; "the fall inaugurates a time of banishment, wandering, and perdition, symbolized successively by the expulsion of Adam and Eve from the garden of Paradise, the wandering of Cain, the dispersion of the builders of Babel, and the undoing of creation in the flood" (Ricoeur 1967, 331). Even the notion of exile in the body can be found in Hebrew literature. Ezekiel and Jeremiah use images of sin drawn from the body, the heart of stone, the lewdness of the adulterer compared to a beast in heat.

St. Paul, though he never falls into the soul-body dualism of the Orphic myth, reinforces the notion of sin as connected with the "flesh" understood as a symbol for everything opposed to the Spirit. But it is above all through a sort of "contract with Neo-Platonism" that Christianity moves "towards a quasi-dualism, accredited by the inner experience of cleavage and alienation" (Ricoeur 1967, 333). As this "contract" is lived out, the distance between the Adamic Myth and the myth of the exiled soul, "still very perceptible in St. Paul, will become smaller when the peculiar traits of the Adamic Myth become attenuated and new traits of Christian experience make the myth of the exiled soul more seductive" (Ricoeur 1967, 334). Adam will become less and less the symbol of our humanity and his innocence will become "a fantastic innocence, accompanied by knowledge, bliss, and immortality. . ." (Ricoeur 1967, 334). Adam's fault will become a "fall" comparable to the fall of the soul into a body in the Orphic myth, "an existential downgrading, a descent from the height of a superior and actually superhuman status . . ." (Ricoeur 1967, 334). Ricoeur does not believe that Christianity ever yielded completely to the contamination of the myth of the exiled soul, but its persistent presence underscores the importance of understanding the difference between the Adamic Myth and the Orphic and the influence of the Orphic myth on Christianity.

REFLECTIONS AND THEOLOGICAL RETRIEVAL

Ricoeur claims to be doing neither philosophy nor theology in this hermeneutics of myth. What then does this "symbolism of evil" have to offer to the theologian? Without attempting to develop a theology based on Ricoeur's work, I would like to give some indication of how I find it useful. Most importantly, Ricoeur provides a map that allows us to situate the various approaches to the relation of God and evil. Ricoeur takes his place in the Adamic Myth. This fixed point relativizes the value of the other myths, places them in orbits closer to or farther from the Adamic Myth, and thus allows the truth of each to emerge. A second helpful feature of this study is Ricoeur's treatment of hermeneutics. The notion of "demythologizing," though not original with Ricoeur, is crucial to his approach because it allows the myth to be myth. It is thus a remythologizing. When one accepts the fact that the myth of Adam and Eve is not a historical explanation of

how sin came into the world, one is free to explore how it reveals the existential structure of human sin. This is the stage of criticism that moves
us out of what Ricoeur calls a "first naïveté." A "second naiveté," on the
other side of the critical analysis, returns us to our beginning in faith, now
a critical faith.

A third significant contribution to theology is the richness of Ricoeur's
analysis of each of the myths on the origin and end of evil. Even though
he takes his stand in the Adamic Myth and views the other myths from that
vantage point, Ricoeur enters sympathetically into each myth to retrieve the
truth that each contains. Particularly helpful is Ricoeur's emphasis on the inner logic of each myth. They are myths of the *beginning* and the *end* of evil,
and the end is coherent with the beginning.

The beginning of evil in the violent struggle of the gods portrayed in the
myth of chaos, a struggle out of which human beings are born, leads logically
to the holy war as a way of overcoming evil in the realm of politics. The act of
salvation reenacts the act of creation. Once one understands this coherence in
each of the myths, one can see how incoherent transpositions take place. For
instance, the presence of a kind of holy war theme in the Hebrew Testament
is inconsistent with the idea of God contained in the Adamic Myth and with
the Hebrew understanding of sin that predates the Adamic Myth. Holy war
as an exercise in salvation has its ground in the myth of chaos and appears in
Jewish literature only as "cut flowers."

If the symbol itself, and Ricoeur's meditation on the myths of evil, give
rise to thought, they give rise also, by that very fact to questions. I would
like to consider one of those questions and sketch some answers that might
lead to further reflection. The question concerns the centrality Ricoeur gives
to the Adamic Myth. Though Ricoeur considers his choice a presupposition,
he does offer a rationale. The presupposition is that "the place where we can
best listen to, hear, and understand what all the myths together have to teach
us is the place where the pre-eminence of one of those myths is proclaimed
still today—namely, the Adamic Myth" (Ricoeur 1967, 306). The "theological retrieval" that I propose in this essay begins at this very point. Ricoeur's
"presupposition" is neither theological nor philosophical. But a theological
motive does exist for choosing the Adamic Myth; that motive is faith. As late
as 1995, Ricoeur refers to his pact not to mix the non-philosophical sources
of his conviction with the arguments of his philosophical discourse (Hahn
1995, 50). To retrieve Ricoeur's position for theology requires another pact,
the Anselmian commitment to proceed from a faith that seeks understanding.
Anselm claims to write his *Proslogium* "in the person of one who strives to
lift his mind to the contemplation of God, and seeks to understand what he
believes" (Anselm 1968, 2).

Having stated his presupposition, Ricoeur moves to the reasons for his choice. These reasons seem to me more like clarifications about how he understands the Adamic Myth rather than reasons for choosing it. His first reason is that the Hebrew consciousness of sin expressed in the Adamic Myth is the appropriate counterpart of the Christian doctrine on the forgiveness of sin. Second, the Adamic Myth is "revealed because it is revealing." In other words, the verification of this myth and the justification for choosing it as a privileged standpoint, lie in its power to reveal the deep structure of human evil. This is, Ricoeur acknowledges, a philosophical argument and would have been developed in the third volume of Ricoeur's study on the voluntary and the involuntary. The final argument for choosing the Adamic Myth as privileged standpoint, is that it serves to illuminate the other myths, reaffirming in various degrees their essential truths.

Even when one has made explicit the theological motive of faith as the basis for designating the Adamic Myth as the privileged standpoint, another challenge arises about the legitimacy of this choice. The challenge comes from critiques of the centrality long given to the Adamic Myth in Christian theology and the consequent emphasis on guilt and sin rather than suffering. To pick one example of this critique, Wendy Farley of Emory University challenges the pride of place given to this myth in the Christian tradition by making suffering rather than sin the center of the problem of evil and by working from a conceptual environment of tragedy rather than of the fall. Moreover, Ricoeur himself, in his "Intellectual Autobiography" published in 1995 as the opening essay in Lewis Hahn's collection of studies on Ricoeur, credits to his study of Freud that took place after the writing of *The Symbolism of Evil* "a decreased concentration . . . on the problem of guilt and a greater attention to undeserved suffering . . . (Hahn 1995, 21). These are precisely the issues raised by Wendy Farley.

Although the choice of the Adamic Myth as privileged standpoint from which to view the other myths could, in 1967, be presented as a presupposition with some accompanying clarification of what the choice meant, it may require further justification forty-five years later. That further justification, beyond the clarifications cited above, can be found in a deeper look at the inner logic of Ricoeur's study on the symbolism of evil.

First, *The Symbolism of Evil* is part of Ricoeur's larger project on the philosophy of the will, inaugurated with the publication of *The Voluntary and the Involuntary* and continued ten years later with *Finitude and Guilt* of which *The Symbolism of Evil* is the second volume. This overarching goal already sets Ricoeur on the path toward choosing the Adamic Myth as the privileged place to stand because only the Adamic Myth offers the possibility of a fully free will. The first section of *The Symbolism of Evil* on the primary symbols of defilement, sin, and guilt, ends with the concept of "the Servile Will." This concept is self-contradictory because will means freedom by its nature and servitude means "the unavailability of freedom to itself" (Ricoeur 1967, 151). St Paul expresses this "unavailability of freedom to itself" in his famous lament in Romans: "For I do not do what I want, but I do what I do not want to do" (Rom. 7:15). The Adamic Myth is the only one of the four myths that Ricoeur treats which both recognizes and resolves the dilemma of the servile will. This myth contains three elements related to freedom. First, it sees God as the Source of human freedom as of all other goods. Then, it sees Adam and Eve separating themselves from that Source and thus from the actuality of freedom. Finally, it sees God, the Source of freedom, reconciling human beings to himself through a series of interventions that culminate in the sending of his own Son, Jesus Christ. As St. Paul says, God was in Christ reconciling the world to himself (2 Cor. 5:19).

None of the other three myths can solve the dilemma of the servile will. For each the limiting factor against which the will struggles lies outside itself. In the tragic myth the limit lies in the jealously of the god that is pleased to pre-destine the hero to unavoidable evil. The lesson of the tragic myth is "do not aim too high, for the gods will bring you down." The lesson of the Adamic Myth is that all things are possible with God. The Creation myth locates evil within the sphere of divinity itself. Human beings achieve salvation, but not real inner freedom, by fighting the battles of the gods. The Orphic myth locates evil in the body, not in the servile will. The Adamic Myth alone sees God as fully on the side of human freedom. Only the Adamic Myth opens the way for a healing of the human will. This is why Ricoeur says that in the Adamic Myth evil is radical but not primordial, deeply rooted, in other words, but not the ultimate reality of human existence. Since evil is *only* radical, it rests on a primordial goodness and can be overcome by the original Source of that primordial goodness. That Source of goodness available to human beings for the healing of the will, we call grace. Ricoeur makes much of Paul's claim in Romans that where sin abounded grace abounded all the more. No other myth offers this miracle of abounding grace. How could they? In all of them evil is not just radical, but primordial. In all the other myths, evil shares with good the status of ultimate reality. In the Adamic Myth only the good is the ultimate reality. Goodness shares itself first through the gift of creation, then through the gift of grace. The vehicle of grace is forgiveness. Ricoeur notes, as we have seen above, that the tragic vision of the world excludes forgive-ness, precisely because the gods are jealous of human success. The God of the Adamic Myth wants human beings to thrive. Irenaeus' famous dictum sums it up "The glory of God is human beings fully alive. The life of human beings is the vision of God" ("Gloria enim Dei vivens homo, vita autem hominis visio Dei) [Irenée de Lyon 1965, 649].

The ultimate justification, then, for the choice of the Adamic Myth is that it alone sees ultimate reality as purely good and thus makes possible the miracle of forgiveness. The Ultimate Reality, God, wills the good for human beings even more that they will it for themselves. God rejoices in the freedom of the human will. If this is true, then a hermeneutic of suspicion toward God, though it may have its place for a time—as in the case of Job—cannot be the final attitude of a believer.

CONCLUSION

I have called this essay on Ricoeur's hermeneutic of religious symbol "a theological retrieval." What I have attempted to retrieve is the role of faith in grounding the choice of the Adamic Myth as the privileged place from which to view the other myths. This retrieval does not entail a critique of Ricoeur but a completion of something he did not include in the project of *The Symbolism of Evil*. In a second retrieval, this time using Ricoeur's own analysis of the Adamic Myth, I have tried to show how the logic of that myth justifies its choice as the standpoint from which to view the other myths. I remain convinced that Ricoeur's work as a whole is a fruitful source of reflection for theology. Though Ricoeur methodically separates the non-philosophical sources of his conviction from his philosophical discourse, those non-philosophical sources are at work in his thought. Ricoeur reveals how profoundly this is true in his admission that he found the lineaments of his book *Oneself as Another* (Ricoeur, 1992) in the "magnificent lines that conclude the priest's diary—not the final lines of the novel—in Bernanos' *Diary of a Country Priest*: 'It is easier than one thinks to hate oneself. Grace is to forget oneself. But, if all pride were dead in us, the grace of all graces would be to love oneself humbly, as any of the suffering members of Jesus Christ'" (Hahn 1995, 50). Compassion, in other words, begins with oneself.

Chapter Two

The Adamic Myth in the Hebrew Testament

> The primeval history, which the Yahwist constructed from elements of very different kinds, proclaims first of all with impressive one-sidedness that all corruption, all confusion in the world, comes from sin; but it also testifies that the continually widening cleft between God and man is matched by a secret increasing power of grace.
>
> —Gerhard Von Rad, *Genesis: A Commentary*, 24

Having examined the Adamic Myth in relation to other ancient myths accounting for the origin and end of evil, we now turn to its context in the Hebrew Testament, to trace the history of a story and its successive interpretations. The first chapter of that history concerns the place of the Adam and Eve narrative in the Hebrew Bible. Surprisingly, after its appearance in the book of Genesis, the story disappears from Israel's scriptures. "The contents of Gen., ch 2, and especially ch. 3" [the story of the fall], says Gerhard von Rad, "are conspicuously isolated in the Old Testament. No prophet, psalm, or narrator makes any recognizable reference to the story of the Fall" (Von Rad 1961, 98). But we must not, Von Rad hastens to add, let this isolation blind us to the fact that between this story of the Fall and "the subjects which Israel's faith was usually careful to mention [i.e., the Exodus from Egypt, the covenant, the entry into the promised land]" there are "manifold and important connecting lines running back and forth between here and there" (Von Rad, 99). Another biblical theologian, David Clines, speaks of *recurrent patterns* in various accounts within the Pentateuch. The exploring of those "connecting lines" and "recurrent patterns" is the aim of this chapter. We will discover that the story of Adam and Eve is an expression of Israel's covenant theology. We will also find here the origins of the sin that will spread like a virus in the primeval history and continue in the life of Israel. And the divine compassion that will abound in Israel's history begins in this story with a small, intimate gesture toward the couple after their disobedience, ashamed for the first time of their nakedness (Gen. 3:21). This act, small in comparison to God's acts of saving Noah from the flood or delivering the people of Israel from slavery in Egypt—is full of significance as a revelation of God's compassionate nature at the very beginning of the history of sin.

A couple of important qualifications need to precede the treatment of God's compassion in the Old Testament. First, recognizing with Von Rad that the story of disobedience connected with Adam and Eve is isolated to the first eleven chapters of Genesis, we mainly explore that story while attending to some of the "manifold and important connecting lines" that Von Rad also mentions. We need also to keep in mind a crucial limit to God's compassion. In the story of Adam and Eve itself and the narratives that follow it in the first eleven chapters of Genesis, God's compassion is universal because the characters in these stories are portrayed as the ancestors of all human kind, not just of the Jews. But as we move into the history of Israel proper, especially in the account found in Exodus, God's compassion is notably partisan. God has compassion on the Jews, not on their enemies. The divine treatment of the Egyptians, for instance, especially the killing of their first-born children in the last plague, strikes modern readers as harsh. On the other hand, God does forgive the people of Nineveh in the story of Noah. This is a complicated topic that would have to be explored carefully in a work that claimed to cover the topic of compassion thoroughly in the entire corpus of the Old Testament. This is not such a work.

ADAM AND EVE IN THE HEBREW BIBLE

If we start reading the Hebrew Bible from the beginning, we first encounter this drama of human sin and divine grace in the story of Adam and Eve and the primeval history of which the story is a part. The story recounts God's creative goodness, human refusal to accept the terms entailed in the gift of creation, the disastrous consequences of that refusal, and God's determination to repair the damage. It is a story of love met with refusal, refusal met with punishment, punishment yielding to compassion, compassion leading to forgiveness. This is the core of Israel's faith, powerfully expressed in the primeval history but not expressed there exclusively. This chapter will focus primarily on the context of Adam and Eve in the Pentateuch with some references to the wider context in the Hebrew Bible as a whole.

Biblical scholars have followed different methods for exploring the meaning of the Pentateuch and the connections of its constitutive parts. Gerhard von

Rad (1901–1971) and Martin Noth (1902–1968) have explored the *sources* brought together to form the text as we have it today. That text, they maintain, is the work of a final editor who collected various written sources already in existence. These sources, in turn, drew from a variety of preexisting written and oral material. According to Von Rad and Noth, the principal sources that make up the Pentateuch, designated by significant features of each source rather than by clearly identifiable "authors," are the Yahwist (J), the Elohist (E), the Deuteronomist (D), and the Priestly (P) documents. The theory based on the identification of these sources is called the "documentary hypothesis." An important feature of Von Rad's approach is that he treats the first six books of the Hebrew Bible, the Hexateuch, rather than the first five. This means the addition of the book of Joshua in which the people of Israel actually enter the Promised Land. Von Rad begins with what he considers the most primitive core of the Hexateuch and shows how its principal editor, the Yahwist, adds various traditions to make up the final product that he calls the Hexateuch.

Although the place of Von Rad and Noth in the history of Old Testament studies is assured, more recent scholars, while recognizing the importance of their work, criticize their reliance on the search for sources and their concern with the development of those sources into a final text. One such scholar, David J. A. Clines begins, not with a search for sources, but with the final text itself. He attempts to determine whether he can detect a pentateuchal theme and, if so, discern what the theme is. I will take advantage of both methods to help us locate the story of Adam and Eve in its larger context and thus to shed light on its meaning.

VON RAD'S GENETIC ANALYSIS

A movement toward reinterpreting the Bible through a return to the original languages in which it was written, attention to internal inconsistencies, repetitions, and other features indicating the unlikelihood of a single author began as early as the late medieval period and continued during the Renaissance and Reformation (Hillers 1982, 17). Baruch Spinoza, more famous as a philosopher than as a biblical scholar, recognized in his *Tractatus Theologico-Politicus* (1670) that "Moses did not write the Pentateuch, which is the work of 'someone else, who lived many centuries after Moses,' maybe Ezra" (Hillers, 18). Spinoza, anticipating the method later exegetes would follow, outlined his criteria for interpreting the Bible. Hillers paraphrases: "The exegete needs to examine the nature and properties of the language in which the Bible was written; then analyze the subject matter and outline it to show the contents; next study the environment of the books—who wrote them? what do we know of the author's life? what was the occasion for his writing? the age in which he lived? for whom did he write? and in what language—last, investigate the subsequent history of the book" (Ibid.). We do not need to trace the history of biblical interpretation as it developed in the centuries following Spinoza except to say that it continued to refine the methods referred to above and to develop theories about how our present Bible came to be. Following the "documentary hypothesis" outlined above, Von Rad developed a theory about how the Hexateuch developed into its present form. I am particularly interested to determine how the story of Adam and Eve functions in its context, the Pentateuch or, for Von Rad, the Hexateuch.

From Creedal Formulas to Adam and Eve and the Primeval History

Von Rad begins with the conviction that the historical core of Israel's faith embedded in the Hexateuch consists in God's loving care for the people of Israel, carried out in a series of divinely guided events. First, through Joseph, God leads the people into the land of Egypt (Genesis 37, 39–50) where they eventually become slaves; then, through Moses, God leads them out of slavery in Egypt (Exodus 1–15), and finally, through Joshua, into the Promised Land (Joshua). God's actions and the circumstances surrounding them, says Von Rad, are described in certain creedal formulas that constitute the earliest formulation of Israel's faith. Von Rad describes the path that leads from these earliest formulations to the much later development of which the story of Adam and Eve is a part.

Von Rad identified three creedal statements that he considered the most primitive articulation of Israel's faith, as just described, and he attempted to show how a subsequent editor built the edifice of the Hexateuch on them. First, Von Rad noted that these succinct formulations of Israel's faith contain no reference to the primeval history (Gen. 1–11), of which the Adamic Myth is part, nor are there present other key features of the final formulation of Israel's faith. Next Von Rad showed how the Yahwist editor (J), beginning with these creedal formulas, added other materials now included in the Hexateuch. Von Rad has a high regard for the Yahwist's contribution. "For it was the Yahwist who, so far as we can see, gave to the entire Hexateuch its form and compass. The Yahwist marks that decisive line of demarcation in the history of culture which we can observe for so many peoples; he was the collector of the countless old traditions which until then had circulated freely among the people" (Von Rad 1961, 17).

Von Rad includes three versions of the creedal formula, Deut. 26:5–9, Deut. 6:20–24, and Joshua 24:2–13. In spite of superficial differences among them, each of these three texts embodies the same foundational elements of

Israel's faith. We can see those elements by considering one of these texts in its entirety and the final lines of another. From Deuteronomy:

> A wandering Aramean was my father; and he went down to Egypt and so-journed there, few in number; and there he became a nation, great, mighty, and populous. And the Egyptians treated us harshly, and afflicted us, and laid upon us hard bondage. Then we cried to the Lord the God of our fathers, and the Lord heard our voice, and saw our affliction, our toil, and our oppression; and the Lord brought us out of Egypt with a mighty hand and outstretched arm, with great terror, with signs and wonders; and he brought us into this place and gave us this land, a land flowing with milk and honey (Deut. 26:5–9).

The last chapter of the Book of Joshua offers us a longer and more embellished version of the same simple formula. Its final lines emphasize a crucial feature of these early formulations of Israel's faith, the absence of any contribution on their part to the benefits conferred on them: "And I sent the hornet before you, which drove them out of your way; it was not by your sword or by your bow. I gave you a land on which you had not tilled, and cities which you had not built, to dwell in; you have eaten of vineyards and olive groves which you did not plant" (Josh. 24:12–13). These succinct narrations, says Von Rad, not the story of Adam and Eve, constitute the earliest expression of the core of Israel's faith. And yet the story of Adam and Eve, incorporated into the final version of the Yahwist source comes to have a resonance with this foundational expression of faith and, more important, with the fundamental themes of the Hexateuch of which the formulas are the core. How does it happen?

A *possible* answer to this question lies in Von Rad's account about how the Yahwist enriched these original creedal formulas by adding to them other ancient traditions that had, before his editorial genius laid hold of them, re-mained separate and disconnected one from the other. Three elements make up the essential content of the creedal formulas: the people of Israel descend into the land of Egypt and eventually became slaves, God liberates the people from Egypt, God leads them into the Promised Land, "a land flowing with milk and honey." These recitations are full of gratitude for the wonderful works of God toward the people of Israel, works that God carried out without any effort on their part. But the creedal formulas omit some of the central elements in the biblical story that we now have in the Hexateuch, namely, the primeval history that includes the creation accounts, the story of Adam and Eve and the saga of increasing sin that follows (Gen. 4–11), and the establish-ing of the Covenant at Sinai (Exod. 19). Moreover, says Von Rad, the account of the patriarchal period found in the creedal formulas is sketchy compared to the final version. Without losing the essential content of the original for-mulas, the Yahwist editor adds the missing elements, incorporating the Sinai tradition, extending the account of the patriarchal tradition, and including the primeval history (Von Rad 1961, 20–23).

The Incorporation of the Sinai Tradition

The "incorporation" of the Sinai tradition (Exod. 19:1–Num. 10:10) adds to the original creedal formulas the notion of covenant between God and his people. The creedal formulas, Von Rad notes, "witness to God's gracious leading; it is a sacred history" (1961, 20). The Sinai tradition adds the notion of a covenant based on obedience to God's will. After reminding Moses on Mount Sinai "how I bore you up [the people of Israel] on eagle wings and brought you here to myself" (Exod. 19:4), God draws a momentous conclusion: "Therefore, if you hearken to my voice and keep my covenant, you shall be my special possession, dearer to me than all other people, though all the earth is mine" (Exod. 19:5). So now, beginning with the creedal formulas' proclamation of God's leadership of his people, the Yahwist has added a second strand, the notion of a covenant and the obedience it entails. "In the union of these two traditions," says Von Rad, "the two basic elements of all biblical proclamation are outlined: law [Sinai] and Gospel [God's leading into the Promised Land]" (Von Rad, 20).

The Extension of the Patriarchal Tradition

A second addition, the "extension" of the patriarchal tradition, adds the notion of *promise* to the tradition of God's leading the people of Israel into the Promised Land. The creedal formulas, as identified by Von Rad, speak of a deed God has already accomplished: ". . . he brought us into this place and gave us this land . . . "(Deut. 26:9), only briefly mentioning "the God of our fathers," i.e., the patriarchs. The Yahwist extension of the patriarchal narrative, beginning with Abraham, imagines a time before the events described in the creedal formulas and *projects* into Israel's future a *promise* of land and multiple descendants. The creedal formulas regard the gift of land as an accomplished fact; the extended patriarchal history regards the gift only as a promise. This notion of promise, never fully realized even when Israel's God leads his people into the Promised Land, introduces an element of openness toward the future that will remain a permanent feature of Israel's faith. This openness allows for a continuous revision of the first formulations of Israel's faith.

The Inclusion of the Primeval History

We come, finally, to the Yahwist's inclusion of the primeval history (Gen. 2:4b–12:3), which includes the story of creation and fall and the continuing descent into sin that follows the first act of disobedience. Von Rad's words, which appear at the head of this chapter describe primeval history: "The primeval history, which the Yahwist constructed from elements of very different kinds, proclaims first of all with impressive one-sidedness that all corruption, all confusion in the world, comes from sin; but it also testifies that the continually widening cleft between God and man is matched by a secret increasing power of grace" (Von Rad 1961, 22–23). Paul's proclamation from Romans expresses the same idea more succinctly, "Where sin increased, grace has abounded all the more . . ." (Rom. 5:20b).

Now we are in a position to ask how the story of Adam and Eve comes to have a resonance with the creedal formulas that, according to Von Rad, express the earliest form of Israel's faith and, more importantly, with the fundamental themes of the Hexateuch of which these formulas are the core. The creedal formulas record the fact of God's saving actions on behalf of Israel, making a case for the gratitude owed by the people to their benefactor. By incorporating the Sinai tradition, extending the patriarchal tradition, and including the primeval history, the Yahwist editor situates the story of Adam and Eve in the context of *covenant* (Sinai), *promise* (the patriarchs), and the unfolding drama of sin and redemption (primeval history). We can, then, understand Adam and Eve not only as disobeying a command but as breaking an implied covenant, not only as forfeiting their beautiful life in the land of Eden, but as participating in a promise of new land in the future, with multiple progeny, and a renewed relation with God. We will return to the subject of the story of Adam and Eve as covenant theology.

DAVID CLINES: THE THEME OF THE PENTATEUCH

David Clines, following a different method, gives his own answer to the question about how the story of Adam and Eve is related to larger themes in the Pentateuch (not the Hexateuch). Protesting against the "primacy of the genetic method" (Clines 2001, 12), Clines begins with the Pentateuch in its final form and looks for a theme drawn from indicators in the biblical material. As it turns out, Clines' determination of the overall theme of the Pentateuch—and especially, his statement of "patterns" in the primeval history—though following a different method, closely resembles Von Rad's conclusion.

Clines carefully defines "theme": "The theme of a narrative work may first be regarded as conceptualization of its plot" (Clines, 19). Or, a theme can be regarded as "the central or dominating idea in a literary work . . . the abstract concept which is made concrete through its representation in person, action, and image in the work" (Clines, 20; Thrall and Hibbard, 486). A third definition of theme is "a rationale of the content, structure and development of the work" (Clines, 20) in terms of the final form of the work not its genetic development. Theme orients one to a work, "it makes a proposal about how best to approach the work. *Theme* is not identical with the author's *intention*; it "refers only to that aspect of the author's intention that is expressed in the shape and development of the literary work" (Clines, 21).

Clines identifies a theme for the Pentateuch as a whole. *"The theme of the Pentateuch is the partial fulfillment—which implies also the partial non-fulfillment—of the promise to or blessing of the patriarchs. The promise or blessing is both the divine initiative in a world where human initiatives always lead to disaster, and are* [sic] *an affirmation of the primal divine intentions for humanity"* (Clines, 30). Clines notes three elements in the promise: "posterity, divine-human relationship, and land." The posterity element is prominent in Genesis 12–20 where we find the promise made to Abraham that his descendants will be as numerous as the sands on the seashore (Gen. 15). The divine-human relationship element is found in Exodus and Leviticus with the giving of the law that sets forth how God will relate to the people and the people to God. The land element belongs particularly to Numbers and Deuteronomy where movement toward the land dominates the material. How the story of Adam and Eve participates in this larger theme will become evident from looking at Cline's identification of a theme for the primeval history.

Clines returns, in a later chapter, to the material that is not considered in the elements of the pentateuchal theme; namely, the primeval history. Since the primeval history forms the immediate context of Adam and Eve's story, it is particularly important for our study. Considering the primeval history offers an interpretive lens that will enable us to relate the Adam and Eve narrative, not only with the first eleven chapters of Genesis, but with the rest of the Pentateuch as well. Clines identifies three formulations that might express the theme of the primeval history: "A Sin-Speech-Mitigation-Punishment Theme;" "A Spread-of-Sin, Spread-of-Grace Theme;" and "A Creation-Uncreation-Re-creation Theme."

The Sin-Speech-Mitigation-Punishment Theme

Clines, with the help of Gerhard Von Rad and Claus Westerman, identifies a recurring pattern in the Pentateuch: sin, speech, mitigation, and punishment. Von Rad noted that the first eleven chapters of Genesis manifest a pattern of human sin, followed by divine punishment, and finally divine forgiveness or mitigation (Von Rad 1961, 152 ff; Clines, 67). Westerman observed that between the sin and the punishment occurs a "divine *speech* announcing or deciding the penalty" (Westerman 1961, 47; Clines, 25). And Clines observed something that neither Von Rad nor Westerman had noted: the event of mitigation or grace takes place between the divine speech and the divine punishment. Clines lists five examples of this pattern, the first of which occurs in the story of Adam and Eve. In Genesis 3:6, the sin takes place, Eve eats of the fruit and gives it to Adam. In 14–19, God speaks first to the Serpent, then to Adam and Eve, telling them of the consequences of the sin. The mitigation occurs in v. 21 when God makes leather garments for Adam and Eve. Then, in vv. 22–24 follows the punishment, expulsion from the Garden. The same pattern can be found in four other episodes of Genesis 1–11:

Table 2.1.

Episode	Sin	Speech	Mitigation	Punishment
Fall	3:6	3:14–19	3:21	3:22–24
Cain	4:8	4:11–12	4:15	4:16
Sons of God	6:2	6:3	?6:8, 18ff	7:6–24
Flood	6:5, 11ff	6:7, 13–21	6:8, 18ff	7:6–24
Babel	11:4	11:6f	?10:1–32	11:8

Clines seems to be stretching the hypothesis in designating a mitigation element in the Babel episode. Perhaps that is why he includes a question mark before the relevant verses. Von Rad was of the opinion that no gesture of mitigation can be found in the punishment inflicted on the builders of the tower of Babel. The mitigation in the case of the Sons of God and the Flood— it is one mitigation for both episodes—does not affect those who committed the sins but only those who did not participate in the sin, namely, Noah, his family, and his animals. God mitigates the punishment by instructing Noah how to avoid the flood. For the sinners the punishment was unmitigated. The clearest examples of the sin-speech-mitigation-punishment motif are the stories of Adam and Eve and Cain. God made leather garments for Adam and Eve. And for Cain—who complained, "My punishment is too great to bear. Since you have now banished me from the soil, and I must avoid your presence and become a restless wanderer on the earth, anyone may kill me at sight" (Gen. 4:13–14)—the mitigation is God's promise: "Not so! . . . If anyone kills Cain, Cain will be avenged sevenfold" (Gen. 4:15).

The mitigation that Clines refers to is a softening of, or an exception to, the punishment resulting from sin. We can also look at this same phenomenon of mitigation and frame it in terms of what it says about God. What kind of God would regularly mitigate punishment? Why did God make leather garments for Adam and Eve, or promise to protect Cain from possible killers, or exempt Noah and his family from destruction by the flood? The answer to these questions touches a central aspect of Israel's idea of God and provides another way to view Clines' very helpful formula. We can look at God's mitigations as compassionate gestures. Presumably, God made leather garments for Adam and Eve, not because their nakedness was an offense to the divine majesty, but because God recognized the disarray of the hapless couple after their sin. Presumably, God was moved by Cain's anguished cry and took pity on him. Presumably also, God recognized the injustice of punishing Noah and his family along with the guilty. The divine mitigations arise from divine compassion. Jonah's explanation about why he did not want to accept God's call to preach repentance to the Ninivites—"I knew that you are a gracious and merciful God, slow to anger, rich in clemency, loathe to punish"—constitutes a basic motif in Israel's history (see also Exod. 34:6–7; Num. 14:18).

The Spread-of-Sin, Spread-of-Grace Theme

As a second possible theme of the primeval history, Clines proposes "A Spread-of-Sin, Spread of Grace" motif (Clines, 70). Von Rad had already suggested this theme, noting that although increasingly severe punishments followed on the spread of sin, a parallel spread of grace on God's part accompanied the sin and its punishments (Von Rad 1972, 152f). Clines' criterion for the adequacy of a theme is the extent to which it provides a unifying explanation of the materials being considered. A significant advantage of the spread-of-sin, spread-of-grace theme is that it gives the underlying rationale not only for the narrative sections—the stories of Adam and Eve, Cain, the flood, etc.—of the primeval history but for the creation account in the first chapter of Genesis as well as the genealogies (Gen. 4:17–26; 5; 11:10–26), and the Table of Nations (Gen. 10). This theme differs from the "sin-speech-mitigation-punishment" pattern in that it refers not just to a mitigation before the punishment occurs, but to state of blessing following on the punishment. Adam and Eve do not die immediately after their disobedience even though God had threatened that they would. The go on to have children, fulfilling God's command to "Be fertile and multiply" (Gen. 1:28; 4:1, 25). Cain, after his sin and its punishment, continues to live his life under God's protection, having descendants and even founding a city (Gen. 4:17–24). God promises Noah and his descendants never to destroy all bodily creatures by the waters of a flood; "there shall not be another flood to devastate the earth" (Gen. 9:8–11). And even the sinful ambition of the builders of Babel, not mitigated before the punishment, unfolds into the promises given to Abraham.

A Creation-Uncreation-Recreation Theme

As a third possible theme, closely related to the second, Clines proposes that we look at the primeval history as a sequence of God's creation, human undoing of creation through sin, and God's re-creation of what humans have dismantled. Creation, as described in chapters 1 and 2 of Genesis, has proceeded "by the forging of bonds: between humans and the soil, humans and the animals, the man and the woman, humanity and God" (Clines, 81). But Adam and Eve, Cain, the generation that existed before the flood, and the builders of the tower of Babel, have, in a variety of ways, brought about the dissolution of the harmony envisioned by God in creating the world. The undoing of creation results in punishment. God even seems to despair of creation altogether at one point and threatens to destroy it. But the renewed creation once again accomplishes the separation of sea and land after the flood as God had first done in the account of creation of Genesis 1. Clines concludes that this theme too is pervasive enough to be taken into account in stating the theme of Genesis 1–11.

A combination of the second two proposed themes, says Clines, serves as the most adequate thematic statement of the primeval history. Clines concludes that the first theme (sin-speech-mitigation-punishment) is not sufficiently representative "of the total content of the primeval history to be regarded as part of its theme (though it is, obviously, a recurrent motif" (Clines, 83). If we combine the two themes—in fact, they seem to be different ways of making the same point—two possible readings of the primeval history emerge, one pessimistic, the other optimistic. The pessimistic reading says that no matter what God does, no matter how many times God dispenses grace, mitigates punishment, forgives, and recreates, human sin always re-emerges. Sin seems to have the last word. The optimistic version says that God's grace has the last word: "Even when humanity responds to a fresh start with the old pattern of sin, God's commitment to [the] world stands firm, and sinful humans experience the favour of God as well as [God's] righteous judgment" (Clines, 83).

How do we know which interpretation most adequately represents the primeval history? It all depends, says Clines, on where we place the ending of the primeval history. The last story, the Babel episode, ends without mitigation, recreation, or redeeming grace. God punishes Babel with the multiplication of languages and the dispersal of the city's inhabitants throughout the earth (Gen. 11:8–9), an action that suggests the total breakdown of society for which we are still paying the price. But perhaps the story of Babel is not the final significant word in the primeval history, even though it is the final narration. Clines locates the clue that allows us to choose the optimistic ending in the genealogy that follows the story of Babel. We tend to discount genealogies but they contain important clues. The concluding genealogy of the primeval history mentions both Shem, Noah's son on whom he pronounced a blessing (Gen. 9:26) and Abraham to whom God will give the promise of descendants and land. The inclusion in this genealogy of Shem, "firmly linked into the primeval history (Clines, 85), and Abraham, the first of the patriarchs and the figure on whom the promise to Israel rests, suggests a *transition* from the primeval history to the patriarchal history rather than a clean break. So the primeval history ends, not with the vision of the inhabitants of Babel wandering around the earth unable to communicate, but rather with a forward look toward the story of promise that begins with Abraham and continues through his descendants. This connecting of the primeval history with the patriarchal history and the promises to Abraham also enables us to see how the story of Adam and Eve is an expression of the larger theme of the whole Pentateuch. This will become even clearer when we consider the story of Adam and Eve as an expression of covenant theology.

Convergence of Von Rad and Clines

So we have seen that Gerhard von Rad and David Clines, each following a different methodology, come to the same conclusion regarding the theme of the primeval history (Gen. 1–11). Even though these chapters recount a history of sin and punishment, they narrate even more profoundly a story of grace, forgiveness, and a re-creation of what sin has dismantled. The pattern that begins in the primeval history will be evident in the whole, of the Pentateuch and, indeed, of the Hebrew Bible.

ISRAEL'S NOTION OF SIN AND SALVATION

We have been considering the place of the Adamic Myth in the Hebrew Bible, particularly the Pentateuch (or, according to Von Rad, the Hexateuch) of which it is an integral part. Now, as we consider its relation to a wider theology of sin and salvation in the Hebrew Bible, we will go deeper into the recognition of the Adamic Myth as an expression of covenant theology. We begin by noting Paul Ricoeur's description of Israel's different levels of consciousness regarding sin.

Three Levels in the Consciousness of Evil

In the first part of *The Symbolism of Evil,* Paul Ricoeur speaks about the "confession of the evil in man by the religious consciousness" (Ricoeur 1967, 3). He speaks of a "re-enactment" of that confession as a preliminary step towards a "philosophy of fault." In his re-enactment of the religious confession of evil, Ricoeur distinguishes between three levels in the consciousness of evil: defilement, sin, and guilt. Defilement, the most primitive level, refers to a physical contamination or impurity, analogous to a stain prior to any moral culpability. For the most part, our modern consciousness has left behind this conception of evil, relegating it to the realm of superstition. To get in touch with evil as defilement, "we have to transport ourselves into a consciousness for which impurity is measured not by imputation to a responsible agent but by the objective violation of an interdict" (Ricoeur, 27). The consciousness that sees evil as defilement, as misfortune rather than misbehavior, faring ill rather than doing ill, "transforms all possible sufferings, all diseases, all death, all failure into a sign of defilement (Ricoeur, 27). The violation of sexual prohibitions and prohibitions against spilling blood account for a large part of the category of defilement.

Examples of evil-as-defilement abound in Scripture and even in contemporary consciousness. Robin Cover refers to these as "cultic and unintentional sins" and cites multiple instances in the Hebrew Testament (Cover 1992, 34). One example occurs in the Second Book of Samuel, as the ark was being brought to Jerusalem, "Uzzah reached out his hand to the ark of God and steadied it, for the oxen were making it tip. But the Lord was angry with Uzzah; God struck him on that spot, and he died there before God" (II Sam. 6:6b–7). This ritual violation suggests a contamination of impurity completely separated from any ethical fault. To the objective side of defilement—the defiling force itself, impurity, taboo, ritual prohibition—there is a corresponding subjective side, the dread of violating the prohibition and incurring the consequent sickness, failure, ritual impurity, etc. Ricoeur calls it "ethical dread" because it fears not physical danger but moral contamination. "Man enters the ethical world through fear not love" (Ricoeur, 30). And redemption in this level of consciousness consists in purification, healing, removal of the symbolic stain, restoration of wholeness.

Ricoeur's second level of the consciousness of evil, sin, he defines as: "The category that dominates the notion of sin is the category "before God" (Ricoeur 1967, 50). In this sense, sin is a personal and interpersonal transgression rather than a quasi-material infection. The central historical element of Israel's faith that defines sin is the covenant. We can never understand Israel's mature conception of sin unless we begin with the covenant and particularly the covenant that came through Moses: "Therefore, if you hearken to my voice and keep my covenant, you shall be my special possession, dearer to me than all other people, though all the earth is mine" (Exod. 19:5). The Ten Commandments and all the other prescriptions that follow constitute the spelling out of this covenant. The possibility always remains of reducing these commandments to ritual prohibitions and requirements and thus falling back into the notion of evil as defilement. The Pharisees did it. But the covenant is essentially interpersonal and dialogic. It involves a tension between what Ricoeur calls "the infinite demand and the finite commandment" (Ricoeur, 54 ff).

But why should the people of Israel love God and obey his commandments? The motive is clear. Israel's love and obedience are born out of gratitude. George Mendenhall and Gary Herion illustrate this feature of Israel's covenant tradition by comparing it to Late Bronze Age (LB) treaties that, according to them, have a historically significant relation to Israel's Sinai covenant traditions (Mendenhall, Herion 1992, 1191) and contrasting it with the Iron Age Loyalty oaths. The LB treaties emphasize gratitude for deeds previously done by the sovereign as motivation for obedience. The Iron Age loyalty oaths appeal to "brute military force" as the only motive for obedience (Mendenhall, Herion, 1182). Israel's covenant tradition bases obedience on gratitude. The divine announcement of the covenant that we saw above: ". . . if you hearken to my voice and keep my covenant . . . ," etc., begins with a "Therefore;" it is the final step of an argument of which God has already stated the premise: "You have seen for yourselves how I treated the Egyptians and how I bore you up on eagle wings and brought you here to myself. (Exod. 19:4). *Therefore*, if you hearken to my voice . . . "(Exod. 19:5). The creedal formula in Joshua 23 that we considered earlier occurs in the context of a covenant renewal ceremony. The formula recalls the wonderful deeds of God for his people, his leading them out of slavery in Egypt with great prodigies, his delivering into their hand the people inhabiting the land they were about to enter, and his conducting them into "cities which you had not built, to dwell in . . . "(Josh. 24:1–13). Then Joshua, who has been reminding the people of God's goodness, concludes: "Now therefore, fear the Lord and serve him completely and sincerely. Cast out the gods your fathers served beyond the River and in Egypt, and serve the Lord" (Josh. 24:14). And the Ten Commandments begin, not with the first commandment but with a statement of historical fact that serves as the rationale for all the commandments: "I, the Lord, am your God, who brought you out of the land of Egypt, that place of slavery" (Exod. 20:2). Then follows the commandment, "You shall not have other gods besides me" (Exod. 20:3). In light of the other texts we have considered, it seems fair to assume a causal connection between "I, the Lord . . . who brought you out of Egypt" and *therefore* "You shall not have other gods before me."

Israel's sins, then, are always some form of ingratitude, or forgetfulness, or some other kind of turning away to other gods from the God who has brought them out of Egypt into the Promised Land. The essential ingredient of sin in the faith of Israel is the amnesia that leads to infidelity—we might call it the originating original sin. And just as the objective consciousness of evil as defilement entailed a subjective dread of the consequences of violating, even unconsciously, an interdict, so the objective consciousness of evil as sin, turning away from God, entails the subjective dread of God's wrath toward those who turn away from him. This wrath, says Ricoeur, "is no longer the vindication of taboos, nor the resurgence of a primordial chaos, as old as the oldest gods, but the Wrath of Holiness itself" (Ricoeur, 67). This wrath will eventually be revealed as what it really is at its root, the sadness of love (Ricoeur, 67). It "will have to be converted and become the sorrow of the 'Servant of Yahweh' and the lowliness of 'the Son of Man'" (Ricoeur, 67). The "wrath" of God is ultimately the anger of a rejected lover toward those who have failed, through their disobedience, to express the gratitude they owe to the one who has conferred benefits on them.

In discussing the "Wrath of God" in the Hebrew Bible, Gary Herion, distinguishes between two kinds of anger, "passion," and "pathos." "Passion," says Herion, "can be understood as an emotional convulsion which makes it impossible to exercise free consideration of principles and the determination of conduct in accordance with them" (Herion 1992, 991). Passion indicates a lack of self-control and, in humans at least, is censured in Old Testament writings. "Pathos," on the other hand, "is an act formed with care and intention, the result of determination and decision" (Herion, 991). The wrath of God in the Old Testament, especially the prophets, says Herion "tends to be portrayed in this way . . . it seems not to be an essential attribute or fundamental characteristic of Yahweh's *persona,* but an expression of his will" (Herion, 991). Herion finds only five examples in the Hebrew Bible of God's anger as "passion," Genesis 32:22–32 (Jacob wrestling with the angel/God); Exodus 4:24–26 (God is about to kill Moses until his wife Zipporah circumcises their son); Exodus 19:21–25 (God, speaking to Moses, threatens to vent his anger on the people if they try to come up to the Lord); Judges 13:21–23 (Manoah fears that God will kill him and his wife because they have seen God); II Samuel 6:6–11 (God is angry with Uzzah and strikes him dead for reaching out to steady the Ark in danger of falling). Only the last of these examples seems a clear example of God actually behaving irrationally out of anger. We considered it above as an example of sin as defilement.

Most often, God's anger is a response to human sin. Herion notes that it is the Eden narrative that "acquits Yahweh of any charge of capricious "passion" precisely "by associating the miserable aspects of human life with some fundamental act of disobedience by the prototypical human being . . ." (Herion, 993). And yet, in spite of the many "provocations by human sin" the book of Genesis never explicitly says that God "became angry" (Herion, 993). None of the punishments catalogued in Genesis, the expulsion of Adam and Eve from Eden, the refusal of Cain's offering and cursing Cain to wander the earth, the sending of the flood, etc., "is explicitly tied to divine 'wrath'"

(Herion, 993). Fishbane notes that human violence and lawlessness motivated God's decision to destroy humankind in the time of Noah, not some "whimsical eruption of divine wrath and the consequent disruption of the natural order—features well-known from world folklore. . . . By directly linking divine punishment to human evil, the narrator undercuts the terror known to ancient Mesopotamians of whimsical, even narcissistic gods" (Fishbane 1979, 31–32). The first expression of God's anger occurs in Exodus 4:13–14, where God becomes angry at Moses when he shows reluctance in accepting the mission God wants to give him. The next expression of God's anger occurs after the Sinai covenant and in the context of the special relationship that now exists between God and God's people. God warns what will happen if they neglect the justice toward one another that is implied in the Covenant: "You shall not wrong any widow or orphan. If ever you wrong them and they cry out to me, I will surely hear their cry. My wrath will flare up, and I will kill you with the sword; then your own wives will be widows, and your children orphans" (Exod. 22:22–23).

But whatever punishments follow on the sins of Israel, pardon is always waiting for them. Once they turn back to God, God will receive them. The prophet Hosea announces what Israel can expect if she turns away from her sins of idolatry and false worship: "I will heal their defection, I will love them freely: for my wrath is turned away from them. I will be like the dew for Israel; he shall blossom like the lily; He shall strike root like the Lebanon cedar and put forth his shoots" (Hos. 14:5–7). If turning away from God produced a kind of sterility that kept the people from being productive, turning back and the pardon that greets the repentant Israel will heal them and make them fruitful.

The category "sin" names the *objective* relation of the people in their relation to God. The *subjective* pole that corresponds with the ontological condition of sin, Ricoeur calls "guilt" (Ricoeur, 101). "Sin designates the real situation of man before God, whatever consciousness he may have of it. . . . Guilt is the awareness of this real situation . . . "(Ricoeur, 101). Guilt is not an awareness of being tainted or afflicted, as is the case with evil considered as defilement, but the voice of my conscience accusing me of what I have done, "the evil use of my liberty," as Ricoeur puts it (102). Through my sin, I am cut off from my origin. "Guilt is the loss of the bond with the origin, insofar as that loss is felt" (Ricoeur, 103). For Ricoeur, the phenomenon of guilt constitutes a "revolution in the experience of evil" (Ricoeur,102). The experience of guilt also involves one objective pole and a subjective pole. The objective pole is the person against whom sin has been committed, God. "Against you alone I have sinned," says Psalm 51. The Psalm also names the subjective pole: "For I know my offense; my sin is always before me." I have done it, not a collectivity, but I personally. This is very different from the notion of collective guilt that was characteristic of Israel in the beginning. After the first commandment, the prohibition against worshipping false gods, God pauses for a moment before delivering the second commandment to emphasize the seriousness of what he is saying: "For I, the Lord your God, am a jealous God inflicting punishment for their fathers' wickedness on the children of those who hate me, down to the third and fourth generation (Deut. 5:9).

Later in the prophets Jeremiah and Ezekiel, this notion of collective responsibility in the sense of inherited guilt will be reversed. Jeremiah speaks of a new day and a new covenant. "In those days they shall no longer say, 'The fathers ate unripe grapes, and the children's teeth are set on edge,' but through his own fault only shall anyone die the teeth of him who eats the unripe grapes shall be set on edge" (Jer. 31:29–30). And in those days, the Lord will make a new covenant. "But this is the covenant I will make with the house of Israel after those days, says the Lord. I will place my law within them, and write it upon their hearts; I will be their God and they shall be my people" (31:33). The new internalization of the ancient covenant paves the way for the new law of the New Testament. Ezekiel preaches essentially the same message (Ezek. 18:1–4). Thus guilt comes to have an individual meaning. Even though the leaders of the nation of Israel will be exiled to Babylon—a collective punishment—still individuals will be judged personally on the basis of their own behavior.

So we have three stages in the consciousness of fault, defilement, sin, and guilt; each stage marking a progression over its predecessor. The impersonal and mechanical working of defilement gives way to the interpersonal, I-Thou dynamics of sin. And the objective character of sin as rupture with God evolves into the personal responsibility of individuals for their fidelity to the covenant. Ricoeur ends the discussion on "The Primary Symbols: Defilement, Sin, Guilt" that constitutes the first part of *The Symbolism of Evil*, with a brief chapter on the "Recapitulation of the Symbolism of Evil in the Servile Will" which provides a bridge from the Old Testament material to the New Testament (Ricoeur1967, 151–157). The idea of a "servile will" is paradoxical. The will is by definition the principle of freedom. It can of course be inhibited by the action of others, as happened to the Jewish people in Egypt. But the will can also be the cause of its own enslavement. We will later see Paul's famous expression of this notion: "What I do, I do not understand. For I do not do what I want, but I do what I hate" (Rom. 7:15). And later still Augustine speaks of his will in chains through his own fault. Ricoeur considers this paradoxical notion—he calls it a "schematism"—of a "servile will" as a "recapitulation" of the symbols employed in the confession of fault that he has presented, defilement, sin, and guilt.

The Adamic Myth as an Expression of Covenant Theology

We return now to the story of Adam and Eve as an expression of covenant theology. Though the text does not present God's relation with Adam and Eve in expressly covenantal terms, we can hardly understand it outside the framework of covenant. We have already seen Von Rad's contention that by including the Sinai covenant tradition in the first six books of the Bible along with the primeval history, the Yahwist editor has framed the story of Adam and Eve in the context of covenant. I believe we can make an additional and even more compelling argument by considering the Adam and Eve story in the context of the tightly structured primeval history in which it occupies a crucial place.

Within the primeval history, with its description of the origins of human sin in the disobedience of Adam and Eve and the proliferation of sin in following chapters, we have the covenant God concluded with Noah, God's promise never to destroy the human race again. This covenant, unlike the covenant with Moses, is unconditional. No matter what sins humans commit, God will not, according to this promise, destroy them with a flood. Noah is a second Adam, participating in the new creation of the world just as Adam had participated in its un-creation. The re-creation, described in Genesis 8:1–3, begins with the receding of the flood waters. In language clearly reminiscent of Genesis 1:26ff, God speaks to Noah:

> And God (*Elohim*) blessed Noah and his sons and said to them: 'Be fertile and multiply and fill the earth. Dread fear of you shall come upon all the animals of the earth and all the birds of the air, upon all the creatures that move about on the ground and all the fishes of the sea; into your power they are delivered. Every creature that is alive shall be yours to eat; I give them all to you as I did the green plants. Only flesh with its lifeblood still in it you shall not eat. For your own lifeblood too, I will demand an accounting: from every animal I will demand it, and from humans in regard to his fellow humans I will demand an accounting for human life. If anyone sheds the blood of a human being, by a human being shall his blood be shed; For in the image of God have humans been made. Be fertile, then, and multiply; abound on earth and subdue it (Gen. 9:1–7).

Michael Fishbane comments on this passage: "Noah is thus portrayed as a new Adam in a renewed creation. The hopes of comfort and consolation anticipated in 5:29 ["Out of the very ground that the Lord has put under a curse, this one (Noah) shall bring us relief from our work and the toil of our hands"] are now consummated (Fishbane, 34).

Noah, stands precisely in between Adam and Abraham, ten generations from Adam, ten generations from Abraham (Gen. 5; 11:10–26). "Abraham is, like Noah, a new Adam and a renewal of human life in history" (Fishbane,

39). The whole primeval history thus functions as a kind of prologue to the story of Abraham and his descendants. In the light of this tight structuring of the primeval history, Adam and Eve at the beginning, Noah in the middle, and Abraham at the end, the disobedience of Adam and Eve takes on the aspect of breaking a covenant. Rather than being grateful for what God had lavished on them, they sought to improve their status and become like God. This is the central sin of the primeval history. Fishbane calls it the "*Issue of Will, Desire, and Aggressive Rebellion:* Eve, Adam, and the serpent; the serpentine sin and Cain; the gods and the daughters of the earth; the builders of Babel" (Fishbane, 38)—all of them set out to challenge the prerogatives of God.

The covenant with Noah is the centerpiece. We can read backward from it to Adam and forward to Abraham. Adam received the gift of creation and a special place in the Garden of Eden. He also received a prohibition with a curse attached; if he ate the fruit of the tree in the middle of the Garden, he would die. He and Eve do eat the fruit and thus initiate the unraveling of creation. Cain and the Nephilim, continue the degeneration until God decides to destroy the earth totally. In Noah, God mitigates the punishment, begins re-creating the world, and makes a unilateral covenant never to destroy the earth again, no matter what sins human beings commit. When the builders of the Tower of Babel also challenge God, God causes confusion by multiplying human languages and scattering people across the earth, thus bringing about yet another element of chaos in the creation that God had originally created good. Thus ends the primeval history, which, as we have seen earlier, ends with an opening to the patriarchal history. In the patriarchal history, beginning with Abraham, God begins again with another covenant.

Violating God's prohibition set in motion a process that will become the prototype of sin and salvation in the entire history of Israel. As soon as Eve and Adam eat, even before God announces their punishment and exiles them from the Garden, an internal dislocation takes place in the couple; "Then the eyes of both of them were opened" and for the first time they became ashamed of their nakedness and made loincloths for themselves (Gen. 3:7). And then, "when they heard the sound of the Lord God moving about in the garden at the breezy time of the day" (Gen. 3:8) they hid themselves from the Lord God. Adam and Eve have lost the comfort they once had with their own nakedness— "The man and his wife were both naked, yet they felt no shame" (Gen. 2:25)—and the fearless relation they had had with God. The relation between the two of them seems altered too. Adam blames his wife for his disobedience and later God announces to Eve that, along with bearing children in pain, " . . . your urge shall be for your husband, and he will be your master" (Gen. 3:16b). The author reveals that the subordination of woman to man was not the original state of things but came about through the couple's disobedience. The Yahwist account has introduced a dimension of interiority that gives his account a strikingly modern tone. In a few simple lines, the author explains the loss of the four intimacies that define us a humans, intimacy with one's self, intimacy with God, intimacy with one another, and intimacy with nature. We will return to these three intimacies later in a chapter on forgiveness.

From the very beginning, then, we have an example of Ricoeur's "servile will" i.e., the will estranged from itself by its own doing. Before God banishes Adam and Eve from the garden, they have earned for themselves an internal exile. They have turned a stony heart to God. Ezekiel will represent the Lord's salvation as a kind of heart transplant: "I will remove the stony heart from their bodies and replace it with a natural heart so that they will live according to my statutes, and carry out my ordinances . . ." (11:19–20). Distrust of God leading to disobedience has produced this stony heart that only God can repair. We could also use the language of the Orphic myth that thinks of the human being as a spiritual soul exiled in a material body. Paul Ricoeur, as we have seen, cautions about the use of this imagery but he also notes that as long as we take our stand clearly in the logic of the Adamic Myth, the Orphic vision has a certain relative truth.

The full story of God's restoration of the natural heart and the return from exile takes up the whole of the Hebrew Bible and continues into the New Testament. The first step of God's mercy appears even in the story of Adam and Eve, with the Creator's gesture of making leather garments for the couple. Other steps follow in the primeval history, the "mitigations" that Clines refers to, God's protective care of Cain (Gen. 4:15), the divine choice of Noah and his family to survive the flood (Gen. 7:1–7), and the promise to Noah never again to destroy the human race by flood (Gen. 9:8–17). The story of salvation continues in God's call and promise to Abraham, the divine kindness shown to Isaac and Jacob, God's guidance of Joseph for the salvation of the chosen people, and the leadership of Moses on behalf of the people enslaved in Egypt. God's mercy is evident throughout the Hebrew Testament.

ADAM AND EVE AND ORIGINAL SIN

We now come to a question that is crucial for our understanding of the history of Adam and Eve's story and its interpretations. Does Israel's notion of sin, drawn from its own historical experience and universalized, as we have seen, in the story of Adam and Eve, contain elements of what, in the Christian tradition, would come to be called original sin? We read Adam and Eve's story through the complicated and finely ground lens of historical interpretations.

Most potent have been the interpretations of Paul and Augustine who see the human will as affected by a hereditary weakness received from Adam and Eve. For Augustine, the affliction of will is transmitted by the act of sexual intercourse that perpetuates the human race. Although we will discuss Paul and Augustine in later chapters, for now we have to remove our Christian lenses and, as much as we can, look at sin from a Hebrew perspective. We concentrate on the intent of the story of Adam and Eve, its dynamism, as indicated in the *text* itself in the *context* of the primeval history, remembering that the story does not recur in later books of the Hebrew Bible.

In his book, *The Biblical Doctrine of Original Sin,* A. M. Dubarle examines the notion of original sin in Old and New Testaments and focuses on the story of Adam and Eve as the central text of the Old Testament related to original sin. To what extent does the story of Adam and Eve in itself suggest a doc- trine of original sin? A traditional distinction provides a helpful guide as we set out to answer the question. Original sin turns out to be a compound notion; its two component parts being originating sin and originated sin. *Originating* sin is a free act that brings about an unfree state that gives rise to further sins. The unfree state is not itself a freely committed sin but a predisposition to sin; this is *originated* sin. We can reformulate the question about Adam and Eve and original sin: "Does the story present an *originating* sin? In other words, does the disobedience of Adam and Eve—note that the text never calls it "sin"—set something in motion that continues in the descendants of this first couple? Does the Hebrew Bible treat the sins that follow the story of Adam and Eve, in the primeval history and the rest of the story of Israel, as *effects* of the disobedience in the garden?

Confining ourselves to the story itself, we can begin by looking at the *originating* sin of Adam and Eve and its *originated* consequences. Beginning with the originated consequences, we will work back to the originating sin. The process is simple enough.

We need to consider what life was like in the Garden of Eden *before and after* disobedience. The text provides six indicators of life before the fall: nakedness without shame (Gen. 2:25), familiarity with God (Gen. 3:8–10), the absence of hardship, mutual equality between the man and the woman, death as a natural condition of human existence (Gen. 2:17b), and the pres- ence of temptation in the figure of the serpent. Each indicator presents us with a different challenge. The first, nakedness without shame, is a clear indicator. The others require some deductive reasoning.

Dubarle, examining what we can know of the state of things in the garden before the disobedience of Adam and Eve, points to the simple observation at the end of Genesis 2, "The man and his wife were both naked, yet they felt no shame" (Gen. 2:25). He focuses his discussion on the importance of being clothed as a way of preserving human and social dignity. ". . . Clothing is the epitome of all the dissimulations that make social life possible, and not merely the precautions taken to avoid sexual excitement" (Dubarle 1967, 75). In the time of innocence, Adam and Eve did not need such dissimulations because they did not live in a hostile society. We can better understand the meaning of nakedness by looking at Jewish practice in the Bible. Stripping people of their clothes was a common form of punishment in Israel. Isaiah speaks of the exiles from Egypt and Ethiopia, young and old, who will be led away by the king of Assyria "naked and barefoot, with buttocks uncovered" Is. 20:4); the nakedness will be a source of shame. Jeremiah speaks of the humiliation to come on the inhabitants of Jerusalem: "Because you have forgotten me, and trusted in the lying idol, *I now will strip off your skirts from you so that your shame will appear*" (Jer. 13:26). Adam and Eve, before their disobedience, did not experience nakedness as a source of shame. Besides these cultural meanings of nakedness, we can also think of "feeling no shame at their nakedness" as a symbolizing a kind of inner harmony with themselves in their natural condition, an intimacy with self, that Adam and Eve lost through their disobedience.

The incident of Adam and Eve hiding from God as he walked in garden also reveals life before the fall. We must deduce that they hid because they had eaten the forbidden fruit. When they enjoyed an easy familiarity with God, they would, as the text appears to suggest, not have needed to hide. Life before disobedience is without hardship, since as punishment God pronounces there will be pain in childbearing for Eve, and the soil will resist Adam's efforts to cultivate his crops. We can conclude that these conditions did not exist before Adam and Eve disobeyed. A fourth indicator lies in God's words to Eve, "Your urge shall be for your husband, and he shall be your master" (Gen. 3:16b). This edict suggests a change in the status of the woman vis-à-vis the man, a mysterious combination of desire and subordination. Continuing our consideration about life in the garden before disobedience requires a look at the precise role of death as the end of life. We note God's original command to Adam: ". . . the moment you eat from [the tree] you are surely doomed to die (Gen. 2:17b). Fishbane says that Genesis 3 "deals with the profound interconnection between knowledge and death" (Fishbane, 21). The promise of death announced in Genesis 2:17, "is not only mortality but also the human awareness of mortality" (Fishbane, 21). Would they not have died had they not eaten? Why didn't they die when they did eat? The sentence God pronounces refers to death only in a subordinate clause, suggesting that dying was an event to be expected even before the disobedience: "By the sweat of your face shall you get bread to eat, *until you return to the ground from which you were taken; for you are dirt and to dirt you shall return*" [italics added] (Gen. 3:19). The punishment appears related to the anticipation of death rather than death itself. "To know pain, to be conscious of desire, and to anticipate death are, from the perspectives of this text, indicative of mankind's rupture from an aboriginal, primal harmony" (Fishbane, 21). Taking the changes explicitly noted in the story, we can generalize to a loss of harmony, tranquility, and order in human life. The author seems to suggest that death would henceforth be subject to turmoil rather than a natural, non-traumatic event.

A sixth feature of life in the garden before disobedience takes us to the originating sin. Even before Eve, then Adam, contradicted God's command, the serpent, "the most cunning of all the animals that the Lord God had made" (Gen. 3:1a) dwelt in the garden as an external power of temptation. And Eve showed a *susceptibility* to the serpent's wiles as did Adam, following her lead. This is worth dwelling on for a moment. Even in the state of innocence and harmony before the fatal act of preferring their will to God's, Adam and Eve were *susceptible* to temptation. The Christian tradition has interpreted original sin as an inherited *tendency* toward sin. Here we have a *susceptibility* to sin even before the act that gave rise to the tendency to sin. This susceptibility will become clearer as we look more closely at the precise nature of the temptation that makes up a part of the originating sin.

The temptation and the sin are complex. The serpent questions Eve about the prohibition, exaggerating it: "Did God really tell you not to eat of any of the trees . . ." (Gen. 3:1b)? Eve corrected the exaggeration (2–3). The serpent moves from exaggeration to denial: "You certainly will not die . . . your eyes will be opened and you will be like gods who know what is good and what is bad" (5). The woman ate and gave some to her husband. "Then the eyes of both were opened and they realized that they were naked; so they sewed fig leaves together and made loincloths for themselves" (7). The originating sin is the eating of the fruit, but the eating comes out of a deeper, *more original*, sin, doubting God's motives for forbidding them to eat the fruit. The serpent persuaded Eve that God was keeping something from them, preventing them from enjoying a benefit that would be theirs if they ate. Augustine says that Adam and Eve "began to be evil" in a secret way before the outward act of disobedience became visible. The secret invisible evil was pride which Augustine calls "a perverse kind of elevation" (*City of God,* XIV, 13, 608). We will treat Augustine's view at length in another chapter.

So the ultimate originating sin consists in doubting the goodness and veracity of God, treating God with suspicion rather than with gratitude, regarding the Creator as a competitor. The story presents all of this as occurring in discrete moments with specific consequences laid out one by one. Taking the story not historically but symbolically, we can regard it as an allegory. Sin originates with turning away from God in doubt, suspicion, forgetting of his benefits, preferring our own will to his. From this fertile soil arise all the particular sins that we know. As we will see, Paul found among the "idolaters" this sequence of turning away followed by specific sins: ". . . for although they knew God they did not accord him glory or give him thanks. . . . Therefore God handed them over to impurity . . ." etc. (Rom. 1:21a, 24).

In Adam and Eve's story do we have the foundations of a doctrine of original sin? We can certainly see the foundations but not the fully developed doctrine of Augustine. The effects described in the story, intended first for Adam and Eve for the rest of their lives, seem to carry forward to their descendants. God stations "the cherubim and the fiery revolving sword, to guard the way to the tree of life" (Gen. 3:24b). Eve is called the "mother of all the living" (Gen. 3:20), implying that her descendants will share her fate. The subsequent chapters of the primeval history reveal an unfolding history of sin that repeats the turning from God first undertaken by Adam and Eve. "Furthermore Genesis as a whole," says Dubarle, "and the Yahwist section in particular, is convinced that the ancestor's conduct and fate condition the destiny of his posterity, without it being necessary for the same free decision to be taken anew in each generation" (Dubarle, 67). On the other hand, Dubarle also cautions that though "the author of Genesis emphatically states the existence of a physical and moral legacy passing from one generation to another" (Dubarle, 69), ". . . it would be asking much more of him than he meant to give, if in his work we sought a theory of the relationship of these two factors [physical and moral] and the exact part played by each" (Dubarle, 70). Paul and Augustine, as we will see, emphasized the inherited character of sinfulness and located its effects in a certain weakness of the will. Modern society still debates the relative weight of heredity and environment in the constitution of character for good or ill.

If we move beyond Adam and Eve and the primitive history into the rest of the Hebrew Bible, we find some elements of what has become the doctrine of original sin. Robin Cover affirms that not only Israelite theologians, but their Hittite and Mesopotamian contemporaries recognized that "sin was a universal moral flaw, pandemic in the human race" (Cover 1992, 36). References to the universal character of sin occur throughout the Hebrew Testament. We have seen texts from the primeval history. Job's "friend" Eliphaz puts the rhetorical question: "Can a man be righteous as against God? Can a mortal be blameless against his Maker? Lo, he puts no trust in his servants, and with his angels he can find fault. How much more with those who dwell in houses of clay, whose foundation is in the dust . . ." (Job 4:17–19). We can find in the psalms references to a universal human frailty expressed in images like smoke, grass that fades, the dust to which we return: "For my days vanish like smoke; my bones burn away as in a furnace. I am withered, dried up like grass, too wasted to eat my food" (Ps. 102:3–4). Psalm 53 shows us the image of God who "looks down upon the human race, to see if even one is wise, if even one seeks God. All have gone astray: all are perverse. Not one does what is right, not even one" (Ps. 53:3–4). Psalm 51 comes closest to suggesting something like original sin: "True, I was born guilty, a sinner, even as my mother conceived me" (Ps. 51:5). In the *New Jerome Biblical Commentary,* John Kselman and Michael Barre call this passage "poetic hyperbole meaning 'thoroughly sinful'" (Kselman and Barre 1990, 534). Richard Clifford comments that "Before the all-holy God a human being can plead no self-righteousness but can only ask for God's purifying favor" (Clifford 1989, 765). Mitchell Dahood is more explicit in finding in this passage the equivalent of a teaching of original sin: "All men have a cogenital [probably a misprint for "congenital"] tendency toward evil; this doctrine finds expression in Gen. viii 21; I Kings viii 46; Job iv 17, xiv 4, xv 14, xxv 4; Prov xx 9" (Dahood 1968, 4). All the passages cited by Dahood affirm the universality of sin; none connect that sin with the disobedience of Adam and Eve. Humans sin, in the theology of the Hebrew Bible, out of the frailty that is intrinsic to their constitution, not from an inherited sin passed along from a first ancestor, a frailty that seems akin to the susceptibility to temptation that we found in Adam and Eve even before the fall.

CONCLUSION

The articulation of Israel's faith came out of a struggle that lasted over centuries, a struggle involving God's creative activity and generosity toward humans and their disobedience, ingratitude, and forgetfulness of God. The pattern of gratuitous initiatives on God's part and disobedience on Israel's part emerged in the history of the chosen people long before the inclusion of the story of Adam and Eve in the Hebrew Bible. But Adam and Eve, represented as the archetypical parents of the human race, play out the drama in a tightly knit narrative. All the elements appear, God's generosity, the ingratitude and disobedience of the recipients of that mercy, the consequences of that disobedience, including expulsion from the delights of garden into a life of hardship, and God's compassion. God showed compassion first in the simple gesture of making clothes for Adam and Eve and then in the events of the primeval and patriarchal histories, the deliverance from Egypt and, ultimately, in the whole history of Israel.

R. E. Friedman points out the extraordinary intimacy of Israel's God in the early chapters of the Hebrew Bible and the gradual diminishment of that closeness as the Bible progresses: "In the first few chapters of the Bible God is utterly involved in the affairs of the first humans. The text pictures God and humans in a state of intimacy that is unmatched in subsequent biblical narrative" (Friedman, 8). The breathing of life into the first man, the formation of the first woman, the planting of the Garden of Eden and the fashioning of the animals (Gen. 2:7–8, 19–23)—all of these were accomplished personally by God. "God personally walks in the garden, and the humans hear the sound (3:8). And God speaks familiarly to the humans in conversation (3:9–19)" (Friedman, 8). Friedman traces the diminishment of this intimacy throughout the Bible, beginning as early as the account of the story of the Flood. And while God is gradually "disappearing," says Friedman, the involvement of humans in their own destiny is increasing. Friedman is careful to point out that God's "disappearance" is a "diminishing *visible* presence just as the increasing control of human beings over their own destiny is an *apparent* increase (Friedman, 58). God is still present and active. Is this God's ceding power to human beings or their taking it for themselves? "Or is it neither of these; but rather, like children growing and separating from their parents, the biblical story too is about the growing, maturing, and natural separating of humans from their creator and parent" (Friedman, 59).

Within this dialectic of God's presence and absence, and human dependency and freedom, is the ongoing drama of sin and redemption. Israel's theology developed out of conflicting elements and moved in a definite direction—from God's anger to God's compassion. God's anger and mercy alternated, but mercy trumped anger. God threatened to destroy the human race by a flood then, after preserving Noah from the consequences of the flood, promised never to destroy the human race by flood again. Psalm 89, referring to the permanence of David's dynasty, expresses this coincidence of opposites: "If they fail to observe my statutes, do not keep my commandments, I will punish their crime with a rod and their guilt with lashes. But I will not take my love from him, nor will I betray my bond of loyalty. I will not violate my covenant; the promise of my lips I will not alter" (Ps. 89:32–35). We have seen how Israel's theologians sometimes looked at sin as a kind of defilement, to use Ricoeur's term, that could come about by the unintentional violation of a ritual prohibition. But the theology of the covenant transformed sin into a rupture between an infinitely generous God and a reluctant, vacillating, and disobedient people. As soon as the people ceased to resist and turned back to God, the Lord was there to receive them.

The quality of God's mercy is wonderfully captured by a creedal formula that recurs throughout the Hebrew Bible. Sometimes the formula embodies the tension between God's righteous anger and his mercy. But always it tilts to the preponderance of mercy over justice. "The Lord is slow to anger and rich in kindness, forgiving wickedness and crime; yet not declaring the guilty guiltless, but punishing children to the third and fourth generation for their fathers' wickedness" (Num. 14:18; Exod. 34:6–7). The two poles of the formula as expressed here seem almost contradictory, but, as we have seen, in the evolutionary progress of Israel's theology, Jeremiah and Ezekiel will pronounce a reversal of this passing on of collective guilt. This formula provides the key to understanding the Book of Jonah in its contrast between the abounding mercy of God toward the repentant sinner and the reluctant prophet's desire to see the guilty suffer. At the end of the delightful and instructive drama of Jonah's story, the prophet confesses to God the reason he fled from the mission God had called him to, preaching repentance to the wicked people of Nineveh. Jonah was not afraid he would fail but that his preaching would in fact bring the people to repentance and thus set them up for God's mercy. "This is why I fled at first to Tarshish. I knew that you are a gracious and merciful God, slow to anger, rich in clemency, loathe to punish" (Jon. 4:2b). After recalling the wonders God had worked among his people, Nehemiah praises God's mercy in the face of the sins of Israel's insolent, stiff-necked, and disobedient fathers: "But you are a God of pardons, gracious and compassionate, slow to anger and rich in mercy; you did not forsake them" (Neh. 9:17; see also Ps. 86:15; 103:8; 145:8; Joel 2:13).

Isaiah 52 expresses Israel's abiding hope in God, appealing to the dialectic of divine wrath and divine mercy. The prophet speaks to God's people, calling them out of their former suffering: "Awake, awake!/Arise, O Jerusalem,/ You who drank at the Lord's hand/ the cup of his wrath;/ Who drained to the dregs/ the bowl of staggering" (Is. 51:17). And to the awakened listeners Isaiah promised a new reality: "But now, hear this, O afflicted one,/drunk, but not with wine, Thus says the Lord, your Master,/your God who defends his people:/ See, I am taking from your hand/the cup of staggering;/The bowl of my wrath/you shall no longer drink" (Is. 51:21–22).

This brief look at Adam and Eve's story, with its dynamic of sin and forgiveness in the context of the Hebrew Bible, prepares the way for the chapter that follows, which discusses the Adamic Myth in the New Testament and the dialectic expressed by Paul: "Where sin abounded, grace has abounded all the more" (Rom. 5:20).

Chapter Three

The Adamic Myth
in the New Testament

If because of the one man's trespass, death exercised dominion through
that one, much more surely will those who receive the abundance of grace
and the free gift of righteousness exercise dominion in life through that
one man, Jesus Christ.

—Romans 5:1, NRSV[1]

We have been following the history of Adam and Eve's story and its interpretations and tracing the drama of human sin matched by divine compassion.
The first chapter of that history dealt with the emergence of the narrative
in the Hebrew Testament where it recapitulates and universalizes Israel's
experience of sin and grace already narrated in other accounts. The Hebrew
Bible, however, does not "remember" the saga of Adam and Eve in the way
it remembered its slavery in Egypt and God's deliverance, or the divinely
engineered restoration from the Babylonian Captivity. Adam and Eve's story
disappears from Israel's consciousness. As Paul Ricoeur notes, the story of
Adam and Eve does not become a cornerstone of Israel's faith. The second
chapter of their story must await Paul's treatment in the New Testament.

This chapter establishes the lines of contact between the New Testament
and the Adamic Myth. We turn now to the New Testament with these questions: Can the Adamic Myth be called a cornerstone of Christianity? Does
the dynamic logic of this myth provide a vision that expresses the notion of
salvation in Christianity? Above all, does the New Testament continue to unfold the dialectic of sin and grace that began in Adam and Eve? The answer,
although affirmative, is not obvious—at least not for the whole of the New
Testament. In Paul it is obvious. By making Christ the "Second Adam," Paul,
probably familiar with inter-testamental allusions to Adam and Eve, resurrects

the figure of Adam from its dormancy in the Old Testament and extends its scope, making of it a foundation stone of his theology. The first part of this chapter shows the development of Paul's thought and, in particular, which aspects of the Adamic Myth are crucial to his thought. We must ask, however, do other books of the New Testament, particularly the Gospels, embody the inner dynamic of the Aamic Myth (as opposed to the other myths that Ricoeur explores), and, if so, what aspects of the Adamic Myth find a place in the theology of the Gospels? The second part of the chapter will argue that the inner logic of the Adamic Myth provides a framework for the Gospels, especially the condition of universal moral impotence coupled with the power of freedom through life in Christ that provides a unifying vision to the diverse theologies we find there.

After briefly revisiting the dynamic elements of the Adamic Myth already presented, we will see how Paul, in his *Letter to the Romans*, and to a lesser extent in his First Letter to the Corinthians, elaborates the vision of salvation embodied in the Adamic Myth. Then, guided by the questions about whether, to what extent, and how they might express the logic of the Adamic Myth, we will explore the idea of salvation in the Gospels. A brief schema that lays out three phases of salvation in Christian thought will conclude the chapter and set the stage for an investigation into the dynamics of forgiveness.

This discussion will be guided by the questions implicit in the last chapter: Is the doctrine of original sin a source of liberation rather than the negatively charged vision of human life that many people see in it? How do Paul and the Gospel writers conceive the sinful situation that creates the need for salvation? How does salvation come about? What is God's role? What is our role? Is there a connection between our role and God's role?

ESSENTIAL CHARACTERISTICS OF THE ADAMIC MYTH

Before examining how the dynamics of the Adamic Myth are present in the New Testament, it is helpful to recall the essential elements of that vision. The Adamic Myth is a mythical *type* embodied in a variety of narratives, parables, and myths—among them, the central New Testament narratives and theological developments. The logic of the Adamic Myth extends into the entire primeval history with its history of sin "matched by a secret increasing power of grace" (Von Rad). Finally, we ask what it means to speak of the "dynamics" of the Adamic Myth? It means that this story with its symbolic elements is charged with energy capable of revealing the inner truth of the human spirit. That energy lay dormant in the Hebrew Bible until Paul found a way to tap it as the negative pole of a corresponding positive: salvation in Christ.

The Adamic Myth can be summarized in six points: the goodness of God and everything God has created; the prohibition against eating of the tree of the knowledge of good and evil; the serpent's temptation and Adam and Eve's disobedience; the consequences of disobedience, that is, evil as expressed in the fourfold loss of intimacy with self, God, neighbor, and nature; God's initiative in restoring what has been lost; and human cooperation with God's initiative. The full scope of this vision comes to explicit fullness only in the writings of St. Paul. We might say that Paul makes of Jesus the second pier of a bridge that has as its first pier the figure of Adam. The bridge itself, supported by these two piers, is the historical extension over which walk the figures of Abraham, Moses, and the kings and prophets of Israel.

We now turn to Paul to see how he makes of Jesus the New Testament pier of the Adamic Myth. After considering Paul, we can complete the list of characteristics of the Adamic Myth in its full extension from Genesis to the New Testament.

THE ADAMIC MYTH IN PAUL

In Paul we find transformation of the Adamic Myth in The Letter to the Romans, his most mature work and, to a lesser extent in Chapter 15 of his First Letter to the Corinthians. Romans plays in reverse the turning away from God narrated in the Adamic Myth. Just as the disobedience of Adam and Eve brought about the unraveling of creation, so the obedience of Jesus Christ has knitted it up. The knitting up Paul calls justification, reconciliation, redemptive liberation, or expiation. The argument of Romans unfolds in three phases. First Paul describes the situation that gives rise to the need for salvation, both for pagans and for Jews. All fall under the reign of sin. Then Paul introduces the figure of Abraham, who occupies in salvation history a mid-point between the pagans (or Gentiles) with their knowledge of God through nature and the people of Israel formed by the law. Paul sees in Abraham the prototype of the believer. Abraham embodies, as a type, the answer to the question, "What must *we* do to be saved?" We must believe. Finally, Paul establishes Jesus Christ as the *second* Adam and shows how the gospel of Jesus Christ, by offering salvation from the dilemma of the enslaved will, is the "power of God for salvation to everyone who has faith, to the Jew first and also to the Greek" (Rom. 1:16).

The Situation of Sin is Universal

Paul begins, not with the consequences of Adam's and Eve's disobedience, but with "the ungodliness and wickedness of those who by their wickedness suppress the truth" (Rom. 1:18). These people knew God because what can be known about God is plain from creation. But although they knew God, "they did not honor him as God or give thanks to him, but they became futile in their thinking, and their senseless minds were darkened." They worshipped idols, "images resembling a mortal human being or birds or four-footed animals or reptiles" (Rom. 1:21–23). Their sin, then, was a turning away from God toward gods. The *consequence* of their sin was that "God gave them up" to vices, "degrading passions," in which Paul includes illicit sexual relations and "every kind of wickedness, evil, covetousness, malice . . ." and so forth. He seems to exclude no type of sin. The phrase, "God gave them up . . ." occurs three times in Romans 1:18–32. "God gave them up in the lusts of their hearts to impurity" (Rom. 1:24), "God gave them up to degrading passions" (Rom. 1:26), "God gave them up to a debased mind and to things that should not be done" (Rom. 1:28). The crucial point of Paul's analysis, for this study, is that with the Gentiles, as with Adam and Eve, the originating sin is failing to recognize God or give him thanks. All the other "sins" come as a consequence of the original turning away, the originating sin.

Though Paul himself does not mark the connection, this turning away of the pagans from the knowledge and glorification of God seems to parallel the turning away of Adam and Eve from God through disobedience. The consequences of turning away from God for the pagans, and for Adam and Eve and their descendants, are similar. In case his Jewish listeners might be feeling righteous in hearing this critique of the Gentiles, and congratulate themselves on being righteous for having the law, Paul reminds them that they are under the same judgment to the extent that they do similar things. Just *having* the law does not justify a person, "For it is not the hearers of the law who are righteous in God's sight, but the doers of the law who will be justified" (Rom. 2:13). So then, both Gentiles and Jews stand in need of salvation because they have turned away from God. "Are we [Jews] any better off? No, not at all; for we have already charged that all, both Jews and Greeks, are under the power of sin . . ." (Rom. 3:9). The Gentiles have turned away from God as manifested in nature, the Jews have turned away from God as revealed in the Law.

Abraham as the Model of Justification by Faith

In the second phase of Paul's argument he presents a solution that applies both to Jews and Gentiles: Paul appeals to the figure of Abraham who found salvation not through the law, which God revealed only later through Moses, but through the obedience of faith. Abraham is a universal figure because he is an example for all people, not just for Jews. Paul quotes God's promise to Abraham, i.e., that he would become "the father of many nations" (Rom.

4:18). The key is that Abraham was justified by faith not by obedience to the law. When God promised children to Abraham and Sarah and said that Abraham would become the father of many nations, Abraham believed even "when he considered his own body, which was already as good as dead, for he was about a hundred years old, or when he considered the barrenness of Sarah's womb" (Rom. 4:19).

Justification by Faith in Jesus Christ, the Second Adam

In the third phase of his argument, Paul transitions from Abraham's faith in God's promise, to the Christian's faith in what God has actually done in Jesus Christ. We can discern seven steps in the unfolding of this third phase. First, Abraham's faith becomes the model of the Christian's faith: "Now the words, 'it was reckoned to him,' were written not for his sake alone, but for ours" (Rom. 4:23–24). Abraham's faith is the model, but the object of that faith is different although parallel. Just as Abraham believed that God would bring about the seemingly impossible feat of giving children to a barren couple, so Christians are asked to believe in the seeming impossibility of life coming out of death. This paradox of life coming from death is what Bernard Lonergan calls "the law of the cross" (Lonergan 1961, 524–535), which he believes to be "the essence of redemption" (Ibid., 527). "It [righteousness] will be reckoned to us who believe in him who raised Jesus our Lord from the dead, who was handed over to death for our trespasses and was raised for our justification" (Rom. 4:24–25).

Just as God took the initiative to save a remnant from the flood, by having Noah build an ark, just as God promised Abraham that he would be the father of many nations even though he was old and his wife barren, and just as God raised up Moses to save his people from the slavery of Egypt, so now "God proves his love for us in that while we still were sinners Christ died for us" (Rom. 5:8). Our justification takes place through our believing in what God has done in Jesus Christ, impossible as that might seem.

The second step—the crucial move in the completion of the Adamic Myth—is Paul's teaching that Christ is the second Adam. "Therefore, just as one man's trespass led to condemnation for all, so one man's act of righteousness leads to justification and life for all. For just as by the one man's disobedience the many were made sinners, so by the one man's [Jesus'] obedience the many will be made righteous" (Rom. 5:18–19). Paul refers to Christ's death for us as a "free gift" that leads to justification, just as the sin of Adam lead to condemnation (Rom. 5:18).

In the third step Paul returns to the law—by which he means the Law of Moses—and its role in salvation from a Christian point of view. Paul now shows the true depths of the situation of sin from which humans need to be redeemed. It is not just that a situation of sin exists—that in itself would only mean that *someone* needs to do *something*. The law has *increased* sin and, in fact, produced a situation of "ethical impossibility" (Byrne, 224–233). In chapter 1, Paul referred to the situation of sin that followed on the pagans' turning away from the knowledge of God. God in fact "turned them over" to these sins as a consequence of their refusal to acknowledge and glorify him. Now Paul insists that for those under the law—the Jews, that is—the law has solidified the reign of sin. It is not that the law itself is sin, but the law has revealed sin. The law is a pedagogue. I would not have known that it was wrong to covet, says Paul, if the law had not said, "You shall not covet" (Rom. 7:7). But the law is a pedagogue that has gotten linked to the very thing it is trying to prevent, sin. Sin takes advantage of the law—one commentator says that sin "hijacked" the law (Byrne 1996, 220)—and runs rampant, producing all kinds of covetousness. This is a paradoxical teaching and Paul expresses it forcefully to set up his idea of salvation in Christ:

> Apart from the law sin lies dead. I was once alive apart from the law, but when the commandment came, sin revived and I died and the very commandment that promised life proved to be death to me. For sin, seizing an opportunity in the commandment, deceived me and through it killed me. So the law is holy, and the commandment is holy and just and good. Did what is good, then, bring death to me? By no means! It was sin, working death in me through what is good, in order that sin might be shown to be sin, and through the commandment might become sinful beyond measure (Rom. 7:8b–13).

This extraordinary insight specifies the situation from which humans need to be saved. The law itself has increased sin. The prohibition contained in the law has produced the very thing it was meant to prevent. Paul is thinking of the law of Moses. Can one apply it to the first "sin," that of Adam and Eve? Brendan Byrne suggests that, in fact, Paul was thinking both of Adam and Israel (Byrne, 218). The prohibition against eating of the tree of the knowledge of good and evil became, through the trickery of the serpent, a kind of *incitement* to eat.

The fourth step of Paul's argument is what Ricoeur calls "the servile will," the will enslaved by its own action and incapable of doing what a will is meant to do, i.e., choose the good (Ricoeur 1967, 151–57). Paul expresses the idea in his famous lament: "I do not understand my own actions. For I do not do what I want, but I do the very thing I hate" (Rom. 7:15). And again, "For I do not do the good I want but the evil I do not want is what I do. Now if I do what I do not want, it is no longer I that do it, but sin that dwells within me"

(Rom. 7:19). This bondage of the will constitutes the situation that necessitates a moral and spiritual conversion.

The fifth step is Paul's answer to his own question: "Wretched man that I am! Who will rescue me from this body of death" (Rom. 7:24)? If the law, "weakened by the flesh," produced a situation of ethical impossibility, life in the Spirit brings about in the believer the state of "ethical possibility" (Byrne, 234–41). How does this reversal take place? The answer to this question takes us to the heart of the Adamic Myth as transformed by Paul. God does for us what the law could not do: "by sending his own Son in the likeness of sinful flesh, and as a sin offering, [God] condemned sin in the flesh, so that the just requirement of the law might be fulfilled in us who walk not according to the flesh but according to the Spirit" (Rom. 8:3–4).

Three points in this quotation deserve comment: First, it is God who takes the initiative to free us from sin, and this is consistent with the logic of the Adamic Myth. The second point regards the kind of initiative God now takes. It is different from any of God's earlier initiatives. God has sent his own Son "in the likeness of sinful flesh and as a sin offering," and thus condemned sin in the flesh. In this way, the just requirement of the law—Paul has consistently affirmed that the law is good—is fulfilled. This sending of God's Son represents the closest possible identification of God with the suffering and, indeed, the sin of his people, so close in fact that Paul can say, "For our sake [God] made him to be sin who did not know sin, so that we might become the righteousness of God in him" (2 Cor. 5:21). The third point is that though God takes the initiative, human beings have a role to play and a choice to make. God's initiative requires a human response. The choice Paul puts before the Christian is to live out the logic of our baptismal promise (Rom. 6:1–4). "Therefore we have been buried with him by baptism into death, so that, just as Christ was raised from the dead by the glory of the Father, so we too might walk in newness of life." In Romans 8, Paul expresses this choice as whether to live by the flesh or by the Spirit—"so that the just requirement of the law might be fulfilled *in us who walk not according to the flesh but according to the Spirit*" (Rom. 8:4).

By "the flesh" Paul means all that is opposed to God's Spirit, all egotism, greed, violence, lust, and every other form of idolatry by which humans put their own desires in the place of God's will. "'Flesh' and 'Spirit,'" says Brendan Byrne, "do not denote separate elements in the make-up of human individuals ('body' and 'soul,' for example) but rather two possibilities of existence—the one self-enclosed, self-regarding and hostile to God, the other open to God and to life" (Byrne, 238).

The sixth step considers the place of suffering in the salvific plan of God. Even though Christ, through his death and resurrection, has restored ethical possibility, a possibility actualized through the Christian's faith, suffering and frustration still remain part of life even in the new dispensation, but Paul turns suffering into an argument for hope. "For I reckon that the sufferings of the present time are a small price to pay for the glory that is going to be revealed in us" (Rom. 8:23). Having stated his confidence that suffering will be caught up in glory, Paul goes on to describe three levels of "groaning": the groaning of all creation, our own groaning, and the groaning of the Holy Spirit. The groaning of the Holy Spirit takes place within the groaning of creation and of human beings. This theme in Romans 8 hearkens back to Romans 5 where Paul has already said that we [Christians] "boast in our sufferings, knowing that suffering produces endurance, and endurance produces character, and character produces hope, and hope does not disappoint us, because God's love has been poured into our hearts through the Holy Spirit" (Rom. 5:3–5). What is striking in these passages from chapters 5 and 8 of Romans is the degree to which God, through Jesus Christ and his Spirit, has entered into the very deepest recesses of human sin and suffering. We see here the ultimate expression of the divine compassion that accompanied human beings along the way of suffering and sin beginning with God's gesture of making leather garments to clothe Adam and his wife (Gen. 3:21).

To advance to the seventh step, the superabundance of grace, we must go back to an earlier section of Romans. The restoration of the human situation through the grace of Christ is *better* than the situation lost through sin. Beginning with the situation of ethical impossibility caused by the complicity of sin and the law, Paul goes on to exalt the power of grace: "But law came in, with the result that the trespass multiplied; but where sin increased, grace abounded all the more . . ." (Rom. 5:20). Paul himself, in a rhetorical flourish that highlights the paradoxical nature of what he is saying, poses the question, "What then are we to say? Should we continue in sin in order that grace may abound?" (Rom. 6:1). Paul's rhetorical question, a device common within ancient diatribe, sets up the answer: "By no means! How can we who died to sin continue living in it?" (Rom. 6:2). Paul's resounding affirmation in chapter 8 that " . . . the sufferings of the present time are a small price to pay for the glory that is going to be revealed in us" (Rom. 8:18) seems to be an echo of the earlier statement about abounding grace. So, in the new dispensation of justification in Christ, the Holy Spirit transforms sin and suffering themselves into the hope of glory.

Summary of the Adamic Myth in the Light of Romans

Can we now summarize the phases of Paul's doctrine of salvation as contained in his Letter to the Romans? I have identified three phases: the universal reign of sin, the faith of Abraham as the model of faith to be practiced by all those who want to be saved, and, finally, faith in Jesus Christ, the second Adam, as the source of righteousness, salvation, and reconciliation. Now that we have seen how Paul completes the construction of the Adamic Myth by providing a pier in the New Testament to correspond to the pier in Genesis and allowing us to see the procession of salvific characters in the Old Testament as a bridge, we can at last complete the list of elements of this vision that has been a *leitmotiv* of this work: the goodness of God and everything God has created; the prohibition that appears in the Genesis story as a command not to eat of the fruit of the tree of the knowledge of good and evil, emerges among the pagans as a kind of natural law, and takes the form of the Mosaic law for the historical community of Israel; temptation from the serpent, the only pre-existing evil in the Garden; disobedience or the violation of the prohibition by Adam and Eve, by Israel, and by the pagans; the consequences of the violation, namely, the situation of sin that has hardened into an ethical impossibility requiring salvation from the outside; God's initiative in restoring through a series of mediators—the last of whom is his own Son—what has been lost through disobedience and turning away from God; the super-abundance of grace relative to the abundance of sin; and, finally, the necessity for human beings to accept the gift of the Holy Spirit and to prove that they have accepted it by living according to the Spirit rather than according to the flesh.

If we go back to the questions posed at the beginning of this chapter, we can give Paul's answers. To the question: "From what do we need to be saved?" Paul's answer is *the universal reign of sin.* This reign of sin can be seen in the consequences of Adam's disobedience, in the list of vices to which God "turned over" the pagans when they refused to acknowledge and thank him, and in the situation of the children of Israel who did not obey the law. "All, both Jews and Greeks, are under the power of sin . . ." (Rom. 3:9). This reign of sin entails a loss of intimacy—with self, God, neighbor, and nature—and hardship in the exercise of living, darkness of the mind, violence, and every other kind of vice. Moreover, this reign of sin is a form of slavery that leaves human beings impotent with regard to the moral law. No matter how much they might *want* to live according to the law, they are unable to do so and keep doing what they do not want to do. It is a desperate situation, literally without hope.

To the question, "What does God do about the situation?" Paul answers that God loves us enough to send his Son to die for us. In the midst of a situation without hope, God gives a motive for hope, namely the grace of the Holy Spirit. Paul notes: " . . . and hope does not disappoint us, because God's love has been poured into our hearts through the Holy Spirit that has been given to us" (Rom. 5:5). The gift of the Holy Spirit comes through Jesus Christ, the ultimate proof of God's love. "But God proves his love for us in that while we still were sinners Christ died for us" (Rom. 5:8). The effect of the gift of God's love is to take away condemnation (*katakrima*). "For the law of the Spirit of life in Christ Jesus has set you free from the law of sin and death" (Rom. 8:2). Life in Christ replaces moral impotence, "ethical impossibility" with "ethical possibility" so that those who believe can fulfill the just commands of the law. Finally, the gift of God's love takes the form of a groaning through which the Spirit of God enters into our groaning and turns it into hope. What God does, then, is utterly reverse the consequences of sin. As Brendan Byrne puts it: ". . . all believers (Jewish and Gentile) have been gifted with God's righteousness in Christ. . . . They have been swept up within a 'solidarity of grace' immeasurably more 'powerful for salvation' than the solidarity in sin stemming from Adam" (Byrne 1996, 208–209). God has reversed the sequence of events that followed on the sin of Adam and Eve, the sin of the Gentiles, and the sins of Israel.

It appears that God has opened a door. With regard to our third question "What are human beings to do toward salvation?" Paul's answer—simple to state as it is difficult to put into practice—accept the gift offered. That means, first, to believe as Abraham did. Abraham is the model of the believer because he believed *in the face of the impossible*. Justification for the Christian comes first through faith in what God has done in Jesus Christ. Then the Christian must enter into the death of Christ. The Christian is baptized into the death of Christ so as to share in the resurrection of Christ (Rom. 6). Finally, the Christian is to live by the Spirit, rather than by the flesh, to take advantage of the freedom offered through the gift of the Spirit and not fall back into slavery to sin.

SALVATION IN OTHER NEW TESTAMENT WRITINGS

Paul's development of the notion of salvation in his most influential work, *The Letter to the Romans* seems clearly to be within the framework of the Adamic myth; what about the rest of the New Testament? Romans might be seen as bringing to completion the inner dynamic of the myth. Paul provides us with the most explicit, sustained, and influential account of Christ as second Adam. But other New Testament writers also knew Christ in relation to the beginnings of the human race in Adam, saw his salvific obedience on the Cross as the reversal of Adam's disobedience, and recognized his grace and mercy as the only antidote to sin. An early 5th Century Holy Saturday homily by Epiphanius of Cyprus dramatically draws together hints and clues from the New Testament.

This imaginative recreation of Christ's descent into hell after his crucifixion abounds in gentle irony and the *voluntas* pietatis or "will of tender mercy" described by Hugh of St. Victor (see above, ix–x). Jesus introduces himself to Adam: "I am your God, who for your sake have become your son." The author imagines Christ after the crucifixion as going "to search for our first parent, as for a lost sheep . . . He has gone to free from sorrow the captives Adam and Eve, he who is both God and the son of Eve." Christ contrasts their garden with his: "For the sake of you who left a garden, I was betrayed to the Jews in a garden, and I was crucified in a garden" Christ invites these first humans, once in paradise, now in hell, to see his hands "firmly nailed to a tree, for you who once wickedly stretched out your hand to a tree." Finally Christ invites Adam and Eve to share in the place he has opened through his redemptive death and resurrection: "Rise, let us leave this place. The enemy led you out of the earthly paradise. I will not restore you to that paradise, but I will enthrone you in heaven" (PG 43, 439, 451, 462–463).

If we look closely at the non-Pauline New Testament writings, we can find some of the indications that gave rise to this imaginative vision. Just after his account of Jesus' baptism and before describing the temptations that prepare Jesus for ministry, Luke gives a genealogy that, unlike Matthew's, traces Jesus' ancestry back to Adam. Matthew's genealogy occurs at the beginning of his Gospel, even before Jesus' birth, and traces the savior's ancestry only back to Abraham, suggesting a clear connection with the history of Israel but not with the origins of the human race. In mentioning Adam, Luke establishes a connection with the origins of the humanity itself and implies that Christ's fidelity in ministry will reverse the infidelity of Adam. Luke's account of Jesus' rejection of Satan's temptations in the desert seems to be a reversal of the capitulation of Adam and Eve to the serpent's urgings (Franklin, 2001, 931, col. 2; Karris, 1990, 688, col.2; Stöger, 1981, 80). Stöger compares Luke's account with Paul's claim in Romans 5:19, "As the many became sinners through the disobedience of one man [Adam] so, too, by the obedience of one [Christ] the many were justified" (Stöger, 1981).

Three times in Acts, 5:30, 10:39, 13:29, Luke refers to Jesus' death on a tree, clearly evoking the image of the tree from which Adam and Eve ate and pointing to Jesus' obedience as reversal of their act of disobedience. "The God of our ancestors raised up Jesus, whom you had killed by hanging him on a tree" (5:30). 10:39 also refers to Jesus' death by hanging on a tree and adds, "but God raised him up on the third day and allowed him to appear, not to all the people but to us who were chosen as his witnesses, and who ate and drank with him after he rose from the dead" (see also 13:29). When we hear Luke call the cross a tree through which Jesus entered into his resurrected life, we think of the tree of life to which God closed off access in Genesis 3 after Adam and Eve went against God's command by eating of the fruit of the tree of knowledge of good and evil. By his obedience, Jesus, by passing through death, has opened the door to eternal life once closed by the disobedience of Adam.

If we add to Acts' Cross-as-tree references Revelation's promise of access to the tree of life, we have an even stronger case for seeing Christ as the second Adam. The references in Revelation occur at crucial points, the beginning and the end of the Book. "To everyone who conquers I will give permission to eat from the tree of life that is the paradise of God" (2:7b). The two references in chapter 22, the last chapter of the Book, occur in the context of Revelation's vision of "a new heaven and a new earth" announced at the beginning of chapter 21. Chapter 22 refers to "the river of the water of life" and adds the comment, "On either side of the river is the tree of life with its twelve kinds of fruit, producing its fruit each month; and the leaves of the tree are for the healing of the nations" (22:6b). A few lines later: "Blessed are those who wash their robes, so that they will have the right to the tree of life and may enter the city by the gates" (14b, 19b).

All these promises of access to the tree of life reverse God's preventive measures described in Genesis 3 to keep Adam and Eve from the Tree of Life: "Then the Lord God said, 'See the man has become like one of us, knowing good and evil; and now, he might reach out his hand and take also from the tree of life, and eat, and live forever'—therefore the Lord God sent him forth from the garden of Eden, to till the ground from which he was taken" (Gen. 3:22–23). And the promised new heaven and new earth announce the reversal of the unraveling or un-creating of heaven and earth that followed Adam's disobedience. But the promise is not unconditional. Revelation's last reference to the tree of life, the last words of the book before the closing peroration, raise the possibility of losing once again the access opened by Jesus' death and resurrection: ". . . if anyone takes away from the words of this prophecy, God will take away that person's share in the tree of life and in the holy city, which are described in this book" (22:19). Disobedience still closes off access to the tree of life.

Between these references to the tree of life we have, in Chapter 12 of Revelation, the images of the woman, the child, and the dragon that recall the curse God placed on the serpent in Genesis 3: "I will put enmity between you and the woman, and between your offspring and hers; he will strike your head and you will strike his heel" (Gen 3: 15). Commentators believe the account in chapter 12 of Revelation was put together by the author from two other non-Christian sources, "a narrative describing the conflict between a woman with child and a dragon (vv. 1–6 and 13–17), and a narrative depicting a battle in heaven (vv. 7–9)" (Collins, 1990, 1008, col 2). The identity of the woman, Collins notes, has been disputed. Catholic tradition has identified her with Mary. She could also be "the heavenly Jerusalem, personified wisdom, or the Church" (Ibid). Collins concludes: "In the present form of chap. 12 the woman is the heavenly Israel, the spouse of God" (Ibid.). As for the dragon, this final form of chapter 12 identifies him "with the serpent of Gen 3, who in turn is identified with the devil and Satan" (Ibid). Richard Bauckham also sees in v.9 a reference to the serpent of Eden who is identified "as also the sea-monster or dragon Leviathan, destined for eschatological defeat by the sword of God (Isa 27:1)." In the woman, Bauckham sees not Mary the mother of Jesus, but "the people of God "both Israel and the Church. V.3, not Mary's pregnancy so much as the sufferings of Israel from which the Messiah came and which he bore" (Bauckham, 2001, 1296, col. 2).

This last reference to "the sufferings of Israel from which the Messiah came" suggests the figure of Second Isaiah's Suffering Servant (42:1–4; 49:1–6; 50:4–9; 52: 13–53:12), along with the title Son of Man suggests a path from Christ to Adam. Jesus himself referred to the story of Adam and Eve only once, in connection with the issue of divorce: "Have you not read that the one who made them in the beginning 'made them male and female,' and said, 'for this reason a man shall leave his father and mother . . . '" Three other New Testament passages refer to Adam and Eve in the context of the relation between man and woman (Matt. 19:4–5, I Timothy 2:13–14, and II Corinthians 11:3). These direct references to Adam and Eve do not point to Jesus' role as Second Adam. But the title, Son of Man, and its connection with the Suffering Servant of Isaiah do, upon closer inspection, invite a comparison with Paul's dramatic parallel between Christ and the first parent of the human race, Adam, the Man. The Son of Man is the Son of Adam.

The designation "Son of Man" appears eighty-four times in the New Testament, most often in the Gospels but also twice in Revelation (1:13, 14:14), once each in Acts (7:56), and Hebrews (2:6). In all the Gospel references, it is Jesus who uses the title of himself; it is the characteristic way in which Jesus speaks of himself. The Son of Man is the sower of good seed (Matt 13:37), the judge who will come in glory "to reward all people according to their works" (Matt 16:27), the one who has power to forgive sins (Mark 2:10), Lord of the Sabbath (Mark 2:28). In almost half of the Gospel references, Jesus couples the designation Son of Man with the notion of the suffering servant or simply suffering (for example, Matt. 8:20, 17:12, 20:18; Mk. 8:31, 9:12, 10:45; Lk. 9:22, 18:31, 22:22; Jn. 8:28, 12:34, 13:31). Christ, then, is the Son of Man (Adam) who voluntarily shares in the sufferings brought to all Adam's children through their parents' disobedience, and who, paradoxically, accomplishes human salvation through that very suffering.

Paul Ricoeur argues that Christ's self-designation in the synoptic tradition, as Son of Man and Suffering Servant, situates that tradition firmly within the vision of the Adamic Myth. We will also discover that the synoptic tradition manifests other key characteristics of the Adamic vision, among them, the universality of the reign of sin, the inability of human beings to save themselves, the abounding mercy of God who sent his Son as liberator of sons and daughters longing for freedom, and the teaching that salvation comes from God alone. They do not contain Paul's central affirmation that "by the one man's transgression the many died . . ." (Rom. 5:1b).

The Adamic vision consists, as we have seen, of the following elements: the absolute goodness of God and God's creation, the presence of prohibition, restriction, or law that sets conditions for human life in the created world; temptation from the serpent, the turning away from God through disobedience, the loss of intimacy with self, God, neighbor, and nature that are the consequences of turning away; the initiative of God toward reconciliation, the superabundance of grace compared with the abundance of sin, and the necessity on our part to accept the gift of salvation. The questions posed at the beginning of this chapter are again a framework for what follows: What do we need to be saved from? What is God's role in salvation? What is our role? And what is the connection between our role and God's role?

The Son of Man and the Suffering Servant in the Gospels

Ricoeur holds that Paul's designation of Christ as the Second Adam both incorporates and transcends the designation Son of Man. "This new figure [the second Adam] at the same time consecrates the preceding ones and adds a decisive trait to them" (Ricoeur 1967, 271). The decisive trait is the superabundance of life that comes with the intervention of the second Adam, as expressed in Paul's phrase, "Where sin increased, grace abounded all the more" (Rom. 5:20). In other words, Christ's coming not only restores the state of things before Adam and Eve's disobedience, it makes possible a higher state of existence. Ricoeur suggests that it may be necessary to have assimilated the succession of figures, Messiah, Son of God, Son of Man, Suffering Servant in order to understand the one "which insures the ultimate symmetry between the Adamic figure of the myth of origin and the series of eschatological figures—namely, the figure of the 'second Adam'" (Ricoeur 1967, 271). My concern here is to show that the gospel figure of the Son of Man is indeed an Adamic image even though it lacks some of the fullness that Paul attributes to the figure of the second Adam in *Romans* and *1 Corinthians*.

We must recognize from the beginning that the term "Son of Man" applied to himself by Jesus in the Gospels does not establish him as the Second Adam with the same clarity that we find in Paul. The expression "Son of Man," as it turns out, has a complicated history. Scholars suggest that it comes into the Hebrew Scriptures from other sources than the story of Adam in the book of Genesis. The most notable occurrence of the figure of the son of man in the Old Testament is in Daniel 7: The context is Daniel's apocalyptic dream that presents a vision of a new kingdom of God to replace kingdoms that will pass away. Daniel recounts that in the dream, "I saw in the night visions, and behold, with the clouds of heaven there came one like a son of man, and he came to the Ancient of Days and was presented before him" (Dan. 7:13). Son of Man also appears in Old Testament books other than Daniel, notably, Ezekiel (93 times), The Wisdom of Solomon, 1–6; 4 Ezra, 11–13; 2 Baruch, and in other texts such as Psalm 8. The term also appears in the non-biblical book, I Enoch. Its origin does not seem to be directly the figure of Adam from Genesis. "Broad consensus sees this chapter [Daniel 7] as the product of a complex history of tradition with deep roots in non-Israelite mythology" (Nickelsburg 1992, 137). It also has roots, as Nickelsburg makes clear in this same article, within the Hebrew tradition.

Paul Ricoeur, on the other hand, makes the connection with the Adamic myth of Genesis. "This figure [the son of man]," says Ricoeur, "the most distant from the figure of the earthly king, will lead us back . . . to the initial figure: To Man, to Anthropos" (Ricoeur 1967, 267–68). But, Ricoeur adds that though the figure of the Son of Man leads us back to the initial figure, it is not identical with the Adam of Genesis: "The Son of Man is Man; but he is no longer the First Man, but a Man who is coming; he is the Man of the end, whether he be an individual or the personification of a collective entity, of the remnant of Israel, or of the whole of humanity" (Ricoeur 1967, 268). The figure of the Son of Man looks toward the future, to a kingdom that is to come, something we have not yet seen, rather than to the simple restoration of a state of being that was lost. In this sense, the figure of the Son of Man shares something of the "grace abounding" so prominent in Paul's designation of Christ as the Second Adam. The important point here is that the figure of the Son of Man is thoroughly anthropological and thus radically connected with the anthropological myth, the myth of Adam.

This figure of the Son of Man, as applied to Jesus, is transformed by its coupling with the figure of the suffering servant into a radically new vision—incomprehensible to many of Jesus' followers, even to his disciples in the beginning—that transforms suffering into a source of hope. So the Adamic vision of the Gospels, expressed in the figures of the Son of Man and the Suffering Servant, is indeed very like that of Paul who finds in Jesus the Second Adam. But the Adamic vision is also expressed in other ways in the Gospels.

The Gospel View of God's Role in Salvation

Having reviewed in the non-Pauline New Testament writings these various resonances with the story of Adam and Eve—the Cross as tree (Acts), the Tree of Life, the serpent, the new creation (Revelation), the Son of Man and the Suffering Servant (the Gospels)—we can now look for other features, in the New Testament outside of Paul that might express what I would call the logic of the Adamic Myth so thoroughly developed by Paul and alluded to in other New Testament writings. Three features predominate: the universality of the reign of sin, the inability of humans to save themselves, and the abounding mercy of God who sent his Son as liberator of those who would believe in him.

The Universal Reign of Sin in the Gospels

As we have seen, Paul maintains not only that all have sinned but that a power of sin is at work in the world challenging the power of God. According to E. P. Sanders, the general Jewish view that all people sin, at least in the sense that they "commit a sin at some time or other," is accepted throughout the New Testament (Sanders 1992, 41). Sanders refers to Paul's affirmation that "all have sinned and fall short of the glory of God" (Rom. 3:23) and points to the "assumption of universal sinfulness . . . seen in the Lord's Prayer, where the disciples are told to say, 'forgive us our debts' (Matt. 6:12) or 'forgive us our sins' (Lk. 11:4)" (Ibid.). "All four Gospels and Acts," says Sanders, "place early a passage which displays the assumption that all have sinned" (Ibid.). Sanders points to Matthew's affirmation that "Jesus shall save the people from their sins" (Matt. 1:21), Mark's reference to John the Baptist's preaching of "a baptism of repentance for the forgiveness of sins," to Jesus' preaching that his hearers should "repent" (Mk. 1:4, 15) and to John's reference to John the Baptist's saying of Jesus that "he takes away the sins of the world" (Jn. 1:29). At the end of what Sanders calls "the first Christian sermon" we find Peter's call to his hearers: "Repent, and be baptized every one of you in the name of Jesus Christ so that your sins may be forgiven . . ." (Acts 2:38).

Henri Rondet says of Jesus, "Like the precursor, he preaches penance. All men are sinners and should repent" (Rondet 1972, 20). The texts Rondet cites, Matt. 4:17, Mk. 1:15, and Lk. 13:3, address the call of repentance to all Jesus' listeners and thus imply that all have sinned. The text from Luke says explicitly that the Galileans who died in Pilate's sacrifices and others who died as a result of the fall of a tower were not worse sinners than other Galileans or others living in Jerusalem; "No, I tell you; but unless you repent, you will all perish as they did" (Lk. 13:3). This seems to imply that all Jesus' listeners and, presumably, all those who would hear or read his message are sinners.

The New Testament teaching about the universality of sin is not as unambiguous as Paul's affirmation in Romans that "all have sinned and fall short of the glory of God" (Rom. 3:23). In fact, several passages in the Gospels seem to suggest that the world is divided into two groups, those who humbly acknowledge their sins and ask for God's mercy and those who refuse to admit that they are sinners. Luke's Jesus says "I have come to call not the righteous, but sinners to repentance" (Lk. 5:32). Taken by itself, this passage might be seen to suggest that a class of people exists, the righteous, who have no need of salvation. Yet another more plausible way of reading the Gospels suggests that "the righteous" are simply those who refuse to admit their sins, the Pharisees and Scribes (Jn. 9), the older son in the story of the Prodigal Son (Lk. 15), or the debtor who refused to forgive a debt owed to him (Matt. 18).

A striking example is the familiar parable told by Jesus "to some who trusted in themselves that they were righteous and despised others" (Lk. 18:9). A Pharisee and a tax collector go to the temple to pray. The Pharisee thanked God that he was not like other people, "thieves, rogues, adulterers, or even like this tax collector" (Lk. 18:10) and went on to recount his virtuous deeds. The tax collector, on the other hand, "would not even lift up his eyes to heaven, but beat his breast, saying, 'God be merciful to me a sinner'" (Lk. 18:13). After declaring the tax collector justified rather than the Pharisee, Jesus ends with a generalization: "for every one who exalts himself will be humbled, but he who humbles himself, will be exalted" (Lk. 18:14). No one has the right to exalt himself. Why not? It seems legitimate to read this text as implying that all are in some way sinners. If such a reading is correct, then for Jesus, any righteousness that one might claim as one's own does not exist. The only way to be authentic would be to admit one's need for redemption and cast oneself on God's mercy.

Matthew's parable of the forgiven debtor who refused to forgive someone who owed him much less than what his master forgave him (Matt. 18) gives two motives for forgiveness. The most striking and the one readers are most likely to remember comes at the end of the parable: if we do not forgive our brothers and sisters from the heart, God will be merciless to us. (Matt. 18:35). But the more compelling, if more subtle, motive is that all who follow Christ have been forgiven a debt much larger than anything they will be asked to forgive. All Christians are forgiven sinners and should never forget God's mercy to them.

Not only can we find indications also in the Gospels of Paul's clear teaching that all have sinned, we encounter references to a power of sin. John's Gospel, for instance, speaks throughout of a power comparable to Paul's notion of a sin that dwells in us making us do what we do not want to do and not do what we want to do (Rom. 7:17–20). Sometimes John characterizes the power as darkness; sometime he refers to the devil. And just as in Paul the liberating power of Christ frees the enslaved will, in John the light of Christ overcomes the darkness, and the power of Christ overcomes the power of the devil. The back and forth struggle between light and darkness recurs at key points in John. In the Prologue, ". . . the light shines in the darkness and the darkness does not overcome it (or the darkness did not comprehend it" (1:5). Speaking to Nicodemus, who comes to him at night (Jn. 3:2), Jesus says: "And this is the verdict, that the light came into the world, but people preferred darkness to light, because their works were evil. For everyone who does wicked things hates the light and does not come to the light, so that his works might not be exposed" (Jn. 3:19–20). Before Jesus appears to his disciples walking on the water, John tells us, "It had already grown dark and Jesus had not yet come to them" (6:17b). The story of the man born blind revolves around light and darkness (9:1–40). At the end of "The Book of Signs," Jesus says, "I came into the world as light, so that everyone who believes in me might not remain in darkness" (12:46) . . . After the Resurrection, Mary Magdalene came to the tomb "while it was still dark" and did not recognize Jesus.

Rondet finds in the story of the man born blind of John's Gospel (Jn. 9) a further indication of a universal reign of sin (Rondet 1972, 20). However, instead of tracing human sin to Adam, John traces it to the devil (*diabolos*). In the passage just before the story of the man born blind, Jesus refutes the Pharisees' claim to be children of Abraham: "You are of your father the devil, and your will is to do your father's desires. He was a murderer from the beginning, and has nothing to do with the truth because there is no truth in him. When he lies, he speaks according to his own nature, for he is a liar and the father of lies" (Jn. 8:44). The first letter of John warns his hearers not to be like Cain "who was from the evil one and murdered his brother" (I Jn. 3:12). We might well see in the Serpent who tempted Cain's parents the first manifestation of the "father of lies."

The powers of sin in John, darkness and the devil, might seem to constitute a dualism. In fact, E. P. Sanders has noted a sort of incipient dualism in Paul's conception of sin as an external force that could take over the law. In his article on sin in the *Anchor Bible Dictionary,* Sanders finds some inconsistencies in Paul's case for the universality of sin and even speculates on a kind of dualism in Paul's treatment of sin as an alien power. But, says Sanders, even though such a dualism might exist in Paul's thought, he never takes the step of making the power of sin a Being. We must say the same of whatever duality we might detect in John. Even in these hints of an incipient dualism that never comes to maturity, we find an echo of the Adamic Myth. The striking presence of the serpent in the Genesis narrative, in the midst of a world that has been created good, indicates a kind of externality of evil in an otherwise good creation. Eve's response to the serpent and Adam's response to Eve, also indicate a subjective vulnerability to temptation even before the event of disobedience. Ricoeur, as we have seen, interprets the externality of evil as a residue of the tragic myth. The presence, however, of a power of evil in the form of temptation does not negate the fundamentally anthropomorphic origin of evil in the form of Adam's disobedience. And, as we have seen, the power of sin in Paul and the powers of light and the devil in John, though formidable adversaries, are infinitely subordinate to the power of light and grace coming from Christ.

Inability of Human Beings to Save Themselves

So it seems that the Gospel authors present Jesus as teaching that all human beings are subject to a reign of sin—and not only subject to sin, and even to a power of sin outside themselves, but also without a way to escape by their own power. All are subject to the moral impotence that Paul laments and that we have seen as one of the key features of the Adamic Myth. Matthew recounts the story about the servant with the huge debt who has to beg his master for forgiveness; he cannot forgive himself. The tax collector of Luke's gospel prays for mercy and is justified, even while the Pharisee who imagines that he needs no forgiveness is not justified. Those who deny this impotence are blind. The whole of John 8 is a condemnation of the Pharisees who are going to die in their sin "unless you believe that I am he" (Jn. 8:24). They will die in their sin precisely because they do not recognize that they are sinners in need of salvation. At the end of the story of the man born blind in chapter 9, the Pharisees will say: "Surely we are not also blind, are we"? And Jesus replies: "If you were blind, you would have no sin; but now you are saying, 'We see,' so your sin remains" (Jn. 9:40–41). By thinking that salvation comes from themselves, specifically from their punctilious observation of the Law, the Pharisees put themselves beyond possibility of salvation.

Humble recognition of one's inability to save oneself is a necessary condition for salvation. Especially in the Gospel of John, but also in the Synoptics, Jesus does not even claim for himself some independent righteousness apart from his Father. "I will no longer talk much with you, for the ruler of this world is coming. He has no power over me; but I do as the Father has commanded me, so that the world may know that I love the Father" (Jn. 14:30–31).

The temptation by which the serpent tricked Adam and Eve into disobeying God was the illusion that behind God's prohibition against eating the fruit of the tree of the knowledge of good and evil was divine jealousy, a desire to keep something back from his creatures, and that Adam and Eve would, in fact, become like God if they disobeyed his command. The reign of sin begins with that temptation, not historically but existentially. And liberation from sin occurs when people accept creation as God's gift and submit to the divine order established when God created the world. Having blighted the harmonious order of creation by claiming for themselves prerogatives that belong to God alone, human beings introduced alienation and hardship into their relations with themselves, with nature, with other humans, and with God. As a consequence, human beings can only hope for restoration through God's gracious favor.

The Doctrine of Redemption Precedes the Doctrine of Sin

The Gospels, then, echo Paul's teaching that the reign of sin is universal and that human beings are incapable by themselves of attaining salvation. It would be a distortion, however, to make this teaching about sin the central doctrine of either Paul or the Gospels, or later of Augustine. The New Testament's principal message is the redemption that is offered in Christ for those willing to accept it. Sin is simply that from which people need to be redeemed. To return to Paul, Sanders' conclusion is important: "If there is some truth in the suggestion that Paul was influenced by dualistic thought, there is more in the view that his discussions of sin are the reflex of his soteriology" (Sanders 1992, 46). In other words, the teaching that Jesus is redeemer precedes the teaching about the power of sin. The stories about Jesus' interaction with sinners—and his parables—express concretely this abstract theology. Jesus is interested primarily in opening up possibilities, not in accusing or condemning. When he exposes those who want to condemn the woman taken in adultery, Jesus refuses to condemn her himself and instead offers her advice that seems to carry with it the power to fulfill what he is recommending: "Go your way, and from now on do not sin again" (Jn. 8:11).

Paul's anguished lament in Romans 7, "Who will save me from this body of death?" opens the door to the next verse, "Thanks be to God through Jesus Christ our Lord!" and to the opening cry of Romans 8, "There is now no condemnation for those who are in Christ Jesus. For the Law of the Spirit of life in Christ has set you free from the law of sin and death" (Rom. 8:1–2). Jesus' words to the adulterous woman say concretely to her: "There is now no condemnation for those who follow me" (Jn 8). Perhaps the most inviting words of the New Testament are Jesus' "Come to me all you that are weary and are carrying heavy burdens, and I will give you rest" (Matt. 11:28). And who is not weary and heavily burdened? If some such people exist, they need not, it would seem come to Jesus. So the central message of the New Testament is salvation, healing, rest, freedom from sin, hope for the future even to eternal life through Jesus Christ. "For in Him fullness was pleased to dwell, and through Him to reconcile to himself all things whether on earth or in heaven, by making peace through the blood of his cross" (Col. 1:19–20).

Summary of Gospel View of Salvation

The Gospels teach that God saves us through his mercy toward sinners. This teaching, dramatically illustrated in Luke's story of the Prodigal Son, is also expressed in his Sermon on the Plain. Moreover, Jesus ate with sinners, he welcomed them into the circle of his intimate followers, he came to find those who were lost and rejoiced more over one sinner found than over ninety-nine righteous persons who need no repentance (Lk. 15:7). This constant teaching of the Gospels echoes Paul's affirmation in Romans, "But God proves his love for us that while we were still sinners Christ died for us" (Rom. 5:8). Christ ultimately expresses God's mercy through his own humiliation and death. This is what Lonergan calls "the law of the cross." I will return to it. If this is what God does, what does God expect us to do?

God created us without our collaboration; he cannot save us without it. A cryptic statement of what we must do to be saved appears in Mark's account of Jesus' words at the beginning of his ministry just after he has returned from the encounter with Satan in the wilderness: "The time is fulfilled, and the kingdom of God has come near; repent *(metanoiete)* and believe (*pisteuete*) in the good news" (Mark 1:15). This repenting and believing represent a complete change of mind and heart, a new way of seeing the world and responding to it. What that means in detail I have set out above. These are the main points.

It is clear that Christ expects his followers to obey the commandments. The fact that Jesus invites his hearers to go *beyond* the keeping of the commandments suggests that obedience by itself is not enough for salvation. In this the gospel accounts echo Paul who insists that salvation comes not through observance of the law but by believing in Christ. Renunciation in order to follow Christ even to the point of death, universal love that reaches to strangers, that is, to those outside our familiar circle, and even to enemies; forgiveness, humility, rejoicing in wrong done to us—all of these belong to the path of salvation indicated by Christ.

If we ask about the relation between God's role in salvation and ours, the answer is clear. God is the initiator of salvation. This is a key feature of the Adamic Myth reflected in Paul and in the Gospels. Our role in salvation, what *we* have to do to be saved, is subordinate to God's role. It consists first in *accepting through faith* the gift of salvation. Having accepted the gift of salvation, we then *imitate* God's mercy toward us through our love of neighbor.

CONCLUSION

Having summarized the synoptic teaching about salvation, we may now return to the question posed at the beginning of this chapter, namely, whether, to what extent, and how the non-Pauline New Testament writings express the logic of the Adamic Myth. We have noted significant references in Acts and Revelation, the resonance between the gospel designations "Son of Man" and "Suffering Servant" on the one hand and Paul's term designating Christ as the "Second Adam." We have also considered the notion of the universality of sin and, in fact, of a power of sin at work in the world, an idea prominent in Paul and in the Gospels. Finally, an exploration of central parables and narratives of the Gospels has manifested key elements of the logic of the Adamic Myth.

This discussion of salvation in Christianity in the framework of the Adamic Myth, more precisely of the Adamic Myth as stretching from Genesis to Romans, places the New Testament within the logic of the Adamic Myth rather than any of the other four myths described by Paul Ricoeur in his work, *The Symbolism of Evil.* The other three myths, the Creation myth, the tragic myth, and the Orphic myth, all see the origin of evil as external to human beings. The Adamic Myth sees evil as coming into the world through human sin. It sees the all-good Creator of the world, and of human beings, as taking the initiative—not once, but repeatedly—to overcome the consequences of sin in human life. God's initiative always requires human cooperation because, although God created humans without their collaboration, he cannot save them without it. We can schematize this program of salvation in three steps that correspond to the evil consequences that followed on the disobedience of Adam. The first step in salvation, corresponding to the loss of intimacy with self, God, and neighbor that followed Adam's sin, is a restoration of that intimacy, ending in the healing of the moral impotence that afflicts the human will. The second step, corresponding to the fact of suffering and death, is the transformation of suffering through renunciation, the law of the cross, and forgiveness. The last step, corresponding to the loss of hope produced by death, is the new hope founded on the resurrection of Christ and the promise that those who die grounded in hope and love will share in that resurrection. In a later chapter we will return to an issue central to the New Testament teaching and a key theme of this book, the role of forgiveness.

NOTE

1. This scriptural quotation is from the New Revised Standard Version Bible: Catholic Edition, copyright © 1989, 1993 National Council of the Churches of Christ in the United States of America. Used by permission. All rights reserved worldwide.

Part II

THE SYMBOL GIVES RISE TO THOUGHT: FROM BIBLICAL NARRATIVE TO AUTOBIOGRAPHY, THEORY, AND DOCTRINE

Chapter Four

Augustine

Original Sin and Compassion

For I do not do the good I want, but the evil I do not want is what I do.
Now if I do what I do not want, it is no longer I that do it, but sin that
dwells in me.

—Rom. 7:19–20, NRSV[1]

For Augustine of Hippo (354–530 AD) the fundamental theological category was grace, the divine help given to human beings who labor under
the burden of sin. When Jesus says, "Come to me all you who labor and
burdened and I will give you rest" (Matt. 11:28), he speaks of grace. Augustine called the burden original sin, an inherited condition that gives rise
to the evil people do. Grace implies not only sin but also compassion. Jesus
Christ, the bearer of grace, did not just take away sin by a kind of magic;
he entered into it, bore its consequences, and thus freed humans from its
burden. So if Augustine is doctor of grace, he needs to be doctor of compassion, too. That is, we need to be able to find in him that deep experience
of human nature that will allow us to say of him, as John's Gospel says of
Jesus, that he knew what it was to be human (Jn. 2:25). Jesus knew humanity, its grandeur and its perversity. Such knowledge made him both wary
and compassionate. This study began with the claim that a consciousness of
sin in ourselves—original and actual—tends to move us to compassion (see
introduction). If we are aware of being under the same burden of weakness
as everyone else, we tend to judge others more favorably. Do we find in
Augustine, chief architect of the Church's tradition regarding original sin,
this connection between original sin and compassion? The answer requires
some nuance.

On the one hand, key features of Augustine's teaching seem to imply a God lacking in compassion. Augustine held, for instance, that unbaptized infants are subject to condemnation, the mildest condemnation of all, but still condemnation. Augustine also held that God grants the grace of conversion and final perseverance to a limited number of people—predestines them even before creation—and leaves the rest to suffer the consequences of Adam's sin in whom they have all sinned and deserved condemnation. And Augustine maintained that the original sin that all inherit from Adam is transmitted through the power of lust that is "both the consequence and the agent of transmission of original sin" (Lancel, 425). Augustine saw in the concupiscence that accompanies the act of sexual intercourse a crucial element in the transmission of original sin. Note that Augustine did not consider marriage evil, nor even the act of sexual intercourse itself evil; but the concupiscence which arose because of the disobedience of Adam and Eve is evil. Before the fall, God exhorted Adam and Eve to "increase and multiply" (Gen 1:28). But it was only after the fall that the first couple felt shame at their nakedness. Augustine interprets this shame mentioned in Genesis 3:7 as indicating that concupiscence or sexual desire was awakened by the sin of disobedience. "Why then did they experience shame because of those [sexual] members after their sin, except that there arose in them that indecent motion which would certainly not be part of marriage, if human beings had not sinned" (*Marriage and Desire,* 5, 6). These doctrines seemed harsh to Augustine's contemporaries and they seem so to us.

And yet, in spite of these teachings that seem inconsistent with the notion of a compassionate God, we can find within and throughout Augustine's teachings, including his doctrine of original sin, evidence of a deep humanity. It is a characteristic feature. Henry Chadwick, who, as we will see, had reservations concerning the notion of predestination, says of Augustine, "When he tells a story, its dramatic force is given the maximum effect by consummate artistry, with an exact eye for the differing motives of human character, *but above all by the manifest affection that he feels towards frail mortals whose actions he thinks far from a model of conduct"* [italics added] (Chadwick, 1–2).

One cannot say the same of Pelagius whose more optimistic view of human nature thinly veiled a program of rigorous moral expectations. "Pelagius never doubted for a moment that perfection was obligatory; his God was, above all, a God who commanded unquestioning obedience. He had made men to execute his commands; and He would condemn to hell-fire anyone who failed to perform a single one of them" (Brown, 342; Augustine, *The Deeds of Pelagius,* 3, 9, 11). Since, according to Pelagius, we have no innate vulnerability of will that keeps us from choosing the good, we have no excuse not to choose it and therefore no claim to compassion. When Augustine himself, arguing against Pelagius' contention that all sin is pride, asserts, "Many sins are, after all committed out of pride, but not every wrong action is done with pride. Many wrong actions are done by the ignorant, by the weak, and often by persons weeping and groaning" (*Nature and Grace,* 29.33) he shows that his pessimism about human nature unaided by grace is more merciful than Pelagius' optimism. People sin out of weakness.

Augustine did, of course, recognize the work of pride. But for Augustine pride is both more subtle than it is in Pelagius and more insidious. So subtle, in fact, that only grace can heal it. Pride not only sometimes leads to evil deeds but "lies in ambush for the human spirit, even in good actions" (Ibid., 31, 35). And unaided human efforts to overcome the pride that rises from virtuous deeds fail just as surely as efforts to persevere in good works. "For its healing, pious souls entreat him with tears and mighty groans to stretch forth his right hand to those who are trying to overcome [pride] and in some sense to trample it under foot and destroy it" (Ibid.). For as soon as we rejoice at overcoming pride in the midst of our good works, "pride raises its head as a result of this joy and says, 'See I am still alive. Why are you triumphant? And I am alive precisely because you are triumphant'" (Ibid.). Only radical humility before the work of God in us roots out pride.

We have here a tension between two voices of Augustine, one harsh, one gentle. How resolve the tension? One could simply lop off the unacceptable teachings that violate the universal sense of the faithful that God must be loving and compassionate. In a way the Church did this by not approving some aspects of Augustine's thought. This chapter will follow a different course. Beginning with these difficult teachings of Augustine, working our way through them rather than setting them aside, we will explore the humaneness at the heart of Augustine's thinking and preaching, especially the compassion implicit in his doctrine of original sin, even in the midst of the troubling elaboration of it called predestination, an elaboration in which Augustine placed himself "on the frontiers of heresy" (Lancel, 425). I say "in the midst of" his elaboration because I do not mean to claim that the doctrine of predestination itself is compassionate. But when it came to preaching Augustine showed ambivalence about his own teaching, recognized its difficulty, and admitted quite openly that he found it troubling. After looking at these more difficult and troubling aspects of Augustine's teachings we will consider the foundational teachings from which they arose and of which they were distortions or exaggerations, namely the doctrines of grace and original sin. We will explore the sources of these doctrines, in scripture and Augustine's own experience, and the gradual emergence of the Bishop of Hippo's mature thinking through a long course of development, including the great controversies with Manichees, Donatists, and Pelagians.

With respect to his place in the larger arc through which Christian belief developed over centuries, we can identify three levels in Augustine's thought. First, in predestination Augustine proclaimed a doctrine never incorporated into the tradition through official Church recognition, a doctrine explicitly repudiated by the Council of Orange a century after Augustine's death[2]. We might call this an outlandish teaching, so outlandish in fact that Augustine himself showed discomfort with it. Second, in teaching that unbaptized infants suffered condemnation Augustine found support in the magisterium of his time. But the tradition eventually abandoned this teaching, recognizing it as inconsistent with the mercy of God. And, in the Council of Trent, the Church abandoned Augustine's teaching that concupiscence is sin. Finally, Augustine's doctrine of the necessity of grace for salvation and of the condition of original sin that makes that grace necessary has become, in the official teaching of the Church at least, a permanent cornerstone of Christian belief. The claim of this chapter will be that in all these levels, even the most difficult, Augustine's deep pastoral instincts ultimately prevail over the rigor of his reasoning.

ON THE FRONTIERS OF HERESY

We begin by looking at the most extreme expression of Augustine's theology of grace. Augustine's teaching on predestination seems unfair and arbitrary and a contradiction of the New Testament affirmation that God wills all people to be saved (I Tim. 2:4; II Peter, 3:9). Even some of Augustine's most ardent followers and faithful defenders in his own time like Prosper of Aquitaine and a certain Hilary, both laymen, had difficulty with the doctrine and wrote to Augustine for help in explaining it to the monks of southern Gaul who objected to Augustine's teaching. These monks had, in fact acknowledged the errors of Pelagius, and "accepted the doctrine of original sin and the need for rebirth through the grace of God (Teske, 1990, 22). But they also believed that all people had been offered this grace and therefore objected to Augustine's doctrine that only some had been predestined to grace. If "vessels of honor" are distinguished from "vessels of dishonor" before the creation of the world, then "sinners lose any motive to rise up from their sins and the saints find an occasion for tepidity" (ibid).

The Church never officially accepted the position of Augustine on predestination (Teske, 1999, 25). His highly sympathetic biographer, Henry Chadwick, briefly summarizes the outcome of Augustine's controversy with Pelagius over grace and freedom: "The subsequent verdict of the Church on the controversy about grace has been to reject Pelagianism without fully endorsing the rival predestinarianism of Augustine" (Chadwick, 2010, 165). Chadwick observes further that restatements of Augustine's views on predestination by Thomas Bradwardine in the Middle Ages, John Calvin in the Reformation, and the Jansenists in the 17th Century have "never failed to provoke a strong counter-reaction. Within the mainstream of traditional western Christianity, this side of Augustinianism has not been comfortably digested" (166). It does not do "sufficient justice to freedom" (166).

In *The Gift of Perseverance*, Augustine himself recognized that preaching this doctrine could be problematic "so that," as Augustine says, "the multitude of those who are uneducated or slower to understand think that [the doctrine] is somehow refuted by its being preached . . ." (*The Gift of Perseverance*, 57). In other words, why preach repentance if God has already chosen who will be saved and who will be left to suffer the consequences of their solidarity in the sin of Adam? A few paragraphs later, Augustine suggests a subterfuge that seems highly artificial, namely that one not preach this doctrine in the second person, "'And if some of *you* (italics added) obey, but have been predestined to be rejected, the power to obey will be taken away so that you cease to obey.' For what else does saying this seem to do but to curse or somehow foretell evil" (61). Rather, the preacher should say these things, not of those listening, but of a universal and impersonal *they*, "That is, we should not say 'If any of you obey, but are predestined to be rejected,' but 'If any obey,' with the rest in the third person, not in the second" (Ibid).

Then Augustine adds, as if to indict his own teaching. "For one does not speak of something desirable, but of something dreadful, and with great harshness and hatefulness it is thrown as if into the face of the listeners . . ." (Ibid). It would be hard to find a more stinging criticism of Augustine's doctrine from his most ardent opponents. Serge Lancel finds in this passage about preaching the voice of the pastor whispering to the theologian to tone down the harshness of his teaching at least in form, but doubts the effectiveness of the ploy. "These manipulations of pure form sometimes cause a smile: what kind of hearers could the preacher put off the scent by addressing them impersonally in the third person plural" (Lancel, 2002, 433). We might also find in Augustine's words a startlingly honest admission of something indigestible in his own teaching.[3]

More convincing than his advice about preaching, which might seem contrived, we have Augustine's own performance as a preacher, humbly standing before his listeners and acknowledging the difficulty of his doctrine. In one of his sermons preached during the height of the Pelagian controversy, probably about the year 417,[4] Augustine acknowledged his hearers' resistance, "'But it troubles me,' you say, 'that this one perishes, that one is baptized. It troubles me, it troubles me as a man.'" And Augustine adds immediately, "Well if you want to know the truth, it troubles me too, because I too am human" (Sermon 26, 15).

Toward the end of *The Gift of Perseverance*, Augustine gives additional advice from the pastoral side. He cautions against the manner of speaking which he has said should be used in preaching predestination unless the preacher adds "this or something of the sort and says, 'And so, you ought to hope for this perseverance in obedience from the Father of lights from whom comes down *every best gift and every perfect gift* (Jas. 1:17). And you ought to ask for it by daily prayers and, in doing this, you ought to be confident that you are not strangers to the predestination of his people, because he himself also grants that you say these prayers and have his confidence'" (*Gift of Perseverance,* 62). Then Augustine adds what is really the whole point of his teaching on predestination: "But heaven forbid that you despair about yourselves because you are commanded to place your hope in him, not in yourselves" (Ibid).

In all this pastoral sensitivity of Augustine we can find the expression of a certain humility that characterized his attitude toward his own writings. Toward the end of Augustine's *The Gift of Perseverance*, after reminding his readers that he has been consistent in teaching that God's grace is necessary for final perseverance, Augustine adds, "And yet, I would not want anyone to embrace all my views in order to be my follower, but only those points on which he sees that I am not mistaken . . . For I speak with more arrogance than truth if I say that I have now at this age come to perfection without any error in my writing" (Ibid., 55). In the same spirit, at the end of his *De Trinitate* (399–419) Augustine prays, "O Lord, the One God, God the Trinity, whatsoever I have said in these books is of you, may those that are yours acknowledge; whatsoever of myself alone, do you and yours forgive. Amen (*On the Trinity,* 51, last par.).

In concluding his chapter on Augustine's long dispute with Julian of Eclanum over predestination and the necessity of grace for the beginning, middle, and end of our acts of willing, Serge Lancel asks why the "doctor of grace" held on to this doctrine of predestination. We have seen the trouble this doctrine caused for Augustine himself. His opponents and even some of his supporters were even more troubled. Not only is the teaching difficult to accept because of our image of God as merciful, it also contradicts the explicit teaching of the New Testament that God wills all people to be saved (I Tim. 2:4; II Peter, 3:9). Lancel recognizes that the way Augustine "skirted around" these texts of Paul and Peter is widely considered the weakest point of his attempt to understand the Christian faith, but quickly adds: "No one would dream, however, of drawing the conclusion that [Augustine] felt some morose pleasure by leaving a good proportion of his fellow men abandoned by God" (Lancel, 434). The problem, in Lancel's view, was that Augustine in the last twelve years of his life "was a prisoner of his Anti-Pelagian polemic" (434). He was afraid to give an inch to his adversaries in the dispute over the necessity of God's grace in every stage of the path to salvation. This may be true, but if we go back to the pivotal document "To Simplician—on Various Questions," written in 396, even before Augustine had taken up arms against Pelagius, we find, in the second part of that work, the doctrine on predestination already well formed. Perhaps Augustine would have softened that doctrine if it had not been for his battle with Pelagius. Whatever the case, it remains a troubling teaching.

Another factor in Augustine's articulation of predestination was his excessively narrow and literal interpretation of certain texts from Scripture. In the same crucial work of 396, which we have already considered above, "To Simplician," Augustine refers to God's choice of Jacob and rejection of Esau in Genesis, discussed already by Paul in his letter to the Romans (Rom. 9: 10–13). Augustine cites first God's prediction to Rebecca, mother of Esau and Jacob, "Two nations are in your womb, two peoples are quarreling while still within you: but one shall surpass the other, and the older shall serve the younger" (Gen. 25:23). Augustine also cites the prophet Malachi: "I have loved Jacob but hated Esau" (Mal. 1:3b) and points out that neither the love of Jacob nor the hatred of Esau had anything to do with prior good or bad deeds of the two brothers. Augustine is also careful to point out that God hates not the man Esau, but the sinner. We ask what sin God hates since Augustine has already said that God's choice of Jacob and rejection of Esau was not based on any virtue or sin of theirs. The sin God hates in Esau is the sin of Adam in which he participates. So does Jacob of course, but God has chosen to rescue him from the consequences of that sin. If we read the texts Augustine cites from Genesis regarding Esau and Jacob in the context of the whole story—as Augustine could have done—their value is minimized. The choice of Jacob and the rejection of Esau appear more the result of maternal intrigue than of divine predestination. Isaac preferred Esau since he was a good hunter, but Rebecca preferred Jacob and Rebecca cooked up—literally—a scheme to get the paternal blessing for her preferred son (Gen. 25:27–34). Moreover, the choice of Jacob and the rejection of Esau are not a matter of eternal salvation or damnation but of position within the family and its consequences for the brothers' posterity. We have here one example of how Augustine used scripture in a way that seems to wrench it from its context to support his own position.

DOCTRINES GRADUALLY ABANDONED
IN THE COURSE OF HISTORICAL DEVELOPMENT

Augustine taught that "little ones who leave the body without baptism will be under that mildest condemnation of all. But," he adds immediately, "one who preaches that they will not be under any condemnation misleads others very much and is himself very mistaken" (*Punishment and Forgiveness of Sins,* 21). Augustine claimed that his opponents, the Pelagians, made precisely this mistake in ascribing "salvation and eternal life to unbaptized little ones as a recompense for their innocence" (*Punishment,* 26, 48). The Church, too, condemned this view along with other key Pelagian teachings in the Council of Carthage in 418. "If any say . . . that in the kingdom of heaven there will be some intermediate place or any place anywhere in which the little ones will live happily who have left this life without baptism . . . let them be anathema" (Canon 3). The Church's later belief in limbo, a place of natural happiness without the vision of God, better reflects the view of the Pelagians than the view of Augustine. And now the Church has dropped even the narrow vision of God's mercy implied in Limbo.[5]

Augustine and the teaching Church of his time felt compelled to maintain this severe teaching by their reading of the key passage, Romans 5:12. We read in contemporary versions of this passage variations on the following: "Therefore, just as through one person [Adam] sin entered the world, and through sin, death, and thus death came to all, *inasmuch as all sinned* [italics added] . . . "The Latin version of this passage available to Augustine and his contemporaries translated the Greek, "*eph ho*"—now translated as "inasmuch as"—as "*in quo*" or "in whom." So the rendering Augustine and his contemporaries read was something like this: "Therefore, just as through one human being [Adam's] sin entered the world, and through sin death, and so it was passed on to all human beings *in whom* (i.e., in Adam) all sinned." Augustine recognized the distinction between the actual sins that adults commit and infants cannot commit and the sin inherited from Adam. But, based on his understanding of Romans 5:12, he came to think of the inherited sin as really sin and deserving of condemnation unless one is saved through Baptism.

This crucial aspect of Augustine's belief, a belief he shared with the Church of his time, explains much of the other material we find troubling, including the notion of predestination. Augustine justifies predestination on the assumption that all humans *deserve* condemnation because of their share in the sin of Adam. "The whole mass of humanity owes a debt of punishment, and if all suffered the penalty of damnation they deserved, they certainly would not be paying an unjust penalty" (Augustine, "Nature and Grace," 5,5). If God chooses to select out some from that fate, he is justified in doing so. In "To Simplician" Augustine compares this strategy to the gospel passage from Matthew in which the master pays the late comers just as much as those who had showed up at the beginning of the day (Matt. 20:11ff; *To Simplician,* Book Two, 16). Not easy, Augustine admits, for human beings to understand. "[God] decides who are not to be offered mercy by a standard of equity which is most secret and far removed from human powers of understanding" (Ibid).

Once we acknowledge that human beings, though affected by the sin of Adam, do not deserve condemnation—as the Church now teaches—then the whole structure of the doctrine of predestination is shaken at its foundations. Predestined to holiness perhaps but not rescued from condemnation.

To understand how Augustine came to teach a doctrine that he recognized as harsh—a doctrine that troubled him as a man—we must turn to the theology of grace and original sin that constitutes Augustine's most lasting contribution to the life of the Church. For it was in pushing to an extreme limit a theology at the heart of Christian belief that Augustine went to the frontiers of orthodoxy.

THE AUGUSTINIAN TEACHING
OF GRACE AND ORIGINAL SIN

Augustine developed his theology of grace out of a meditation on the writings of Paul. Other biblical texts from Old and New Testaments reinforced Paul's teaching but the foundation is Pauline. The question is how human beings are to be saved. Paul interpreted the Old Testament as teaching that salvation is based on merit, specifically on the merit that comes from observing the Law. Paul argued that, though the Law can tell us what is right and what wrong, it does not give us the power to actually choose the good and reject the wrong. We have reviewed Paul's teaching in chapter 3 above. The crucial point here is that the human will after the fall is not capable by itself of consistently choosing the good and rejecting evil. Paul's famous lament sums up the human condition: "For I do not do the good I want but the evil I do not want is what I do" (Rom. 7:19). The grace of Christ is precisely what saves the believer from this chronic impotence of the will.

Augustine accepts Pelagius' stages in the unfolding of acts of will, the ability, the will, and the action: "That is the ability by which one can be righteous, the will by which one wills to be righteous, and the action by which one is righteous" (*The Grace of Christ and Original Sin,* I, 4). According to Augustine, Pelagius taught that the first of these three, the ability, "was given to nature by the creator and is not in our power" (Ibid). But the other two elements, the willing and the doing, come from us alone without any help of grace. Pelagius cites a passage from Paul on which Augustine also relies; but the two interpret it differently. "It is God, after all, who produces in you the willing and the accomplishment" (Phil. 2:13). For Pelagius God's producing in us the willing and the accomplishment is the law and teaching. (*Grace of Christ,* I, 10, 11, par. 1). But, says Augustine, "we want the Pelagians at some point to admit not merely the grace by which we are promised the great glory to come, but that by which we believe in and hope for it; not merely the grace by which wisdom is revealed, but that by which we love it as well; not merely the grace by which we are urged on to everything good, but that which moves us to action" (Ibid., I, 10,11, par 2).

"That by which we love it as well"—here is the heart of Augustine's doctrine of grace. Only love, delight in doing good can overcome in us the power of concupiscence. Augustine speaks of fulfilling the law out of fear rather than from a love of righteousness (*The Spirit and the Letter,* 8, 13). Perhaps his fullest statement comes a few paragraphs later in this same work. If one obeys the law out of fear of punishment, one obeys in the manner of a slave. "For there is lacking that good fruit that springs up from the root of love. But if *faith that works through love is present* (Gal. 5:6), one begins to find delight in the law of God in the interior human being" (Ibid., 14, 26).

Augustine's teaching on original sin developed over time out of three sources. As a theological position, original sin was a corollary of the belief that the grace of Jesus Christ is the only source of salvation. Original sin and the actual sins that proceed from it were, for Augustine, precisely what Christ saves from. This line of reasoning proceeded deductively. Another source of Augustine's teaching about original sin was his observation of the behavior of human beings which, inductively, provided evidence of a deep wound in human nature. Finally, Augustine's own interior struggle for freedom, recorded in his *Confessions*, provided a personal foundation elaborated in all of his mature writings. We will consider each of these, beginning first with the last mentioned since it was chronologically first.

Serge Lancel claims that the years 396–397 stand out as one of those "specially favored periods" one often finds in the course of an author's development. These were the beginning years of Augustine's time as Bishop of Hippo, first as coadjutor, then as full bishop. To these years belong "the richest results, in both the pastoral field and in [Augustine's] development of fundamental texts" (Lancel, 187). Among the fundamental texts of those years are two that mark the beginnings of Augustine's doctrine of original sin, *To Simplician,* and the *Confessions. To Simplician* contains Augustine's answer to two questions posed by his mentor and friend who would soon succeed Ambrose as Bishop of Milan. Simplician had asked for an interpretation of two passages from Paul's Letter to the Romans. Simplician's first question had to do with Romans 7:7–25 which contains Paul's famous lament, "For I do not do the good I want, but the evil I do not want is what I do" (Rom. 7:19). The second had to do with Romans 9:10–29 in which Paul addresses the issue of predestination. The first question, the one that concerns us here, was whether Paul meant his lament to apply to the person under the law or the person under grace. Augustine is quite clear: Paul, although he had himself by the time of this writing come under grace, was speaking as someone under the law, thus not able to do what he wanted and avoid what he did not want. Under the impulse of his dispute with the Pelagians, Augustine, as we will see, later changed his interpretation of this passage, recognizing that even under grace the Christian struggles to be faithful.

We come to the crucial document that has a special place in the writings of Augustine and a foundational role in the development of his doctrine of original sin, the *Confessions.* This account of Augustine's struggle to free his will from its chains not only lies under his doctrine of original sin, but provides the foundation of all his subsequent thought and writing. John O'Meara finds the *Confessions*, with its description of the human struggle, at work in Augustine's, *The City of God.* ". . . the *City of God* is the application of the *Confessions* to the history of mankind" (O'Meara, xvii).

It is surely significant that Augustine wrote his *Confessions* between 397 and 401, shortly after his answer to the first question of Simplican about the meaning of Romans 7:7–25 in 396. The question of Paul's famous lament about not doing what he wanted to do and doing what he did not want to do as well as his liberation from this situation through the grace of Christ was on Augustine's mind. Paul's brief account of the enslaved will and its liberation expresses the inner logic by which Augustine developed his own life story. On several occasions Augustine speaks of his will in chains. ". . . I was held fast, not in fetters clamped upon me by another, but by my own free will which had the strength of chains" (*Conf.*, VIII, 5). And a little later as the moment of conversion was approaching: "I was in torment, reproaching myself more bitterly than ever as I twisted and turned in my chain. I hoped that my chain might be broken once for all, because it was only a small thing that held me now (VIII, 11). As his struggle intensified just before his famous liberation in the garden, Augustine referred quite explicitly to Paul's lament: "*My action did not come from me, but from the sinful principle that dwells in me* [Rom. 7:17]. It was part of the punishment of a sin freely committed by Adam, my first father" (*Conf.,* VIII, 10).

Augustine's quite personal struggle brought him to a consciousness of the basic truth of original sin, a term he used for the first time in his response to the first question of Simplician (*To Simplician,* Book I, 10). Also in his first book to Simplician, Augustine discusses the division Paul makes in three stages of human liberation from sin. First comes a stage before the law when sin is dead or latent (Rom. 7:8b). Second, when the law comes, it awakens sin: "but when the commandment came, sin became alive" (Rom. 7:9). Paul says he didn't know what it meant to covet until the law said "thou shalt not covet" (Rom. 7:7). So law awakens the consciousness of sin but does not give the power to avoid it. The third stage is liberation through the grace of Jesus Christ: "For the law of the spirit of life has freed you from the law of sin and grace" (Rom. 8:2). Augustine explicates at length Paul's three stages of bondage to and liberation from sin in his answer to Simplician's first question.

If we apply these three stages elaborated by Paul to Augustine's development of his own life journey, we find an amazing parallel. The nine years during which Augustine found himself under the influence of the Manichees was really a time prior to the law. The Manichees taught that the evil substance in us sins, not our own will. In this sense, Augustine was not "under the law." The law did not apply to him because another substance acted in him. Eventually, as Augustine struggled free of the Manichee influence, he came to recognize his own responsibility toward the law: "When I chose to do something or not to do it, I was quite certain that it was my own self, and not some other person who made this act of will . . ." (*Conf.*, VII, 3, par 2). But though Augustine recognizes that he has a will and has thus come under the law, he is not able by his free will alone to conform to the law, the second phase. The struggle that comes from this situation moves him toward the third phase, liberation through grace. This comes about in a dramatic way in his conversion experience in the Garden. In what may be the most dramatic scene of his *Confessions*, Augustine describes how, under increasing frustration and longing he hears a child's voice call "take and read" (Ibid., VIII, 13, par 2). Taking up the Scripture, Augustine read the words from chapter 13 of Romans, "not in rioting and drunkenness . . . ," and experienced a flood of release. It was the beginning of his surrender to grace.

In his relatively brief response to the first question of Simplician and his longer *Confessions,* we have Augustine's first articulation of his doctrine of original sin. We need to pause and note what this first articulation contained and did not contain. At stake was the freedom of the will, that is, the freedom to do what one desires to do and avoid what one desires not to do. Grace frees the will in the sense of empowering it. We do not yet have the issue of final salvation or final condemnation. We do not have a resolution of the question of whether the original sin is truly sin for which Adam's progeny must pay the price. The "originating sin" appears in these writings as the cause of the concupiscence in the will that draws one toward evil away from the good. Only later, facing the issue of infant baptism in the heat of the controversy with Pelagius, will Augustine affirm that the sin we have inherited entails not just the origin of a weakness of the will in adults but the condemnation referred to above, of infants who have not been baptized.

Augustine's personal struggle and gradual liberation ground his own compassion toward those who struggle in a similar way. His personal experience kept him from the harshness of Pelagius in judging the faults of others. Even after his liberation through the conversion in the garden, Augustine continued to feel the pull of concupiscence.

Later, in the midst of the Pelagian controversy, Augustine would reverse his response to Simplican's question about whether Paul's lament is spoken by someone under the law or someone under grace. In 396, Augustine thought it was someone under the law, not yet under grace.

Augustine's observation of human behavior served as a second source of his conviction about what original sin was. Not only did he recognize his own confusion and turmoil, he saw it in those around him. Augustine was not, as Serge Lancel notes, "an egghead theologian poring over texts" (Lancel, 422). Julian's ardent adversary, Julian of Eclanum shared the Pelagian confidence about what human beings could do on their own unaided by grace. Not Augustine. "Against Julian's naturalism and optimism [Augustine] mainly set the daily findings of his experience as a man and pastor. He had only to look around him to fuel a pessimism whose anthropological foundations his meditations on St. Paul had begun to give him some thirty years earlier . . ." (Ibid). We will see later Augustine's observations on the behavior of his family and friends recounted in his *Confessions* that also confirmed his conviction of the universality of original sin. Augustine's interior journey with its struggle from slavery to freedom and his observations of human behavior give the experiential grounds of his doctrine of original sin.

The third source, the theological foundation for the doctrine of original sin, lay in the doctrine of Christ as universal savior that Augustine inherited from St. Paul and other scriptural readings. Though Augustine was not "an egghead theologian poring over texts," he had pored over texts throughout his life and the texts influenced him. As he pursued the restless quest that led him to Christianity, Augustine found texts that awakened something in him at each stage only to disappoint in the end until St. Paul opened the door to salvation through the grace of Christ. Augustine was, as he himself tells us, "trying to find the origins of evil," to reconcile the fact of evil with the existence of God (*Conf.,* VII, 5). Ideas about what evil is and where it comes from also entail prescriptions for salvation. The Manichees offered Augustine the doctrine of two substances, one evil, one good. The evil substance, quite apart from the human will, produces evil deeds. We have seen how Augustine came to reject this solution and to accept responsibility for his own deeds. Through Cicero's *Hortensius* (now lost), Augustine learned to love truth for its own sake (Ibid., III, 4). The Platonists, especially Plotinus, prompted him, "to look for truth as something incorporeal" (Ibid., VII, 20), thus opening him to interiority and the transforming power of contemplation. Finally he began to study "the venerable writings inspired by your Holy Spirit, especially those of the Apostle Paul (Ibid., VII, 21).

Augustine discovered in St. Paul whatever truth he had found in the Platonists and something more as well, namely that whatever good we do comes as the gift of God's grace, and not as an achievement of our own (Ibid.). Whereas Platonic contemplation was a method for lifting the spirit out of its enslavement to flesh, a method that one could perfect through practice, Christian discipleship was a matter of surrender to the power of the Word of God who had become incarnate. Though the Platonists recognized the word of God, they did not acknowledge that the Word had taken on flesh and died for our sins (*Conf.,* VII, 9). Theirs was a path of salvation through knowledge. In the Christian scriptures Augustine found the path of charity. Augustine's portrait of himself during his Platonist days explains the difference: "I was full of self-esteem, which was a punishment of my own making. I ought to have deplored my state, but instead my *knowledge only bred self-conceit* [I Cor. 8:1]. For was I not without charity, which builds an edifice on the firm foundation of humility, that is, on Jesus Christ? But how could I expect that the Platonist books would ever lead me to charity" (*Conf.,* VII, 20)? Along with charity went humility, the best antidote to thinking of oneself as better than the others.

Charity implied not only love of God but love of neighbor. In his work, *On Christian Teaching*, written during this same fruitful period, 396/97, Augustine spoke of "the counsel of compassion" (*concilium misericordiae*). This counsel, the fifth of seven stages Augustine lays out for the ascent of the Christian soul to the vision of God, arises from the command of charity. "Here," says Augustine, "[the Christian] strenuously occupies himself with the love of neighbor and becomes perfect in it (*On Christian Teaching*, VII, 21). In the thirteenth book of the *Confessions,* Augustine elaborates the point more fully. In an allegorical interpretation of the seven days of creation, Augustine compares the seed-bearing fruits to the works of mercy. "When we love our neighbor by giving him help for his bodily needs, our souls bear fruit in works of mercy proper to their kind, for they have seed in them according to their species" (*Conf.,* XIII, 17). From these good deeds, the Christian passes on "to that more sublime harvest, the joy of contemplation" (Ibid., 18).

These works of mercy designate for Augustine a crucial difference between the Platonic and the Christian path to contemplation. The Christian way takes into account the incarnational character of human existence, and not only its incarnational character but also that fact that humans have sinned and thus incurred dissolution and death. This human situation entails recognition of bodily and spiritual poverty and the consequent need for works of mercy. And because we all share the same humanity wounded by sin, our works of mercy come out of a profound humility. "For from our weakness we are moved by pity (*compatimur*) to serve those in need, aiding them as we would wish to be aided ourselves if we were in like distress" (XIII, 17).

In the passages cited above, Augustine refers to the help we give our neighbor "for his bodily needs." A little further on in chapter 13 of the *Confessions,* Augustine addresses the neighbor's moral situation. Consistent with what we have seen in his letter, *To Simplician,* Augustine distinguishes between those under grace and those not yet under grace. The person under grace "who has spiritual gifts and has been refitted for closer knowledge *so that the image of God who created him is his pattern* must obey the law, not pass judgment on it" (Ibid., XIII, 23). Being under grace does not give a person the right to judge those not under grace. God knows them, we do not. "Furthermore no man, even though he has the gifts of the spirit, can pass judgment on the peoples of this world who still struggle on without your grace. *How can he claim jurisdiction over those who are without,* (I Cor. 5, 12), when he does not know which of them will come into the sweet domain of your grace and which remain forever in the bitter exile where you are not loved" (Ibid., XIII, 23)?

This reservation of judgment relative to those not under grace does not, at this stage of Augustine's development, apply to the relation between those under grace and those who share the gift of grace with them. "The man who has spiritual gifts also judges the faithful, approving what he finds to be right, blaming what he finds to be wrong" (Ibid, final paragraph). The person with special gifts under the regime of grace can judge others under grace by their almsgiving, by their practice of chastity, by fasting, "and by the soul's regard for its duty to God when it reflects upon the sensations of which it is conscious through the body" (Ibid.). Finally, Augustine gives the rationale for this exercise of judgment, fraternal correction. "For he judges only those things which he also has the power to correct" (Ibid).

At this stage of his development, Augustine, as we have seen above in discussing the letter, *To Simplician*, still took Paul's famous lament in Romans 7 about doing the things I do not want to do and not doing the things I want to do as applying to the person not yet under grace but not to the person under grace. But later, under the pressure of the controversy with Pelagius that dominated Augustine's attention from 412 until his death in 430, Augustine came to recognize that even under the regime of grace the Christian still experiences the strange waywardness of the will that provoked Paul's lament and thus deserves compassion. This is a crucial point in coming to understand the connection between Augustine's teaching on original sin and his radical compassion. We will return to this point in the discussion of Augustine's struggle with the Pelagians that provides the context for his final elaboration of the doctrine of original sin.

Even at the period of Augustine's development we are now considering, the early years of his episcopate from 396–400—the period of his letter, *To*

Simplician, the *Confessions,* and *On Christian Doctrine*—Augustine has moved beyond the first hopes evoked by his conversion in 386. Between the time of his conversion to Christianity (386) and the writing of his *Confessions* (397–98), Augustine underwent, as we have seen, a dramatic shift brought about by two influences, the experience of resistance in his own life to the platonic ideal he had set before himself, and a close re-reading of St. Paul. The reading of Paul helped him make sense of his own experience. "His re-reading of Saint Paul in the mid-390s is one of the great divides of Augustine's intellectual development" (Markus 1989, 22). This re-reading, coupled with his personal experience of continuing temptation, put an end to Augustine's "belief in human self-determination" and introduced him to "the beginnings of the theology of grace he would deploy against Pelagius" (Markus, 22).

Markus refers to Peter Brown's biography of Augustine that examines this period of Augustine's life in a chapter provocatively entitled, "The Lost Future." The chapter title suggests disappointment and, indeed, this period of Augustine's life required him to let go of something that had sustained him since his earliest "conversion." But, paradoxically, the disappointment opens Augustine to what will be most liberating in his theology of original sin, the doctrine that has seemed to many full of pessimism about human life. Brown describes the world Augustine will have to give up: ". . . From 386–391 . . . Augustine was still rooted in the old world. The ideal on which he had based his life still belonged to the Platonic tradition of the ancient world. He would be a '*sapiens,*' a wise man, living a life of contemplation, determined, as were his pagan contemporaries . . . 'to grow god-like in their retirement'" (Brown 139, Augustine, *Ep.* 10, 2). Observing that "Ten years later this great hope had vanished," (Brown, 140), Brown cites Augustine: "Whoever thinks that in this mortal life a man may so disperse the mists of bodily and carnal imaginings as to possess the unclouded light of changeless truth, and to cleave to it with the unswerving constancy of a spirit wholly estranged from the common ways of life—he understands neither what he seeks, nor who he is who seeks it" (Augustine, *de cons. Evang.,* IV, x, 20).

In reading Paul's account of liberation from slavery through the grace of Christ, Augustine found the story of his own conversion. His captivity had been deeply rooted in his will. Not only was Augustine the victim of his own sinful habits, which had become a chain holding him back, he believed he was subject to a more profound weakness that he shared with the human race, an originating sin. And until that was healed, no amount of self-discipline would free him, not even Platonic contemplation. Once having surrendered to the power of grace, Augustine found that it had its own logic and its own demands. Working out the implications of that logic occupied the last thirty years of Augustine's life. The more Augustine reflected on the logic of grace, the more he came to recognize the utter dependence of human beings on the redemptive action of Christ.

A DOCTRINE DEVELOPED THROUGH CONTROVERSY

Augustine's doctrine of original sin developed, as we have seen, from his own experience, from his observation of human beings, and from his reading of Scripture, especially Paul. At stake in this first stage of development was Augustine's own personal struggle for liberation that brought him to conversion. But Augustine soon recognized an even higher set of stakes, the Christian tradition itself, the integrity of Catholic teaching, and the community of the Church. When Julian of Eclanum, the last and most formidable of Augustine's Pelagian adversaries, attacked Augustine, he attacked the fathers who had preceded Augustine in teaching the doctrine of original sin. That at least was Augustine's view. Julian had found in Augustine's doctrine of original sin a resurgence of Manichaeism. If he is guilty, says Augustine, so are the many fathers who have held the doctrine of original sin. "You frequently accuse of us of being Manichees, but also consider, if you are awake, the many great and good men, defenders of the Catholic faith, whom you dare to attack with so hateful an accusation (*Against Julian*, I, 3, 5). In the pages that follow Augustine lists by name and cites their works church fathers from the East and the West who have maintained the doctrine of original sin. When he comes to John Chrysostom, Archbishop of Constantinople and a contemporary of Augustine whom Julian had cited as holding that unbaptized children are without sin, Augustine makes the all-important distinction between actual and original sin which Julian has obscured, "But you transform [Chrysostom's] words into your teaching. He said that little ones do not have sins, that is personal sins. For this reason, we rightly call them innocent . . ." (I, 6,22).

What is crucial to note here is that Augustine's position on original sin, which began in a personal struggle, came to maturity through controversy. Three formidable adversaries, the Manichees, the Donatists, and the Pelagians, impelled Augustine to define and clarify the teaching of the tradition. When Julian found lurking under Augustine's doctrine of original sin the heresy of Manichaeism, he threw his adversary back to the struggle that had marked his early years. Augustine had spent nine difficult years of his youth personally caught in the web of these people he calls "those would-be saints, who were such frauds both to themselves and to others" (*Conf.*, Bk. V, Ch 10, 103). His efforts to disentangle himself and his subsequent writings against the Manichees constitute the first great controversy of his life. The second, lasting from about 393–411, involved him in conflict with the Donatist heresy. From 411 to the end of his life, Augustine pursued the third controversy with Pelagius and the Pelagians.

A thread runs through all these controversies that leads us into the heart of the texts we are considering here. The thread is the extent of the will's freedom. Augustine's thinking develops and his final position is complex; the development itself is crucial to understanding his thought. One's belief about freedom influences one's attitude toward compassion. If people are fully free, fully responsible for their actions, they seem to deserve less compassion, as Pelagius illustrates. People not fully free, Augustine believed, people laboring under constraints not of their own making, call forth more compassion.

As we have seen above, Augustine's Manichee period, from about 375 to 484, embroiled him in their doctrine of two wills, one evil, one good. In his *Confessions,* Augustine describes his state of mind at this time: "I still thought that it was not we who sin, but some other nature that sins within us" (*Conf.,* Bk. V, Ch 10, par 2). In his darkness, Augustine found this a convenient place to dwell, not having to admit guilt and confess so that "you [God] might bring healing to a soul that had sinned against you" (Ibid., Bk. V, Ch 10). But gradually, Augustine came to find liberation in the idea of his own will: "One thing lifted me up into the light of your day. It was that I knew that I had a will, as surely as I knew that there was life in me. When I chose to do something or not to do it, I was quite certain that it was my own self, and not some other person, who made this act of the will, so that I was on the point of understanding that herein lay the cause of my sin" (Ibid., Bk. VII, Ch 3). Augustine returns to this idea in Book IX: " . . . by now I had learned to tremble for my past, so that in future I might sin no more. And it was right that I should tremble, because it was not some other nature belonging to the tribe of darkness that had sinned in me as the Manichees pretend" (Ibid., Bk. IX, ch 4).

During this time also, Augustine was trying to resolve the problem of evil: "I was trying to find the origin of evil, but I was quite blind to the evil in my own method of research" (Ibid., Bk. VII, Ch 5). Augustine expresses the classic dilemma simply: "Where then does evil come from, if God made all things and because he is good, made them good too" (Ibid., Bk. VII, Ch 5)? For the Manichees, good and evil are two different substances. Their position is a variation of the mythic type that Paul Ricoeur calls "The Creation Myth" (chapter one). But for Augustine, the idea of God's infinite substance being limited by another reality completely different from God contradicted the very notion of God. Augustine came to see that God is good, that all God has created is good and—another way of saying the same thing—that everything that has being is good. "They are in you because you hold all things in your truth as though they were in your hand, and all things are true in so far as they have being. Falsehood is nothing but the supposed being of something which has no being" (Ibid., Bk. VII, Ch 15). And to his further question about what wickedness was he answers, "I saw that it was not a substance but perversion of the will when it turns aside from you, O God, who are the supreme substance . . ." (Ibid., Bk. VII, Ch 16).

Augustine continues to struggle with the division in his will: "My inner self was a house divided against itself" (Ibid., VIII, 8). Because of this phenomenon of the divided will, which the Manichees also recognized in themselves, they had claimed the existence of two wills, one good, one evil. But for Augustine, now liberated from his false teachers, the divided will revealed something other than the existence of two different wills: "All this [his habit of sin] happened to me although I did not want it, but it did not prove that there was some second mind in me besides my own. It only meant that my mind was being punished" (Ibid., VIII, 10). Here Augustine shows his dependence on St. Paul: "My action did not come from me, but from the sinful principle that dwells in me. It was part of the punishment of a sin freely committed by Adam, my first father" (Ibid., VIII, 10).

Two opposed, but not contradictory affirmations, contain Augustine's final position. First, against the Manichees, the human will is free. When I commit sin it is truly my will that performs the act not some other will dwelling in me. I am responsible for my acts. But though my will is free in principle and demands that I accept responsibility for my acts, my will is not free in an unqualified way. It is free in principle but divided in fact, subject to my intentions but subject also to a certain weakness that Augustine, following Paul, calls sin, "the sin that issues from a more voluntary sin, for I was Adam's son" (Ibid., VIII, 10). It is here, the heart of Augustine's doctrine of original sin, that Pelagius thrusts the sword of his denial. According to Pelagius and his followers, including Julian of Eclanum, we are free in an unqualified way, without any prior inclination to evil. Adam's sin was only a bad example that we are free to follow or not. And Julian uses this qualification that Augustine introduces into human freedom as a warrant to accuse him of Manichaeism. Pelagius and Julian do not have that bold quality of thought that F. Scott Fitzgerald admired so much as the mark of a great mind, "the ability to think opposed thoughts at the same time and still retain the ability to function" (Fitzgerald 1993, 69). For them only two alternatives existed. Either the will was free or it was not free. They did not see how it could be both free and not free at the same time.

This issue of free will, at the center of Augustine's controversies with the Manichees and the Pelagians, was also relevant to his position in the Donatist controversy. The Donatists were hardliners. They maintained that the Christian priests who had apostatized, handing over the holy books to be burned in the face of Roman threats, could not validly perform the sacraments after they returned to communion with the Church since they were apostates and that anyone baptized by them needed to be re-baptized. Augustine's position was that the Donatists did not understand the true nature of the sacraments, which depend not on human virtue for their efficacy but on the grace of Christ which operates through imperfect human instruments.

Augustine spent enormous energy opposing the Donatists. "For ten years he spent all his energies as a writer and a diplomat in combating them, his object being first to defeat their leaders in argument and then, as a result of a general conference, to persuade the mass of the Donatist Church to reunite with the Catholics" (Frend 1971, 228). Although Augustine's victory over the Donatists did not last beyond his death because, at least according to Frend (Ibid., 234), he did not understand the depth of resistance that sustained the movement, his writings against them reveal his own view of Church and sacrament and, more important still for the subject of this paper, his compassion toward those who had betrayed their faith through human weakness. Augustine understood that the human will is not perfectly free and that, out of weakness, it can engage in sinful acts. But that does not prevent God from acting even in sinful people to bring about the effects of the sacraments.

Augustine's response, spelled out at length in his treatise, *On Baptism, Against the Donatists*, contains several crucial elements that will continue within the Christian Church even to the present. One is that the effect of the sacraments does not depend on the virtue of the one administering or the one receiving but on the power of Christ present in them. Closely related to this affirmation is the distinction between the sacrament itself and its "grace." People can have validly received the sacrament in such a way that they never need to receive it again, says Augustine, but the valid reception does not guarantee that they have achieved a holy life.

Augustine makes these points repeatedly in *On Baptism, Against the Donatists.* To the hypothetical question: "If the unrighteous may baptize, and give remission of sins, why do we destroy their credit and call them unrighteous?" he answers, ". . . in the first place, that the baptism with which they baptize is not theirs . . ." In other words it is Christ's. ". . . and secondly, . . . it does not follow that whosoever has the baptism of Christ is also certain of the remission of his sins if he has this only in the outward sign, and is not converted with a true conversion of the heart so that he who gives remission should himself have remission of his sins" (*On Baptism,* VI, 32–36). The baptized Christian, in other words, though a member of the Church, is still on the way, still evolving into the fullness of life in Christ.

From these two points follows Augustine's discussion of different ways of "being in the Church." For Augustine, it is not as easy as the Donatists, with their rigid standard of purity, believed it was, to determine who is inside and who is outside. Only God knows who is inside and who outside: "For in that unspeakable foreknowledge of God, many who seem to be without are actually within, and many who seem to be within, yet really are without" (Ibid., V, 27–38). Augustine describes different levels of participation, from those who are deeply at home in the Church to those who struggle mightily to secure a foothold in the midst of their weakness (Ibid., V, 27–38).

What emerges in the course of the controversy are two radically different ways of conceiving of the Church. "On the one hand, there is the orthodox Catholic Church, prepared to compromise with the evils of this world for the sake of unity and peaceful progress" (Frend 1971, 112). This is the Church that Augustine will defend. "On the other hand, there is the Church of the Holy Spirit, of enthusiasm, of open hostility to the world, individualistic and intolerant" (Ibid., 112–113). The Donatists follow this second way of thinking. The terminology might be confusing. The "orthodox church," in this instance, is orthodox precisely because it is filled with the compassion that recognizes God's power at work even through sinners, and the Church of the Holy Spirit, as conceived by the Donatists, is not orthodox in as much as it fosters an unreal and unattainable idea of holiness. It was, of course, the conversion of Constantine and the subsequent establishment of Christianity that gave rise to these two views of the Church. The Donatists were still attached to the Church of martyrs and could not tolerate the return of those who had defected by turning over the holy books to be burned, the *traditores,* without demanding of them a second baptism. Augustine, on the other hand, recognized that though the Church, as the bride of Christ, was pure, it was also a collection of sinners reaching toward the holiness of the bridegroom. Peter Brown expresses the difference: "The Donatists had claimed, against the Catholics, that, as the church was a unique source of holiness, so no sinner could have a part in it . . . The Catholicism of Augustine, by contrast, reflects the attitude of a group confident of its powers to absorb the world without losing its identity" (Brown 1967, 2000, 208–209).

Along with these two views of the Church are two views of the individual Christian. For Augustine, Baptism was only a beginning of a long development. "Augustine," as Brown explains, "endowed the concrete rites of the Catholic Church with a mysterious and enduring validity. Yet he did so in order to make the Church itself a field of innumerable, personal evolutions. The individual Catholic was only 'guarded' by his sacraments; he still had before him the long process of spiritual growth" (Ibid., 218). And the integrity and validity of the sacrament does not depend on the holiness of the recipient: "Nor is it material, when we are considering the question of the genuineness and holiness of the sacrament, 'what the recipient of the sacrament believes and with what faith he is imbued.' It is of the very highest consequence as regards the entrance into salvation, but is wholly immaterial as regards the question of the sacrament'" (*On Baptism*, III, 14–19).

Underlying all this is the Augustinian conviction that, even after Baptism, a certain weakness of the will, a darkness and confusion, a reluctance to conform one's life totally to the demands of holiness still afflicts the Christian. For the Donatists, such weakness, at least as it was manifested in the handing over of holy books, is a clear indication that baptism did not take. Since Augustine sees baptism as a beginning not of itself guaranteeing salvation, he can be compassionate with the sinner.

We come full circle to the doctrine of Pelagius to which Augustine turned after he had finished with the Donatists. The Donatists shared with Pelagians the conviction that the human will was possessed of all the freedom it needed to resist evil; for the Donatists evil took the form of temptation to apostasy. When Christians did not resist, they had only themselves to blame and could not be excused on the basis of some chronic weakness of will which only God's grace could heal. And Peter Brown notes the connection between Augustine's anti-Donatist and anti-Pelagian writings: "Augustine's writings against the Pelagians follow closely on his campaign against the Donatists. Between them, they are a significant landmark in that process by which the Catholic church had come to embrace, and so to tolerate, the whole lay society of the Roman world, with its glaring inequalities of wealth and the depressing resilience of its pagan habits" (Brown, 351).

This is the Augustine who responds to Julian of Eclanum's denial of the reality of original sin, taking umbrage at Julian's efforts to enlist the authority of Chrysostom. What is at stake is nothing less than the foundations of compassion, forgiveness, and the restoration of the sinner through God's grace. Paradoxically, the Pelagian denial of original sin leads away from compassion toward severe righteous judgment, away from Jesus' willingness to eat with sinners toward the Pharisees' ritual purity, away from the recognition of the Church as a communion of sinners to an unbridgeable divide between the righteous and the unrighteous. And the affirmation of an original sin shared equally by all paves the way of forgiveness by establishing from the beginning a solidarity in weakness that rules out any firm distinction between those *inside* and those *outside* the Church.

At the height of his controversy with the Pelagians, about the year 420, Augustine returned to the lament referred to in Romans of a person choosing what he does not want and not choosing what he wants. In the first part of his letter *To Simplician,* as we have seen above, Augustine interpreted these as the words of someone still under the law, not yet under grace. But now, twenty years later, he sees that even the person under grace has reason to utter this lament. "I had once thought that this passage from the apostle described a human being under the law. Later, however, these words *but now it is not I who do this* (Rom. 7:17) made me feel their force" (*Answer to the Two Letters*, I, 10.22). Augustine makes clear what he means. Not that people under grace consent to sin but that they struggle with the resistance of the flesh. They "are not yet in that perfect peace in which death will be swallowed up in victory" (Ibid., I, 11.23). This struggle between the spirit that proclaims "I delight in the law of God in the interior self" (Rom. 7:24; *Answer to Two Letters*, I, 10.22) and the flesh that resists the law of God finds expression in Paul's admission, "We too who have the first fruits of the Spirit groan in ourselves as we await the adoption of our body" (Rom. 8:23; *Answer to Two Letters*, I, 11.23). In other words, even those who have surrendered themselves to the grace of Christ still struggle against the powerful urges of the flesh.

It is certainly possible that Augustine has been instructed by his own experience. At the time of his conversion in 386, a life of virtue and contemplation of God seemed like an easy thing. Already ten years later, by the time of his writing the *Confessions* and other works of this period, Augustine had realized that a life of Christian virtue was a struggle, as he affirms in Book X of the *Confessions*. God had given him the grace of continence. "But in my memory" he says, ". . . the images of things imprinted upon it by my former habits linger on. When I am awake they obtrude themselves upon me , though with little strength. But when I dream, they not only give me pleasure but are very much like acquiescence in the act" (Bk. X, Ch 30). And now, after the lapse of another twenty years, Augustine has come to recognize that the struggle never ends until death. In his *Answer to Two Letters* Augustine speaks of those who do not consent to sin, but still struggle with temptation. In another work written a few years before the *Answer to Two Letters,* Augustine even manifests, in opposition to Pelagius, an understanding of those who do consent to sin. "Many wrong actions are done by the ignorant, by the weak, and often by persons weeping and groaning" (*Nature and Grace,* 29, 33). By exalting the freedom of the human will, Pelagius, in effect, removed the grounds for a sympathetic view of sinners.

Augustine's final position on sin lies midway between the Manichaeism that denies the freedom of the will altogether and the Pelagianism that exaggerates it. Against the Manicheans, Augustine affirms that we are free. It is truly we who sin. Against the Pelagians, he affirms that we sin as those afflicted by a weakness that affects all humans. Forgiveness is not relevant in the Manichaean worldview because we ourselves do not sin. In the Pelagian view forgiveness addresses individual acts of wrongdoing; it does not reach to a healing of a deep wound that affects the will even before individual wrong acts are committed. In Augustine's view, a view adopted by the Church, the redemption brought about by Christ, is a healing, not just of particular sins, but of the of the whole person afflicted by a tendency toward sin.

AUGUSTINE ON FREEDOM

These three great controversies through which Augustine came to his mature position on original sin, involve a gradual clarification of his notion of freedom. We find a delicate balance between freedom and determinism on the one hand and freedom and grace on the other. An understanding of these two very different polarities will help us situate Augustine's position on freedom, which lies between the Manichaean denial of freedom on the one hand and the Pelagian affirmation of unlimited freedom on the other. Human freedom is neither non-existent as the Manichees taught nor unlimited as Pelagius taught. The human will in the actual order of things after the disobedience of Adam and Eve is a divided will. As a consequence of Adam's disobedience of God's will, human beings are now justly afflicted with a will that does not obey itself. The punishment fits the crime. "To state it briefly, then," Augustine says, "in the punishment of that sin, what is the retribution for disobedience if not disobedience itself? For what is man's misery if not simply his own disobedience to himself, so that because he would not do what he could, he cannot now do what he would" (*City of God*, XIV, 15)? This, of course, echoes St. Paul's lament in the seventh chapter of Romans, "For I do not do the good I want, but the evil I do not want is what I do" (Rom. 7:19).

Augustine's mature interpretation of the sin of Adam expressed in the *City of God* suggests not an ambivalence about freedom or an outward hostility but a *regret* for something humans could have had but do not have because of Adam's disobedience. What is sinful in Adam's act is not the exercise of human freedom in itself, but the exercise of that freedom contrary to the command of God, and not a difficult command at that: "Man held in contempt the command of the God Who had created him . . ." (Ibid., 611). Adam and Eve, who, according to Augustine, should have experienced gratitude toward God for his abundant generosity, instead saw themselves as competitors, interpreting God's command as an attempt to keep from them knowledge of good and evil and eternal life. If Adam and Eve had obeyed, they would have achieved authentic freedom, spiritual freedom grounded in acknowledging their existence from and in God. "What followed, therefore, [on Adam's disobedience] was a just condemnation; a condemnation such that man, who would have become spiritual even in his flesh had he kept the commandment, now became fleshly even in his mind . . ." (Ibid., 611).

What emerges from these passages and from others throughout Augustine's mature work is his conviction that full freedom for human beings can be found only in God. Freedom exercised in opposition to the benevolent, life-giving will of God, is illusory freedom, a kind of slavery really. Anyone who does not grasp this conception of Augustine's will continually be misreading what he says, finding in his theology a negative weighting of what he actually affirms. An example is Augustine's description of his grief over the death of his friend in the fourth book of *The Confessions.* In deeply moving language, Augustine describes the grief he felt over the sudden loss of his friend. "My soul was a burden, bruised and bleeding. It was tired of the man who carried it, but I found no place to set it down to rest" (*Conf.,* IV, 7). Though the reader might be touched by this account of Augustine's grief, Augustine found signs of disordered affection in his own excessive sadness. The problem was that he had loved his friend outside of God, in whom he did not believe at this point in his life. "Blessed are those who love you," he says, "and love their friends in you and their enemies for your sake" (Ibid., 79).

Augustine resists the notion that humans can be free outside of God. If freedom means the power to do what we want and avoid doing what we do not, then, for Augustine, we can be *actually* free only with the grace of God. Adam and Eve were in principle free to eat or not eat the forbidden fruit, but in eating they chose, without knowing it, a loss of freedom. In Augustine's view, seeking to be free outside of God is precisely the beginning of all sin: ". . . the first evil act of the will, since it preceded all other evil acts, consisted rather in its falling away from the work of God to its own works than in any one act" (*City of God,* XIV). And the first sin entailed all the others that followed because it perverted the order by which alone human beings can thrive. "For man has been so made that it is to his advantage to be subject to God, and harmful to him to act according to his own will rather than that of his Creator" (Ibid., XIV, 12). Augustine says that Adam and Eve "began to be evil" in a secret way before the outward act of disobedience became visible. And this secret, invisible evil was pride, which Augustine calls "a perverse kind of elevation." "For it is," he says, "a perverse kind of elevation indeed to forsake the foundation upon which the mind should rest, and to become and remain, as it were, one's own foundation" (Ibid., XIV, 13). The characteristic in Adam and Eve that made it possible for the devil to successfully tempt them was a certain complacency. "The first evil came, then, when man began to be pleased with himself, as if he were his own light; for he then turned away from that Light which, if only he had been pleased with It instead, would have made the man himself a light" (Ibid., XIV). These passages raise the interesting question regarding whether Augustine believed in some kind of "sinful" state, some kind of defect in the will in Adam and Eve even before the act of disobedience that got us all in trouble.

THE EVOLUTION OF AUGUSTINE'S FINAL POSITION

The question remains—and it is the central question—regarding whether and how Augustine's position on original sin embodies a liberating vision or a constricting vision, a vision that leads to an abundant humanity or one that leads to a narrow prison of guilt. The simple answer is that, through a series of conversions that involved deep shifts away from previously held convictions, Augustine became more and more liberated in his personal life and thinking. Throughout his life, Augustine's thought evolved; he had a restless heart and mind that pushed him from one conquered stronghold to another. First came a conversion to the love of wisdom itself through the reading of Cicero's now lost *Hortensius* (*Conf.,* III, 4). We might say Augustine discovered that he had a mind. His concern with the problem of evil led to his involvement with the Manichees: "I fell in with a set of sensualists, men with glib tongues who ranted and raved and had the snares of the devil in their mouths" (Ibid., III, 6). Augustine's falling out from his nine-year Manichaean phase took another laborious conversion in which he discovered he had a will. The great conversion that put an end to Augustine's long struggle with sensuality and false ambition by opening him up to God's grace took place in a garden reminiscent of the Garden of Eden where the anguished seeker heard a voice inviting him to "Take and Read," *Tolle, lege* (Ibid., VIII, 12). We might say that Augustine re-discovered his will, this time under the influence of grace.

ORIGINAL SIN AND THE
SEPARATION OF THOUGHT AND FEELING

Brown goes behind this last profound shift in Augustine's thinking to the insight that provoked it. In what Brown describes as "a reassessment of human motivation" (Brown, 148), Augustine discovered that the will was moved by feelings, particularly by the feeling of delight (*delectatio*). Humans can only sustain a course of action if they feel drawn to it. This helps to explain Paul's famous lament already referred to in this work, "For I do not do the good I want, but I do the evil I do not want" (Rom. 7:19). Why don't I do it? Augustine's answer is simple: because I don't *feel* like it. Though I might "want" it intellectually, my feelings do not want it; I do not "delight" in it. "It is this psychological discovery," says Brown, "which gives cogency to the interpretation that [Augustine] placed on Paul. Briefly, Augustine had analyzed the psychology of 'delight.' Delight is the only possible source of action, nothing else can move the will" (Brown 148). And that delight, as Paul goes on to say, can enter into us only as a gift of the Holy Spirit; we cannot summon it by act of the will.

Another step in the evolution of Augustine's thought, in response to a further question, brings us closer to the liberating power of his doctrine of original sin. The question is "*Why* can we not summon our feelings in support of what we know we should do?" Augustine's answer may be the most radical aspect of his teaching about the condition we call original sin. We suffer from a separation between the realm of thought and the realm of feeling. Choosing is not just a matter of knowing, "it is a matter in which loving and feeling are involved. And in men, this capacity to know and to feel in a single, involved whole, has been intimately interrupted" (Brown, 375). "The understanding flies on ahead," says Augustine, "and there follows, oh, so slowly, and sometimes not at all, our weakened human capacity for feeling" (Augustine, 2003, *Exposition of Psalm* 118 (119), 4). The originating sin of Adam and Eve's disobedience has afflicted us with a deep division between what we want intellectually and what our feelings will support.

Pelagius and Caelestius, the men whose teaching impelled Augustine to develop his doctrine of original sin, maintained that it was an easy matter to choose the good. Not for Augustine. They did not detect any radical weakness in the human will and thought that all we had to do was decide to choose. But Augustine gradually came to see how deep was the disengagement of intellect and feelings in human beings and how much they needed healing to restore the unity of these two faculties that make choice possible. The healing involved the coincidence of two opposite realities, a growing ability of the will to choose what the understanding puts before it as good, we might call it a capacity for self-actualization, and, on the other hand, a submission of the will to the One who alone can give it the freedom to self-actualize. This is a paradox that Alcoholics Anonymous understands perfectly. In order to achieve the sobriety they so much desire—at least with their mind—alcoholics must first surrender their will to a higher power. And the higher power will give them the capacity to choose what they want. Self-surrender opens the door to self determination.

Augustine was keenly aware of the force of addiction; he called it "habit," (*habitus*). Examples occur throughout the *Confessions*. The prime example, of course, is Augustine's own persistent sensuality: "I was bound down by this disease of the flesh. Its deadly pleasures were a chain that I dragged along with me, yet I was afraid to be freed from it . . ." (*Confessions* VI, 12). And, like most addicts, Augustine shunned help: "I refused to accept the good advice of Alypius, repelling the hand that meant to loose my bonds . . ." (Ibid.). Augustine was also held down for a long time by his vain ambition of being a rhetorician from which his reading of Cicero's *Hortensius* delivered him. "It altered my outlook on life" (Ibid., III, 4). As Augustine approached the time of his conversion in the garden, he still clung to his addiction: "Habit was too strong for me when it asked 'Do you think you can live without these things'" (Ibid., VIII, 11).

And Augustine's friend Alypius, who was "quite remarkably self-controlled in matters of sex" (Ibid., VI, 12), "became obsessed with an extraordinary craving for gladiatorial shows" (Ibid., VI, 8). Augustine describes how his friend, after resisting mightily the invitation of his friends to attend the games, agreed to go, resolving to close his eyes to the scene before him. But he did not close his ears and, when the crowd roared at an incident in the fight, he opened his eyes and "and fell more pitifully than the man whose fall had drawn that roar of excitement from the crowd" (Ibid.). "When he saw the blood, it was as though he had drunk a deep draught of savage passion. Instead of turning away, he fixed his eyes upon the scene and drank in all the frenzy, unaware of what he was doing" (Ibid.). And even Augustine's saintly mother, Monica, when she was a young woman "developed a secret liking for wine" that was satisfied at first with a few drops from the cask, then bit by bit "became a habit, and she would drink her wine at a draught, almost by the cupful" (Ibid., IX, 8). Augustine even speaks of an intervention. Monica was able to break the habit when God's "healing power" was shown to her through the "harsh words of rebuke" of a servant girl who "called my mother a drunkard" (Ibid.). Augustine also alludes to what we would call today, wife-abuse. After describing how adroitly him mother, Monica, handled her hot-tempered husband, Patricius, Augustine notes, "Many women, whose faces were disfigured by blows from husbands far sweeter-tempered than her own, used to gossip together and complain of the behaviour of their men-folk" (Ibid., IX, 9). All that spared Monica from similar behavior from her husband was the rule she followed of not resisting him when he was angry but waiting "until he was calm and composed" before explaining what she had done. Augustine's awareness of sin as habit and disease requiring healing—we would use the word "addiction" in the cases described above—opened him to the necessity for compassion.[6]

Augustine's meditative re-reading of Paul and his attention to the experience of continuing weakness in himself awakened him to his own need for the help of the Holy Spirit. The same awakening also opened up the possibility of compassion for other sinners. It is important that we recognize how signifi-

cant a development this was in Augustine's thought. In the time of his arguments against the Manicheans, Augustine was at pains to assert the *freedom*
of the human will and the responsibility that went with that freedom. With
the emphasis on freedom and responsibility came some harshness in response
to the laxness of the Manichees who claimed that we were not responsible
for our acts. We *are* responsible for our acts, Augustine insists. Brown cites
Augustine's response of 390 to the Manichees: "O pig-headed souls, give me
a man . . . who stands up to the senses of the flesh, and to the blows which
it rains on the soul; who stands up to the habitual thinking of men . . . who
carves away at his spirit" (Brown 144; Augustine, *de vera religione,* xxxiv,
64). Ten years later, having gone through the journey of transformation noted
above, Augustine will adopt an entirely different tone: "Let them deal harshly
with you, who do not know with what efforts truth is found and with what
difficulty errors are avoided; let them deal harshly with you, who do not know
how rare and exacting it is to overcome imaginations from the flesh in the
serenity of a pious intellect, let them deal harshly with you who do not know
with what pain the inner eye of man is healed, that he may glimpse his Sun"
(Brown, 144; Augustine, *Answer to the Letter of Mani,* 2).

CONCLUSION

Augustine inherited an interpretation of the effects of Adam's sin inaugurated
by St. Paul and passed along through the early Fathers of the Church. His genius transformed the tradition, not in an opposed direction, but into a deeper
dimension of interiority. Augustine's theology, nourished by the tradition,
comes to life through his interiority. The God who is utterly beyond us dwells
within us. He expresses the idea in one of those succinct, hard-to-translate
Latin sentences:[7] "You are more inward to me than my inmost self and higher
than my highest self—*interior intimo meo et superior summo meo"* (*Conf.,*
III, 6). In his reflection on the dynamics of his own consciousness, Augustine
is extraordinarily modern. In Book X of the *Confessions,* he explores the sub-
terranean ways of memory, recognizing how thoroughly our identity resides
in it, noting how much of ourselves is hidden from our consciousness, how
much we forget, and how laborious it is to recover it. "O Lord, I am working
hard in this field, and the field of my labours is my own self. I have become
a problem to myself—literally "a land of difficulty and much sweat (*terra
difficultatis et sudoris nimis*)—like land which a farmer works only with difficulty and at the cost of much sweat" (Ibid., X, 16). The image of the worker
sweating over the land recalls the curse laid on Adam after his disobedience:
"Cursed be the land because of you! In toil shall you eat its yield all the days

of your life" (Gen. 3:17b). That Augustine would interiorize the curse is typical of his allegorizing method that turns images from Scripture into a way of exploring the interior world of consciousness.

Has any serious writer ever shown us more of the inner workings of his own thought? Augustine refined his thinking under the pressure of controversy but he brought forth arguments tested first in the realm of his reflection on Scripture and his personal experience. Augustine's recognition of the mystery of his own inner self opened him up to the mystery of the other sinners with whom the planet is populated. He could be angry, at times he was harsh, but gradually the evolutions of his own thought led him to a humility that could not possibly stand in judgment on the hearts of others.

Augustine's thought is summarized by his mentor Paul who also recognized his inner weaknesses and lamented them in the famous cry: "So, then, I discover the principle that when I want to do right, evil is at hand. For I take delight in the law of God in my inner self, but I see in my members another principle at war with the law of my mind, taking me captive to the law of sin that dwells in my members" (Rom. 7:22–23). But when Paul—and his student Augustine after him—looks for a remedy, he finds it not in self-mastery but in Christ: "For the law of the spirit of life in Christ Jesus has freed you from the law of sin and death" (Rom. 8:2).

NOTES

1. This scriptural quotation is from the New Revised Standard Version Bible: Catholic Edition, copyright © 1989, 1993 National Council of the Churches of Christ in the United States of America. Used by permission. All rights reserved worldwide.

2. The Council of Orange, which met in 529, set out the relationship between grace and freedom, "entirely in the spirit, and to a great extent in the words of St. Augustine" (Neuner, Roos, Rahner, *The Teaching of the Catholic Church,* 378). The Council's teaching on predestination sets a clear frontier which Augustine approached without crossing: "This too we believe according to the Catholic faith, that all baptized persons, once they have received grace by baptism, can and must, with the help and cooperation of Christ, achieve what is necessary for the salvation of the soul if they are willing to work loyally." In other words, salvation is open to all, not just to a predestined few. The Council also vigorously rejects the notion of predestination to evil: "Not only do we not believe that some by divine power are destined for evil, but if any there be who wish to believe so much evil, we anathematize them with all detestation" (Ibid. 381). It is important to note that, though Augustine taught that God predestines some but not all to salvation, he did not teach, with a few exceptions, that God predestined any to evil. Those who are not predestined to salvation simply endure the condemnation they have merited through sharing in the sin of Adam. This may not be encouraging but it is not predestination to evil.

3. Perhaps Augustine's distinction between teaching and preaching calls for a new hermeneutical principle to be added to the already well known, *"Lex Orandi est lex credendi*—the law of prayer is the law of belief." Augustine, in the words quoted above, already paid tribute to such a principle by his counsel that we must pray with hope. If we pray with hope, he seems to be saying, then we can also *believe* that God has chosen us. But when he teaches a doctrine such as predestination that he counsels against preaching, Augustine raises a question that he himself did not consider. Does not the fact that we ought not preach a doctrine, raise questions about the doctrine's validity? In other words, can we say that "the law of preaching is the law of belief." That is, if you cannot preach it you ought not teach it. A doctrine that cannot be preached does not stand up as doctrine.

4. Hill, E. 1990.

5. Recently the Church has dropped even the teaching on Limbo. On April 20, 2007 Pope Benedict XVI approved a report of the International Theological Commission that recommended revising the official Catholic Church opinion and opening up the possibility that unbaptized babies can go straight to heaven. The Commission report agreed that no definitive answer exists in past church documents but that sufficient evidence exists for changing the position. This revision comes after years of deepening awareness of the extent of divine mercy.

6. Gerald May, in his book *Addiction and Grace,* suggests that "addiction" might well be a contemporary name for original sin.

7. I find that the translation of R. S. Pine-Coffin, for instance, in the Penguin Classics series fails to capture the force of Augustine's Latin: "You are deeper than my inmost understanding and higher than the topmost height that I could reach" (*Saint Augustine, Confessions,* Penguin Books, 1961, III, 6, 63).

Chapter Five

Adam and Eve and Original Sin

Classical Formulations and Modern Developments

When they heard the sound of the Lord God moving about in the garden at the breezy time of the day, the man and his wife hid themselves from the Lord God among the trees of the garden.

—Gen. 3:8, NRSV[1]

Thomas answered and said to him, "My Lord and my God."

—Jn. 20:28, NRSV[2]

We have considered at some length Augustine of Hippo's foundational formulation of the doctrine of original sin. Augustine, as we noted, was not a mere theoretician. He began with a personal struggle and in the process became a keen observer of human behavior illuminated. His struggle and his observations were guided by scripture, especially the writings of Paul. From experience Augustine moved to theory. Both the experiential ground of Augustine's theory, recorded in his *Confessions,* and the polemical works through which he refined and developed his theory—the anti-Pelagian writings—gave renewed energy to a tradition that began before him and continued long after him. We turn now to the developments that have continued long after Augustine. We will not examine these developments with the same care we devoted to Augustine. But some sampling of the thought to which the archetypal symbols of the myth of Adam and Eve have continued to give rise will help to fill out the long history through which the "truth" of the myth has evolved.

We begin with a review of official church teaching, both Catholic and Protestant, contained in papal pronouncements, conciliar documents, confessional statements, and declarations. We will then examine certain key theological developments as well, developments that witness to the amazing fecundity of the originating symbols and to the restless speculative instinct that has propelled the development of doctrine. The focus in this chapter is on the theoretical formulations of the doctrine. The connection between original sin and compassion so central to this study will, for the moment, remain in the background. The reason is simple; the theoretical elaborations have focused on the doctrinal issues rather than explorations of consciousness. The source of original sin, its effects in human life, its remedy—these have been the focus. The Church's teaching on original sin remained relatively unchanged from the fifth century to the twentieth. Then in the 1950s and 1960s new theological interpretations began to emerge. Since that time, theologians have continued to engage in revisions of the traditional interpretation.

PAPAL DECREES AND CHURCH COUNCILS ON ORIGINAL SIN

The overarching question in all the disputes about sin and grace is how we are justified, or made right, in our relationship with God. The Catholic Church and the churches of the Reformation believed that human relations with God had been permanently damaged through the sin of Adam. How were they to be made right? Both Luther and the Council of Trent speak of "justification." that is, restoring a right relationship with God and attaining salvation. The general response of the Christian tradition was that human beings could be restored to a right relationship with God and gain eternal life only through God's initiative. We have seen this insight expressed in the powerful image of Julian of Norwich's servant who, rushing off to do the lord's will, fell into a ditch from which he could not get out by his own efforts. The issue, then, is what human beings are capable of on their own and what they can do only through the help of God called "grace."

Early Decrees: the Pelagian Context

The provincial Council of Carthage in 418, attended by 200 bishops, formulated the Church's first official teaching on the doctrine of original sin. As with almost all councils, the teachings of Carthage in 418 responded to positions considered contrary to the Church's authentic teaching. The heretical teaching in this case came from Pelagius and the theological inspiration of the Council's teaching came from Augustine. We have already considered their controversy. Condemned first in an episcopal synod of 416 and then in the Sixteenth Council of Carthage in 418, the key elements of Pelagius' teaching were as follows: Adam was created mortal; Adam's sin harmed only himself not the human beings descended from him; newborn children are in the same condition as Adam before his fall; and Christ's death and resurrection are not the cause of people's rising from death since some people were free of sin even before Christ's coming (Neuner and Depuis, 135). These teachings went contrary to the Church's foundational position that human beings cannot save themselves without Christ's grace.

A second document, the *Indiculus*, a summary of official teachings published sometime between 435 and 442, confirmed the teachings of the Council of Carthage but dealt with a further refinement of the Pelagian heresy that had arisen since the Council. This heresy—called semi-Pelagianism because its followers, though they accepted the Church's condemnation of Pelagius for teaching that human beings could be saved without the grace of Christ—affirmed that at least the *desire* for salvation was entirely natural and did not require grace. This also the Church condemned in the *Indiculus*. "God so works in the hearts of people and in the free will itself that a holy thought, a good counsel and every movement of a good will comes from God" (Neuner and Depuis 1982. #1911, 548). Even more clearly, the *Indiculus* states: "Therefore, with the help of the Lord, we are so strengthened by these Church norms and these documents [earlier pronouncements] derived from divine authority that we acknowledge God as the author of all good desires and deeds, of all efforts and virtues by which from the beginning of faith human beings tend toward God" (#1914, 549).

Heresies do not disappear just because the Church condemns them. In spite of the *Indiculus*, the semi-Pelagian controversy continued. The last definitive doctrinal statement of this early period comes from the Council of Orange (529). The Council's declarations were based on a document put together by Pope Felix IV, with the help of Caesarius of Arles and Prosper of Aquitaine, from some, but not all, of Augustine's positions on grace. Neuner and Depuis call the Council "a moderate Augustinianism" (550) that upholds key elements of Augustine's teachings on grace.

The teachings of the Council of Orange were meant to put an end to the heresy of the semi-Pelagians, once and for all, reaffirming the Church's teaching that even the desire for God comes from grace. "If anyone says that the grace of God can be conferred because of human prayer, and not rather that it is grace itself that prompts us to pray, such a one contradicts the prophet Isaiah, or the apostle [Paul] who says the same thing: 'I have been found by those who did not seek me; I have shown myself to those who did not ask for me'" (Rom. 10:20; Is. 65:1; Neuner and Depuis #1915, 550). The Council's "Canons on Grace" repeat the same point in various ways: anyone who "contends that God awaits our will before cleansing us from sin, but does not confess that even the desire to be cleansed is aroused in us by the infusion and action of the Holy Spirit, opposes the Holy Spirit. . . ." A comprehensive statement sums up all the variations on the theme:

> If anyone says that mercy is divinely conferred upon us when, without God's grace, we believe, will, desire, strive, labour, pray, keep watch, endeavour, request, seek, knock, but does not confess that it is through the infusion and inspiration of the Holy Spirit that we believe, will or are able to do all these things as is required; or if anyone subordinates the help of grace to humility or human obedience, and does not admit that it is the very gift of grace that makes us obedient and humble, he contradicts the apostle who says: "What have you that you did not receive?" (1 Cor. 15:10; Neuner and Depuis #1918, 550–51).

The "Conclusion redacted by Caesarius of Arles" reaffirms these points and clearly rejects a position that seems to have been present in some way in Augustine and will recur in the teaching of Calvin, divine predestination to evil. After affirming that all those baptized "if they are willing to labour faithfully, can and ought to accomplish with Christ's help and cooperation what pertains to the salvation of their souls," adds an explicit rejection of predestination to evil. Not only does the Church not believe "that some are predestined to evil by the divine power," it anathematizes any who "believe such an enormity" and "with great abhorrence" condemns them.

The Lutheran Context: Augsburg and Trent

The papal pronouncements and conciliar decrees of the fifth century responded to the dangers perceived in Pelagianism. The sixteenth century Council of Trent responded to what the Catholic Church saw as threats to true doctrine from Martin Luther (1472–1546). If the Church saw in Pelagius an excessive optimism about what human nature could accomplish by itself, without the aid of divine grace, it saw in Luther an excessive pessimism. Further, just as Augustine, the "doctor of grace" provided the teaching incorporated into official pronouncements in the fifth century, Thomas Aquinas (1225–1274) provided the theological framework for the teaching of Trent. Before looking at Luther and Trent, it will be helpful to consider how Thomas Aquinas (1225–1274) refined the Augustinian teaching on original sin. Crucial to Thomas' teaching on original sin is the distinction between the natural and the supernatural. The "original justice" of which the tradition speaks, was for Aquinas, not a justice given to Adam and Eve as a natural endowment. It was rather supernatural destiny given to them at the time of their creation. This original justice, says Thomas, "held all the soul's parts together in one" (Aquinas, ST, I–II, q. 82, art. 2, reply to obj. 3). The disobedience of Adam and Eve broke down the proper subordination of the human will to God, of moral choice to reason, and of the powers of the body to will and reason (Wiley 2002, 85). Once Adam and Eve lost this harmony, maintained by a special gift of God's grace, among all the soul's parts, they could not regain it by their own efforts. Adam and Eve and their descendants were thus thrown back onto their own resources without the possibility of attaining the destiny God had intended for them. The redemptive grace given through Christ gave human beings the power to achieve their supernatural end.

To explain how the aspects of original sin worked together, Aquinas turned to the four causes of Aristotle (384–322 BC) that he had found in studying works of the Greek philosopher recently discovered by the Arabs.[3] A *cause* for Aristotle is "that from which . . . a thing comes into being" (*Metaphysics,* 1013b, Bk. V, Ch. 2). The four causes are material, formal, efficient, and final. Each of the four causes enters into the being of the thing in a different way. The material cause is the stuff of which something is made, e.g., marble in a statue. The formal cause is what makes the matter intelligible, e.g., the shape of a human being carved from marble. The formal cause answers the question "What is it?" as the perplexed observer might ask in front of an amorphous lump of stone or metal. The efficient cause is the agent who brings about the product, e.g., the sculptor of a statue. A subdivision of the efficient cause is the instrumental cause, that is, the instrument the agent uses to produce an effect; for instance, the chisel in the hand of the sculptor. The final cause is the purpose of the thing produced, e.g., the statue is made to honor some individual or to give pleasure to the beholder.

Aquinas applies the four causes to original sin, beginning with the formal cause, that which defines original sin as sin. Just as original justice consisted formally in the subjection of the human will to God, so original sin consists formally in turning away from God and thus losing original justice. And the loss of original justice leads to the material aspect of original sin, disorder in the powers of the soul. (ST, q. 82, art 3, response). "Accordingly, the privation of original justice, by which the will was made subject to God, is the formal element in original sin, while every other disorder of the soul's powers is a kind of material element in respect of original sin" (Ibid.). This disorder of the "powers of the soul" Aquinas calls "concupiscence" (reply to first objection). Augustine was speaking of this material element in original sin when he spoke of his sinful habits as chains.

The efficient or principal cause of original sin is the free choice of Adam not to obey God's command. The instrumental cause is the semen through which the condition of the soul called original sin is transmitted to Adam's posterity (Aquinas, q. 83, art 1, Response). Aquinas does not speak of a final cause of original sin, a purpose served by original sin. This makes sense since sin is precisely a turning away from the purpose God had in mind for human beings. However, one can speak in a paradoxical way of original sin as having the purpose of bringing about the redemptive activity of Christ. Paul hints at this when he says: "For if, by the transgression of one person, death came to reign through that one, how much more will those who receive the abundance of grace and the gift of justification come to reign in life through the one person, Jesus Christ" (Rom. 5:17).

Luther and Trent

Aquinas' analysis of original sin in terms of causality is a useful way to approach the definitions of the Council of Trent. Since the teachings of Luther and the other reformers serve as the particular context of Trent, we will have to consider the reformers' ideas of original sin and justification. I will limit myself to the positions of Luther. Whether the Catholic bishops understood Luther correctly or not—and there is evidence that they did not—Luther's positions, precisely as interpreted by the Roman Church, became a catalyst for setting out as clearly as possible the Church's understanding of sin and justification. If we set the Catholic teaching of Trent opposite the teaching of the Lutheran confessions, we will find the two not as far apart as Trent seemed to think. It seems likely, from the perspective offered by five hundred years of distance from the Reformation and the Catholic response to it, that both sides misread each other's positions. The "Joint Declaration on the Doctrine of Justification" approved by the Lutheran World Federation and the Catholic Church in 1998 clearly moves beyond the misunderstandings and mutual suspicion of the sixteenth century.

On October 31, 1517, Luther posted his "95 Theses" under the title "Disputation of Dr. Martin Luther Concerning Penitence and Indulgences." The theses did not lay out Luther's teaching on original sin but only his views on the granting of indulgences. At this point it seems that Luther did not intend a complete break with the Roman Church, but only wished to denounce what he saw as an unacceptable abuse, the selling of indulgences to raise money for building St. Peter's Basilica in Rome. During the year 1520, Luther published three significant works that laid out his teachings. In the "Address to the Christian Nobility of the German Nation" Luther attacked church corruption and abuses of authority and stated his belief in the right of lay persons to spiritual independence. "Concerning Christian Liberty" contains Luther's doctrine of justification by faith and his basic theological positions. In the "Babylonian Captivity of the Church," Luther criticized the sacramental system as practiced in the Roman Catholic Church and established the Scriptures as the supreme authority in Christianity.

In 1520, three years after Luther had posted his "95 Theses" and twenty-five years before the Council of Trent, Pope Leo X condemned what he saw as certain errors of Luther. Among the condemnations are the following: Luther seemed to teach that original sin was actually a sin that kept a person who died without baptism from entering into heaven even though there is no actual sin. Leo also condemned Luther's teachings that "In every good work the just man sins," and that "A good work perfectly performed is a venial sin" (Neuner and Depuis 1923/31, 554). The *Confession of Augsburg* (1530), based on Luther's Articles of Schwabach, but written by Philip Malencthon, express clearly the first position condemned by Leo. The second article "Of Original Sin," states that all people are born into sin and "that this original disease or flaw is truly a sin, bringing condemnation and also eternal death to those who are not reborn through baptism and the Holy Spirit" (Bettenson 1963, 210).

The sixth session of the Council of Trent (1547) lays out the position of the Catholic Church on justification. Trent's "Decree on Justification" agreed with Lutherans in condemning the errors of Pelagius, repeating the same doctrine laid out in the councils of the fifth and sixth centuries and expressly confirmed in Lutheran confessions of faith. The "Canons on Justification," brief summaries of the Decree's teachings, condemn certain positions the Council attributed to the reformers. We can divide the issues under three questions. First, what are the material effects of original sin in the sinner? Second, what is the role of believers in their justification? Third, what is the effect in the sinner of the justification offered by Christ? Regarding the material effects of original sin, the Catholic Church understood the reformers to say that freedom of will disappeared after the Fall and that the more people strove for salvation, the more they sinned. Trent affirmed the freedom of the human will even before justification and condemned those who held the opposite (Canon 5). Trent also condemned anyone who would say "that all works performed before justification, no matter how they are performed, are truly sins or deserve God's hatred; or that the more earnestly one tries to dispose himself for grace, the more grievously he sins . . ." (Canon 7). The Catholic position is thus that, even though the human will is afflicted with a certain impotence regarding its own salvation, it is not utterly devoid of the ability to do good.

The bishops at Trent also rejected certain positions regarding what believers are able to do or need to do in order to attain salvation and regarding who can be saved. Trent understood Luther's affirmation of the necessity of faith for salvation as excluding the need for good works and affirmed the opposite (Canon 9). To attain salvation, people must perform good works (Canons 18, 19, 20). And not only are these good works "the fruits and signs of the justification obtained," as the reformers held, but they are also "a cause of [justification's] increase" (Canon 24). Trent clearly attributes to human good works a real causality in obtaining justification. Human beings participate in their own salvation "through the grace and charity which is poured into their hearts by the Holy Spirit and inheres in them" (Canon 11). The theologians of Trent understood some of the reformers at least—no one is mentioned by name in the text—to be saying that people are justified "either by the imputation of Christ's justice alone or by the remission of sins alone" (Canon 11) and not through any participation on their part made possible by grace. Perhaps the clearest affirmation of human participation in justification is found in Canon 32. "If anyone says that the good works of the justified person are the gifts of God in such a way that they are not also the good merits of the justified person," let the one holding such a position be, as the Council puts it, "*anathema.*"

Trent also rejected the requirement, attributed to the reformers, that "to attain the remission of sins, everyone must believe with certainty and without any hesitation based on his own weakness that he is absolved and justified . . ." (Canon 13). Human salvation is conditioned not on subjective certainty in the one saved but by the saving work of Christ. The bishops of Trent also rejected the position that some are predestined to salvation, some to evil by the divine power (Canon 17).

Trent's tone of condemnation, expressed in its repeated formula "*anathema sit,*" is offensive to modern ears, both Protestant and Catholic. Trent never names those it condemns, nor does it cite texts expressing the positions it rejects. The reformers had no chance to speak at the Council. Nevertheless, in spite of the absence of dialogue before or during the Council, Trent sets forth a remarkably balanced picture of original sin and salvation. It avoids Pelagius' excessive optimism about justification, already rejected a thousand years before Trent convened. In defining original sin, Trent carefully distinguished between the *tendency* toward sin that it called "concupiscence" and the actual sins that deserve punishment: "The Catholic Church has never understood that [concupiscence] is called sin because it would be sin in the true and proper sense in those who have been reborn, but because it comes from sin and inclines to sin" (Neuner and Depuis, 139, Trent, Decree on Original Sin, 512).

Lutheran Positions

The positions of the Catholic Church are clear from Trent, as are their opinions of what the reformers held. What is not clear from Trent is what the reformers themselves actually held. To determine that, we will need to consider the reformers' confessional statements. I will limit myself to documents setting forth the Lutheran positions. Differences among various reformers were significant. Even among Lutherans, differences emerged, and doctrines developed from earlier statements of Luther, through the Augsburg Confessions of 1530, based on teachings of Luther but authored by Malencthon, up to the Formula of Concord (1577) and, finally, the completed Book of Concord put together in 1580.

As would become evident five hundred years after the Lutheran Confessions and the Council of Trent, during the dialogues on justification between Catholics and Lutherans, the differences between the two sides were not as great as the hardened traditions of opposition had made them seem. The Augsburg Confessions (1530) affirmed a doctrine of original sin and justification very close to the teaching of Trent. Augsburg, while denying that people are saved by good works, recognized their necessity. "Further, it is taught that good works should and must be done, not that a person relies on them to earn grace but for God's sake and to God's praise" (Augsburg Confession, XX, "Faith and Good Works," (*Book of Concord,* #27, 56). Good works, says Augsburg, come from the Holy Spirit. "When through faith the Holy Spirit is given, the heart is moved to do good works. Before that, when it is without the Holy Spirit, the heart is too weak" (Augsburg XX, 29–31). Augsburg also taught the freedom of the human will. The Confession recognizes both the freedom of the will that enables people "to live an outwardly honorable life and to make choices among the things that reason comprehends" and the inability of human effort to make a person acceptable to God "without the grace, help, and activity of the Holy Spirit" (Augsburg XVIII, 1–2).

The question still remains about the effect of original sin in the human spirit. That Lutherans struggled among themselves to determine the extent of damage done to Adam's descendants by his disobedience is evident from the "Formula of Concord" of 1577. The subtitle of the Formula sets forth its purpose: "A thorough, pure, correct, and final restatement and explanation of a number of articles of the Augsburg Confession on which for some time there has been disagreement among some of the theologians adhering to this Confession, resolved and reconciled under the guidance of the Word of God and the comprehensive summary of our Christian teaching." The Declaration sets forth a kind of diagnostic of original sin and justification that helps interpret not only the Lutheran position, but also the Catholic. At stake was the question of how deeply the disease had entered into human nature.

The "Solid Declaration," second part of the "Formula of Concord," describes the terms of the "dissension among a number of theologians of the Augsburg Confession about what original sin, strictly understood, is" (*Book of Concord,* 508). One side held a view the Formula calls "nature sin" or "person sin," meaning that "the nature, substance, and essence of fallen man, at least the foremost and noblest part of his essence . . . is original sin itself" (Ibid.). In this view no difference exists between human nature and original sin. The other side maintained that human nature remains God's handiwork and cannot be identified with original sin. Original sin is rather "something in man's nature, in his body, soul, and all his powers, . . . an abominable, deep, and inexpressible corruption thereof . . ." (Ibid.). The corruption consists in a lack of the righteousness in which Adam was originally created such that "in spiritual matters he is dead to that which is good and is turned to everything evil, and that, because of this corruption and this inborn sin which inheres in his nature, all actual sin flows out of his heart" (508–09). One side, then, sees human nature as so utterly corrupted by original sin as to be identified with it. The other side, desiring to preserve the integrity of nature as God's creature, claims only that original sin "inheres in [man's] nature" (509).

The "Declaration of Concord" clearly rejects identification of original sin with human nature. In effect, says the Declaration, such identification is equivalent to Manichaeism. The Declaration, then, locates the Lutheran position between Pelagianism and Manichaeism. Lutherans, according to the Declaration, reject and condemn "the following and related Pelagian errors: That human nature even after the Fall is incorrupt and, especially, that in spiritual matters it is good, pure, and in its natural powers perfect" (Article 1, 511). The argument against the Manichaean identification of original sin with human nature is twofold. If we identify human nature with original sin, we thereby claim that God has created sin. If, on the other hand, we say that God created human nature good but that "Satan created or made something essentially evil and blended this with their nature" (512–513), then we say that it is not human nature that sins "but a strange and foreign something within man, so that God . . . does not accuse and condemn man's nature, corrupted by sin, but only the original sin" (513).

The Lutheran position of the Declaration echoes Augustine's rejection of both Manichaeism and Pelagianism. Against the Manichees, Augustine affirmed that the human will is free. Against the Pelagians, he affirmed that it is not completely free. Lutheran documents affirm a limited freedom for the human will. The Augsburg Confessions concede "that the human will has some freedom for producing civil righteousness and for choosing things subject to reason," but add immediately "However, it does not have the power to produce the righteousness of God or spiritual righteousness without the Holy Spirit . . ." ("Confessions," XVIII, *Book of Concord,* 51). Augsburg also acknowledges the necessity of good works but denies that such works "reconcile us with God or obtain grace" ("Confessions," XX, *Book of Concord,* 54). Good works, rather than earning God's favor, depend on it: Because the

Holy Spirit is given through faith, the heart is also moved to do good works" ("Confessions," XX, *Concord,* 56).

Reading the "Augsburg Confessions," one realizes that Lutherans and Catholics were not, even at that time, as far apart as some of their rhetoric suggested. The passage of five hundred years since Augsburg and the Council of Trent and the growing desire to look for common points rather than differences led finally to the Lutheran-Catholic dialogues of the late 20th century that culminated in the *Joint Declaration on The Doctrine of Justification.* "Together we confess," says the *Declaration:* "By grace alone, in Christ's saving work and not because of any merit on our part, we are accepted by God and receive the Holy Spirit, who renews our hearts while equipping and calling us to good works."

MORE RECENT THEOLOGICAL REAPPRAISALS

The classical texts I have been citing, including the *Joint Declaration,* are doctrinal statements that express the traditional Christian position on original sin. Christians have held that the exercise of human freedom led to a fall from which human beings cannot rise without the help of God. The fall, according to the tradition, has also left humans with concupiscence, a tendency to sin, as an inheritance from the first human couple. The human will remains free, and good works are necessary to achieve salvation but neither the freedom nor the exercise of good works can merit salvation except through the grace of Christ. Though the human will cannot by itself achieve salvation, the integrity of human nature remains intact as something good but infected by an inherited vulnerability.

What the official teaching says is one thing. Theological speculation is another. While respecting the doctrines set down in official Church teaching, theologians explore the meaning of those doctrines to illuminate them and make them fruitful in the lives of believers. Theology always reflects the culture from which it arises and tries to answer questions posed by dominant cultural expressions such as philosophy, science, literature, and even the common concerns of believers struggling to make their faith real. As cultures succeed one another, theologians shed new light on the mystery of salvation. A consideration of some theological reappraisals from the second half of the twentieth century and the first ten years of the twenty-first will give evidence of a continuing interest in the subject of original sin as an abiding aspect of human life and show some possibilities for reinterpretation. All of these reappraisals come out of the intellectual revolution that began before the Second

Vatican Council, took shape in the Council's 16 documents, and has continued to mature during the fifty years since the Council.

Historic developments in the twentieth century have brought about changes
in conceptions of human development that raise new questions about the
meaning of original sin. The philosophical turn to the subject, expressed in
various forms of phenomenology, personalism, and cognitional theory, has
profoundly influenced the way theologians look at original sin. The emergence of evolution as a scientific hypothesis to explain the origin and development of the human race challenges the traditional explanation of human
evil as coming from the sin of a first historical couple. Evolution offers no
verification of the hypothesis that the human condition, as we now experience it, originates in a fall from some earlier state of perfection. Whatever
perfection human beings might be capable of lies in the future, not the past.

We have become profoundly conscious in the past century of the frighten-
ing power of human violence. The manifestations of violence include two
world wars, many smaller but still destructive instances of armed conflict
between nations, the presence of gang warfare in cities, drug wars, genocidal
campaigns within nations—the Nazi "final solution" of eliminating the Jews
and the Rwandan massacre of Tutsis by Hutus come powerfully to mind—and
the institutional violence that keeps whole classes of people from participating
in human progress. The pervasiveness of violence suggests a way of looking at
the aspect of original sin the churches have called "concupiscence."

Men and women of the twenty-first century are also conscious of living in
a global community. Financial crises that begin in one corner of the globe,
quickly spread to the whole global community. The environment knows no
national boundaries. Communicable diseases spread across the globe. AIDS
began in Africa. Now the infection occurs in every country. All nations
share one atmosphere whose degradation through pollution affects all. The
development of communication technology, television, and especially the
Internet, make far-off events immediately available. Modern educated people
have also largely, with notable exceptions, accepted the evolutionary view
of the development of human beings from the animal kingdom. Pope John
Paul II, in a 1996 address to the Pontifical Academy of Sciences, recognized
evolution as "more than an hypothesis" and acknowledged a convergence of
independent studies that "constitutes in itself a significant argument in favor
of the theory" (John Paul II, 1996, 4, par 2). These cornerstones of modern
consciousness require a rethinking of the traditional notions of original sin.

We turn briefly to look at some efforts to rethink original sin in light of
these heightened areas in modern consciousness. We have already considered above Aquinas' analysis of original sin according to the four causes of
Aristotle. Aquinas' analysis will provide a useful way of understanding the

approaches taken by various authors. The perspective offered by evolution, for instance, gives rise to questions about the efficient cause of original sin, which Aquinas, following the tradition, located in the free choice of Adam and Eve to disobey God's command. In the light of evolutionary theory it seems naïve to think of a single couple as cause for all the fragility of the human condition. The epidemic character of violence suggests a new way of looking at the material cause of original sin, what the tradition has called concupiscence. The heightened conscience moderns have of living in a global community, has led some authors to look at the formal cause of original sin as a break with humanity rather than a break with God. Feminist perspectives offer a way of looking at what original sin consists of, that is, its materiality.

Evolutionary Perspectives

Several authors have reinterpreted the traditional understanding of original sin in the light of evolutionary theory. I will consider the work of three authors, Piet Schoonenberg (1964), Alszeghy and Flick (1965–67), and Daryl Domning (2006).

Piet Schoonenberg's 1964 work, *Man and Sin,* carefully reviews the traditional teaching about original sin "in the spirit of Teilhard de Chardin" (192). This Teilhardian spirit means fundamentally that paradise lies not at the beginning of human history but at the end. The "old static view" of the world, according to Schoonenberg, sees the world coming from God's creative hand as simply good and ignores "the slow development of order and all the travail involved in it . . ." (193). In the older static view, "all disorder, all suffering, including biological death have entered the world only on account of sin (193). Thus, as just mentioned, in the view of Teilhard and Schoonenberg, "Paradise lies not at the beginning, but at the end . . . (194). From this it follows that the redemptive work of Christ is aimed not at restoring a condition lost by sin but in countering by grace the effects of sin in the evolutionary development of human beings. This "evolutionary picture," says Schoonenberg "may be outlined in two sentences" as follows:

"The whole evolution of creation is crowned by a historical ascent of mankind, crowned in its turn by Christ's presence, which keeps growing too towards his manifestation in the parousia, the beginning of "God all in all." That ascent is crossed by a similar ascent of sin, but God brings about the triumph of the ascent in Christ" (194).

Schoonenberg's understanding of that "ascent of sin" is the key to his understanding of original sin. He describes this ascent first in terms of what we have been calling the material cause of original sin, that in which original sin consists as its material expression. Schoonenberg enumerates three manifestation that he calls "the sequels of sin" (63). First is "sin itself as punishment" (63). Sin has its external manifestation and its inner core that leaves a residue as a form of punishment. "That core of each action is the decision through which the person realizes himself in some direction; it is the attitude which he gives to himself" (63). That attitude is the "state of sin" and it constitutes a kind of intrinsic punishment for the sin. The intrinsic punishment for smoking is addiction to smoking. A second sequel is "the inability to love" (70). The third is "the inclination to evil" (80). "After murder there remains hatred, after impurity, egoistic desire" (80). This is more than just an inability to do something good; it is an inclination to evil.

Having enumerated some of the material aspects of original sin, Schoonenberg, turns to its efficient and instrumental causes. How does "the ascent of sin" get started? How does it get transmitted? Schoonenberg recognizes the beginning of sin in Adam's disobedience but attributes its continuance not just to heredity, but to what we might call environmental or situational causes. The ascent begins somewhere, of course, but its upward movement is explained not by that first sin alone but by the accumulated sins that follow. Schoonenberg calls this accumulation of sin "the sin of the world" and the "situation of sin" (chapter 3, "The Sin of the World")." "The biblical warrant for Schoonenberg's position here lies in his interpretation of Romans 5:12. Schoonenberg cites the version common in modern translations: "Therefore sin came into the world through one man and death through sin, and so sin spread to all men *because all men sinned*" (italics added). Earlier translations, certainly the translation with which Augustine would have been familiar, said that "sin came into the world through one man *in whom all sinned*" (italics added). Schoonenberg considers the difference of translations crucial. The earlier translation seems to suggest that all humans sinned in Adam even before they had committed any personal sins of their own. The modern translation suggests that "this domination of sin is undergone only when one sins personally" (134).

The accumulation of personal sins and their consequences on the human situation constitute the sin of the world or "the situation caused by sinful acts" (111ff). Schoonenberg enumerates them: bad example (112), bad example with pressure (113), obscuration of values and norms (115), total obscuring of values and norms (115). Through all of these circumstances "Sin embodies itself in the transgression of certain commandments, in the offense against a certain virtue or value, in the production of some disorder in our world" (118). These are manifestations of something deeper. "But the soul of sin, its deepest personal core, consists in opposing the whole reality of God and world, in conflicting with love, both natural and supernatural" (118). This is what Aquinas calls the "formal cause" of sin, what defines sin as sin.

Alszeghy and Flick: Personalism and Evolution

In a series of articles dating from the 1960s, two Jesuits from the Gregorian University in Rome, Zoltan Alszeghy and Maurice Flick, reappraise original sin from the twin perspectives of personalism and evolution. Noting that "Original sin is a theological theme that needs radical rethinking" (Alszeghy and Flick 1967, 190), these two authors rethink the traditional doctrine by moving beyond what they call an exclusively "juridical or ontic order" toward the relational category of dialogue between persons. Humans, unlike other living beings, become what they are meant to be through interaction with other human beings and God. Original sin interrupts that dialogue.

Contrary to those who might want to explain original sin as simply a breakdown in the horizontal dimension of communication among human beings, Alszeghy and Flick believe that only an interruption of communication with God explains the phenomenon of original sin. If we try to explain original sin as the distortion in human life that comes from "a selfish society that prevents his development" (192), we interrupt the link with Adam's sin described in Trent's declaration that original sin is "transmitted by propagation, not by imitation" (DS 1513, Bettenson, 138). This line of thinking makes clear that Alszeghy and Flick wish their reinterpretation to remain within the framework of the Church's defined teaching. This means that they see original sin as rooted in a freely chosen break with God whose consequences affect all human beings through propagation. We will see shortly the reinterpretation these authors introduce into this traditional teaching in light of evolution.

The personalist viewpoint adopted by Alszeghy and Flick leads them to an understanding that is both traditional and radical, radical precisely because it gets to the roots of the tradition. The break with God, say these two authors, is not just something that occurs in the order of objective being, a kind of unconscious break with God that dooms us to a kind of blindness. Rather, the break consists in something we can recognize in our own subjectivity, the inability of each human being to recognize God as *his* or *her* own God. The relation of children to their human parents illustrates the point. "One does not assume the role of son by simply knowing the fact that a person is one's father. One's father is discovered by immediate practical experience in which the other's presence as father makes one *become* son" (Alszeghy and Flick 1965, 194).

We find this personalist interpretation already in biblical passages and later developments of the tradition. Adam and Eve hid themselves from God's presence when, after they had disobeyed God's command, God walked in the garden "in the breezy time of the day" (Gen. 3:8). God was no longer *their* God. In Romans Paul talks about the origins of sin among the Gentiles who

"exchanged the truth of God for a lie and revered and worshiped the creature rather than the creator" (Rom. 1:25). The Gentiles' refusal to worship
God, that is, to enter into intimacy with God, recognizing God as *their* God,
explains why God "handed them over to degrading passions" (Rom. 1:26).
Later in the same letter, Paul speaks of salvation for the believer as receiving
"a spirit of adoption, through which we cry, *'Abba,* Father'" (Rom. 8:15b).
Julian of Norwich, as we shall see in chapter nine, gets at the same truth when
she describes her servant/Adam as fallen into a ditch from which he can no
longer see his loving master.

The personalist reinterpretation of Alszeghy and Flick takes Aquinas'
formal cause of original sin, the break with God brought about by Adam's
disobedience, and makes it part of the materiality of original sin. The loss of
intimacy with God that prevents me from seeing God as *my* God and keeps
groups of people as seeing God as *theirs,* is a "material" consequence of the
break with God. It is part of the *stuff* of original sin. In chapter six, we will
consider at greater length the loss of the four intimacies, intimacy with God,
with self, with the neighbor, and with nature. Modern psychology recognizes
the importance of bonding with parents, especially with the mother, as the
foundation of a healthy human existence. The break with God as formal cause
of original sin and the loss of intimacy as the material cause provides a helpful explanatory account.

Alszeghy and Flick approach original sin not only from the perspective of personalism but from the viewpoint of evolution. As noted above,
these authors understand their reappraisal as a legitimate extension of the
tradition. They consider the Council of Trent statement on original sin (DS
1510–1516) as the Church's most important statement of this doctrine (Alszeghy and Flick, 1967, 199). The authors introduce a variation that they
believe preserves the authoritative teaching while recognizing an evolutionary perspective. If we assume that the human race repeats in its evolutionary
development the steps followed by individuals, we can suppose that several
generations of truly human beings "go through life without any more use of
reason than we observe in babies" (199). And at a certain moment, just as
happens in each human being's development, our human ancestors "become
capable of a *free* decision" (200). God's plan, says the hypothesis, intends to
produce human beings "vivified by grace" (200). The passage over to this
new stage requires a "leap" specifically different from all the preceding ones,
even hominization. Bringing man to divinization surpasses absolutely all possibilities of any created order. This leap is precisely what human beings fail
to make: "But at the moment for this option man sets himself in opposition to
God's will and refuses to follow the plan of evolution with which he is asked
to cooperate" (200). Since human beings have failed to choose the condition

intended by God, God introduces a new way of fulfilling his still intact plan of divinization. That way is Christ.

By introducing the hypothesis that Adam and Eve are the first humans beings capable of free choice, these two authors suppose a stage of human development prior to the emergence of free will, followed by a state in which humans could finally choose whether to follow God's divine plan. Adam and Eve chose not to. Alszeghy and Flick claim to have preserved the orthodox tradition and, at the same time, given due recognition to the theory of evolution. Still claiming to give due recognition to the tradition and to the theory of evolution, Alszeghy and Flick explain the transmission of original sin to all human beings in a new way. "According to our hypothesis the sin of the first man who reached the use of reason affects all men whether they are his descendants or not" (201).

Alszeghy and Flick, always concerned to reconcile their views with authentic church teaching, next address the task of explaining how their theory of transmission preserves the tradition. First, they deny that "physical descent of all men from one Adam is a certain element of revelation" (201). What is crucial, say these authors, is Trent's affirmation of the universality of sin and "participation in it through natural generation" (201). But the Church has not defined "that the generative act is the cause of the transmission of original sin" (201), it might only be the occasion. Still, even with these qualifications, Alszeghy and Flick see the difficulty of explaining why all people share in a common sinfulness. The answer lies in an appeal to the unity of humankind.

Two possible explanations of the unity of humankind emerge. The first is offered by "theistic evolutionism," which says that the unity of humankind is "not diminished but rather widened by being anchored on an earlier level than hominization" (201). That earlier level is the time of incomplete development when human beings have not yet collectively reached the age of reason. The second, "more important and helpful," in the eyes of our two authors, "is the biblical notion of corporate personality" according to which "a whole community determines its stand before God in the acts of a single person" (201). This would certainly seem to be the Pauline view expressed in Romans in which Paul correlates the gift of universal salvation accomplished by Christ with the universal sin brought about by Adam. "For just as through the disobedience of one person, the many were made sinners, so through the obedience of one, many will be made righteous" (Rom. 5:19).

We can summarize the views of Alszeghy and Flick by relating the two focal points of their revision of the traditional view to the Thomist "causes" of original sin set out above. These authors appeal to personalism and evolutionary theory. The personalist reinterpretation has to do with the material side of original sin and answers the question of what exactly original sin in human beings consists in. For Alszeghy and Flick—they do not actually use Aristotle's four causes as Aquinas did—the "material" side of sin is the direct correlative of its "formal" side. The formal cause of original sin in Aquinas' analysis, is the separation from God through disobedience and the material side is concupiscence, the tendency toward selfishness, lust, disharmony, etc. Alszeghy and Flick hold that the result of the disobedience of Adam and Eve (formal cause) is a chronic inability (material cause) to think of God as "my God," "our God," as belonging to us and being for us. This identification of the condition of original sin with the modern category of alienation seems to me the most satisfying element of the Alszeghy and Flick analysis.

The second part of their analysis responds to the evolutionary context of modern thought, the challenge to think of the original perpetrators of original sin in an evolutionary perspective. These two authors respond to this challenge by projecting a time of growth before the first human beings were capable of committing sin.

Sin as Selfishness: Another Evolutionary Perspective

Daryl Domning's 2006 work, *Original Selfishness: Original Sin and Evil in the Light of Evolution,* responding to the same evolutionary hypothesis that motivated the work of Alszeghy and Flick, offers an even more radical reinterpretation of the doctrine of original sin. A brief editorial comment at the beginning of the book summarizes the import of its contribution:

> Daryl P. Domning explains in straightforward terms the working of modern evolutionary theory, Darwinian natural selection, and how this has brought forth life and the human mind. He counters objections to Darwinism that are raised by some believers and emphasizes that the evolutionary process necessarily enforces selfish behavior on all living things. This account of both physical and moral evil is arguably more consistent with traditional Christian teachings than are the explanations give by most contemporary "evolutionary" theologians themselves ("Original Selfishness," opening summary).

The opening summary also notes that "The prominent theologian, Monika K. Hellwig dialogues with Daryl Domning throughout the book to present a balanced reappraisal of the doctrine of original sin from both a scientist's and theologian's perspective." The thesis of the book, encapsulated in its title, is that the root dynamism of human development, the engine, so to speak, of human progress, is selfishness. The human race did not begin, as *Genesis* suggests and as the tradition has maintained, in some state of perfection from which, through an original act of disobedience by the first couple, the human race has fallen. Perfection lies not in the past but in the future.

The evolutionary perspective forces us to acknowledge that Scripture is, above all, not about the past but about the *present* in every age: about our existential problems, about our relationship to God, about our [present] hopes for the future, and even about creation itself—not as something *made* "very good" once upon a time, but as a *creatio continua,* something God is *making* "very good." As Jesus put it, "My Father is at work until now, and I am at work as well" (Jn. 5:17; Domning 2006, 107).

Included in Domning's thesis is the conclusion embraced by almost all the reappraisals since the Second Vatican Council that the biblical story of Adam and Eve is not an historical account of events that took place in the life of the first human beings. The story of Adam and Eve expresses a profound truth, a symbolic, "mythical" truth, not a historical one. We have already seen this conviction expressed in the work of Paul Ricoeur (chapter two, above). For Ricoeur and Domning, It is just as important that we hold firmly to the symbolic truth as it is that we let go of the historical truth. Domning's is a work that merits detailed study. I will only note aspects of the argument that seem particularly important to me. I am particularly interested in Domning's reinterpretation of the story of Adam and Eve (Domning, Chapter Ten).

Domning gives a useful "working definition" of original sin that he claims is "uncontroversial" (Domning 2006, 140). Original sin "is simply *need for salvation (by Christ) which is universal to all human beings and acquired through natural generation*" (140). Domning notes the observation of Alszeghy and Flick that "any hypothesis capable of explaining these two dogmatic truths [universality of sin, and participation in it through natural generation] is . . . to be considered tenable" (Domning 2006, 140, Alszeghy and Flick 1967, 201).

Domning's theory, though radical in its application of evolutionary theory to original sin, is more traditional than some modern interpretations that resist the notion of transmission of original sin by generation. The radical element lies in Domning's rejection of the traditional assumption "that the *universality* and the *moral character* of original sin both necessarily stem from *one and the same* individual act, and moment in time" (Domning, 140). Domning thus separates the "universality" of original sin and its "moral character." The universality of original sin comes not from Adam and Eve or from any other human ancestor, but from "the common ancestor not only of all humans but of all living things on Earth as well" (140). What interests Domning is not the ancestor itself but the natural descent through which it passed on its characteristics. This process is "governed by natural selection and the selfish behavior it requires" (141). The first human beings, whoever they were and whenever they appeared, inherited this natural selfishness. Domning thus reaffirms in different terms the traditional insistence of transmission of origi-

nal sin by generation rather than solely by imitation, as Pelagius is accused
of teaching and as some modern theologians have taught under the name of
"cultural transmission."

Once again, the language of Aquinas is useful though Domning himself
does not employ it. This natural selfishness is the "material" cause of original
sin. In the traditional view, this material cause, the actual sinful situation of
human beings, follows from the efficient cause, namely the sin of Adam and
Eve. The formal cause, alienation from God, and the consequent alienation
from self, neighbor, and nature, gives the intelligible ground of a condition
that is in itself mysterious, our tendency toward selfishness. For Domning,
the material element comes down, not from human actions but from the original selfishness that governs the development of all living things. Among all
living beings, humans were the first to have the possibility of going against
the natural selfishness they inherited by choosing to be selfless. But humans,
represented symbolically by Adam and Eve, failed the test and introduced
"sin" into the process of human development.

The sinfulness of human acts thus "proceeds from a source that is logically
and temporally separate from their common genealogical origin . . ." (141).
Though Adam and Eve *symbolize* the beginnings of human sin, it is not necessary to posit a historical first couple in order to explain the universality of
sin. That universality comes from the original selfishness that characterizes
the development of all life forms. It seems implicit in Domning'a theory that
we must say that each time human beings were confronted with the reality
of inherited selfishness and offered the possibility of overcoming it through
a free choice to be selfless rather than selfish, they failed to realize the possibility. If some humans, confronted with this choice, actually did transcend
inherited selfishness, then we would expect to see a strain of human beings
who had grown accustomed to overcoming selfish tendencies. Domning
avoids this possibility by defining original sin as *"that need for salvation (by
Christ) which is universal to all human beings and acquired through natural
generation"* (140). This means that the human will, though offered the *possibility* of overcoming selfishness, is incapable of *actually* doing so without
the grace of Christ.

Domning notes that his account of original sin does not exclude Schoonenberg's account, but "broadens and deepens" Schoonenberg's central
explanatory notion of cultural transmission (142). Schoonenberg and most
other post-Vatican II theologians "tend to equate it [original sin] with the sinful situations or structures into which each person is born" (142). Domning
reaches into the time before the advent of human beings to posit a "'society
before (human) society' which was molding our ancestors' behavior (both
learned and genetically determined) for millions of years before they became

human" (142). Domning's broadening and deepening of the notion of cultural transmission corrects what he finds to be a defect in Schoonenberg's position, namely the lack of any explanation of how culture first got infected.

Domning's account of the origins of original sin has the advantage of using evolutionary theory to explain what is often left unexplained in the story of Adam and Eve. Why were they so susceptible to what seems like a crass temptation of the serpent? The hapless couple, first Eve, then Adam, seemed all too ready to swallow the hook dangled in front of them. Domning takes his place in a line of thinkers who have spoken of a condition of sin prior to the sin itself. Irenaeus in the third century maintained that Adam and Eve were like children, not yet mature enough to resist temptation. Näiveté, then, becomes the precondition that sets Adam and Eve up for a fall. For Augustine, the precondition was a certain complacency. "The first evil came, then, when man began to be pleased with himself, as if he were his own light; for then he turned away from that Light which, if only he had been pleased with it instead, would have made the man himself a light" (Augustine, *City of God,* XIV, 13).

ORIGINAL SIN AS VIOLENCE

In her reappraisal of the doctrine of original sin, *The Fall to Violence: Original Sin in Relational Theology* (1995), Marjorie Hewitt Suchocki redefines both the formal and material causes of original sin. Instead of the traditional designation of the formal cause as rebellion against God, Suchocki maintains that the formal definition of original sin consists in a "rebellion against creation" (Suchocki 1995, 16). And instead of the traditional designation of the material cause as concupiscence, Suchocki speaks of original sin as violence (28–29).

Suchocki recognizes the depth of the tradition that defines original sin as rebellion against God, but gives her own strong reasons for suggesting another formality. The concept of sin as rebellion against God, says Suchocki, "tends to cast the primary function of God as the moral lawgiver who establishes the boundaries of acceptable human conduct" (17). It also tends all too easily to translate "into a social formula for keeping marginal and oppressed peoples in places of poverty and/or powerlessness, since it tends to interpret rebellion against any form of political, social, or personal power as rebellion against God" (17). Hiding all sin, "the enormity of political torture, massive wars, cruel oppressions, child abuse . . . under the one umbrella of rebellion against God effectively levels the distinction between sins" (17–18). It also hides the real victims of sin, contributes to the devaluation of creation, "fosters rather than illuminates the Christian problem of sin," and "makes the fundamental conflict of human beings a promethean defiance of deity which is probably remote from the experience of most people" (18).

Given her formal definition of original sin as rebellion against creation, it is not surprising that Suchocki finds the material element of original sin in "human brutality" and "our penchant for violence" (28). Suchocki prefaces each chapter of her book with a brief newspaper or journal report. All deal with violence or environmental pollution and its effects. These reports, say Suchocki, make sin concrete, help us avoid the "trivialization of sin"—such things as "going off one's diet or telling a white lie"—and keep us from treating sin "as if it were synonymous with sex" (28). All these examples of violence against human beings and against the earth complement the theoretical accounts that are never "fully adequate to the awful reality of human ill-doing" (28).

Suchocki's identification of original sin as violence that is primarily a sin against creation and only secondarily a sin against God, comes out of a feminist critique of Reinhold Niebuhr. Niebuhr, says this feminist critique, along with Augustine and Aquinas, places the core of original sin, its formal causality, in pride or rebellion against God, making one's self the absolute rather than God. The feminist critique embraced by Suchocki places the core of sin in rebellion against one's essential relatedness to creation or nature. Sin is an offense against creation rather than a sin against God.

Both Niebuhr and his feminist critics place original sin in a failure of self-transcendence. But for Niebuhr the self fails to transcend itself by failing to recognize its essential relation of dependence on God. For Suchocki and the other feminists she cites, the self fails to transcend itself in violating its essential relatedness to other creatures. The failure can take place in a couple of ways. One can make one's self absolute, independent of other selves for whom one has no sympathy or care. This is the sin of the privileged and powerful. One can also absolutize other human beings, granting them real objective value and turning the self into an unreal subordinate reality. "One can so identify with the other that one effectively loses—or never develops—a sense of self" (40). Suchocki and other feminists call this phenomenon "hiding" (32–33, 40). This is the sin of the marginalized, among them women, who never emerge from the shadow of the dominant other into their own selfhood. It may well be that these two perspectives can be reconciled, as the prophets of Israel do, by identifying sins among human beings as sins against God. Suchocki, however does not want to reduce sins against human beings to sins against God.

FEMINIST PERSPECTIVES

Suchocki stands out for her emphasis on violence as the material embodiment of original sin. Her grounding of that emphasis on feminist principles naturally leads us to a wider look at feminist perspectives. Christian feminist theologians, including Suchocki, accept much of what the tradition proposes on the subject of original sin. Rosemary Radford Reuther, for instance, affirms that original sin arises "out of the misuse of human freedom" (Wiley, 175), that "humanity has become *radically alienated* from its true relationship to itself, to nature, and to God" (Wiley, 175; Reuther, *Sexism and God Talk,* 37). Reuther accepts the Pauline-Augustinian teaching that "we derive a profound existential recognition of the divided self, acting against its own interests and desires" (Wiley 2002, 175; Reuther 1992, 142).

Rather than new insights into the efficient or instrumental causes of original sin, feminist perspectives offer insight into the materiality of original sin, answering the questions, "What does original sin consist of?"[4] According to Wiley, Reuther "places the critique of the classical doctrine of original sin at the heart of the feminist theology. The very purpose of feminist theology is to name evil rightly" (Wiley 2002, 157). And that name is male domination. What the tradition has obscured, say feminist theologians, is the patriarchal structure that has ruled human consciousness unchallenged until recent times. At the root of the social arrangements that embody male domination lie hidden structures of consciousness. Elizabeth Johnson uses Bernard Lonergan's term "scotosis" to characterize the resistance to feminist efforts to bring out of hiding the structures of patriarchal consciousness. Scotosis is a blind spot that obscures unwanted insights, preventing them from emerging into consciousness (Johnson, *She Who Is,* 13). The title of Johnson's book is a feminist translation of the Hebrew name YAHWEH given by God to Moses at the Burning Bush (Exod. 3:13–14). The Hebrew is difficult to translate because it is a verb form and has several possible meanings. A common translation, the one from which Johnson is working, is "I am who am," or "He who is." This very name of God as it has been translated embodies the patriarchal structure to which Johnson objects and entails the scotosis that prevents us from understanding the true nature of God.

The problem begins with interpretations of the story of Adam and Eve in Genesis 2 and 3. Early church theologians found three key gender-related elements: woman was created inferior to man; woman's sin is the cause of the fall; the male is created to rule the female (Wiley, 155). The earliest scriptural embodiment of this interpretation, according to Wiley, is found in 1 Tim. 2:8–15. "Let woman learn in silence with full submission. I permit no woman to teach or have authority over a man; she is to keep silent. For Adam was formed first, then Eve; and Adam was not deceived, but woman was deceived and became a transgressor" (1 Tim. 2:12–14). This letter is probably not from the hand of Paul, but rather from one of his followers.

Some scriptural texts embody this unconscious assumption of male superiority and are products of it, others counter the assumptions. But even texts that might seem to challenge the patriarchal view have been interpreted from a patriarchal perspective and subordinated to texts that seem to give a biblical warrant to male domination of society. Feminist theologians see Jesus' teaching as anti-patriarchal. Jesus treated women differently than did members of the religious and political establishment of his time. "In his words and actions—parables, stories, healings, exorcisms, friendships, and encounters—Jesus signaled domination as *sin* and freedom from subordinate status as *redemption*" (Wiley 2002, 168). And Paul cites baptismal formulas that show continuity between Jesus' teaching and the reality lived by the communities formed in his name. "There is no longer Jew or Greek, there is no longer slave or free, there is no longer male or female; for all of you are one in Jesus Christ" (Gal. 3:28). But the deutero-Pauline letters written later using his name but actually written by different authors "provide evidence of the patriarchalizing of the church in the late first and early second century C.E." (Wiley 2002, 170).

In contrast to the liberating texts of Paul that seek to transcend the polarities of male/female, etc., Elizabeth Schussler-Fiorenza identifies "patriarchal submission texts" that "seek to bring the communal structure of the *ekklesia* into line with the structure of the patriarchal household" (Wiley, 170; Schussler-Fiorenza, 73). The complete form of these texts, according to Schussler-Fiorenza, is found only in two passages from deutero-Pauline letters, Col. 3:18–4:1 and Eph. 5:22–6:9. In these passages, the relations between man and woman, master and slave, parents and children are hierarchical. "Wives, be subject to your husbands, as is fitting in the Lord" (Col. 3:18). And "Wives, be subject to your husbands as you are to the Lord. For the husband is the head of the wife just as Christ is the head of the church, the body of which he is the Savior" (Eph. 5:23–24).

The "appropriation" of these patriarchal submission texts, says Wiley, "submerged" the vision of Jesus and Paul that had rejected patriarchal structures. "The Christian church created its own separate and unequal spheres for women and men" (Wiley 2002, 171). This submerging, in later New Testament writings, of the incipient movement toward equality and the elimination of hierarchical distinctions found in the teachings of Jesus and the writings of Paul has, according to the feminist perspective, continued in the development of church tradition. The systematic distortion of the proper relation of equality between men and women is intertwined with the history of original sin, specifically in assigning an unwarranted role to women in the originating of sin.

CONCLUSION

The feminist attention to male dominance as a principal manifestation of original sin belongs to a larger category of oppression in general. Paul in Galatians mentions the polarities of men and women, masters and slaves, Jews and Greeks (Gal. 3:28) as divisions to be overcome in the Christian's new life in Christ. We can extend the list to include every kind of division exploited by oppression, differences of race, social class, degrees of physical perfection. This universal unconscious tendency to exploit whatever advantage one has against those who have less leads to the pervasive violence identified by Suchocki and, as we will see in chapter seven, by René Girard. But even the tendency toward exploitation and the violence to which exploitation gives rise, finds its place within a wider category, selfishness (Domning). Selfishness seems to be a basic category that has many manifestations, exploitation of others, self-complacency, and covetousness, to name a few. All of these can be taken as names for the material aspect of original sin.

I speak of original sin here in its "material" reality. The material aspect tells us what original sin consists of. If the formal aspect consists in a separation from God, or in Suchocki's view, a separation from creation, and the efficient and instrumental aspect consists in the act(s) of free will and their consequences perpetuated by inheritance and cultural conditioning, the condition that results from the formal, efficient, and instrumental causes is the material cause, the stuff of original sin in its manifestations in human living.

We have been considering original sin from a theoretical perspective, leaving aside some of the fundamental themes of this work that belong to the realm of subjective consciousness rather than to the realm of speculation, themes like compassion and forgiveness. The development of doctrine and the historical succession of theoretical explanations may seem to have taken us away from the central preoccupation of this work, the connection between original sin, compassion, and forgiveness. At the conclusion of her work, *The Fall to Violence,* Marjorie Suchocki offer some reflections that can serve to bring us back to home base in the midst of our theoretical reflections. In the next-to-last chapter of her book, "Forgiveness and Transformation," Suchocki reminds us of what is our central theme, the solidarity in sin that can, if realized and accepted, lead to compassion. We all have varying degrees of guilt, says Suchocki, depending on our level of freedom and the possibilities given to us in life. But, she adds, "there is no one who does not bear some degree of responsibility for what he or she has done with the inherited past, no one who does not in some sense integrate the sins of others into the self through solidarity, no one who does not experience an inherent inclination toward aggression that entails a capacity of violence" (*Fall to Violence,* 149).

This "inherent inclination toward aggression that entails a capacity for violence" forms the subject matter chapter seven, "René Girard: Original Sin as Covetousness." Girard has developed an impressive system based on an interpretation of original sin as the innate desire in human beings to have what the other has precisely because the other has it. The inclination, not evil in itself within bounds, can lead to the war of all against all when it becomes generalized. Girard's work may be the most influential elaboration of original sin in our time.

NOTES

1. This scriptural quotation is from the New Revised Standard Version Bible: Catholic Edition, copyright © 1989, 1993 National Council of the Churches of Christ in the United States of America. Used by permission. All rights reserved worldwide.

2. This scriptural quotation is from the New Revised Standard Version Bible: Catholic Edition, copyright © 1989, 1993 National Council of the Churches of Christ in the United States of America. Used by permission. All rights reserved worldwide.

3. Aristotle describes the four causes in Book V, Chapter 2 of his *Metaphysics.* Aristotle. 1952. *Metaphysics.* Translated by W. D. Ross in *Great Books of the Western World.* Chicago: Encyclopedia Brittanica.

4. Tatha Wiley's comprehensive work, *Original Sin: Origins, Developments, Contemporary Meanings,* after tracing the historical development of original sin, gives a useful summary of feminist positions. See chapter 7, "Original Sin in Feminist Theology."

Chapter Six

Compassion as Prelude to Forgiveness

While he was still a long way off, his father caught sight of him and was filled with compassion.

—Luke 15:20b, NRSV[1]

For it belongs to humanity to suffer-with and to be moved by compassion for the suffering of others. An animal is able to suffer but to suffer-with is proper to humanity. For this reason, the will of tender pity is called the will of humanity, because it belongs to a human being to be moved with tender pity. And, in as much as he is human, we find this compassion in Christ.

—Hugh of St. Victor (1096–1141), *On the Four Wills of Christ*

We have considered how the Adamic Myth is situated in the world of ancient Near Eastern accounts of the origin and end of evil, and we have explored its place in the Old and New Testaments. We have examined the notion of original sin and argued that a personal consciousness of original sin in oneself can lead to compassion. This connection between original sin and compassion seems to have occurred, as described in the chapter four, even in the thought of Augustine. Now it is time to look more closely at the dynamic interconnections among the three key terms of this study, sin—original and actual, compassion, and forgiveness. What is sin? How does compassion work? How does compassion lead to forgiveness?

Sin is an action against someone, an injury, an insult, a slight, an act of disobedience. Even original sin, which is inherited, begins with an actual act of disobedience. Ultimately, in the theologies of Judaism and Christianity, sin is an action against God, but it can also be a sin against the neighbor. And forgiveness is a response; it consists of letting go, sometimes of forgetting, of passing over, of releasing from the debt that sin incurs for the sinner. Mediating between sin and forgiveness is *compassion*. Examples abound in both the Hebrew Bible and the New Testament. Compassion was at work in God's forgiveness of the people of Nineveh. "And should I not be concerned over Nineveh, the great city, in which there are more than a hundred and twenty thousand who cannot distinguish their right hand from their left?" (Jon. 4:11). The human agent, Jonah, did not share God's compassion. One can bypass compassion in forgiving, but then the forgiveness is likely to be false or shallow, a mere act of the will without any support from the heart. Compassion expands the heart and opens it to forgiveness, which follows as something spontaneous, more like a gift than an act of virtue.

Compassion plays a crucial role in the dynamics of the Adamic Myth. The sin of Adam and Even evokes God's compassion. Even within the framework of the narrative of Genesis 3, which ends with disastrous consequences for the disobedient couple, God shows compassion, fashioning leather garments for the man and his wife with which he clothed them (Gen. 3:21). In fact, even God's question when Adam and Eve hid from him, "Where are you?" seems more compassionate than reproachful, as if God regretted the chain of events that the couple had unleashed. And the multitude of sins that followed the first disobedience, beginning with Cain's murder of his brother, Abel, and continuing through the prehistory and history of Israel, continued to call forth God's compassion. When God saw the wickedness of the people he had created and that all the desires of their hearts were evil, "he regretted that he had made man on the earth, and his heart was grieved" (Gen. 6:6). So even God's decision to wipe out all men and beasts seems to have been motivated more by grief than anger. And, as it turned out, God relented of that decision, mitigated it in favor of Noah, and promised after the flood never again to strike down all living beings. God became for Israel, as we have seen, "The Lord, the Lord, a merciful and gracious God, slow to anger and rich in kindness for a thousand generations, and forgiving wickedness and crime and sin . . ." (Exod. 34:6–7). Though the Old Testament does not refer to the story of Adam and Eve after chapter 3 of Genesis, the Hebrew Scriptures do affirm and reaffirm the pattern of God's mercy in the face of the continual sin of his people. This pattern will be the model that Jesus follows and also transforms in the New Testament.

FORGIVENESS AS NECESSARY, POSSIBLE, AND ACTUAL

Through Paul's *New Testament* transformation of the story of Adam and Eve found originally in the book of Genesis, and through the more subtle but nonetheless clear expression of it in the Gospels and other New Testament writings, the Adamic Myth has become a privileged, if controversial expression of the logic of salvation in Christianity. At the heart of the Adamic Myth lies the notion that separates it from the other three myths described, as we have seen, by Paul Ricoeur in *The Symbolism of Evil*, the notion that evil came into the world through the free choice of the man and woman created by God. This choice to prefer their own will to God's and eat of the fruit God had commanded them not to eat, sets up the archetypal situation in which forgiveness first becomes a necessity, a possibility, and a reality. Forgiveness becomes a *necessity* because Adam and Eve and their descendants have no way to overcome by themselves the consequences of their act, a *possibility* because God does have the power to reverse the situation caused by disobedience, and a *reality* because God chooses in fact to take the initiative in offering salvation to human beings.

Forgiveness is a *conditional* necessity, necessary for human beings if they are to be restored to wholeness and necessary for God if the Creator wishes to see the original purpose of his creation realized. We take for granted the *possibility* of divine forgiveness. We should not. For forgiveness is *possible* only if the one offended is willing to pardon the "wickedness and sins" of his "stiff-necked people" and receive them as his own (Exod. 34:9b), as Moses prayed in the refashioning of new tablets to replace the ones he had destroyed; only if he is "The Lord, the Lord, a merciful and gracious God, slow to anger and rich in kindness for a thousand generations, and forgiving wickedness and crime and sin . . ." (Exod. 34:6–7). Forgiveness is *possible* if this God is willing to forgive iniquities and heal diseases (Ps. 103:3), no longer to remember" (Jer. 31:34) when they pray, "the sins of my youth and my transgressions do not remember" (Ps. 25:7). Forgiveness is *possible* if God can choose to tread underfoot his people's guilt, to cast into the depths of the sea all the people's sins (Mic. 7:18–19). These are all expressions of God's habit of mercy.

Can we imagine Oedipus praying to Apollo or to the Fate that condemned him to horrible deeds that they not remember the deeds of his youth or tread underfoot his guilt or cast his sins into the sea? In the tragic vision of predestination to evil such forgiveness is not *possible.* Or what god can a follower of Orphism appeal to for forgiveness? That we are essentially spirit imprisoned in a body is not our fault but the result of divine atrocities before we were born. Or where could a follower of one of the creation myths, which see human beings as the result of a cosmic struggle between the gods, turn for forgiveness? According to this mythic type, we are essentially victims of powers beyond ourselves and prior to our existence, not free beings who have in some way chosen our destiny. Only if one has offended a caring and loving god, as is the case in the Adamic Myth, can the god forgive. But forgiveness is *only* possible because even this caring and loving God can refuse forgiveness. Abraham understood as much when he begged God to spare the people of Sodom even if only ten righteous ones could be found (Gen. 18:16–33). But as we have seen, the God of Israel, who is also the God of Jesus, is predisposed to forgiveness, inclined to mercy, slow to anger—at least for those who turn and ask. And so forgiveness has become a *reality*. And this forgiveness is *real*, because it has actually happened in the history of Israel and the New Covenant of Christ.

Forgiveness in the Christian Dispensation

Chapter three traced the lines of connection between the New Testament and the Adamic Myth. The New Testament also builds on the Old Testament image of a "gracious God and merciful, slow to anger, and abounding in steadfast love, and ready to relent from punishing" (Jon. 4:2b) *and* the Jewish belief that all have sinned and need God's mercy. We now turn to the distinctively Christian notion of forgiveness to see what it adds. The biblical notion of compassion works like a leaven in the Christian tradition. We have already seen how Augustine's teaching on original sin evolves toward a theology of compassion. We begin not with the New Testament itself, but with a follower of Augustine, Hugh of St. Victor (1096–1141), considered by some the most influential theologian of the twelfth century. He catches the teaching of the New Testament in the magnifying lens of a brief reflection on the compassionate will of Christ entitled, "The Four Wills of Christ."[2] Beginning with Hugh's reflection, we will explore how compassion operates in the New Testament and why, though central to Christ's teaching, it is so hard for us to achieve.

Hugh of St. Victor's "The Four Wills of Christ"

Hugh begins with the traditional distinction, enunciated by ecumenical councils, between the human and divine wills of Christ. If Christ were to be considered both fully human and fully divine, so the argument went, he had to be possessed of both human and divine wills. Hugh goes beyond this received distinction, while in no way contradicting it, by finding within the human will of Christ three further "wills." It is evident that these are not separate wills, but aspects of the one human will. The rational will (*voluntas secundum rationem*) is the aspect of Jesus' human will by which he chose to follow the decree of God for him, especially regarding the Passion. A second aspect, the will of the flesh (*voluntas secundum carnem*), was the aspect by which Jesus naturally resisted in his flesh the prospect of his suffering and death. Hugh finds these two aspects of will, not only in Jesus himself but in the disciples as well: "The spirit is willing but the flesh is weak" [Matt. 26:41]. The rational will and the will of the flesh appear strikingly of course in Jesus' prayer recorded a few verses earlier in Matthew: "My Father, if it is possible, let this cup pass from me [will of the flesh]; yet not as I will, but as you will" [rational will] (Matt. 26:39).

But the tension between Jesus' rational will, by which he assented to God's plan for him, and the will of the flesh by which he resisted it is not the main concern of Hugh of St. Victor's treatise. The third aspect of Jesus' human will, the "will of compassion" (*voluntas pietatis*) or tender pity [Coolman's translation][3] takes up most of Hugh's treatise. In Christ, says Hugh, the will of compassion (*voluntas pietatis*) "sighed deeply over another's evil through co-suffering (*per compassionem*) [Hugh of St. Victor, 176.841b]. In other words, this is the aspect of the will by which Christ suffered over the evil, deserved or undeserved, that befalls another. As examples of this will of compassion, Hugh cites Luke's account of Christ weeping over Jerusalem: "As he drew near, he saw the city and wept over it, saying, 'If this day you only knew what makes for peace—but now it is hidden from your eyes" (Lk. 19:41–42). Luke does not say that Jesus thought the coming downfall of Jerusalem was undeserved, just that he wept over it. "Hugh interprets Jesus' tears as an expression of felt sorrow over the eternal fate of Jerusalem's unbelieving inhabitants, which he does not will, *secundum pietatem*," (Coolman, 536), that is, according to his compassionate will. Presumably, though Hugh does not say so explicitly, Jesus also recognized, with his rational will, that the punishment was deserved and so accepted the fate of Jerusalem though he grieved over it. This nuance is worth dwelling on for it relies on a distinction that escapes many people wrestling with forgiveness. Hugh finds in Christ a willingness to *regret* and feel sorrow over the sufferings that arise from a just punishment even while he is upholding the justice of the punishment.

The second passage cited by Hugh is Jesus' weeping over the death of Lazarus, described in John 11. Hugh's text, slightly different from that used in modern translations, reads: "Jesus groaned in spirit and troubled himself" (Jn. 11:38). Hugh asks whether it was a "good troubling" and answers that it was: Jesus' humanity meant that just as he bore suffering in his body, he also bore co-suffering in his mind (*compassionem in mente*). Note that in this case Jesus is grieving over a natural phenomenon, death, and not over a destiny brought about by sin. Clarifying the parallel between passion and compassion, Hugh says of Jesus that: "He bore his *passion* that he might die for those who were going to die; he bore *compassion* that he might weep for those who were going to perish" (Hugh of St. Victor, 844d–845a).

COMPASSION AS PRECONDITION FOR FORGIVENESS

Hugh uses his analysis of the four wills of Christ as a foundation for a much larger claim, that compassion is the form of ideal humanity: "For it belongs to humanity to suffer with (*compati*) and to be moved with tender pity (*pietate*) for the misery of others" (Hugh of St. Victor, 842). This is, of course, the teaching of the New Testament. Moreover, the New Testament makes a connection that Hugh does not pursue in this brief treatise, the connection between compassion and forgiveness. Paul urges the Colossians, and through them all Christians: "Put on, then, as God's chosen ones, holy and beloved, heartfelt compassion (*splangkna*), kindness, humility, gentleness, and patience . . ." (Col. 3:12). This is to be done in imitation of Christ: ". . . as the Lord has forgiven you, so must you also do" (Col. 3:13b). We can use Hugh's three aspects of the human will of Christ as the foundation for a meditation on forgiveness. The argument of this chapter is that compassion is a necessary precondition for forgiveness. The connection may seem obvious, but discussions of forgiveness that bypass compassion, suggesting that forgiveness is a matter only of rational willing, miss an essential ingredient of the process. Forgiveness is less an act of the rational will than of the movement of tender mercy. We may say "I know I ought to forgive" [rational will], "but I can't bring myself to do it" [will of the flesh]. The only power that can overcome the natural resistance of the flesh is the "compassionate will" described by Hugh. Or we might even say, "I see no reason to forgive; the one who offended me does not deserve forgiveness and forgiveness would seem to justify the injury [rational will]. Again, it is the compassionate will that would have to mediate between the rational will and the act of forgiveness. It is difficult, whatever our resistance might be, to forgive someone for whom we have no compassion.

The New Testament, especially the Gospels, illustrates this connection repeatedly. In the famous "sermon on the plain" in Luke's Gospel, Jesus expresses this teaching in sweeping terms that include not only friends but enemies: ". . . love your enemies and do good to them, and lend expecting nothing back; then your reward will be great and you will be children of the Most High, for he himself is kind to the ungrateful and the wicked. Be merciful (*oiktirmones*) just as your Father is merciful" (Lk. 6:35–36). A parallel passage from Matthew, "Be perfect, therefore, as your heavenly Father is perfect" (5:48) defines perfection in terms of mercy. To be "perfect" like the heavenly Father is to imitate him in loving enemies as well as friends, "for he makes his sun rise on the evil and on the good, and sends rain on the righteous and on the unrighteous" (5:45b).

Probably the most famous parable of forgiveness, also from Luke, is the story of the Prodigal Son. "While he [the son] was still a long way off, his father caught sight of him and was filled with compassion (*esplangnisthe*). He ran to his son, embraced him and kissed him" (Lk. 15:20b). Note that the father expresses compassion even before his son has come close enough to acknowledge his fault. The parable illustrates not only how compassion leads to forgiveness—in this case the compassion and the forgiveness are hardly distinguished—but how the lack of compassion prevents forgiveness. The older brother, hearing the commotion and learning what has happened, becomes angry and refuses to go in to the feast. He feels no compassion toward his brother but only jealous resentment. After all my years of service, he says, "you never gave me even a young goat to feast on with my friends. But when your son returns who swallowed up your property with prostitutes, for him you slaughter the fatted calf" (29b–30). And, even with this older angry son, the father speaks compassionately: "My son, you are here with me always; everything I have is yours" (31). Neither of the brothers grasped what it meant to be son of such a loving father. Then the father reveals what has touched his gentle heart and gives the reason for his rejoicing: "But now we must celebrate and rejoice, because your brother was dead and has come to life again; he was lost and has been found" (32).

Another parable, this one from Matthew, emphasizes the need to render mercy for mercy received. When the man who owes a huge debt comes to his master asking for forgiveness, the master begins with a movement of compassion: "Moved with compassion (*splangnistheis*) the master of the servant let him go and forgave him the loan" (Matt. 18:27). The story ends, as we know, with the failure of the servant to forgive a fellow servant who owed a much smaller debt, a failure that invoked the wrath of the master and the withdrawal of the original forgiveness. The master's anger toward the ungrateful servant swallows up his compassion. Mark's account of Jesus' cure of the leper includes a mention of compassion not included in Matthew's and Luke's versions. When the leper approaches him with the bold request "If you wish, you can make me clean," Mark tells us that Jesus "moved with pity (*splangnistheis*), . . . stretched out his hand, touched him, and said 'I do will it,' be made clean" (Mk. 1:41). In a passage that follows immediately, the healing of a paralytic, Jesus makes clear the equivalence of healing and forgiving sin: "Which is easier to say so the paralytic, 'Your sins are forgiven,' or to say 'Pick up your mat and walk'" (2:1–12)?

Not only does the New Testament vividly illustrate the connection between compassion and forgiveness, but it also urges the necessity of forgiveness and stresses the reciprocity of forgiving and being forgiven. The parable from

Matthew 18, cited above, is an example. Jesus tells his disciples in the sermon on the plain of Luke 6, "Stop judging and you will not be judged. Stop condemning and you will not be condemned. Forgive and you will be forgiven." Judging and condemning set us up to be judged and condemned in our turn. Forgiving sets us up to be forgiven. The prayer that Jesus taught his disciples when they asked him how to pray, also contains the admonition to forgiveness: " . . . forgive us our debts as we forgive our debtors . . ." (Matt. 6:12). In Matthew's version of the Lord's Prayer, Jesus returns to the point at the end in case the disciples might have missed the point: "If you forgive others their transgressions, your heavenly Father will forgive you. But if you do not forgive others, neither will your Father forgive your transgressions" (14–15).

So we have the clear example of Jesus' compassion and its connection with forgiveness. But even with Jesus' example and his clear teaching, his followers, to say nothing of humanity in general, find it difficult to feel compassion, and therefore to forgive, in spite of Hugh of St. Victor's claim that is belongs to humans to be compassionate. Pelagius would be scandalized. Why, he would ask, are the example of Jesus and his clear teachings not sufficient motive for obeying his laws? And surely one of those laws, probably the most important of all, is that we forgive one another. So why does compassion come so hard? We have to look to Paul, for the answer, to the other New Testament writers, and to Augustine and, more generally, to the Christian tradition that recognizes the weakened condition of the human will and the internal conflicts that tear at it. Compassion leading to forgiveness is the expression of a free will, and our freedom is compromised. In the next chapter, we will look at the thought of René Girard who sees the primary evidence of original sin in what he calls "mimetic rivalry," the desire to have what the other has simply because the other has it. The Bible calls it covetousness. The older son in the story of the Prodigal Son provides the archetypal example. One suspects that he only desired a party because his brother had one. The Letter of James anticipates Girard by two millenia: "Where do the wars and where do the conflicts among you come from? Is it not from your passions that make war within your members? You covet but do not possess. You kill and envy but do not receive" (Jas. 4:1–2). After his admonition to "be merciful just as your Father is merciful" (Lk. 6:36), Jesus addresses some of the obstacles to mercy: "Stop judging and you will not be judged. Stop condemning, and you will not be condemned. Forgive and you will be forgiven." These passages suggest a circular relationship between compassion and forgiveness. The gesture of forgiving can lead to the compassion that is its real ground. Sometimes we have to start from the outside and work our way in.

But we need to push our questioning further. *Why* are we given to rivalry, and envy, judging, and condemning rather than to the works of mercy? The easy answer, of course, is original sin. We do not know how to will what we really want and avoid what we really do not want. Paul, speaking of our knowledge of God, says that we "see indistinctly (*en ainigmati*), as in a mirror" (I Cor. 13:12). *Ainigma* in Greek means a riddle or an indistinct image. Not only do we see God indistinctly, but we know ourselves and others *en ainigmati,* confusedly. We have seen how, in the intense reflection that followed his conversion, Augustine had become a "problem" for himself, "like land which a farmer works only with difficulty and at the cost of much sweat" (*Conf.* X, 16). Enigma, riddle, problem—these are all words that describe the mystery of our human condition that we call original sin. But what is its inner constitution? Can we find a structure that reveals its inner essence? Can we perform a diagnostic of the dis-ease that characterizes our own lives and our relations with one another? A patient might come to her doctor for an explanation of her lack of energy. He might trace it to anemia, or depression, or a tumor. And the remedy, if there is one, would be related to the underlying condition. Can we do this with original sin?

What follows will be the first of several attempts to explore the pattern of elements that make up original sin. We have seen that Augustine, in the years before he developed his doctrine of original sin, became conscious of the role of feelings in the operation of the will. It is one thing, he recognized, to know intellectually what we should do, quite another to experience the effective support necessary to actually choose the good our mind sets before us. Augustine came to recognize a certain chaos in his feelings, a darkness, a resistance to the known good. Assuming that Augustine is right, we might expect that this same chaos in our feelings is what makes it hard to forgive even though we might want to do so. To carry this line of thinking further, I suggest we look at a suggestion made in the second chapter that the disobedience of Adam and Eve resulted in the loss of four intimacies crucial to human living, intimacy with self, intimacy with God, intimacy with one another, and intimacy with nature. The healing of these damaged intimacies opens us to the possibility of compassion and forgiveness just as the treatment of someone's anemia might restore their energy.

Restoration of Intimacy with Self

"Then the eyes of both were opened, and they knew that they were naked; and they sewed fig leaves together and made loincloths for themselves" (Gen. 3:7). This account from Genesis symbolizes the loss of innocence and the beginning of shame. This shame at nakedness, coming as an immediate consequence of the first act of disobedience, reveals something profound about the constitution of sin. Shame, contempt for self, and even the feeling of condemnation,

afflict human beings in a literally radical way; they are the *roots* of a luxuri-
ant growth of other evils that the subsequent chapters of Genesis describe in
detail. Modern writers have also explored this phenomenon of self-loathing.
The first chapter of this book on Paul Ricoeur's treatment of the four myths
of the origin and end of evil ends with a quotation from Bernanos' *Diary of a
Country Priest*: "It is easier than one thinks to hate oneself" (Bernanos 1936,
252). This theme of self-hatred runs throughout the novel. The human being is
"a secret and cunning enemy to himself" (Ibid., 92). Contrary to the common
opinion that peasants are simple people, Bernanos' country priest, himself a
son of peasants, finds them "complicated." "A peasant rarely loves himself"
(Ibid., 23) and is indifferent to those who love him, not because he doubts their
sincerity but because he despises them for loving him. At their death, some old
men may let slip an anguished word that testifies to a hatred of self for which
there may be no forgiveness. It is a kind of despair.

If contempt for self is radical in human beings, then salvation needs to involve a *radical* mending of the torn relationship. How does such healing take
place? Bernanos suggests a way, the grace of self-forgetfulness. Bernanos
contrasts *forgetfulness* of self with self-hatred. The work of grace, he says is
to help us forget ourselves, and "if all pride were dead in us, the grace of all
graces would be to love oneself humbly as any suffering member of Christ."
To hate oneself is to be tied up in oneself. Self-hatred is a form of egotism.
Self-forgetfulness, on the other hand, opens up the possibility of compassion
toward oneself and toward others who suffer. And so salvation—perhaps the
first grace of salvation—is to restore intimacy with self, paradoxically in the
form of a self-forgetfulness that leads to compassion.

Related to a sense of shame and contempt for self, is a feeling of condemnation. Joseph Day, hero of Julian Green's novel *Moira,* suffers from a
rigid Protestant background that leaves him at times with a crippling sense
of being condemned. Sexual desire is the problem. Joseph is consumed with
desire, yet believes it is evil. At a crucial point in the story, Joseph turns to his
memory of a verse from the first letter of John: "If your heart condemns you,
God is greater than your heart" (Green 1950, 185). John actually says, "Little
children, let us love, not in word or speech, but in truth and action. By this
we will know that we are from the truth and will reassure our hearts before
him whenever our hearts condemn us; for God is greater than our hearts, and
he knows everything" (1 Jn. 3:19–20). Joseph believed that these were God's
personal words to him.

Finally, the alienation of the self from itself finds expression in the
enslaved (or "servile") will and its attendant moral impotence to which I
have already referred (see above, 52, 71). The will no longer obeys its own
commands, does not do what it wants or avoid what it does not want. The

expression "enslaved will," of course, has meant various things in the history of Christian theology, including the utter depravity that Calvin attributed to humans after "the fall." Here it corresponds to what modern society calls addiction. Gerald May suggests that to be human is to be addicted (May, 1988).

Restoration of Intimacy with God

Genesis shows Adam and Eve moving inexorably from shame at their nakedness to embarrassment before God. "They heard the sound of the Lord God walking in the garden at the time of the evening breeze, and the man and his wife hid themselves from the presence of the Lord God among the trees of the garden" (Gen. 3:8). The passage seems to imply that Adam and Eve would normally have joined God in his evening stroll in the garden. But shame over their nakedness has made such familiarity with God impossible. For Augustine, intimacy with self and intimacy with God, are correlative. *"Tu autem eras interior intimo meo et superior summo meo,"* he says, "You were more inward to me than my inmost self and higher than my highest self." (Augustine 1950, Bk. III, Ch. 6, 118–21). Therefore, to be excluded from intimacy with God is to be excluded from intimacy with myself, and exclusion from the deepest part of myself excludes me from God.

In her diary, *An Interrupted Life*, Etty Hillesum, a young Jewish woman from Holland who died in Auschwitz, explores this notion of intimacy with God in a variety of ways, perhaps most strikingly through the image of kneeling. "The story of the girl who gradually learned to kneel is something I would love to write in the fullest possible way" (Hillesum 1983, 61). The whole aim of what Christians call the spiritual life is to dispose oneself for intimacy with God. Augustine's whole intellectual and spiritual development consisted in an increasing intimacy with himself that was at the same time an intimacy with God.

The Restoration of Intimacy with Neighbor

The story of Adam and Eve suggests the loss of intimacy with the neighbor by describing a distortion in the relation between Eve and her husband: "Yet your urge shall be for your husband and he will be your master" (Gen. 3:16b). We can take this brief notice as a symbol of the tensions that exist not only between husbands and wives but in all our human relationships. These are precisely the tensions we noted in the Letter of James. They make forgiveness a complicated matter. A circular relationship exists between intimacy with self, intimacy with God, and intimacy with the other. Insecurity in myself tends toward troubled relations with others. Improved relations with others can help heal my relation to myself. Without proper love of self and God, true love of neighbor is not possible. On the other hand, John uses love of neighbor as a test of love of God. "Those who say, 'I love God,' and hate their brothers and sisters, are liars; for those who do not love a brother or sister whom they have seen, cannot love God whom they have not seen" (1 Jn. 4:20). John's admonition extends, of course, not only to individual brothers and sisters but to social groups. We have become conscious in modern times of structures of alienation that embody patterns of hatred for neighbor so deeply embedded that they go unnoticed by individuals caught in them. Racial prejudice, gender bias, and class divisions are all examples.

Christianity teaches that healing of the relation with one's neighbor and healing of the distortions that come from violence, indifference, and greed, is also necessary. This healing affects not only interpersonal relationships, but relations with people outside our circle of intimates. When the priest and Levite in the story of the Good Samaritan passed by the man who had been beaten by robbers, they were practicing the art of evasion, walking with eyes closed to the suffering of their neighbor. But the Samaritan, a foreigner, who finally came to the man's aid "was moved by compassion (*esplangnisthe*) at the sight" (Lk. 10:33) and took care of him. Compassion opens us up not only to forgiveness but to action on behalf of our neighbor. Compassion is really another name for intimacy with the suffering neighbor. The ability to suffer-with is the surest sign of friendship and true love in all its forms.

Intimacy with Nature

We can take God's words to Adam after his disobedience, "Cursed be the ground because of you! In toil shall you eat its yield all the days of your life" (Gen. 3:17b), as symbolizing the human being's difficult relation with nature. It yields its fruits grudgingly, we exploit it and it punishes us. There is never enough of it for our needs, we fight over it, and claim it for our exclusive use. In the process, we lose our ability to enjoy it, to share it, to properly appreciate it. Our age has dramatically revealed the limits of the human environment to meet human needs and the tragic results of centuries of exploitation. Here, too, we need healing before we can experience the compassion that leads to forgiveness. The lust for land and its products is at the root of chronic illnesses that afflict modern society, war, starvation, and poverty. Here compassion takes the form of "suffering with" the land, the water, the air, grieving at the degradation of the earth brought about by abuse of nature.

If we want to find the obstacles to the compassion that leads to forgiveness, we have to look at the distortions in these four intimacies. Some examples can help illuminate the complexity of the processes necessary for authentic forgiveness.

SOME EXAMPLES

In his book, *Wounds Not Healed by Time,* Solomon Schimmel retells the story of Eric Lomax, a British soldier captured by the Japanese during the Second World War. For the next fifty years, Lomax harbored a hatred for Japan and the Japanese, for his torturers and, in particular, for the translator/interpreter who passed along to him in English the questions of his interrogators. Finally, Lomax's dreams of revenge ended when he was able, through a complicated series of events, to meet the translator fifty years after the torture took place. The translator had felt genuine guilt and had made extraordinary efforts to atone for his part in these war crimes. When the two men finally met in Japan, the deep grief of the translator took away all the feeling of anger on Lomax' part and led him to a formal act of forgiveness. Basing his account on Lomax's own memoir, Schimmel describes the various stages Lomax went through on his long journey to forgiveness. A key point in Lomax' process was the realization that the man whom he had identified in his memory with the tortures had himself suffered in the aftermath and deserved Lomax' compassion.

Sometimes forgiveness involves not just the parties injured but the communities of which they are a part. A striking example is the story of forgiveness recounted in *The National Catholic Reporter* article of November 7, 1997, "Parish Turns Murder to Grace." The story began in June 1996, when a Hispanic boy shot and killed an Anglo youth on the border between Chicago and Evanston, Illinois. In July 1997, a Cook County judge sentenced the 19-year-old killer, Mario Ramos, to a sentence of forty years in prison without possibility of parole. The real drama of the story took place during the fifteen months between these two dates. The Catholic parish of which Mario Ramos and his parents were members responded to this tragedy by reaching out to Mario in jail awaiting trial and to his parents who were overcome with shame. A parishioner organized a group of Hispanic youth to address the divisions and alienation that characterized them. Stephen Young, father of Andrew, the murdered boy, also nineteen, said he was overcome with rage but vowed that his son's death would not be in vain. He carried out that vow by working for gun control. Maureen, Andrew's mother had fallen away from her Catholic faith, but later experienced "an extraordinary encounter" with "some evangelistic women," and recommitted her life to Jesus.

Through the intervention of his pastor and members of the parish, Mario Ramos became truly repentant and turned his life around. The story reaches its dramatic high point when Mario, before his sentencing had taken place, writes to Andrew's parents. "Though I could spend the rest of my life in jail, I don't even come close to the hurt your family must be going through. I hope that some way you may find it in your heart to forgive me." At the same time

Mario was composing his letter, Andrew's mother, Maureen, was typing a letter to him. "You don't know me, though I suspect you have heard of me," she opens, "I am Maureen, Andrew's mom. I've thought of you and prayed for you many times since you shot and killed my son." After telling about her own religious conversion, she ends her letter with these words: "You've probably heard Jesus is the way, the truth, and the life. I'm writing to tell you IT'S TRUE. He desires to lead you on a new adventure. If He is for you, who can be against you? Well, I don't know whether you'd ever feel up to asking my forgiveness for killing my son, so I'll go first. . . . "I FORGIVE YOU." "The two letters crossed in the mail," says the author of the article. This simultaneous apology and forgiveness, so rare in an era accustomed to angry cries for retribution, struck the parish and the entire community" (McClory 1997).

This account illustrates some key points regarding forgiveness. It shows first that forgiveness is a process, a process that can involve a whole community as well as the individuals immediately involved. The individual act of murder was rooted in the alienation of the Hispanic community, particularly its youth, from meaningful involvement in the life of their city. Both the Anglo and the Hispanic communities in the parish were willing to face the deeper implications of what had happened and accept their complicity in the situation that gave rise to the murder. Maureen Young, mother of the murdered youth, because of her own religious conversion to Christ, was able to draw on the resources of her faith to offer forgiveness even before she had received an apology. Forgiveness arose in her as a form of gratitude for her own healing by Christ. Mario's repentance was a factor too, even though Maureen did not know that he had written a letter asking for forgiveness. The justice system also did its work. Given the transformation that had taken place in Mario, the punishment seemed harsh to his friends, but all of them accepted the sentence and set their sights toward creating a supportive network that would help him withstand the corrupting influence of prison life.

MOTIVES FOR FORGIVING

The article, "Parish Turns Murder into Grace," with its description of process of forgiving, suggests another important category, motives for forgiveness. Why should we forgive? Why should a family ever forgive the father who has abandoned its members, especially if he has never repented? Why should the black majority of South Africa forgive the atrocities that were committed against them by the white minority for so many years? Nelson Mandela and Desmond Tutu have provided an eloquent answer to this question—there is no future without forgiveness. This will not satisfy everyone. Is it meaningful to speak of Jews "forgiving" the horrors of the Holocaust, or as many Jews prefer to call it "The Shoah?" The question here is what motivates forgiveness. We have already considered compassion as a key motivator. But compassion needs its motives too. What might move people to compassion?

One of those motives, of course, is the repentance of the injurer. Nothing moves more powerfully toward forgiveness than a sincere apology from the one who has done the injury. A central claim of this book has been that the Christian doctrine of original sin is itself a significant motive for forgiveness. By original sin I mean the condition, shared by all human beings, of the weakness and confusion that lead us to evil deeds. We have already seen Augustine's recognition of a universal weakness of the human will as a mitigating factor in an individual's responsibility for sin. No one, says the doctrine of original sin, escapes the infection and this should make us more understanding of sin. Christian theology can never be satisfied with the division of human beings into the good and the bad. Everyone, both the worst criminals and the most holy people, are good and bad at the same time.

The prayers of the psalmist, "I do not sit with the worthless, nor do I consort with hypocrites; I hate the company of evil doers, and will not sit with the wicked" (Ps. 26:4–5) or from another psalm, "Do not drag me away with the wicked, with those who are workers of evil, who speak peace with their neighbors, while mischief is in their hearts" (Ps. 28:3), do not fit easily into Christian theology. Jesus offers a very different view of the attitude that justifies in the sight of God. The parable of the Pharisee and the tax collector is an instance. The Pharisee offers this prayer: "God, I thank you that I am not like other people: thieves, rogues, adulterers, or even like this tax collector." The tax collector, on the other hand, standing far off and not even looking up to heaven, says simply, "God, be merciful to me a sinner" (Lk. 18:11–13). Jesus responds that the tax collector rather than the other went home justified. Contemporary Christian theology still remembers this admonition. Desmond Tutu, the former Anglican Archbishop of Capetown, insists that the perpetrators of Apartheid were not utterly different from their victims and warned the victims against considering themselves morally superior.

Etty Hillesum expressed this truth of solidarity in evil with startling clarity. Speaking with her friend Klaas, Etty insists on the need to look at our own sin rather than the sin of others: "And I repeat with the same old passion, although I am gradually beginning to think that I am being tiresome, 'It is the only thing we can do, Klaas, I see no alternative, each of us must turn inward and destroy in himself all that he thinks he ought to destroy in others: (Hillesum 1996, 212). And Klaas responds "But that—that is nothing but Christianity!" "And I," says Etty, "amused by your confusion, retort quite coolly, 'Christianity, and why ever not?'" (Ibid.). What make Etty's insistence on this point particularly striking is that the evil-in-others that confronted her as she wrote this advice was the genocidal program of the Nazis.

Another theological motive for forgiveness is the conviction that God can bring good out of evil. The fundamental instance of this for Christians, is of course, their belief that God brought the good of redemption out of the evil of the crucifixion. The suffering servant songs of the Prophet Isaiah express this same belief within the Hebrew tradition. In fact, one of the images the New Testament writers apply to Jesus is that of the suffering servant. Isaiah portrays God as saying to his Servant, "It is too light a thing that you should be my servant to raise up the tribes of Jacob and to restore the survivors of Israel; I will give you as a light to the nations, that my salvation may reach to the ends of the earth" (Isa. 49:6). A clear example of this theological motive for forgiveness occurs in the story of Joseph, to which I have referred. Joseph recognized his brothers' sin for what it was, but found the strength to set it aside through his conviction that God used their sin and his own suffering to fulfill the divine promises made to Abraham and his descendants that they would be a lasting people.

In his last novel, *Deep River,* the Japanese novelist, Shusako Endo, has his hero affirm that God has even used his sin to draw him closer to God. Speaking to the unbelieving woman, Mitsuko, who had many years earlier tempted him to have sex with her in order to destroy his faith, then rejected him, Otsu says "After everything that happened to me I began to think that God, like a magician, can turn any situation to the best advantage. Even our weaknesses and our sins" (Endo 1994, 63).

The ultimate motive for forgiveness in Christian theology is the conviction that God has forgiven us when we were sinners and that God loves both the good and the bad. If deeply experienced in a personal way, this conviction gives rise to gratitude. God does not love us because we are good; we are good because God loves us. In fact, we *are* because God loves us. God's love first brought us into existence and when we sinned, it offered us the gift of forgiveness. Christian scripture is clear on this point. First Paul, in his Letter to the Romans:

> For while we were still weak, at the right time Christ died for the ungodly. Indeed, rarely will anyone die for a righteous person—though perhaps for a good person someone might actually dare to die. But God proves his love for us in that while we still were sinners Christ died for us. Much more surely then, now that we have been justified by his blood, will we be saved through him from the wrath of God (Rom. 5:6–9).

The First Letter of John puts it this way: "In this is love, not that we loved God but that he loved us and sent his Son to be the atoning sacrifice for our

sins. Beloved, since God loved us so much, we also ought to love one another" (1 Jn. 4:10–11). In Luke's sermon on the plain, Jesus clearly states that
we should not just love those who love us, but should love even sinners. ". . .
Love your enemies, do good, and lend, expecting nothing in return. Your reward will be great, and you will be children of the Most High; for he is kind to
the ungrateful and the wicked. Be merciful as your Father is merciful. Forgive
and you will be forgiven; give, and it will be given to you" (Lk. 6:35–38a).

The knowledge that justice has been done can also open the way to forgiveness, though not necessarily. Sometimes seeing a criminal punished can
barely satisfy the desire for vengeance of the victim's family. But it may also
happen that the rendering of justice can fulfill a legitimate desire of injured
persons to see their cause vindicated and thus free them for compassion and
forgiveness. This may well have been the case in the story "Parish Turns
Murder to Grace." Justice and mercy are dialectically related. The Hebrew
Testament clearly shows the connection between justice and mercy in God.
Neither substitutes for the other, but both are connected. To substitute forgiveness for justice can be a terrible mistake. Solomon Schimmel tells the
story of a nun brutally raped who refused to turn in her assailant, reasoning
that her forgiveness would have more effect on him than the process of criminal justice. This seems misguided. Aside from the tension her forgiveness
would leave in her own consciousness, there is the issue of protecting society
from a dangerous person. Yet justice does not remove the need for forgiveness. Ultimately, only God knows how to perfectly balance justice and mercy
but the reconciliation of humans among themselves demands that they try to
achieve some kind of equilibrium.

The Difference between the Hebrew Bible and New Testament with Respect to Forgiveness

Since our study has been based on both the Hebrew and New Testament
treatments of compassion and forgiveness, it seems appropriate to conclude
this chapter with a comparison of their teachings on this subject. Christianity
differs from Judaism in three principal ways. First, the Christian God, while
still One, like the God of Israel, is also Three, Father, Son, and Spirit. Second, the Father out of compassion for his people, sends his Son to become
a human being. One can see the difference of the two testaments through a
comparison of the parable of the unproductive vineyard found first in Isaiah
and repeated in Matthew. To the owner's frustrated "what more was there
for me to do for my vineyard that I had not done?" of Isaiah's version (Isa.
5:4), Matthew's version responds: "Finally, he sent his son to them, thinking,
'They will respect my son'" (Matt. 21:37). The result was no more positive

in Matthew's version, for they killed the son, but the degree of commitment on the part of the owner was greater. The owner of the vineyard, in both cases God, submits in Matthew's version to violence and death through the death of his son who is also God. The degree of God's involvement, even to the point of a humiliating death, is so enormous that even Christians refer to it as the scandal of the Cross.

The third difference between Christianity and Judaism lies in Christianity's emphasis on forgiveness. Dennis Praeger, who describes himself as "a religious Jew who has come to admire many Christians and appreciate Christianity . . . as a holy path to God for non Jews," says that weekly conversations with Christians over a decade have convinced him that "aside from the divinity of Jesus, the greatest—and even more important—difference between Judaism and Christianity . . . is in their different understanding of forgiveness and, ultimately, how to react to evil" (Wiesenthal 1997, 216). Praeger separates the two differences, but they are connected. In Jesus, the divinity is subject to evil, not sovereign over it. He is the Suffering Servant and so can teach about forgiveness both by his example and by his words. By his own forbearance, by his willingness to suffer evil and unwillingness ever to inflict it—think of Jesus' refusal to resort to violence during his Passion (Matt. 26:51–54)—Jesus reveals the primacy of forgiveness. But he also instructs his disciples that they should forgive one another, not seven times, but seventy times seven times (Matt. 18).

While recognizing a basic truth in Praeger's view, it would be a mistake to exaggerate the difference between Christianity and Judaism with respect to forgiveness. The Hebrew Scripture may not have the same universal teaching about forgiveness of the neighbor under all circumstances, even for an unrepentant offender—admittedly an important difference—but it does present a sublime vision of divine and human compassion. The Law of Moses celebrates the importance of compassion; toward aliens, widows, orphans, in lending money to the poor, in taking the neighbor's cloak (Exod. 22:20–26), in the provisions for the poor in the Jubilee Year (Lev. 25), and in the prohibition against reaping the fields to the very edge or picking the vineyard bare, or picking up the grapes that have fallen so as to leave something for the poor (Lev. 19:9–10). Though compassion is not yet forgiveness, it is, as we have seen, a crucial mediator between sin and forgiveness. Israel's Scripture makes atonement for one's sins and the sins of one's household central to Israel's faith (Lev. 16:11) and urges God's people to love their neighbor as themselves (Lev. 19:18). And though sorrow for our own sins is not the same as forgiving sins committed against us, repentance even in Christianity is a normal requirement for forgiveness. And even if loving one's neighbor as one's self does not specify what one is to do in the face of injury, this equating of self-love and love for the other, lies at the foundation of forgiveness.

And the Hebrew Scripture does contain examples of forgiveness of injuries done, even in the absence of repentance from the offender. Esau forgives his younger twin Jacob for stealing the birthright that belongs to Esau as well as his father's blessing without any expression of sorrow from Jacob. Esau seems to have *forgotten* these injuries when he meets Jacob returning from the home of their uncle Laban and embraces him warmly (Gen. 33:4), a form of forgiveness. Joseph forgives his brothers who sold him to some passing merchants as an alternative to killing him (Gen. 45:4–8) even in the absence of any real repentance on their part. We will return to this example and particularly to the motive for Joseph's forgiveness. In the First book of Samuel, Abigail takes on herself the blame for the rude behavior of her husband, Nabal, and David grants it (1 Sam. 25:25–35). And we can even find in Judaism the general admonition to forgive even if the offender does not repent. In these cases, the offended person should "forgive him from the heart and leave vengeance to God" (*T. Gad* 6:7—cited in Gary Shogren, 1992, 837, col. 2). But we must still recognize that Jesus' teaching to forgive even one's enemies constitutes a distinguishing feature of Christianity.

The distinctiveness of Jesus' teaching about forgiveness is further underlined if we consider that Greek culture, for all its ethical greatness, did not arrive at a doctrine of forgiveness. An extended treatment of forgiveness in the poetry, drama, and philosophy of ancient Greece is beyond our scope but it is useful to note that Hellenism never developed a comprehensive and consistent teaching about forgiveness of the neighbor. The Judaic and Greek traditions, of course, differ radically. In Judaism, God was one and compassionate, in Greek literature the gods were multiple, caught up in rivalry, jealous of one another and human beings as well, and *therefore* no models for forgiveness. "Greek gods do not command us to forgive . . . they themselves are not conspicuously forgiving" (Dover 1991, 178). Christianity is obviously closer to the Jewish tradition than the Greek. The Christian teaching that human beings should forgive one another arises out of and completes Israel's teaching about the compassion of God and the compassion required of God's people.

CONCLUSION: DEFINING FORGIVENESS

Wide reading in the literature of forgiveness makes one wonder if we all define forgiveness in the same way. A touching article by the Holocaust survivor, Elie Wiesel, illustrates the point. In a *New York Times* op-ed piece of October 2, 1997, entitled "A Prayer for the Days of Awe," Wiesel states his intention to "make up" with God after being angry for more than fifty years. Wiesel makes clear that his problem is not with God, but with those who perpetrated the crimes. Much healing has taken place in the hearts of the survivors. He says of them:

> They learned to build on ruins. Family life was recreated. Children were born, friendships struck. They learned to have faith in their surroundings, even in their fellow men and women. Gratitude has replaced bitterness in their hearts. No one is as capable of thankfulness as they are. Thankful to anyone willing to hear their tales and become their ally in the battle against apathy and forgetfulness. For them every moment is grace.

This description seems to correspond to a first level of forgiveness, "laying down the burden" of injuries experienced so that they no longer prevent a person from living fully. Solomon Schimmel calls this "internal forgiveness." But Wiesel clearly does not see this renewal of life as a stage on the way to forgiveness. Immediately after his ringing affirmation that for the survivors "every moment is grace," he affirms just as clearly, "Oh, they do not forgive the killers and their accomplices, nor should they. Nor should you, Master of the Universe." What does Wiesel mean by forgiving? Does he mean to forget, to excuse, to justify? If he does, then one must agree no one should forgive the Nazis. But it may mean something else. Wiesel did not, as far as we know, have the experience described by Eric Lomax of meeting one of the people responsible for his suffering and finding him full of repentance and deep wounds of regret, vigorous in making amends as far as he could. Would he have forgiven in that case? It is reasonable to suspect he might have. At least many Jewish theologians would say he *should.* That could do much, as we saw in the case of Eric Lomax, to open the heart to forgiveness and justify it. But what if repentance on the part of the perpetrators does not take place?

This might also be the place where Jewish and Christian theologies of forgiveness differ. Wiesel's unwillingness to forgive is not just a case of personal inability. It is a theological position. In Christian theology, forgiveness has a certain absolute value independent of justice and independent of repentance. I say "a certain absolute value" because justice retains its importance in Christianity as does repentance. To substitute forgiveness for justice when justice is possible is a perversion of forgiveness. Dietrich Bonhoeffer, the Lutheran theologian who died in Flossenberg prison for opposing Hitler, might call it "cheap forgiveness," just as he talked about "cheap grace." It would be cheap because it tried to do away with the hard work of building a just society where people can live together in peace. Gregory Jones, in his book,

Embodying Forgiveness, talks about Bonhoeffer's notion of cheap grace, commenting that "Cheap grace denies any real need for deliverance from sin since it justifies the sin instead of the sinner" (Jones 1995, 13).

But forgiveness can be costly, even when justice cannot be achieved by the internal mastery it demands on the part of the one who forgives. And, admittedly, forgiving when repentance has not taken place, is an incomplete form of forgiveness. It does not affect the person who has done the injury. It does not arrive at reconciliation. But the change of heart and the substitution of good will for ill will still constitute real forgiveness. A person can, in the Christian theological tradition, stand in the truth, recognizing evil for what it is, and still forgive without illusion, without false expectations. Such forgiveness is profoundly liberating.

And still, the more we pursue the topic of forgiveness in Christianity, the more evident it becomes how deeply rooted Christian teaching is in the Hebrew tradition, in spite of Dennis Prager's insistence that Christianity and Judaism differ radically in their interpretations of the obligation to forgive (Wiesenthal 1998, 225 ff). It should be evident, from what has been said above, the extent to which the two traditions are intertwined with respect to their teaching on forgiveness. But the differences are real, too. And those differences, expressed especially in contemporary authors, have helped us define more clearly what is distinctive in the Christian view of forgiveness. Perhaps that difference can be stated most simply by saying that in Christianity one finds an impulsion toward forgiveness, almost a reckless abandon, a preference to err on the side of forgiving rather than risk a hardening of the heart. And the deepest motive for that propensity is God's own prodigality in forgiving, illustrated in the New Testament through Luke's story of the Prodigal Son (really the prodigal father). Earlier in his Gospel, Luke portrays Jesus as promising his followers that if they forgive their enemies and do good to those who persecute them they will be "children of the Most High; for he is kind to the ungrateful and the selfish. Be merciful, even as your Father is merciful" (Lk. 6:35–36). Yet even here we find ourselves returning to the God of the Hebrew Bible, whom the reluctant prophet Jonah fled because he was "a gracious God and merciful, slow to anger, and abounding in steadfast love . . ." (Jon. 4:2).

NOTES

1. This scriptural quotation is from the New Revised Standard Version Bible: Catholic Edition, copyright © 1989, 1993 National Council of the Churches of Christ in the United States of America. Used by permission. All rights reserved worldwide.

2. I will be following the excellent study of Boyd Taylor Coolman, "Hugh of St. Victor on 'Jesus Wept': Compassion as Ideal Humanitas," *Theological Studies,* vol 69, 2008, 528–557. Hugh's Latin text is not, as far as I know, translated. Translations for the Latin text are my own.

3. The word "piety" that would seem to be the most natural translation of *pietas* is misleading in this context. Piety in English, and also sometimes in Latin, means a relation of respect of a children to parents, of citizens to the state, or of believers toward God. A pious person in English is one who demonstrates an attitude of devotion to God. But the Latin *pietas* can also mean compassion as it clearly does in this treatise of Hugh of St. Victor.

Chapter Seven

René Girard

Original Sin as Covetousness

You shall not covet your neighbor's house; you shall not covet your neighbor's wife, or male or female slave, or ox, or donkey, or anything that belongs to your neighbor.

—Exodus, 20: 17, NRSV[1]

We have already considered what the inner structure of original sin might be. I suggested in the chapter on forgiveness that the wounding of four intimacies that define our relations to self, God, one another, and nature is one approach to analyzing the malaise we call original sin. The distortion of these intimacies gives rise to a seemingly infinite proliferation of evil choices. Another systematic distortion of our willing that seems to come out of our wounded intimacies is covetousness. René Girard, probably best known for his 1972 work, *Violence and the Sacred,* has elaborated a theory on the origins of religion in *mimetic rivalry,* the desire for what the others possess precisely because they possess it. This is what the Bible calls covetousness. Girard sees mimetic rivalry as equivalent to original sin. Mimetic violence, which arises from mimetic rivalry, leads to using mechanism of the scapegoat. Girard also argues that the way Greek mythology deals with this violence and its effects on society differs dramatically from the biblical treatment. This chapter will follow Girard's exploration of two texts, Sophocles' *Oedipus the King* and the biblical story of Joseph, to illustrate the difference between mythic and biblical approaches to violence and then turn to his interpretation of the crucifixion of Jesus. Finally, we will look at the theological significance of Girard's work, especially its relevance to the doctrine of original sin. A look at the general lines of Girard's thought will serve as background.

187

Though he claims that his studies are anthropological rather than theological, Girard also admits at certain points that his analysis brings him to a point where theology has to enter in to provide explanations not available through a study of the human. For instance, to explain the turnabout of Jesus' disciples after the Resurrection when before the Resurrection they had been almost completely overwhelmed by the violent contagion that led to Jesus' death, Girard admits that he must for the first time move beyond "a purely commonsensical and anthropological context" (Girard 2001, 189). We will come back to the connection between methods of anthropology and theology. For now, it is enough to say that the development of an anthropology of original sin—this, in effect, is what Girard is doing—provides a useful foundation for theological reflection.

THE DEVELOPMENT OF GIRARD'S THOUGHT

In a 1996 interview with James G. Williams, Girard speaks of "three great moments in the process of my thinking and writing" (Williams 1996, 262). The first of those moments was "mimetic desire and rivalry." The second was "the discovery of the scapegoat mechanism." The third moment was, in Girard's words, "when I began to see the uniqueness of the Bible, especially the Christian text, from the standpoint of the scapegoat theory" (Ibid., 262). A word about each of these "moments" offers the necessary foundation for understanding Girard's comparison/contrast of *Oedipus* and the Story of Joseph in Genesis and his analysis of the meaning of Gospel accounts of Jesus' Passion. An important clarification at this point will serve not only to put Girard's thought in its proper perspective but also to provide a helpful reminder of the place of a doctrine of original sin in the whole scheme of Christian anthropology and theology. The issue is a proper understanding of the term "desire." Though Girard begins with the notion of desire, in particular *mimetic* desire, he is himself not completely satisfied with the phrase. The word "desire," he says, tends, because of Freud, to connote "the sexual or erotic" (Williams 1996, 268). In his 1996 interview with James Williams, Girard suggests some possible substitutes for the phrase, "mimetic desire": "I don't know, perhaps 'drive,' or *elan vital,* or even Sartre's 'project.' Almost any word that could express the dynamism, the dynamics of the entire personality" (Ibid., 268). Cautious about using Sartre's term too exclusively, Girard also suggests that Kierkegaard's idea of subjectivity as passionate inwardness and choice might be helpful. ". . . Whatever the term," he says, "something bigger and other than 'desire' should be used" (Ibid., 268). The important point here is that desire need not designate something negative. At the root of the human spirit is desire, longing for fullness of life, a dynamism toward human realization. This distinction of a desire that lies at the heart of being human from what has traditionally been called inordinate or disordered desire, concupiscence, addictive attachment (May 1998, 3) is crucial for an appreciation of the doctrine of original sin. Original sin does not name what is deepest in the human being. The name for the deepest is original goodness; it entails longing for God.

In spite of these qualifications, it is still the phrase "mimetic desire" that Girard uses in his works as the foundational concept of his thought, even after this 1996 interview with Williams. So we need to understand its meaning. Human beings, according to Girard, are motivated less by the desire for certain objects in themselves than by the desire for those objects precisely as possessed by someone else. This is the "mimetic" half of the phrase "mimetic desire." According to Girard, we desire what the other has precisely because the other has it. In itself, this desiring of what the other has and what the other desires, especially if we understand mimetic desire as the fundamental dynamism of the human spirit, is a good thing. We become human precisely by imitating the qualities of persons who are our role models as human beings, parents, teachers, and all those who offer examples of human realization. By mimetic desire, the desire to mimic the achievements of others, we learn language, civilized customs, morality and everything that makes up the human world. Mimetic desire is paradoxically even the source of creativity. We not only imitate the objects produced by our models, we also imitate their creativity and, often enough, end up surpassing them in originality. Girard gives several examples, the Germans vis-à-vis the English, the Americans vis-à-vis Europe, Japan vis-à-vis the west (Girard 1994, 70–71). Mimetic desire becomes problematic when we desire to have what the other has, but cannot or will not give to us.

Girard's interpretation of Freud's famous Oedipus complex exemplifies mimetic desire. Freud says that the son is sexually drawn to his mother. Girard says that the son desires his mother, not directly as an object, but only through the mediation of the father whose wife she is. So it is a triangulated desire. But, though the father can share his language and his virtues with his son, he cannot share his wife in the way that the son wants her because that belongs only to the father and cannot be given to the son. This desire for what belongs to the other in such a way that it cannot be shared is the mimetic desire that gives rise to rivalry, and ultimately, when it becomes epidemic in society, to the "war of all against all."

The Bible, both Hebrew and Christian Testaments, calls this *covetousness*. Paul speaks of it in Romans. Girard cites the tenth commandment, which recognizes the destructiveness of mimetic desire precisely by forbidding it: "You shall not covet your neighbor's house; you shall not covet your neighbor's wife, or male or female slave, or ox, or donkey, or anything that belongs to your neighbor" (Exod. 20:17). Covetousness names the form of mimetic desire that gives rise to violence. The sixth, seventh, eighth, and ninth commands name in particular and forbid the forms of violence that lie behind the tenth commandment's prohibition of covetousness. "You shall not murder. You shall not commit adultery. You shall not steal. You shall not bear false witness against your neighbor" (Exod. 13–16). We murder, steal, commit adultery, and bear false witness because we covet. And, of course, these five negative commandments follow on five commands about right worship, honoring God's name, respect for parents, and keeping holy the Sabbath. Covetousness is both the *originating* sin that gives rise to other sins and the *originated* sin that resides in us as a condition. This mimetic desire, when it becomes generalized in society, gives rise to violent contagion, everyone wanting what the other has and doing whatever they need to do to get it.

The Discovery of the Scapegoat Mechanism

The issue then is how to control the violent contagion that comes from generalized mimetic desire. When violence becomes generalized, giving rise to the war of all against all, some mechanism must be found to resolve the crisis. That mechanism is sacrifice, human or animal. Sacrifice can be made for almost any purpose, to induce rain, for instance, or bring fine weather (Girard 1977, 8). But there is, says Girard "a common denominator that determines the efficacy of all sacrifices and that becomes increasingly apparent as the institution grows in vigor. This common denominator is internal violence— all the dissensions, rivalries, jealousies, and quarrels within the community that the sacrifices are designed to suppress. The purpose of the sacrifice is to restore harmony to the community, to reinforce the social fabric" (Ibid.).

As long as the sacrificial mechanism works, society remains at peace. When the sacrificial mechanism breaks down and the sacrificing of ritual victims no longer keeps violence at bay, the result is a sacrificial crisis. The sacrificial crisis is resolved by the mechanism of scapegoating. Since the generalized violence threatens to destroy the social fabric, someone is designated as uniquely responsible for the breakdown and killed or exiled, carrying away with him or her the guilt of the whole society. The scapegoat can be an individual or a group. Mythology is full of examples, the story of Oedipus being one of them. So is modern history. The extermination of the Jews during the Nazi regime is an example, as is the false accusation of Dreyfus in nineteenth century France. Girard mentions Joan of Arc, regarded as a demon by the English and a quasi-divine being by the French. The Church's canonization of

Joan "acknowledges another form of relationship to the supernatural which is different from the demonized-divinized scapegoat" (Williams 1996, 263). It is crucially important in Girard's analysis that in mythology the scapegoat is never seen *as a scapegoat,* never seen, that is, as someone arbitrarily chosen to be sacrificed in order to restore calm in society. Mythology always presents the scapegoat as actually guilty. We will see that as we look at the example of Oedipus. In fact, the scapegoat mechanism always needs to be hidden whether in mythology or in social life.

In mythology we find a second moment in the scapegoat mechanism; the scapegoat, once sacrificed, becomes divinized because of the healing value his death or exile has had for the community. So the scapegoat goes from being the unique cause of violence in the community to being the savior who restores peace. Since the scapegoat has saved society by being ejected from it, he becomes a savior figure.

The Uniqueness of the Bible with Respect to Violence

The final "moment" in Girard's intellectual development was his recognition of the uniqueness of the Bible with respect to the scapegoat mechanism. Whereas mythology disguises the scapegoat mechanism, the Bible brings it to light and shows the scapegoat for what he or she is, someone arbitrarily accused and loaded with guilt in order to draw off the infection that the community is experiencing. We will see this difference between mythology and the Bible illustrated in the stories of Oedipus and Joseph. Girard's thought in this respect also allows him to interpret the sacrifice of Jesus on the Cross in a way that rescues it from certain Christian interpretations that transform it into yet another example of the scapegoat mechanism. Girard claims to be searching "for the anthropology of the Cross, which turns out to rehabilitate orthodox theology" (Williams 1996, 288). We will return to Girard's treatment of the Passion of Jesus in considering the theological implications of his thought. Now we turn to Girard's treatment of the myth of Oedipus and the biblical story of Joseph as illustrations of his theory concerning the difference between mythical and biblical treatments of violence.

Perhaps it is already obvious to readers that Girard's approach to myth differs significantly from Ricoeur's. We are dealing with a difference not a contradiction. Ricoeur, as we have seen, in an attempt to recover the truth of the Adamic Myth, contrasts mythical narration with historical. Myth deals not with events that happened in a particular times and places that we can coordinate with our historical chronology and the geography of our globe. For Ricoeur, myth uses symbols to reveal meaning. Ricoeur regards myth in a positive light. The truth of myth is just as true as the truth of history. In some ways it is more true, because it deals with meaning and not just facts. And of course myth and history overlap in such a way that it is sometimes difficult to distinguish them. That is the task of historians. Without ever denying the point of Ricoeur's comparison of history and myth, Girard takes a different approach. For him, myth serves as a way of disguising the truth of mimetic rivalry by disguising the scapegoat mechanism as a justifiable punishment of persons seen as responsible for the evils afflicting their societies. In reality, these persons, no more guilty than anyone else, are arbitrarily selected as victims and punished in order to restore harmony in society. Our examples will illustrate how it works.

OEDIPUS THE KING AND JOSEPH

Oedipus the King

Sophocles' *Oedipus the King,* as a tragic treatment of an earlier myth, is already a transformation of that myth. The myth on which the tragedy is built tells the story of how the king and queen of Thebes, learning through an oracle that their infant son is fated to kill his father and marry his mother, expose him to die on a mountain top. But their scheme is frustrated without their knowledge when a shepherd finds the baby and gives him to another shepherd who takes him to the home of the King and Queen of Corinth where Oedipus grows up thinking that he is their natural son. When Oedipus grows up, learning from the oracle that he will kill his father and marry his mother, he flees his home in Corinth. On the road, he meets a man with a retinue who prevents him from passing. Enraged, Oedipus kills the man who is actually his father though he does not know it. As Oedipus is approaching Thebes, he hears of the riddle of the Sphinx, solves it, and, as his prize, receives the reward of marrying the widowed queen of Thebes, his mother. All of these events have already taken place before the action of Sophocles' play. The play begins in the midst of a plague afflicting the city of Thebes. Oedipus promises to find the cause and sends to the oracle to find out how to proceed. Sophocles' tragedy, built on this myth, tells of how the adult Oedipus, now king of Thebes, comes to find out that he is the guilty party causing the plague infecting his kingdom, guilty not only of having killed his father but also of marrying his mother. The story of the myth and the story of the tragedy are different but intertwined narratives. There is in fact a tension between the inner logic of the myth and the inner logic of the tragedy. According to Girard, Sophocles' tragic interpretation of the Oedipus myth represents "a progress in the direction of mythical dismantling" (Girard 1977, 84). But it is a dismantling that never, according to Girard, fully exposes the scapegoat mechanism disguised by the myth.

Let us explore a little further the tension between the tragedy and the myth. The myth presents Oedipus as uniquely guilty of the terrible crimes of patricide and incest. True, Oedipus has been predestined to these violations and in that sense we might think of him as innocent. But, according to the myth, he is the cause of the city's plague. What never appears in the myth is any suggestion that Oedipus might have been a scapegoat, no guiltier than anyone else, who has been arbitrarily designated as a substitute victim whose death will rid the community of the violence of all against all. This is the logic of the myth. It disguises the scapegoat mechanism. The logic of the tragedy, says Girard, introduces a dismantling tension that moves in the direction of exposing the hidden logic of the myth. It goes in the direction of exposing, without actually achieving the exposure toward which it tends.

What does the tragedy reveal that the myth conceals? This is the crucial point of Girard's analysis. Sophocles, through the dialectic of discovery that is the subject of his tragedy, reveals the generalized violence infecting the social fabric, a generalized violence that lies hidden in the myth. That violence emerges in the exchanges between Tiresias and Oedipus and between Creon and Oedipus. Sophocles' story also shows a certain reciprocity between two manifestations of violence: on one side, the murderous intent of Laius, Oedipus' father, in exposing his son to death on a mountain top as well as Laius' violent thrusting aside of the stranger—who is actually his son—at the crossroads and, on the other side, the act of murder committed by Oedipus against the person who has treated him so rudely, a person who is actually his father. Both men are guilty of violence.

An important aspect of the violence is the destroying of distinctions essential for the social order; the characters in Sophocles' *Oedipus* mutually violate the distinctions, among them: the distinction between the seer and ordinary citizens, between the king and his subjects, between a husband and his brother-in-law. Oedipus disrespects the seer Tiresias and hurls insults at him; Tiresias responds with rage at Oedipus the King; Oedipus treats his bother-in-law with suspicious contempt, and Creon reciprocates with angry words. This violating of established differences is the heart of the sacrificial crisis which can be defined as "a crisis of distinctions—that is a crisis affecting the cultural order" (Girard 1977, 49). These distinctions are for Girard essential for the cultural order which is "nothing more than a regulated system of distinctions in which the differences among individuals are used to establish their 'identity'" (Ibid.).

Thus, a close look at Sophocles' tragedy makes it clear that Oedipus is not the only one guilty of violence. But his is the only violence that is punished and we are left at the end of the play with the conviction that Oedipus got what he deserved and the others are vindicated. In other words, Sophocles does not push the indications of generalized violence evident in his play to their logical conclusion, namely that Oedipus is no guiltier than anyone else, that, in fact the plague under which the city is suffering is not just physical disease, but a breakdown of culture, a breakdown to which all the key players contribute. The crucial point here for our purpose is that the myth hides the fact of the epidemic quality of violence in society and designates one character alone, the scapegoat, as uniquely guilty.

The Story of Joseph

A look at the biblical story of Joseph reveals how differently the Bible approaches the scapegoat mechanism. In a 1985 essay, "The Myth of Oedipus, the Truth of Joseph," Girard compares and contrasts the two stories. He is at pains to note similarities and differences. The stories are similar in that "Both heroes were rejected by their families, Oedipus by his parents, Joseph by his brothers" (Girard 2004, 107). Both were cast out of the community to which they belonged by birth and the community into which they had been adopted. Oedipus and Joseph both became "highly successful immigrants" (Ibid.) through their skill in interpreting riddles. Oedipus saved the people of Thebes from the plague and became their leader by solving the riddle of the Sphinx. Joseph interpreted Pharaoh's dream and became the leader of the Egyptians, a position that enabled him to save both Egyptians and Israelites from the disaster of famine. Though Joseph, unlike Oedipus, never committed a crime, his brush with seduction at the hands of Potiphar's wife describes a situation that, for Girard, at least invokes comparison with Oedipus' crime of incest. Even though Joseph rebuffs the advances of his Egyptian master's wife, he ends up in jail because Potiphar believes his wife's false accusations rather than Joseph's denial. So both Joseph and Oedipus more than once undergo a kind of expulsion, once from their native land, once from their country of adoption.

Having set out the points of comparison, Girard poses a simple question whose answer leads to a clear statement of the difference between the two stories: "Do the communities to which Oedipus and Joseph belong act justly when they expel these heroes from their midst" (Ibid., 108)? The question never really comes up in the tragedy of Oedipus because the answer, coming from the mythical account on which the tragedy rests, is always taken for granted; yes, the community is justified. It is equally clear in the story of Joseph that the hero is unjustly punished. For Girard the difference is crucial. Though both stories might be considered mythical in that they do not narrate historically verifiable facts, both are not mythical in terms of their ethical content. The ethical content of the myth of Oedipus is the presumption of a unique burden of guilt on the hero's part. The ethical content of the biblical story, whether historical or fictional, is the unjust suffering of the hero. Basing his categories on this ethical difference, Girard distinguishes between "mythical" and "biblical" stories. Girard finds in the story of Joseph a deliberate critique of myth (Girard 2001, 112). The story not only manifests the dynamic of persecution against the hero but, at the end, presents the only response capable of stopping the spiral of violence, Joseph's pardon of his brothers. That pardon, as we have seen, comes about not because the brothers deserved it, but because Joseph saw the redemptive hand of God at work in their evil deed: "But now do not be distressed, and do not reproach yourselves for having sold me here. It was really for the sake of saving lives that God sent me here ahead of you" (Gen. 45:5). Mimetic rivalry and scapegoating work against forgiveness; they are its opposite. The scapegoat temporarily relieves the tension cause by generalized violence in society but ultimately gives rise to a cycle of violence that never ends. Forgiveness heals mimetic rivalry at its root.

One might ask about the significance of this difference between mythical and biblical accounts. Girard's answer is resoundingly clear:

> Far from being minor, the divergence of the biblical account and the myth of Oedipus, or whatever other myth, is so great that no greater difference could exist. It's the difference between a world where arbitrary violence triumphs without being recognized and a world where this same violence is identified, denounced, and finally forgiven. It's the difference between truth and deception, both of them absolute. Either we succumb to the contagion of the mimetic snowballing effect and fall into the lie of victimization, with mythology, or we resist this contagion and rise into the truth of the innocent victim with the Bible (Girard 2001, 114).

THE THEOLOGICAL RELEVANCE OF GIRARD'S THOUGHT

Girard's Anthropology as Foundation for Theology

The difference between the way myth and scripture treat the scapegoat mechanism is admirably illustrated by the stories of Oedipus and Joseph. More central to Girard's thought is the role of Christ's Passion as a reversal of the tendency of myth to disguise society's penchant for scapegoats. The examples of Joseph and Jesus take Girard up to the realm of theology, if not into it. Girard is always respectful of the difference between anthropology and theology, but he also claims that his anthropological approach offers something valuable to theology. While acknowledging that what makes Jesus' suffering unique "is not the violence, but the fact that the victim is the Son of God, which is certainly the main thing from the standpoint of our redemption" (Girard 2001, 43), Girard affirms at the same time that "if we neglect the anthropological substructure of the Passion, we will miss the true theology of the Incarnation, which makes little sense without this anthropological basis" (Ibid., 43–44). Girard sees his thought as giving specific content to an idea of Simone Weil: "She held that even before presenting a 'theory of God,' a *theology,* the Gospels offer a 'theory of man,' an anthropology" (Ibid., 44). Girard summarizes: "My research is only indirectly theological, moving as it does across the field of a Gospel anthropology neglected by theologians. To increase its effectiveness, I have pursued it as long as possible without postulating the reality of the Christian God. No appeal to the supernatural should break the thread of the anthropological analysis" (Girard 2001, 192–93).

But though Girard's thought is mainly anthropological, his anthropology leaves room for theology, even points to the theological and never presents itself as a substitute for theological categories that are always breaking in to the openings provided by his anthropology. We have already seen Girard's admission that to explain the disciples' return to and faithful following of Jesus after their poor showing during the time of the Passion he had to move beyond "a purely commonsensical and anthropological context" (Girard 2001, 189). Other examples of theological categories appear in Girard's work.

In his essay on Proust, for instance, that serves as an introduction to a work he edited, *Proust: A Collection of Critical Essays,* referring to the conversion experienced by the hero of Proust's great novel, *In Search of Lost Time,* a conversion described entirely in secular terms by Proust himself, Girard comments that "The only possible analogy for the Proustian experience has been noted by Georges Poulet, and it is that of Christian grace" (Girard 1962, 11). In answer to those who object to such an interpretation, claiming that Proust himself "never made any effort to live according to Christian morality and probably did not even believe in God," Girard answers: "This biographical fact does not, however, alter the aesthetic one, which is simply that, although Proust was an agnostic, his masterpiece espouses the Christian structure of redemption more perfectly than the carefully planned efforts of many conscientious Christian artists" (Ibid.). We now turn to some areas where Girard's anthropology has relevance for theology.

Mimetic Rivalry as Original Sin

We considered earlier in this chapter the important distinction between mimetic desire as a fundamental dynamism that, on the one hand, opens the way for basic human achievements, such as learning language and developing the skills that belong to civilized life and includes a restless longing for the vision of God, and, on the other hand, mimetic desire as distorted into mimetic rivalry or covetousness, as Scripture calls it. Girard's work is concerned principally with the second kind of mimetic desire, the kind that leads to the war of all against all and, ultimately, to the mechanism of scapegoating.

The question I raise here is how we are to understand the difference between these two kinds of mimetic desire, one positive and constructive, the other divisive and destructive. To answer this question, we have to look more closely at Girard's characterization of mimetic rivalry. The key point here is connected with Girard's own conversion and with the conversion process he came to recognize as necessary for the writing of a really great work of literature. In responding to a question about his own conversion experience, to which we will return, Girard admits that he began work on his first book, *Deceit, Desire, and the Novel*, "very much in the pure demystification mode: cynical, destructive, very much in the spirit of atheistic intellectuals of the time" (Williams 1996, 283). He was engaged in "debunking." The recognition of mimesis "is a great debunking tool because it deprives us moderns of the one thing we think we still have left, our individual desire" (Ibid., 283–84). Girard attributes to this debunking character of his first book the lingering feeling on the part of some that his concept of mimesis is destructive.

At this point in his interview with Williams, Girard makes a cryptic statement that he develops more fully in other places. "Yet I like to think that if you take this notion [the concept of mimesis] as far as you possibly can, you go through the ceiling, as it were, and discover what amounts to original sin" (Ibid., 284). In other words, the difference between mimetic desire as ordered to the human good and mimetic desire as destructive rivalry is another name for the distortion of human nature traditionally called original sin. As we have seen, original sin is the Christian conception of a shared guilt or, better still, a solidarity in sin that can be traced back to the disobedience of Adam and Eve described in chapter three of Genesis. Girard points out that the Hebrew word translated as "covet" in the tenth commandment—"You shall not covet your neighbor's house," etc. (Exod. 20:17)—simply means desire. The same word, says Girard, "designates the desire of Eve for the prohibited fruit, the desire leading to original sin" (Girard 2001, 7). Girard makes it clear he believes that this "desire" is universal: "The notion that the Decalogue devotes its supreme commandment, the longest of all, to the prohibition of a marginal desire reserved for a minority is hardly likely. The desire prohibited by the tenth commandment must be the desire of all human beings—in other words, simply desire as such" (Ibid., 8). Girard makes it clear that he is not referring to the good desire that grounds human achievement, but to the desire that is rivalry. "If individuals are naturally inclined to desire what their neighbors possess, or to desire what their neighbors even simply desire, this means that rivalry exists at the very heart of human social relationships" (Ibid., 8). And, indeed, the text of Genesis 3 presents the serpent's temptation of Eve as an incitement to mimetic rivalry; ". . . your eyes will be opened and you will be like gods who know what is good and what is bad." And the scapegoating mechanism follows. When God confronts Adam and Eve after they have both eaten of the fruit, Adam shifts the blame to Eve, who, in turn shifts it to the serpent.

We can easily recognize the scapegoat mechanism at work in others, catching them in the act of laying blame on others; it is not so easy to recognize it at work in ourselves. Thus, the concept of mimetic desire itself can be falsified by finding in it something that affects others but does not affect me. This possibility of self-deception regarding mimetic desire is based on the fact that the phenomenon, in order to be effective, depends on remaining hidden. The exposing of mimetic rivalry and the mechanism of scapegoating that accompanies it is also a disarming of these practices. The genius of the Bible, especially the New Testament, is that, whereas myth disguises the scapegoating mechanism, the Bible exposes it for what it is.

Girard's appeal to the theological notion of original sin complements his anthropological analysis and subjects it to a more comprehensive interpretation. In another book length interview, Girard professes his belief that mimetic rivalry constitutes a significant component, *un bon morceau*, of original sin. (Girard 1994, 54). His view of original sin and its function in society occupies the center of Girard's thought. Responding to the accusation made against him that he is *frenetique,* because he has no illusions à la Rousseau about the natural goodness of man, Girard says: "nothing teaches moderation like the theory of original sin, which is always just the opposite of what its critics say of it" (Girard 1994, 69). It is in fact belief in the natural goodness of man, a belief always disappointed in the real world, that ends up in the search for scapegoats (Ibid.).

Girard's thought here might remind us of those earlier believers in the natural goodness of man whom we have considered before, Donatus and Pelagius, both of whom fell into controversy with the great articulator of original sin, Augustine of Hippo. As comforting as their theories seemed at first glance, affirming as they did the capacity of humans to do whatever they knew to be good and set out to do, both of these men turned out to be harsh critics of human weakness. We have already considered Augustine's theory of original sin. It seems at first to be needlessly pessimistic, but turns out to be deeply compassionate toward human weakness. Augustine can be compassionate precisely because he knows the weakness that afflicts all humans. We have already seen Peter Brown's contrast of Pelagius' thought with Augustine's. To Pelagius' claim that all sins are a form of pride, Augustine responds, "Many sins are committed through pride, but not all happen proudly . . . they happen so often by ignorance, by human weakness; many are committed by men weeping and groaning in their distress" (Brown 2000, 350–351).

Anthropology of the Cross as Foundation for Theology of the Cross

Just as Girard provides an anthropological foundation for the doctrine of original sin, he offers an anthropology of the Cross. For some time, Girard resisted the notion of taking Jesus as a scapegoat, but by the time of his interview with James Williams he was willing to see Christ as a sacrificial victim (Williams 1996, 280). But Girard posits a difference between Jesus as scapegoat and other scapegoats. He agrees that Jesus is a scapegoat for all, "except now in reverse fashion, for theologically considered, the initiative comes from God rather than simply from the human beings with their scapegoat mechanism" (Ibid.). Girard clarifies what he means by citing Paul's Second Letter to the Corinthians: "For our sake [God] made him to be sin who did not know sin, so that we might become the righteousness of God in him" (2 Cor. 5:21). This position that Girard came to later in his life can only be understood by setting it in the context of his earlier resistance to seeing Jesus as scapegoat. Taking Jesus as a scapegoat for the sins of humans, as some Christian interpretations suggest, places God the Father in the position of an instigator of the scapegoat mechanism, like the Greek gods. For Girard, Jesus' death is rather the unveiling of the mechanism of scapegoating itself. The leaders of the people made a scapegoat of Jesus, accusing him of trying to incite the crowds. God's will was that Jesus should submit to this process, allowing himself to be a victim rather than victimize others. But the Father of Jesus did not initiate or approve the process. "There is nothing in the Gospels," says Girard, "to suggest that God causes the mob to come together against Jesus. Violent contagion is enough" (Girard 2001, 21). A recent work influenced by Girard expresses the same idea: "Jesus' crucifixion in Jerusalem was neither a historical accident nor a death wish on Jesus' part to fulfill God's need for a victim-substitute to discharge divine wrath" (Heim 2006, 101). God the Father is not the originator of the scapegoat mechanism or its ally; the God of the Bible always takes the side of the victim.

Just as Paul had seen the obedience of Christ as the reversal of the disobedience of Adam and Eve, Girard sees the Passion of Christ as the undoing of the scapegoat mechanism. Jesus' submission to violence as a way of overcoming the cycles of violence played out in the human tendency to blame and punish others for our own sins, shows how deeply rooted this original sin is and how radical must be the redemptive action that frees us. Jesus' teaching is, of course, rich in warnings against the scapegoat mechanism—judge not and you will not be judged, do not condemn and you will not be condemned, forgive and you will be forgiven (Matt. 5:21–26, 38–48; Lk. 6). But Jesus' actions are more powerful than his words. His willingness to be a victim rather than to victimize, to suffer death rather than to inflict it, not only gives us an example to follow but brings about our redemption.

The Resurrection

Girard's references to the resurrection occur at each stage of his intellectual development. In the first stage, presented above, Girard's discovery of mimetic rivalry through his analysis of literature, resurrection is identified with a kind of conversion experience undergone by authors. In fact, conversion and resurrection become virtually identical in Girard's thought. James Williams, during his interview with Girard published in 1996, responds to Girard's discussion of his own conversion that culminated at Easter time, by a comment: "So resurrection and conversion are difficult to distinguish . . ." To which Girard responds, "Conversion is Resurrection." Though these two topics are intimately connected in Girard's thought, it seems to me more convenient to develop them separately. We will come back to this aspect of resurrection in the discussion on conversion below.

Girard identifies the second phase of his thought as the discovery of the scapegoat mechanism. In this stage, resurrection consists of the transformation of the victim after the violence inflicted on him or her. It is a "return of beneficence following the paroxysm of malevolence" (Girard 1977, 247). One can see this in the case of Oedipus. Once exiled from the community, he undergoes a restoration, described in *Oedipus at Colonnus*, that turns him into a benevolent force. But it is not only the victim who is transformed. The death of the victim is for the community. "The surrogate victim dies so that the entire community, threatened by the same fate, can be reborn in a new or renewed cultural order" (Ibid., 255). Of course, the renewal is never definitive because the blaming of the sacrificial victim only disguises the generalized violence that exists in the community. Sophocles' *Antigone* tells the story of Oedipus' children and his brother-in-law, now become king, in which violence has again emerged. But at least we find a temporary resurrection that restores peace for a time. Girard's discussion of the ritual violence of shamanistic initiation in certain cultures also belongs to this second phase. The shaman submits to ritual violence that imitates the violence done to mythic characters important to the shaman's culture. "Dismemberment [which the shaman undergoes ritually] is emblematic of triumph and resurrection. . . ." The neophyte experiences the same metamorphosis as the mythical creatures whose help he will later require in the exercise of his shamanistic functions" (Ibid., 286).

Finally, in the third phase of his intellectual development—the recognition of the difference between mythical and biblical treatments of violence— Girard discusses the resurrection that is a central doctrine of Christian faith. Two elements are important in Girard's treatment, first the *truth* of the resurrection, then its *meaning*. For Girard, the resurrection of Jesus is an objective fact, even if "it is visible or comprehensible only to those who are converted or in the process of converting . . ." (Williams 1996, 280). Girard disagrees with Bultmann and others who interpret the resurrection as an event that occurred only in the subjective consciousness of the apostles (Ibid., 280). So, for Girard, the "truth" of the resurrection lies in its objectivity as an event that occurred outside the consciousness of those who witnessed it.

As he enters into the discussion of meaning of the resurrection, Girard acknowledges that he is passing from anthropology to theology. "Until now I have always been able to find plausible responses to the question posed in this book [*I See Satan Fall Like Lightning*] within a purely commonsensical and anthropological context. This time, however, it is *impossible*" (Girard 2001, 189). It is clear also, in spite of what Girard says here, that his interpretation retains its anthropological significance even as it enters the realm of theology. First, the resurrection has a cosmic significance. "It is the spectacular sign of the entrance into the world of a power superior to violent contagion" (Girard 2001, 189). The resurrection is the only power able to break the power of violent contagion. This is the first aspect of the meaning of the resurrection, its cosmic power against victimization.

The second aspect of its meaning, this one not cosmic but occurring in the smaller sphere of a particular community, appears in the effect of the resurrection on the disciples themselves. Very simply, it transformed them from reluctant witnesses to the Passion into courageous preachers of the Gospel. They had fallen asleep in the Garden of Gethsemane, Peter three times denied any association with Jesus, and the others were barely visible during their master's ordeal. The Resurrection "enables [the disciples] to recognize what they had not recognized before and to reproach themselves for their pathetic flight in the preceding days" (Ibid., 189). The power that awakened the disciples was the Holy Spirit. "It would be false . . . to say that the disciples 'regained possession of themselves': it is the Spirit of God that possesses them and does not let them go" (Ibid.). Girard focuses on the examples of Peter and Paul, both of whom went through a conversion experience that broke their connection with the contagious force of violence and liberated them for compassion and forgiveness. In these instances, Girard's phrase, "conversion is resurrection" has an obvious and literal meaning. We now turn to Girard's wider discussion of conversion, including his own. The connection with resurrection is always an aspect of conversion, *metanoia,* turning away from sin, escaping from the hidden influence of mimetic rivalry.

The Necessity of Conversion for a Correct Understanding of Mimetic Rivalry

Girard's idea of conversion relates closely to his concept of original sin, for mimetic rivalry in Girard's thought is original sin. For Girard, essential notes of original sin are its universality and its hiddenness. Original sin afflicts everyone. We cannot say that some people are guilty of mimetic rivalry and others not. No one escapes the web. Yet, though this universality belongs to the internal logic of mimetic rivalry, we do not want to acknowledge, even once we have recognized the idea conceptually, that we too are guilty of putting it into practice. It takes a conversion to awaken people to the reality of disordered affection in themselves. Girard describes conversion as an awakening to the realization that I am not a completely righteous person, as the Pharisee of Luke's Gospel thought he was, condemned to live with the unrighteous: "God, I thank you that I am not like other people, thieves, rogues, adulterers, or even like this tax collector" (Lk. 18:11). Rather, we should make our own the prayer of the tax collector: " . . . who would not even look up to heaven, but was beating his breast and saying, 'God, be merciful to me, a sinner'" (Lk. 18:13).

Girard came to this insight, as a kind of intellectual conversion, when he was working on the last chapter of his first book, *Deceit, Desire, and the Novel.* He noticed that some great novelists moved from an earlier conception of their work to a later one. The first draft was "an attempt at self-justification" (Williams 1996, 184) either focusing on "a wicked hero, who is really the writer's scapegoat, his mimetic rival or "a knight in shining armor, with whom the writer identifies" (Ibid., 284). This first project fails somehow and the author realizes that "The self-justification he had intended in his distinction between good and evil will not stand self-examination. The novelist comes to realize that he has been the puppet of his own devil. He and his enemy are truly indistinguishable" (Ibid., 284). This realization is "shattering to the vanity and pride of the writer" (Ibid.). This experience, which Girard calls "an existential downfall," is often enough "written symbolically, as illness or death, in the conclusion" (Ibid.).

Girard illustrates his point through Marcel Proust's monumental novel, *In Search of Lost Time*, which corresponds to what Girard calls above a "later conception" of his work. The "earlier conception" was Proust's never finished *Jean Santeuil*, in which the hero is an idealized figure exempt from the ills that Proust finds present in the society of which he is writing. But, says Girard, "Jean Santeuil's apparent health and rationality stem from Proust's own failure to *perceive* the irrational and magical elements of his own approach to reality" (Girard 1962, 8). The later conception embodied in the seven-volume novel recognized as Proust's paramount achievement, *In Search of Lost Time,* is expressed in the last volume of that work, *Le Temps Retrouvé,* in a kind of mystical experience the hero undergoes. Following on a period of deep desolation in which the narrator/hero of Proust's work doubted not only his own vocation as a writer, but even the whole project of literature itself, the hero experiences a moment of enlightenment that completely restores his confidence. In the passage that follows this "conversion" experience, Proust comes to see the vanity of the social upper classes that he has been cultivating all through his life up to this moment. In exposing the vanity of the aristocracy and upwardly-mobile bourgeoisie, Proust is also exposing his own vanity for having invested so much of his time with them. His "conversion" has a double effect: it opens up for him the deepest source of his own inspiration and, at the same time, reveals the mechanisms by which he has been escaping the responsibility of living out of that inspiration.

Important to note is the fact that the last volume of Proust's *In Search of Last Time*, the volume that contains the definitive conversion experience— other versions of this experience had occurred in earlier volumes—was written before the volumes that precede it in the novel. Thus, the experience of enlightenment described in *Time Regained* took place before the writing of the novel as a whole. It seems clear that his deep sadness at the death of his mother in 1905, three years before he began work on the work that established him as a great writer, was part of the malaise out of which his conversion drew him. Moreover, Proust was deeply discouraged that as he was nearing his fortieth birthday he had still not even begun to achieve his life-long dream of becoming a great writer. This profound discouragement in Proust's own life provides the background for the despair followed by liberating hope described in *Time Regained.*

Girard found similar experiences in the work of Dostoyevsky and Cervantes' *Don Quixote*. "And so," he concludes, "the career of the great novelist is dependent on a conversion, and even if it is not made completely explicit, there are symbolic allusions to it at the end of the novel" (Williams 1996, 284). Such allusions are "at least implicitly religious" (Ibid.). As he wrote the last chapter of this his first book, Girard realized that he himself was undergoing the kind of experience he had found in the novels he was discussing. This "intellectual-literary conversion," though enjoyable, did not lead to any change in his life until he found out that he had some cancerous tissue, which he had removed. So his intellectual conversion, which he called "a very comfortable experience, self-indulgent even" (Ibid., 285), turned from being an aesthetic experience to a religious one. He went to confession, had his children baptized, and had his marriage blessed by a priest. Girard gave a longer account of his conversion in his 1994 interviews with Michael Treguer (Girard 1994).

Compassion and Forgiveness

Finally, we return to the theme that forms the leitmotiv of this book, the connection of original sin with compassion and forgiveness. We return for a moment to two examples Girard uses to make clear the essential difference of the mythic and biblical approaches to violence: the stories of Oedipus and Joseph. As we saw earlier in this chapter, the myth of Oedipus, and Sophocles' tragedy based on it, conceal the injustice of punishment Oedipus undergoes. The story of Joseph, on the other hand, makes the injustice clear from the beginning, unmasking the scapegoat mechanism. The principal point at this stage of our analysis is that Joseph's story not only manifests the injustice of Joseph's treatment by his brothers, but reveals the redemptive moment that arises from this manifestation. The difference between the mythical and biblical stories, says Girard, is a difference between worlds: "It's the difference between a world where arbitrary violence triumphs without being recognized and a world where this same violence is identified, denounced, and finally forgiven" (Girard 2001, 114). The redemptive moment, the moment that puts an end to the cycle of violence, is forgiveness.

As in all genuine forgiveness, Joseph's exoneration—literally, taking away the burden—of his brothers entails compassion. What the text gives us is Joseph's expression of compassion that implies forgiveness. After revealing to his brothers who he is—"I am your brother Joseph"—Joseph reassures them. "But now do not be distressed, and do not reproach yourselves for having sold me here" (Gen. 45:5a). Joseph's exoneration is the exact opposite of the scapegoat mechanism. The scapegoat mechanism concentrates fault and lays it on the shoulder of one person. Compassion mitigates fault. In this case the mitigating factor is Joseph's recognition of God's providential intention, which Joseph's brothers carried out even through their unjust treatment of their brother: "It was really for the sake of saving lives that God sent me here ahead of you" (Gen. 45:5b).

Girard refers to an even more compelling example, this one from the New Testament, of compassion as an antidote to the scapegoat mechanism. The story from John 8 of the woman taken in adultery shows how Jesus reverses the violent contagion that would have produced a stoning. It is crucial, says Girard, that Jesus prevents the throwing of the first stone. That first stone is what unleashes the contagious violence that follows on the first act of violence. After writing on the ground—probably the sins of those who wanted to throw stones—Jesus says, "Let the one among you who is without sin be the first to throw a stone at her." Here we have the "identification and denunciation" of the scapegoat mechanism at work in the situation. Jesus exposes the hypocrisy of the accusers. Then, when all have gone away without condemning her, Jesus manifests his compassion and forgiveness: "Neither do I condemn you. Go [and] from now on do not sin any more" (Jn. 8:11b). The text seems to imply that Jesus' command carried with it the power to carry it out. This empowerment would be the subject of Augustine's prayer in the *Confessions,* "Give me the grace to do as you command, and command me to do what you will" (*Conf.* X, 29).

And, following the example of Girard's claim that "conversion is resurrection," we can assert that forgiveness is resurrection. It is resurrection for the one who gives and the one who receives. The parable that offers the clearest support for this claim is Luke's Prodigal Son. The father of the prodigal comes to life when he sees his son approaching and runs to meet him, much as the disciples ran to see for themselves after Mary Magdalene announced that the stone had been removed from the tomb (Jn. 20:3–10). Luke's text reveals the connection with the resurrection in the brief dialogue between the father and the older son. To the reluctant brother the Father says: "But now we must celebrate and rejoice, because your brother was dead and has come to life again . . ." (Lk. 15:32). Up to this point in the story the older brother, by his inability to be compassionate and forgive, has refused to enter the joy of his father's and brother's resurrection experience.

CONCLUSION

Girard offers an intriguing version of the inner dynamism of original sin. He finds it first in the mimetic rivalry that emerged from a study of literature published in his first work, *Deceit, Desire, and the Novel.* Through studies in cultural anthropology, he discovered the related phenomenon of the scapegoat mechanism. Finally, through a gradual conversion experience that began in the writing of the last chapter of his first book, *Deceit, Desire, and the Novel,* Girard came to recognize the unique contribution of the Bible to the issue of violence. We have examined these main stages of Girard's work but considered more in detail the last phase, the discovery of the difference between mythical and biblical approaches to violence, by presenting his treatment of the stories of *Oedipus the King* and Joseph. As Girard moved more securely into the realm of faith, he came to recognize that his literary and anthropological studies provided a basis for Christian theology. Theologians have for a very long time built upon the thought of philosophers. In modern times, the range of disciplines on which theology can build is vastly expanded. Anthropology, as the study of the human, can contribute significantly toward understanding the theology that reflects on the one who became human so that we might become divine. Girard calls his work an "evangelical anthropology" (Girard 2001, 182). He cites, in support of his claim for the necessity of an anthropology of the Cross, Simone Weil's observation that the Gospel itself is an anthropology before it is a theology (Girard 2001, 44, 182). John's Gospel confirms them both when it says of Jesus that he "would not trust himself to them because he knew them all, and did not need anyone to testify about human nature. He himself understood it well" (Jn. 2:24–25).

NOTES

1. This scriptural quotation is from the New Revised Standard Version Bible: Catholic Edition, copyright © 1989, 1993 National Council of the Churches of Christ in the United States of America. Used by permission. All rights reserved worldwide.

Part III

THE WORD BECOMES FLESH: FROM THEORY AND DOCTRINE TO LITERATURE

Chapter Eight

Perceval

Compassion Awakened through Conversion

> A man was going down from Jerusalem to Jericho, and fell into the hands
> of robbers, who stripped him, beat him, and went away, leaving him half
> dead. Now by chance a priest was going down that road; and when he saw
> him, he passed by on the other side.
>
> —Luke 10: 29b–31, NRSV[1]

The previous chapter explored the thought of René Girard, especially his
identification of mimetic rivalry or covetousness with original sin and his
contention that only forgiveness enables individuals and groups to move
beyond the cycle of violence that arises from mimetic rivalry. Ricoeur began
his life-long investigation of mimetic desire and its consequences through a
study of literature. I will now move, in the next chapters, to an examination
of four literary texts that illustrate in various ways the thesis of this book, the
medieval romance of *Perceval* by Chrétien de Troyes,[2] the Revelations of
Julian of Norwich, Shakespeare's *Measure for Measure,* and Georges Simenon's Maigret stories.

Chrétien de Troyes' *Perceval* describes the process by which mimetic
desire clouds the consciousness of a good but naïve hero, crowds out compassion, blinds the hero to an opportunity for healing, and eventually invites
its own reversal through conversion, thus opening the door to wisdom. The
story was written during a period still fascinated by the story of Adam and
Eve,[3] and we can legitimately see in this romance a "modern" analogue of
the Genesis account. As a much longer and more elaborate description of
human passage from innocence through sin toward redemption, the story of
Perceval also provides fuller insight into the inner dynamics of original sin.
The twelfth century, in which this story was written, one commentator notes,

209

experienced a significant development in the "capacity of the age to deal with the inner life and to see the mechanics of the soul in sharp definition" (Muscatine 1953, 1168; cited by Fowler 1959, 7).

Commentators acknowledge *Perceval* as one of the great literary works of the Middle Ages. Its twelfth century author, Chrétien de Troyes, "created the Arthurian romance as a literary genre" (Cline 1985, ix) out of elements that existed before it became literature. A review of the commentaries reveals a variety of interpretations, all of them describing various forms of the spiritual quest. "Perceval is the naïve laborer of the French forest carried away by a chivalric vocation, he might also represent an intellectually weakened (*intellectuellement infirme*) humanity, slow to understand and yet seeking for (*en quête de*) perfection" (Frappier 1979, 71). For David Fowler the quest for perfection takes place through a conflict between the ideals of "prowess (*proesce*) and charity." "That these two ideals were inimical and that charity must ultimately prevail over prowess together constitute Chrétien's theme" (Fowler 1959, 3). Robert A. Johnson says of the Holy Grail myth that "Its Christian content, its recent origin, and its source in the European soil make this legend particularly meaningful to the spiritual situation of Western man" (Johnson 1974, 2). Using Jungian analytic categories, Johnson interprets *Perceval* as an example of individuation, "the lifelong process in which a person increasingly becomes the whole and complete person God intended him to be" (Ibid., 2–3). Leonardo Olschki claims that "The idea of sin and redemption was at the ideological core of the whole of [Chrétien's] epic" (Olschki 1966, 34). Brian Murdoch relates the story of *Perceval* and its literary milieu to the story of Adam and Eve. "Adam and the divine economy," says Murdoch, have provided "literary models in various ways." He calls Perceval or Parzifal (Wolfram Von Eschenbach's later version of the story), the Grail King, "another unlikely Everyman, searching for the lost Paradise and for God in the hostile world into which he has been ejected . . ." (Murdoch 2000, ix). And T. S. Eliot found in the Grail legend the inspiration for his poem "The Wasteland."

All these interpretations, revolving around the theme of full human development, seem to me valid expressions of the inner meaning of *Perceval*. I will focus on the affinity this medieval romance has with the story of Adam and Eve and particularly on the movement from naïveté to wisdom. A crucial element of the naïveté, and an image of original sin, is the failure of compassion manifested by the hero at crucial points in the story. Other elements that I have named as constitutive of original sin will also appear in this story: Girard's mimetic rivalry; the loss of intimacy with self and others; alienation from his own creative powers; and ambition cut off from compassion.

THE STORY OF PERCEVAL

The story begins when the hero is young, before he has left his home and mother.[4] One morning in the forest, Perceval sees some knights on horseback. Dazzled by their appearance, he longs to become one of them and decides to follow his newly awakened ambition for chivalry. Perceval's mother is devastated. As he parts from her and passes through the front gate, she faints from grief and, as we find out later in the story, dies.

At first Perceval goes from success to success, overcoming older, more experienced knights and rescuing the maiden Blanchefleur by defeating the evil knight whose armies had besieged her properties. Then, during a visit at a noble castle situated in a beautiful valley, Perceval encounters a challenge beyond his resources. During the meeting between Perceval and the lord of the castle, a young man walks by carrying a lance from which runs a single drop of blood. Perceval is curious about what the lance means and where it is being carried but does not turn his curiosity into a question because his mentor, Gornemant, warned him not to talk too much. Then a young maiden carrying a grail containing a communion host walks by the table. Again, Perceval is curious but does not ask a question because he does not want to talk too much. The lance and grail are carried in procession before the young man several times during the evening, but each time he lets the questions go unasked (3300–3308), thinking that he will get an answer later. The meal ends and everyone retires for the night.

The next morning, surrounded by an ominous and unfriendly silence, Perceval leaves the castle, hoping to find some squires to question about the lance and the grail, for he is still curious. After proceeding a short distance from the castle, Perceval comes upon a maiden weeping under an oak tree for her love who has been killed. The maiden informs Perceval that the castle where he stayed the night before is the home of the Fisher King and that the King, maimed in battle, cannot move himself. Then the maiden asks Perceval if he had seen the lance that bled and the grail and questioned their significance.

When Perceval answers that he had seen the objects but asked no questions, the maiden tells him the consequences of his omission. Had Perceval asked the questions, the maimed king would have been cured, recovered the use of his limbs, and been able to rule his lands with great benefit for the people.[5] Now great misery will come upon Perceval and many others. The cause of his failure to ask the questions, the maiden informs Perceval, was the sin against his mother who died grieving him.

After recounting several more adventures, among them the visit to the court of King Arthur and the appearance of the loathsome damsel who confronts Perceval with the meaning of his unasked questions, the author tells us that "Perceval . . . Had so lost his memory that he had forgotten God," for five years never entering a church to adore God or His saints" (6218–25). Then Perceval runs into a group of penitents observing the passion and death of Christ on Good Friday, and learns from them of a holy hermit. Following their directions he finds the hermit, his mother's brother, to whom he confesses his sins. After telling the hermit what happened at the castle of the Fisher King, Perceval is informed once more that his inability to ask the questions was connected in some way with the sorrow he caused his mother in leaving home. The hermit assigns a penance to Perceval and gives advice on how to live a life of virtue in the future. Here Chrétien's version of the story ends without being completed

Perceval Compared with the Story of Adam and Eve

A comparison of this romantic myth of Perceval with the myth of Adam and Eve, reveals, along with obvious differences, a striking similarity of basic structure. An obvious difference is that Adam and Eve are a couple, Perceval a single man. They are the first humans, and he one of their many descendants. Their sin, as the tradition has interpreted it, was passed along as a congenital weakness in the human will, "original sin." The effects of his sin, though devastating and widespread, are limited to the social milieu he inhabited. But we can find similarities in structure. Both stories begin with a state of "innocence." The short-lived innocence of Adam and Eve is expressed symbolically in the brief note ending the account of their creation, "The man and his wife were both naked, yet they felt no shame" (Gen. 2:25). Chrétien expresses Perceval's innocence by describing the pure joy with which he entered the springtime: "He entered the forest, / And the heart deep inside him Leapt with joy at the sweet Season and the happy sound / Of birds singing from trees All around" (85–90). But in neither story is the innocence absolute or unconditioned. The innocent states—of Adam and Eve, and of Perceval— were qualified by a prohibition meant to protect them. God forbids Adam to eat of the tree of the knowledge of good and evil and names the consequence of eating: "From that tree you shall not eat; the moment you eat from it you are surely doomed to die" (Gen. 2:17b). The protective restriction in Perceval's case is less categorical. It comes from his mother's anxiety. She had worked hard "to keep him from ever seeing knights or learning about them" (316–322). With a little exaggeration, one could turn the mother's anxiety into a command: "You shall not eat of the fruit of knighthood."

In both stories, temptation in the form of mimetic rivalry, the desire to have what the other has, to be what the other is, to be, in fact, like God, leads to the violation of the prohibition. We are familiar with the path the serpent laid out for Adam and Eve—you will be like God knowing the difference between good and evil—and the desire that motivated them to follow it. Perceval, too, was tempted by a desire to be like God. When he first heard the sound of knights "Riding through the forest And making an immense racket" (102–103), he concluded that they were devils and naïvely resolved to "stick the biggest / And strongest with one of these wooden Spears and none of the others / Will come anywhere near me" (121–124)! But when he *saw* them, with "Their gleaming mail shirts and bright, Shining helmets, and such shields / And spears as he'd never seen In all his life . . . (129–132), he concluded that they were angels and even exclaimed of the greatest of them, "That one must be God" (149). And Perceval wanted to be like them (180), asking them endless questions about their equipment, so preoccupied by his intense curiosity that he never answered the question they kept putting to him concerning the whereabouts of five knights and three young girls. Just as Adam and Eve obeyed their desire rather than God's command, Perceval followed his desire rather than his mother's cautious will.

After learning from one of the knights in the forest where the king lives "who makes people knights" (333), Perceval returned home to tell his mother the vision of angels he had seen in the forest. After listening to many protests from his mother and receiving the advice she gave him when she realized he was determined to become a knight, Perceval disregarded his mother's wishes and set off to find the king who made knights. The core of Perceval's sin was not disobedience, but a failure of compassion toward his mother. As he was leaving home, before he had yet gone "as far as a pebble could be thrown" (621), he looked back and saw "that his mother, On the other side of the bridge, Had fallen to the ground, unconscious, And lay as if stone dead, But he bent and whipped his horse . . . And the animal stretched his legs And carried him . . . Into the dark forest" (622–630). This is the originating sin that brings disastrous consequences suggested by the "dark forest" into which he rides. The sin is a violation not primarily of his mother's will to keep him from knighthood but of the care owed a mother by her son. Perceval's failure of compassion will be repeated when he fails to ask the questions that would have healed the Fisher King. Thus, the "original sin" is played out in two stages: one a failure of compassion toward his mother; the other, derived from the first, the missed opportunity to ask the questions that would have healed the Fisher King.

The consequence of Adam's and Eve's disobedience was the loss of their innocence. The serpent had told them, ". . . your eyes will be opened and you will be like gods who know what is good and bad" (Gen. 3:5b). Instead,

" . . . the eyes of both were opened and they realized that they were naked; so they sewed fig lives together to make loincloths for themselves" (3:7). Then, embarrassed by their nakedness, they hid from God. Finally, they heard God pronounce the judgment of hardship that would affect them and their descendants because of their disobedience; this included expulsion from the Garden. Theirs is a punishment with cosmic consequences. The consequences of Perceval's lack of compassion toward his mother unfold more slowly but are just as devastating. Just as surely as Adam's and Eve's disobedience brought about a cosmic "fall," Perceval's lack of compassion brought about a fall that had consequences not only for himself, but for the social situation of a whole kingdom. Perceval's failure, noted above, to ask the questions about the lance that bled and the grail containing a single host, a failure caused by the sorrow he caused his mother on leaving home, was a lost opportunity for healing.

Two denunciations, both from women, announce to Perceval the consequences of his omission. First, the young woman whose lover has been killed speaks: "You're Perceval The Unhappy, the Miserable, the Unfortunate! Ah, how unlucky you are, For had you asked those questions You could have completely cured The good king of all his wounds: He would have become entirely Whole, and ruled as he should" (3583–3590). Sometime later, "on the third day of his coming to [Arthur's] court," a girl, terrifying in appearance—"No creature has ever seemed So awful, not even at the bottom Of Hell" (4619–20)— repeats the denunciation in even more horrible terms. She tells Perceval that the Fisher King will not be healed and be able to rule his kingdom, with the consequence that "Ladies will lose Their husbands, countries will be ruined, Girls will have no guidance And be forced to linger as orphans, And a host of knights will die, And all because of you" (4679–4684). These cosmic consequences compare with the description of hardship—pain in childbearing, the resistance of the soil to cultivation—that followed the disobedience of Adam and Eve.

In both stories, the sin committed is matched by a corresponding grace. But in the case of Adam and Eve the rehabilitating grace does not emerge in their own lifetime—at least we are not told that it did—but only as the history of sin unfolds in their descendants. The story tells us of God's gesture, noted earlier, of making leather garments for Adam and Eve to cover their nakedness (Gen. 3:21), but nothing more. Perceval, on the other hand, experiences a grace of renewal in his confession to his uncle and the advice his uncle gives him, advice very similar to what his mother had told him before he left home. The difference is that now Perceval receives the advice with an awakened consciousness.

We have been examining the structural parallelism between the stories of Adam and Eve and Perceval. To see the pattern of sin and grace at work in

Perceval, we now look more closely at the description Chrétien gives us of this extraordinary knight who moves from naïveté, through shattering failure to wisdom. What is the exact nature of his "original" sin? What are its symptoms? What is the meaning of his downfall and how does it move him to a place of healing?

FROM NAÏVETÉ TO WISDOM

Perceval's Naïveté

The core of Perceval's sin, what is original in it, the originating original sin, is his naïveté.[6] Naïveté is different from innocence. Innocence, though sometimes equated with naïveté, simply means freedom from guilt. Naïveté denotes a lack of awareness, understandable and even attractive in children, but annoying, or merely comical in adults, or tragic. To use Jungian language, naïveté indicates the absence of integration between the two sides of consciousness. For Jung, that would mean the integration of the masculine and feminine sides of the personality. The text of *Perceval* itself suggests a not-yet-achieved integration of ambition—the desire to become a knight—and compassion. Chrétien's description of the young Perceval confirms this interpretation. Most young people are marked by innocence and lack of guile. Perceval was more naïve than most. Though edifying and inspiring at times, his naïveté is merely ridiculous at others and Chrétien capitalizes on the humor. At the beginning of the story, Perceval insistently questions one of the knights he meets in the forest about his armor and weapons, refusing to answer the question the knight puts to him. Finally, the author tells us, "The boy who had little sense, said: 'Were you born like this (in other words, with all this armor)?'" The knight is patient in his response: "Not at all, young sir, no· one can be born like this" (282–84). But when the knight's companions rode up to ask him what he had learned from the youth, he says of Perceval: "As God is my witness, his wits Are distinctly scattered. Whatever I ask him, point blank, he answers Sideways, and off the mark, Asking the names of thing and how they're used" (236–41). This side of Perceval's naïveté makes us want to laugh at him.

Still later, after he had left home, Perceval developed the habit of announcing that he had heard certain things from his mother. When his mentor, Gornemant of Gohort, advises him to go to the church and "pray to the Maker of us all To bless your soul with his mercy And, here in this worldly life, Protect you as the Christian you are," Perceval responds that this is what he had once heard from his mother. "'Please, good brother,' the nobleman

[Gornemant] Said, 'don't explain That your mother told you this Or that. I'm not offended Hearing such things. But others, If you keep announcing the fact, . . . are sure to take you for a fool'" (1665–1684). And Perceval, being docile, accepts the advice and resolves never to say a single word about the lessons he had learned, "except to declare That his host had been his best teacher" (1689–1693). Perceval's slavish following of an earlier piece of advice from Gornemant, that he should not talk too much (1648–1656), prevents him from saying anything when he meets the lovely Blanchefleur whose devastated realm he will restore. "But among themselves, in whispers, the lady's Knights had a great deal to say: 'Good Lord,' they said 'I wonder if this knight can talk at all. What a shame that would be: no better-Looking knight has ever Been born'" (1859–1866).

But if Perceval's naïveté has its comic side, it has a dark side too. Up until the time of his downfall, he doesn't seem to know his own given name. During his first encounter with the knights in the forest, before he left home, one of them asks him what name he should know him by (345). Perceval answers that he is known as "Dear Son" (347). After further probing by the knight, Perceval volunteers two more names, "Dear Brother" (350), and "Good Master" (354). Finally, when the knight asks him if he has no other name, he answers, "I've never had any other" (357). Up to this time in his life, the hero of the story seems to have no way of designating his own proper identity apart from the relationships that define him in his home environment. This may seem comic from one point of view, but it offers a clue to the lack of self-consciousness that will make him stumble. Later in the story, after his failure to ask the questions about lance and grail—his existential downfall—the young woman who reveals to him the meaning of his failure asks for his name. Perceval's remarkable answer reveals a dawning consciousness of identity: "And then, not knowing his name, He somehow knew, and said He was Perceval from Wales, Not knowing if he spoke the truth, But he did, though he did not know it" (374–378).

Finally, after his tragic failure in the Grail Castle, the two dramatic revelations of the meaning of the failure, and five years of engaging in "the wildest exploits, Savage, and cruel, and hard" (6228–6229), Perceval finds himself in a wilderness (6240). In this state, on Good Friday—he didn't know it was Good Friday—he comes, as we have seen, upon five knights and ten ladies in the forest who point him to a holy hermit who will hear his confession. Perceval confesses the whole sorry story of his failure to ask the questions and the five years of wandering that followed. When Perceval has finished his confession but before the hermit responds, the hermit asks him his name. And now, for the first time, he answers with full confidence, "Perceval, sir" (6390). Perceval's confident statement of his own name, after years of not knowing it at all or saying it tentatively without being sure it really was his name, signals the hero's emergence from naïveté to maturity.

On two occasions, Perceval's extraordinary lack of awareness of anything outside the sphere of his chivalric ambition keeps him from responding in a fully human way. First is the sin of galloping away after he looks back and sees his mother fallen, and for all he knows dead, at the gate of their house. This originating sin will precipitate the failure that will, in its turn, shock Perceval into awareness and set him on the road to healing. That failure is his naïve suppression of the questions that arise in his mind when he sees the lance from which a single drop of blood runs down and the grail dish containing the host. The suppression is naïve because it comes from a literal-minded interpretation of the advice his mentor had given him not to ask too many questions. It amounts to a kind of over-obedience that becomes a failure to listen or hear properly. The suppression of the questions produces more than a comic situation. This is the fall comparable to Adam's and Eve's disobedience.

Perceval's Naïveté Moves Toward Its Own Reversal

If Perceval's naïveté is a limitation from one point of view, it has a positive side, too. He may be literal minded in following the advice given to him, but he is open to advice and eager to learn. His naïve wonder and desire to understand everything possible about chivalry is admirable and makes him a quick learner, both within the sphere of his chosen career and the sphere of knightly ethics. When his mentor, Gornemant, advises him to have mercy on those he overcomes in battle when they are unable to defend themselves, he accepts the advice and consistently puts it into practice. The very naïveté that makes Perceval foolish also makes him teachable and, step-by-step, he moves from naïveté to wisdom. Perceval's naïveté is most complete and unchallenged when he is still in the protective atmosphere of his mother's home. Here he is truly innocent, inexperienced, untutored, ignorant, and unformed. Perceval's passage from naïveté to wisdom begins when he sees the vision of the knights in the forest. The vision awakens him to the possibility of a greatness he did not know existed. Though he is still naïve, Perceval is at least aware of a glorious world outside the protective atmosphere of his mother's home.

The movement from naïveté continues with Perceval's separation from the protective atmosphere of home and mother and his setting out on the search for greatness. He develops physical courage, prowess, as it is called in the tradition of chivalry, and the code of ethics, which comes through the advice given by Perceval's mother and his mentor, Gornemant. Perceval also learns from Gornemant the proper use of the equipment of chivalry and the techniques of battle. And, as we have seen above, Gornemant directly challenges Perceval's naïve habit of referring to his mother's advice.

Up to this point, the path from naïveté to wisdom has lead from one success to another. Then comes the moment of failure. Perceval does not ask the questions that occur to him when he sees the lance and the grail, and thus he misses the opportunity to bring about the healing of the Fisher King and the restoration of his kingdom. Failure itself becomes Perceval's tutor, assisted by the women who reveal his fault to Perceval after he leaves the castle of the Fisher King. The revelation is repeated later at the court of King Arthur.

There follows the quest for understanding of his failure and repentance for the sin that caused it. Perceval joins the penitents in their spiritual quest and gains deeper understanding and peace in confessing his sins to the priest, his uncle. As a sign of his repentance, he receives a penance. Though Chrétien de Troyes' account of Perceval ends at this point without telling us what becomes of the hero, it seems Perceval has made a new beginning and discovered a spiritual dimension to his life. He is prepared to be a true knight in the fullest Christian sense of the word. The very naïveté that made Perceval foolish in the eyes of other knights contains a dynamism that moves him to a deeper level of existence. How this is true will be clearer as we look at the stages of Perceval's development.

THREE VISIONS, THREE TRANSFORMATIONS

These, then, are the stages of Perceval's journey from naïveté to wisdom: (1) the vision of greatness embodied in the knights he meets in the forest, (2) separation from his mother's house, (3) meeting a mentor who teaches him the arts of chivalry and its moral code, (4) the successful pursuit of a chivalric career including the liberation of Blanchefleur's realm, (5) the consistent practice of the moral code of chivalry, (6) failure to ask questions about lance and grail, (7) the revelation of the failure, and (8) repentance and conversion. Implicit in these stages of Perceval's journey are three visions and three corresponding transformations that move our hero from naïveté to wisdom. Taken together, these visions and transformations mark the stages of Perceval's education to wisdom, an education that occurs in two ways: through what he learns from others and through his own experience after leaving his mother's home and embarking on his career as a knight. Though Chrétien de Troyes does not refer to three visions, I believe a careful reading of the text uncovers the elements that I am suggesting belong to these three stages of Perceval's development.

First Vision: The Awakening of Mimetic Desire

The first vision takes place at the beginning of Perceval's career. It is a young man's vision, full of naïve wonder and enthusiasm. Awakened in his encounter with the knights in the forest, Perceval is fascinated with each piece of their equipment. More than anything, he wants to be like the angelic characters he has met and asks one question after another without bothering to answer the questions put to him. He wants to know about the lance and its use. He asks about the shield and the coat of mail. This is the vision of a profession, invested with all the wonder young people can experience. Perceval's mentor, Gornemant of Gohort, fills out the picture given by the knight in the forest by instructing Perceval in the use of arms and the skills necessary for a knight. Gornemant advises Perceval, "Every craft requires Clear eyes, and effort, and heart: These three conditions are all one needs" (1466–1469). From the beginning, Perceval is successful in realizing this vision. From the moment he slays the Red Knight just after his first visit to Arthur's court, through all the contests he wins against oppressing knights, Perceval manifests the courage and skill necessary for knighthood.

Second Vision: The Education of Ethical Concern

The second vision is ethical, not in a philosophical sense, but as practical wisdom about how to act nobly. It is expressed in the story through the advice given to Perceval by his mother and his mentor, Gornemant, and by his own conscientious following of that advice. From his mother, Perceval learns that he is to aid maidens in distress if they ask for help. He may take a kiss from a maiden if she offers it, but nothing more; and if she gives him her ring, it will be proper for him to wear it. Perceval should never keep company long with someone before asking his or her name. From his mentor, Gornemant, Perceval learns that when he gains the upper hand against another knight in battle, and the other is not able to defend himself further, Perceval should have mercy on him and not kill him. He should also beware of talking too much and gossiping, advice which he was to follow too literally. If he finds a man or woman in distress and is able to help, he should do so. And, like Perceval's mother, Gornemant advises prayer: "Remember to go to church And pray to the Maker of us all To bless your soul with his mercy And, here in this worldly life, Protect you as the Christian that you are" (1666–1670). Except for the last piece of advice from his mother and his mentor, advice that is really spiritual rather than ethical, Perceval faithfully does everything he has been counseled to do. Each time he conquers a knight, he has mercy and sends the knight to Arthur's court. Several times he helps maidens in distress. After finishing his lessons with his mentor, he asks his name, just as his mother had told him to do. But Perceval does not pray and has, in fact, forgotten God during the five years since he left his mother's home, a fault he acknowledges when he confesses to his uncle. In the professional realm and the ethical realm, Perceval is an outstanding success. And each of these successes moves Perceval further from naïveté and closer to wisdom. For in the practice of his profession and the observance of its moral code, he is forced to abandon the self-absorption that naïveté entails. And yet, Perceval's growing sophistication coexists with a continuing deep naïveté, which though not altogether negative, keeps him from achieving wisdom. As faithful as Perceval is to the requirements of this vision, it is not sufficient to bring the integration he requires to be fully human.

Third Vision: Awakening of Spiritual Consciousness

The third vision has to do with the realm of sin, suffering, and redemption, the realm of the spiritual, the realm of wisdom. Perceval does not easily enter this realm. His failure to do so is the core of the story. We have seen that Perceval did not pray to or even remember God. The full significance of Perceval's spiritual failure is revealed in the encounter with the Fisher King. Though his curiosity is aroused when the lance that bleeds and the grail pass before his eyes, he asks no questions. If he had, the Fisher King would have been healed and able to govern his realm with wonderful effects for all his people. By holding back from asking, Perceval misses an opportunity. Why does Perceval hold back? The superficial reason he himself gives is that he has been told by his mentor not to talk too much. The real reason, as Perceval learns first from the maiden who weeps under the oak tree—the one who first hears him pronounce his name—lies in an unknown sin, the sorrow he caused his mother on leaving home. "You're being punished for the sin You committed against your mother, Who died sorrowing for you" (3594–3596). Much later in the story, when he confesses to his uncle, the hermit confessor, after his five years of absence from self and God—now finally knowing his name—he received the revelation a second time: "Brother, this comes From a sin of which you know nothing. It happened the day your mother Heard you say you were leaving, And she fell to the ground in a faint, near the bridge, in front of the door, And there she died of her sorrow. And that was the sin that caused you Later to ask no questions About the grail or the lance; Everything followed from that" (6393–6403).

Perceval's failure to enter easily into the third realm is all the more striking when contrasted to his success in the first two realms. Even though he had had no experience in the art of chivalry, he learned quickly. And he was easily able to follow the ethical advice he had been given, yet in the realm of the spirit, he seemed to be out to sea. Something is mysterious in Perceval's failure, mysterious and catastrophic. The most bitter accusation against Perceval and the most eloquent recital of the evils which will result from his failure come from an unbelievably ugly girl who rides into Arthur's court on her tawny mule. The damsel's intervention comes at a moment of triumph for Perceval and of great joy for King Arthur and his court. For Perceval, whom Arthur has long sought, has just returned to the court amid rejoicing. "The king and queen and all / The barons with them rejoiced / At Perceval the Welshman's Coming, and led him back to Carlion that very same evening. / They celebrated all night, / And the next day too . . . "(4604–4610). The contrast between the joy at court over Perceval's return and the grim message about to be delivered could not be more stark.

> On the third day of his coming to court A girl came riding up On a tawny mule, her right hand Holding a whip. She wore Her hair in two black, Immense, and ugly braids, And if the book that tells us About her are [sic] truthfully written No creature has ever seemed so awful, not even at the bottom Of Hell. You'll never see Iron as black as her neck And hands, but her hands and neck Were not her ugliest parts. He eyes were two deep caves, Smaller than the eyes of a rat, And her nose was a monkey's, or a cat's, With a donkey's ears—or cow's. Her teeth were as yellow as an egg, But darker, more like rust, And she wore a beard, like a goat A hump grew in the middle Of her chest, and her back was crooked, And her thighs and shoulders were perfectly Made for dancing—oh the hump On her back and her twisted legs Were beautifully made for leading A ball! (4621–4638).

It is hard to imagine the dance for which this damsel was so well suited. Why does the author introduce such a ghastly character into this otherwise joyous scene? What does she symbolize? Robert Johnson suggests that the girl represents Perceval's "anima gone absolutely sour and dark" (Johnson 1974, 67). David Fowler follows an interpretation that considers the "Hideous Damsel" as "a messenger from the other world" (Fowler, 46). "Certainly," Fowler says, "she reminds us of the widespread motif of the supernatural being, beautiful in her own realm, but horribly ugly in this world." Fowler's conclusion is that Chrétien uses this repulsive figure for two purposes. First, she is "a projection of Perceval's conscience" which he would like to ignore but cannot (46). Her second function is to give more information about the meaning of the unasked questions (47). These two explanations converge in suggesting that the message of the loathsome damsel represents an eruption into Perceval's consciousness of a hidden, shriveled part of the hero's spiritual life.

We might also understand this episode in terms of the function of original sin in consciousness. Original sin is a condition rather than a specific act, a condition that sets us in the direction of specific sinful acts. We can call it naïveté, ignorance, lack of integration, concupiscence, mimetic rivalry, addiction, or forgetfulness of the self. It functions at an unconscious level until some kind of awakening brings it to consciousness. For Perceval, the undeveloped side of his consciousness was compassion. He could not enter into the suffering of the other in a redemptive way. And this horrible damsel awakens Perceval from his spiritual slumber. Since this is a crucial episode in the story, we take a moment to look more closely at the damsel's message to Perceval.

After a general greeting to the King and his court, the loathsome damsel addresses Perceval alone:

> Ah, Perceval, my friend, Fortune is bald behind, But hairy in front! May curses Fall on whoever greets you Or wishes you well, or prays For your soul: you found Fortune But didn't know how to keep it. The Fisher King made you His guest, you saw the bleeding Lance, but you couldn't be bothered To open your mouth and speak, Asking why that drop Of blood came rolling down From the point of that shining spear! You saw the grail carried In, and never asked For what great lord it was borne! Those who see their chance But never grasp it, hoping For a better, must suffer for their failure (4646–4665).

The damsel continues her bitter recital: "You're that unlucky man Who watched opportunity Arrive, and held his tongue. What an unlucky fool! How wrong to sit there, silent, When just a simple question Could have cured that rich And noble king of his suffering, Allowed him to rule his kingdom In peace" (4666–4675). If the question had been asked, according to the damsel, the king would have been completely cured and would have been able to rule his land in peace. Since he will never rule his land again and is not healed of his wound, "Ladies will lose Their husbands, countries will be ruined, Girls will have no guidance And be forced to linger as orphans, And a host of knights will die, And all because of you" (4679–4684).

It is a stinging condemnation since the failure seems on the surface so trivial. Perceval certainly did not know that so much depended on whether or not he asked the questions that occurred to him. It does not seem fair to impute guilt to him and to be angry when he had had no idea what was at stake. Yet the damsel is angry and she does judge him harshly, and we instinctively know there is truth in her judgment. We are, of course, in the realm of myth and symbol. Perceval's failure represents far more than the simple omission of a question about objects that pass in front of him. Perceval's deeply ingrained ignorance, rooted in naïveté, is somehow culpable. This hero, otherwise so admirable, noble, and successful, manifests a kind of blindness in the spiritual realm that keeps him from wisdom and leads him to miss the opportunity for healing the king and restoring his kingdom.[7]

But we should not overlook another aspect of Perceval's failure. With all its disastrous consequences, his omission prepares the path for his entrance into a realm of wisdom from which he had thus far been excluded. In this sense, it is a "happy fault." The story ends just at a point where Perceval's new life begins, and we do not know what sort of person he will become; yet it is evident that the successful but naïve hero has been profoundly transformed by what has happened. The nature of the transformation is indicated in Perceval's confession and in the prayer for repentance given to him by his uncle-priest to whom he confessed his failure. Perceval begins his confession with the sweeping admission, "for five years I have not known where I was. I did not love God nor believe in Him, and I have done nothing but evil" (84). The admission is surprising because we have up to this point learned only of Perceval's failure to ask the questions about lance and grail. But now it seems Perceval sees his own life as a spiritual wasteland. The penance assigned by Perceval's priest-uncle is intended to put Perceval on the path of spiritual renewal. It contains the last advice the hero will receive in the story. Every day Perceval is to go to the monastery church before any other place, when the bell rings, or earlier if he has already risen. If the Mass has begun, he is to stay until the priest has finished his prayers and chants. "If your heart is sufficiently willing, It's not too late: return To grace, and then to Heaven!" (3457–3459). Perceval's uncle concludes with the last words of advice Perceval will receive:

Love God, adore Him, believe In Him. Honor good men And women. Stand when the priest Enters: it costs you little, But truly God loves to see it As the sign of a humble spirit. If a girl asks for your help, Give it, and help yourself. Or a widowed lady, or an orphan. These are acts of absolute charity. Help whom you can, as you should. Be careful, never fail them! These are the things I wish you to do, to reclaim God's grace As, once, you used to have it (6460–6474).

The hermit ends as he had begun with a reference to a willing heart, but now in the form of a question: "Tell me: is your heart willing" (6475). This is really the turning point of the whole story. Perceval's future hangs on his answer to this question. The advice his uncle gives is really no different from what the "good son" had received from his mother. Between his mother's advice, and his uncle's, lie his chivalric achievements and, most importantly, the failures that led him into the wilderness. Now he can respond with his whole heart because, for the first time in his life, he knows his name and possesses his heart. "Entirely willing," said Perceval. What his life will actually be we can only imagine, for the story ends abruptly at this the beginning of Perceval's new life: "And Perceval learned, once again, That Our Lord

had died that Friday, Crucified high on the Cross. He made his Easter communion, Humbly, and in perfect simplicity. And here the story breaks Away
from Perceval, About whom the tale turns silent: . . ." (6510–6517). Then
Chrétien tells us that he "will speak a good deal of Gawain Before Perceval
is mentioned again" (6518–6519). As a matter of fact, Chrétien never does
return to Perceval after the long section on Gawain.[8]

THEOLOGICAL REFLECTIONS

I have interpreted *Perceval* as a story analogous to the Genesis account of
Adam and Eve. If this interpretation is justified, Chrétien's medieval romance
should offer some insight into the nature of original sin, and I have suggested
it does. Leonardo Olschki pursues the issue of Perceval's "sin" in his *The
Grail Castle and Its Mysteries* (Olschki 1966). His conclusion is directly opposed to what I propose here. Olschki's view is a convenient beginning point
for these theological reflections. After looking at the nature of Perceval's sin,
we will look at the role of failure and conversion in his return to grace.

Perceval's Sin: Free Will or Fate?

Playing on the similarity of the two Old French words, *pescheor* (fisher) and
pecheor (sinner), Olschki considers both Perceval and the Fisher King as
"two living symbols of a sin that is not caused by their will or by any perversion, but by a destiny that persecutes them" (36). That Perceval was a sinner
becomes clear in the denunciations of the two women, his own repentance,
and the words of the hermit to whom Perceval confesses. These events are
vividly recorded in the text. That the Fisher King might have been a sinner
comes entirely from this play on the Old French words for fisher and sinner.
Olschki offers his theory as a possibility, convinced that medieval readers of
this story would have been aware of the pun. What is of interest relative to
the theme of this study is the theology of original sin that Olschki suggests.
The notion of "a destiny that persecutes them" suggests the kind of fatalism
that we saw earlier in the Greek tragedy of *Oedipus,* and in the Manichaean
teachings that entangled Augustine in his early adulthood. Olschki refers to
a version of the Manichee teaching prevalent in southern France at the time
Chrétien was writing, the Albigensian or Catharist heresy. The Council of
Tours gave this heresy its name and condemned it in 1163, about twenty years
before the writing of *Perceval.* According to the Albigensians, the origin of
the world is dualistic, brought about by a good god, the god of spirit, and an
evil god, the god of matter. The evil god brings about everything evil in the

natural and moral spheres. Sin is caused, not by the will of the sinner but by the evil principle at work in the sinner's life. In this view, freedom of the will does not exist.

We have already seen that Augustine, after a long struggle, came to recognize the falseness of this position, as he realized that he had a will. Augustine also rejected a completely opposite position—Pelagianism—that he encountered later in his life, and which seemed to him to exaggerate the freedom of the human will. Augustine's doctrine of original sin lies between these two extremes. The will is free, and we are responsible for our faults but our will is not completely free. The disobedience of Adam and Eve at the beginnings of our race, damaged the will and inclined it to evil in such a way that it can never be fully free except through the grace of Christ. Olschki, fully aware of Augustine's orthodox position regarding original sin (37, note b), finds in *Perceval* an expression of the neo-Manichean position of the Albigensians. His principle evidence seems to be the absence of liturgical symbols such as the Eucharist and the crucifix.

Without trying definitively to settle the issue of whether *Perceval* expresses an orthodox or heretical view of original sin, I will point to some indications that suggest that Chrétien's theology of sin is closer to Augustine's than to the Albigensians. The whole treatment of Perceval's failure, and its cause, presume a free, but defective will. The first bit of evidence comes during the episodes in which the two women and the hermit reveal Perceval's "sin." The first girl—Perceval encounters her just after he leaves the Grail Castle— informs Perceval: "You're being punished for the sin You committed against your mother, Who died, sorrowing for you" (3594–3596). A failure instigated entirely by an evil spirit inhabiting the one who failed would hardly be a sin deserving of punishment.

The horrible damsel who appears suddenly on the third day of celebrations in Arthur's castle is even more withering in her denunciation. After listing the sufferings that will come because of Perceval's failure, the damsel ends by laying the blame on Perceval, "And all because of you" (4684). Another translation has "And you will be the one to blame" (Cline 1985, 128). This expression imputes personal fault. Finally, as we have seen above, the hermit uncle of Perceval, after the hero's many years of wandering, during which he "Had so completely lost His memory he'd even forgotten God" (6219–6220), hears his nephew's confession. After Perceval confesses what happened in the Grail Castle, the hermit discloses the cause of the failure: "Brother, this comes From a sin of which you know nothing" ("*Uns pechiez don tu ne sez mot,*" 6393–6394). Then the hermit recounts what Perceval has already heard, that his mother died of sorrow as he was leaving. The hermit reveals two important truths: the cause of Perceval's failure was a sin and it was a sin of which he knew nothing. These are the two components of original sin as it first manifests itself. It is sin, but it is largely unconscious and not culpable.

A second indicator that Perceval's "sin" was a personal fault and not the action of an evil principle beyond his will, is his own humble acknowledgment of fault, his sadness at missed opportunity, and finally his repentance. When his mentor Gornemant asks Perceval to continue as his guest "For a month. Or a year, if he cared to" (1574–1575), Perceval's concern for his mother keeps him back. He remembers her fallen at the gate as he left and realizes it was because of him: "She fainted from sadness, because I was leaving, I know she did" (1587–1588). So Perceval continues to look for his mother. This humble admission suggests the stirrings of repentance. From now on, until he learns that she has died, Perceval's quest will be for his mother, not for the grail. This kind of humility makes sense only if some kind of personal responsibility is involved. Later, when his beloved Blanchefleur begs him to stay with her and her people after he has saved them from Clamadeu, he would have liked to stay but "his heart pulled him away, Tugging in a different direction: He remembered his mother, and the sight of her Fainting and falling to the ground, And more than anything else In the world he longed to see her Again" (2918–2924).[9] Perceval seems to be admitting on his own the accusation that will be brought against him by those who reveal his sin to him, the girl and the hermit, seeking to repair something broken through his own fault. This does not square with the notion that Chrétien was following the Manicheans' "the evil principle made me do it."

Theology of Sin

The final expression of Perceval's recognition of fault comes in the last episode: his meeting with the knights and ladies in the forest on Good Friday, his repentance, and his confession to the hermit. Following the directions to the holy hermit indicated by the knights and ladies, "Perceval followed their path, Sighing from the bottom of his heart For all the sins against God He'd committed, which he now repented" (6334–6337). Then, Chrétien tells us, arrived at the hermitage, Perceval enters a tiny chapel as the hermit with a priest—apparently the hermit was not a priest—and an altar boy was "Just beginning the most beautiful, The sweetest service the sainted Church can celebrate" (6346–6348). Perceval dropped to his knees as he entered the chapel. "But the holy hermit called to him, Seeing the honest tears Rolling down his cheeks All the way to his chin. And Perceval, deeply afraid Of having offended God, Clasped the hermit's feet And, bending low, his hands Joined in supplication, Begged for help, for his need Was great" (6351–6361). This moving description of Perceval's repentance coming to full expression has a distinctly Augustinian flavor to it and nothing of the Manichean attribution of sin to an alien principle.

Then the hermit hears Perceval's confession. After confessing his silence in the Grail Castle during the procession of the lance that bled and the grail dish containing the single host, Perceval reveals to the hermit "And ever since I've felt Such sadness that I wished to die; I forgot about God and never Prayed for his grace and mercy Or did what I should to deserve it" (6383–6387). When the hermit asks the penitent his name and learns that he is Perceval—son of the hermit's sister—he understands the cause of Perceval's silence in the Grail Castle. The hermit tells Perceval it is "a sin of which you know nothing" (6394). Though he has in fact heard the same explanation earlier from the maiden who told him of his mother's death, we suspect that Perceval really hears the truth for the first time when the hermit reveals it after his repentance and confession: "It happened the day your mother Heard you say you were leaving, And she fell to the ground in a faint, Near the bridge, in front of the door, And there she died of sorrow. And that was the sin that caused you, later, to ask no questions About the grail or the lance; Everything followed from that" (6395–6403).

The Role of Failure in Perceval's Career

We have been looking at the nature of Perceval's sin and have concluded that it was something for which he was responsible, not merely something carried out by an alien principle dwelling in him. But though he was responsible, he was not fully responsible because the sin was largely unconscious. Only gradually does Perceval become aware of the original, that is, the originating, sin in his life, the sorrow he caused his mother. We can, of course, ask if another even more original sin lies behind the sorrow Perceval inflicted on his mother. Maybe it was, as I have suggested, his ambition cut off from any connection with the compassionate side of himself. But the story says the sin was the sorrow he caused his mother, a sin of which you know nothing, as the hermit tells him. The question now is how does Perceval's sin move from unconscious to conscious? By now, the answer should be clear: through his failures beginning with his silence in the Grail Castle and continuing in his five years of wandering far from God, five years that left him in a wilderness. The full awareness of his failure, already indicated in his lingering sadness, but heightened by the denunciations pronounced by the women, produced a crisis in the root sense of that Greek word, a judgment and a turning point. The first meaning of the Greek word, *krisis*, is "judgment." The two women have rendered the judgment on Perceval's behavior and even his own sadness already implies a judgment on his part. He is sad because he senses something amiss. Another meaning of *krisis* is "turning point of a disease, sudden change for better or *worse*" (Liddell and Scott, *Greek English Lexicon*). That Perceval is suffering from a disease seems evident from what we have seen. Now, in the light of the judgment pronounced against him that clearly states his failure, he could either get better or worse. It is important to realize that failure does not of itself produce healing or growth; that is why it is a *crisis*.

A turn for the worse would have taken place if he had refused to accept the judgment or had blamed others for what happened. This is the Manichean temptation: "it was not my fault." Perceval did not do that. He could turn away through distraction. In fact, his five years of chivalric adventure without any consciousness of God seem to be precisely a diversion from facing up to the meaning of his failure. Despair would have been a third way of turning away, or cynicism, which is basically a form of despair, but Perceval does not choose that path. The change for the better was that the failure actually opened the door to healing. Perceval's uncommon humility, part of the same naïveté that in its first level set him on the path to unconscious sin, left him open to healing when the opportunity came. Sadness over his failure to care for his mother, regret over not asking the questions that his curiosity prompted him to ask, and, finally, sincere repentance as he comes to the end of five years in the wilderness—all of these lead him to healing. During the assigning of a penance, the hermit spoke these words that we have considered earlier: "If your heart is sufficiently willing, It's not too late: return To grace, and then to heaven" (6457–6459). When he finished assigning a penance, the hermit asked him "is your heart willing?" (6475), and Perceval could answer "entirely willing" (6476).

Conversion

And so Perceval experiences a change of heart, *metanoia* and sets his life in a new direction. The text of Chrétien's poem leaves off at the beginning of Perceval's new life. Most commentators believe the text came to an end because Chrétien died, but Robert Johnson suggests that "he stopped where he was. He couldn't say any more" (Johnson, 72). Some of those who continued the story after Chrétien's death, have Perceval return to the Grail Castle and heal the Fisher King. But Chrétien himself only tells us that "Perceval learned, once again, That Our Lord had died that Friday, Crucified high on the Cross. He made his Easter communion Humbly, in perfect simplicity" (6510–6514). And here the story of Perceval ends, just at the beginning of what promises to be a new life. Perceval's conversion recalls René Girard's conviction that conversion is necessary for people to recognize in themselves the presence of mimetic rivalry, the term by which Girard designates original sin. Conversion is necessary precisely because the sin is unconscious, what Perceval's uncle had called, "the sin of which you knew nothing." Conversion, for Girard, is also resurrection. Like the Prodigal Son of Luke's Gospel, Perceval was dead and has come back to life (Lk. 15:32).

CONCLUSION

In her book, *From Ritual to Romance* (1920), Jessie Weston addresses various attempts made to explain the origin of the Grail legend that "consists of a congeries of widely differing elements—elements which at first sight appear hopelessly incongruous, if not completely contradictory, yet at the same time are present to an extent, and in a form, which no honest critic can afford to ignore" (Weston 1920, 2). Weston mentions two ways that scholars have tried to make sense of these differing elements and adds a third of her own that would clarify elements not explained by the other interpretations. "Thus it has been possible for one group of scholars, relying on undeniably Christian-Legendary elements, preponderant in certain versions, to maintain the thesis that the Grail legend is *ab initio* a Christian and ecclesiastical legend, and to analyse the literature on that basis alone" (Ibid.). Another group has seen the tradition as having mainly Celtic origins that were only later "worked over by ecclesiastical writers in the interests of edification." (Ibid.). This group maintains that the "story itself is non-Christian, and Folk-lore in origin" (Ibid.). After showing elements of the grail legend that neither of these interpretations explains, Weston proposed to look at certain "Nature Cults" described by J. G. Frazer's *The Golden Bough,* cults that once had a close union with Christianity (Ibid., 35).

To follow Weston through the detailed presentation of her position would take us away from our subject, but her book produced an effect in the world of literature that itself throws light on the story of *Perceval*. Weston's book influenced T. S. Eliot in the writing of "The Wasteland" (1922). At the end of the poem, in his "Notes on 'The Wasteland,'" Eliot tells us that "Not only the title, but the plan and a good deal of the incidental symbolism of the poem were suggested by Miss Jessie L. Weston's book on the Grail legend: *From Ritual to Romance"* (Eliot 1952, 50). Eliot is so indebted to this book, he tells us, that it "will elucidate the difficulties of the poem much better than my notes can do" (Ibid.) and he recommends that for those interested in understanding the poem, the book is worth reading. What is important here is not the elucidation of Eliot's difficult poem nor the study of Weston's book, but the theme of "The Wasteland" that owes its origin to the Grail legend. That this legend would inspire a poet of Eliot's stature indicates the continuing relevance of its central symbolism.

I have taken *Perceval, The Story of the Grail,* as a medieval symbolization of original sin, and Eliot's image of the wasteland, taken from the medieval romance, is a modern symbol. The wasteland in Eliot, Cleanth Brooks tells us, symbolizes a "Life devoid of meaning . . ." (Brooks 1991, 88). In Perceval's early disregard for his mother's sorrow, we have, as the story makes clear, an "originating" sin. The sorrow he caused his mother brought about the failure to ask questions about the meaning of lance and grail. And, in its turn, the failure to ask the questions brought about a condition that we can call the wasteland, reminiscent of the hardship that came about after the disobedience of Adam and Eve. The wasteland, then, becomes a symbol of the human condition after the fall.

The wasteland imagery comes up in two contexts in *Perceval.* First is the personal wilderness in which Perceval finds himself at the end of five years of wandering away from God. The second—the one on which Weston and Eliot focus—is the wasteland that will follow from Perceval's failure to ask the questions in the Grail Castle, the wasteland predicted by the "dreadful damsel." "Ladies will lose Their husbands, countries will be ruined, Girls will have no guidance. . . ." (4679–4684). Maybe if Perceval could come back after his conversion experience he could undo these consequences, but for the moment these sad consequences follow his sin. The imagery of a wasteland is dark but the paradox of Christian faith is that this somber symbol may be a prelude to redemptive grace, a grace that for St. Paul outweighed the sin that produced it: ". . . where sin increased, grace overflowed all the more" (Rom. 5:20b). The end of Perceval's story leaves us with the impression of overflowing grace.

Perceval's education has taken him from naïveté through wilderness to wisdom, or at least to the threshold of wisdom. A world, including his own name, has opened up for him whose existence was unknown before his failure. What a long distance he has come from the haven of his mother's home. On the way, he has been liberated from his child's naïveté by entering into and practicing a profession, by accepting and carrying out an ethical code, and by accepting a failure which opened the realm of spiritual wisdom. At the end of his journey he has found his mother, not alive but dead from the sorrow he caused her in leaving home. He has learned that this sorrow, which had a crippling effect on him as well, involved a rupture of some sort in him, was a sin. And this sin kept him from asking the questions about the lance and grail. In repenting and accepting the penance imposed on him, he has been healed and has recovered the naïveté that is proper to a man, not a child. He has discovered his own name, found God again, and entered a realm of wisdom whose existence he had not suspected before. Now he is ready to begin again.

What will his life be now? How will the transformed Perceval act? Chrétien de Troyes does not tell us. But, in the penance assigned by Perceval's hermit uncle we have some clues from which to sketch a conclusion.

Perceval's uncle gives some advice meant to help him "return To grace and then to heaven" (6468–6469). During the course of assigning Perceval his penance after confession, Perceval's uncle says: "Now repent! If you care for your soul as you should, You'll open yourself to repentance. The first thing you'll do each day, The first place you'll go, will be church, Where soul and body will prosper" (6440–6445). Perceval is to "Love God, adore Him, believe In him. Honor good men And women" (6460–6462). As he was about to leave home in search of knighthood, still in his first naïveté, Perceval had heard the same advice from his mother. Perceval's response to his mother shows the extent of his naïve ignorance: "Mother," he asked, "What's a church?" (573). His last words to his mother were that he would be happy to go to churches and monasteries (595–598). The young Perceval, that is the "old" Perceval, did not follow the advice but Chrétien leaves us with the hope that the newly awakened Perceval will.

NOTES

1. This scriptural quotation is from the New Revised Standard Version Bible: Catholic Edition, copyright © 1989, 1993 National Council of the Churches of Christ in the United States of America. Used by permission. All rights reserved worldwide.

2. Chrétien de Troyes probably wrote this last and most important of his romances in the mid–1180s. He died before it was finished.

3. See, for instance, *Le Mystère d'Adam: An Anglo-Norman Drama of the Twelfth Century,* edited by Paul Studer, Manchester University Press, 1918.

4. Chrétien de Troyes. 1999. *Perceval: The Story of the Grail.* Translated by Burton Raffel, Yale University Press, New Haven, 1999. All references to the story in the present text come from Raffel's translation.

5. Olschki discusses how the questions that Perceval should have asked would have cured the King. The questions would not have functioned, Olschki suggests, like a magic word found in folk tales, but would rather have drawn some sort of confession from the King that would have freed him from his curse. See *The Grail Castle,* 32. This interpretation is based on Olschki's conviction that, through a wordplay based on the similarity of the French words for "fisher" (*pêcheur*) and "sinner" (*pécheur*), Chrétien means to suggest that the King's wound comes from a sin he committed. However one interprets the King's wound or explains how the questions from Perceval would have healed the King, it seems evident from the story that, without knowing it, the naïve Perceval has wandered into the realm of sin and redemption. He does not know where he is or what to do. And so he fails to act.

6. Irenaeus of Lyon (130–202) treats Adam and Eve as children vulnerable to temptation rather than fully mature adults who would have sinned out of pride (*Against the Heretics,* IV, 38; V, 23, 5). When he sinned, Adam "lost his natural disposition and child like mind, and had come to the knowledge of evil things" (Ibid.). Irenaeus says that God *could* not have made humans perfect from the beginning since they were created and not uncreated. Even if we maintain that God *could* have created humans perfect, says Irenaeus, they would not have been able to receive the perfection any more than infants can receive substantial nourishment (IV, 38, 1). Irenaeus' position differs dramatically from Augustine's who says that Adam and Eve sinned out of a pride that paved the way for their disobedience. "It was in secret that the first human beings began to be evil; and the result was that they slipped into open disobedience. For they would not have arrived at the evil act if an evil will had not preceded it. Now, could anything but pride have been the start of the evil will? For 'pride is the start of every kind of sin' (Ecclesiasticus, 10:13). For it is a perverse kind of exaltation to abandon the basis on which the mind should be firmly fixed, and to become, as it were, based on itself, and so remain" (Augustine, *City of God,* XIV, 13).

7. We are told in the story only that the king was maimed by a javelin through the hips in such a way as to lose the use of his legs. Some commentators think it was a matter of emasculation and that the King had, in fact, lost his fecundity both physically and spiritually. Leonardo Olschki suggests that the King's mutilation and his prolonged martyrdom have a symbolic value and refer to the cause of man's damnation. "He [the King] is injured in his virility which lies at the root of all sin." *The Grail Castle and Its Mysteries* (Manchester: Manchester University Press. 1966), 34. Jessie L. Weston, *From Ritual to Romance* (NY: Doubleday Anchor, 1957), also takes the position that the Fisher King has somehow been wounded in his virility and that his wound affects his whole kingdom. "Now there can be no possible doubt here, the condition of the King is sympathetically reflected on the land, the loss of virility in the one brings about a suspension of the reproductive processes of Nature in the other" (23).

8. Though Perceval is clearly the central character of *Perceval and the Grail Castle,* the story of Gawain is interwoven with the story of Perceval and actually ends the poem since Chrétien died before he could get back to *Perceval.* After Chrétien's death the "unfinished *Perceval* exercised such a fascination that in eleven of the fifteen manuscripts it is followed, without a break, by continuations written between the final years of the twelfth century and around 1230" (Joseph Duggan, "Afterward," *Perceval: The Story of the Grail,* translated by Burton Raffel, Yale University Press, New Haven, 1999, 300).

9. Robert Johnson makes much of what he calls the "mother complex," describing it as "the greatest stumbling block that exists in a man's psychology. Almost no man will admit it, which means that he is probably totally eaten up by it. But as a man grows, he has a chance to make a better relationship with his mother complex. At every point of growth in the Grail myth, Parsifal [Perceval] turns around to redo his mother relationship" (Johnson, 46–47).

Chapter Nine

Julian of Norwich

From Blindness to the Vision of Love

First of all, then, I urge that supplications, prayers, intercessions, and thanksgivings be made for everyone, for kings and all who are in high positions . . . This is right and acceptable in the sight of God our Savior, who desires everyone to be saved and to come to a knowledge of the truth.

—I Tim. 2: 1–5, NRSV[1]

For to this end we struggle, because we have our hope set on the living God, who is the Savior of all people, especially of those who believe.

—I Tim. 4:10, NRSV[2]

Two hundred years after Chrétien de Troyes wrote *Perceval* (between 1181 and 1190), Julian of Norwich (1342?–1416?) wrote her reflective interpretation of sixteen revelations that took place May 8 and 9 of 1373, in the thirty-first year of her life, as she was recovering from a life-threatening illness. Julian's elegant prose pushes to its limit both the orthodox belief in the essential goodness of humans, in spite of their sin, and the belief in the mercy of God. In Julian's thought, God's compassion swallows up justice so that "all things might be well." Julian's writings contribute to the argument of my study in three ways, by their very original interpretation of the story of Adam and Eve, by their conflation of that story with the event of the Incarnation, and by their dramatic presentation of divine compassion.

Julian is considered the first woman to write a work of literature in the English vernacular. Her reflections, to which she gave no title, now appear variously as *Showings* or *Revelations of Divine Love*, or simply *The Revelation of Love*. Over a period of many years, Julian explores, in a "Short Text" (ST) and a "Long Text" (LT), the sixteen visions. Though Julian probably

233

wrote ST shortly after the "showings," or at least before 1388 (Bauerschmidt 1999), she waited almost twenty years to compose the LT, which one author calls "the most remarkable theological achievement of the English late Middle Ages" (Duffy 1992, 314, cited in A.C. Spearing 1998, xxiv). Julian's revelations led her deep into the dialectic of sin and grace, not as humans see it but as the infinitely compassionate God sees it. God's gracious mercy, the tendency to overlook our sins because of Christ, and God's will for our salvation dominate Julian's thought. Reading her work reminds us of the "secret increasing power of grace" that Von Rad noted as God's response to sin in the Primeval History, or the Old Testament refrain, "you are a gracious and merciful God, slow to anger, rich in clemency, loathe to punish" (Jon. 4:2b; Ps. 102, 144), or Paul's proclamation that "where sin increased, grace overflowed all the more" (Rom. 5:20), or Hugh of St. Victor's description of "the will of tender mercy" in Christ and his proclaiming that it belongs to human nature to be compassionate (Ch 5, 6–7, 11). Julian's vision of God's mercy leads her to suggest the possibility of universal salvation even though she realizes this is not the Church's teaching.

Julian's vision is troubling, magnificent, and profoundly challenging. The *Revelations of Divine Love* pushes our understanding of human sin and God's mercy beyond anything we have seen thus far in this study, perhaps beyond a place we would be willing to go. Still, her writings continue to inspire contemporary readers and thinkers. One author even finds in Julian the foundations for "imagining the political" as ideally dominated by compassionate love rather than naked power (Bauerschmidt 1999, Ch. 1).

Julian's texts are profoundly relevant to the study we have undertaken in this book. We will first consider compassion as the unifying principle of Julian's work and then look at her extraordinary retelling of the story of Adam—she does not mention Eve, but takes Adam as the representative of all human beings—as the central theological presentation of God's grace and mercy in the Long Text. We will then examine Julian's writings to see if we can discover her idea of original sin. The revelations Julian received of a divine grace that outstrips sin, bringing about a condition better for us than if we had never sinned, moves her toward the affirmation of universal salvation. We will examine this controversial aspect of Julian's thought in some detail. We will also explore Julian's relations to the tradition that has preceded her, especially the aspects of that tradition that have been part of this study. Finally, there is the question of the importance of Julian's thought for those who have, through a meditative reading of her work, brought to life again in succeeding generations the vision of this fourteenth century anchoress.

COMPASSION AS THE UNIFYING
PRINCIPLE IN JULIAN'S WORK

In her reflections on the 13th revelation, Julian posed the meta-moral question that parallels Heidegger's metaphysical question, "Why is there being rather than nothing?" (Heidegger, *Intro to Metaphysics*). It is the non-being of sin that troubles Julian. She does not ask why human beings commit sin—we will consider her answer to that question in a later section of this chapter—but why God allows sin. Our Lord has reminded her of her great longing to see God and she realized that nothing kept her from the vision of God but sin. "And I thought that if sin had never existed, we should all have been pure like himself, as God made us and so I had often wondered before now in my folly why, in his great forseeing wisdom, God had not prevented sin; for then, I thought, all would have been well" (ST 13, par. 4). In the LT, Julian wonders why God had not prevented "the beginning of sin" (LT 27, par. 1). God's surprising answer leads to a further question that will introduce us into the heart of Julian's message, or rather of God's message to Julian. "But Jesus, who in this vision informed me of all that I needed to know, answered with this assurance: Sin is befitting, but all shall be well, and all shall be well, and all manner of things shall be well" (Ibid.). How can God say that sin is befitting? This is the question we will be pursuing throughout this chapter. For now, it is enough to say that God's answer to Julian's question takes us further into the mystery of the divine compassionate love that makes of sin nothing at all or, even more amazingly, turns it into a source of glory. We will come back to this puzzling answer to Julian's question, but first it will be helpful to explore what it means to say that compassion serves as the unifying principle of Julian's life-work.

The term "work" applies to three interconnected levels of Julian's activity. First and most obvious is the "work" Julian produced and that we are studying, *The Revelations of Divine Love*. Behind the work of writing, and revealed to us through the written work, is the work of Julian's life, a work that began before the writing of this book and continued after it. Julian discloses this life-work, which precedes the "revelations," at the beginning of both the ST (Chapter 1) and the LT (Chapter 2). "I asked for three graces of God's gift. The first was a vivid perception of Christ's passion, the second was bodily sickness and the third was for God to give me three wounds" (ST 1, par. 1). These requests relate to a "life work" because they express not some incidental petition such as, "please heal my asthma!" but the longing for a gift that would give meaning to Julian's whole life. Reflection on these three requests reveals that Julian is, in fact, asking for compassion in three forms. First, Julian "longed by God's grace to feel [the Passion of Christ] more intensely" (ST 1, par. 1) than she ever has before, though she already felt it strongly. "I thought how I wished I had been there at the crucifixion with Mary Magdalene and with others who were Christ's dear friends, that I might have seen in the flesh the Passion of our Lord which he suffered for me, so that, I could have suffered with him as others did who loved him" (Ibid.).

The second gift, bodily sickness to the death, entails compassion in a different sense for it came out of Julian's longing "to be soon with my God" (ST 1, par. 3). She wanted a real sickness, affecting both body and soul, serious enough that she and the others around her would think she was dying and that she would receive the rites of the Church. Julian even wants "all the terror and turmoil of the fiends and all other kinds of torment . . ." (Ibid.). But she did not want to die: ". . . except for giving up the ghost" (Ibid.). Julian makes this request, as she tells us with a little more detail in LT, "because I wished to be purged by the mercy of God and afterwards to live more to God's glory because of that sickness; and that I should die more quickly, for I longed to be soon with my God" (LT 2, par. 2). This request manifests a desire for compassion, not in the ordinary sense of suffering-with, but as suffering-in-order-to-be-with. Julian knew, even before she suffered, that suffering has a privileged role in opening up the human spirit to union with God. Most people learn this by going through sufferings they have not chosen or wished for. We have seen this in Perceval whose stunning and unanticipated failure helped lead him to wisdom. Julian *asks for* the suffering of a life-threatening illness.

Julian asks for these first two gifts, feeling the Passion of Christ more intensely and experiencing a life-threatening illness, with one reservation, saying, "Lord, you know what I would have, if it is your will that I should have it, and if it is not your will, good Lord, do not be displeased, for I only want what you want" (LT 2, par. 2; ST 1, par. 4). But, Julian tells us, she asked for the third gift without any reservation and that "The first two of the longings just mentioned [to feel the Passion and to suffer illness] passed from my mind, and the third stayed with me continually" (ST 1, par. 6). Moved by a story of St. Cecelia according to which the saint "received three wounds in the neck from which she died," Julian "conceived a great longing, praying our Lord God that he would grant me three wounds in my lifetime: that is to say, the wound of contrition, the wound of compassion, and the wound of an earnest longing for God" (ST 1, par. 5). Because they are "wounds," all these gifts involve suffering, contrition as suffering in the form of sorrow over pain caused by her sin; compassion as suffering with those who suffer; and the "earnest longing to be with God" as the desire to be with Christ in his suffering for us on the cross.

Besides the work that Julian did, asking earnestly for three gifts and writing this book of reflections, we have the work of God in her through the revelations. What the revelations reveal is the love of God expressed in the sufferings of Christ and in Christ's extraordinary mercy towards us in our sin in the form of super-abounding grace, God's compassion in Christ. Julian's life-work that begins before the writing of the *Revelations* but is known to us only through that text, the work itself of writing the text, and the work of God in Julian that constitutes the principal content of that text—these are the three aspects of Julian's activity united by the principle of compassion. And, if we can, through the window of the text, discern something of Julian's life before the writing of the *Revelations,* we can also through the same text glimpse a future work that it points to. "This book was begun by God's gift and his grace, but it seems to me that it is not yet completed" (LT 86, par. 1). The completion of the book, Julian tells us in this last chapter of her *Revelations,* will take place in her own life and in the lives of those who will read her work. In the last paragraph of the *Revelations,* Julian prays that:

> this book come only into the hands of those who want to love him faithfully, and to those who are willing to submit themselves to the faith of Holy Church and obey the sound understanding and teaching of men of virtuous life, grave years, and profound learning; for this revelation is deep theology and great wisdom, so it must not remain with anyone who is thrall to sin and the Devil (LT 86, par. 4).

In expressing this hope for the future, Julian is praying that those who read her book will also be drawn into the saving mystery of God's compassion in Christ.

THE PARABLE OF THE LORD AND THE SERVANT

"[Julian's] most penetrating insight into this mystery of salvation comes in the parable of the lord and the servant, expounded in LT chapter 51, by far the longest chapter she wrote . . ." (A.C. Spearing, 1998, xxvii). Nicholas Watson calls this story, which came to Julian twenty years after the original revelation, i.e., 1393, "the heart of the entire work in LT" (Watson 1993, 638). Julian herself says of the parable, ". . . it gives me some teaching, as if it were the beginning of an ABC, through which I may have some understanding of God's purpose, for the mysteries of the revelation are hidden in it . . ." (LT 51, par. 17). Through this parable, Julian found at least a partial resolution of the tension she had been struggling with between two judgments, one the Church's teaching on human sin, the other the content of her revelation according to which God assigns no blame to us. Though God's personal revelation to her was "sweet and delectable," she "could not quite be freed from anxiety" (LT 45, par. 2) because of the Church's judgment according to which she was bound to acknowledge herself a sinner and to recognize that sinners deserve blame and anger one day; "and I could see no blame or anger in God, and then I felt a longing greater than I can or may tell; for God himself revealed the higher judgement at the same time, and therefore I was bound to accept it; and the lower judgement had been taught me before by Holy Church, and therefore I could in no way abandon the lower judgement" (106). This tension between the teaching of the Church, which Julian accepted with her whole heart, and the truth of her revelations, is the place we must enter with her if we are to appreciate the meaning of the lord and the servant. Julian's theological method is to hold the Church's teaching firmly in place and to hold the truth of her revelation equally firmly and attempt a resolution of the tension.

Here is the story. The lord sits with dignity and the servant waits reverently ready to do the lord's will. The lord sends the servant on a mission. "The servant does not just walk, but leaps forward and runs in great haste, in loving anxiety to do his lord's will. And he falls into a slough and is very badly hurt" (LT 51, par. 2). The servant's greatest problem, Julian tells us, was that he had no help to get out of the slough "for he could not turn his face to look at his loving lord" (Ibid.). According to Julian's interpretation, given three months short of twenty years after the vision, the lord is God, and the servant is Adam—she does not mention Eve—who represents all human beings. It is important to note the differences between the servant and the Adam and Eve of the Genesis account and of Christian tradition. The servant, unlike Adam, fell into the slough not through disobedience or any other fault, but through an excess of zeal. "And I watched carefully to see if I could perceive any fault in him, or if the lord would blame him at all; and in truth there was no fault to be seen, for his good will and his great longing were the only cause of his fall; and he was as willing and inwardly good as when he stood before his lord ready to do his will" (Ibid.).

And God's attitude toward the servant's misfortune is different, too. In Genesis, God reproves Adam and Eve for what they have done and assigns a punishment. Not so in Julian's version of the story. "But in the sight of God [the servant's] purpose remained undiminished; for I saw our Lord commend and approve his purpose . . ." (par. 7). God finds no fault with Adam; it is Adam who has lost his sense of purpose: "but the man himself was obstructed and blind to the knowledge of this purpose, and this causes him great sorrow and grievous misery; for neither can he see his loving lord, who is most gentle and kind to him, nor can he see truly how he himself appears to his loving lord" (Julian, Ibid.).

Thus Julian transforms the story of the fall in pushing to their limits both the orthodox belief in the essential goodness of human beings, what Paul Ricoeur calls "primordial goodness," and the Christian conviction about God's mercy. "And this," says Julian, "was the beginning of the teaching revealed to me at this time, through which I might come to know God's attitude to us in our sin. And then I saw that only suffering blames and punishes, and our kind Lord comforts and grieves; he always considers the soul cheerfully, loving and longing to bring us to bliss" (Ibid.).

Continuing her reflection on God's infinite tenderness and mercy, Julian arrives at a striking conception of the identity of Adam and Christ that provides the clue to the parable's meaning and at the same time introduces a note of confusion. "In the servant is comprehended the second person of the Trinity, and in the servant is comprehended Adam, that is to say all men" (par. 13). Even Paul did not go this far in identifying Christ and Adam. Julian identifies Adam's fall and the Incarnation of the Word: "When Adam fell, God's son fell; because of the true union made in heaven, God's son could not leave Adam, for by Adam I understand all men" (Ibid.). Adam fell into "the valley of this wretched world," and "God's son fell with Adam into the valley of the Virgin's womb" (Ibid.). Julian's "servant" represents Christ and Adam as one man, the "strength and goodness which we have" coming from Jesus Christ, "the weakness and blindness which we have" coming from Adam. Julian identifies Christ with the longing of humans to be saved and with all who will be saved: "for the wish and the craving of all mankind that shall be saved appeared in Jesus; for Jesus is all who shall be saved and all who shall be saved are Jesus; and all through God's love, along with the obedience, humility and patience, and other virtues which pertain to us" (LT 51, par. 16).

Julian continues in chapter 52 with the Pauline notion of grace abounding. It seems highly likely that Julian was familiar with this teaching of Paul, twice citing his words on other issues explicitly (ST 9, par. 2; 10, par. 1), and on other occasions expressing ideas that are typically Pauline, especially the notion of grace abounding more than sin and the corollary that both she and Paul reject, namely that we should sin more so that grace will abound even more (Rom. 6:1–2; ST 18, par. 1). In Chapter 52, Julian speaks both of "Adam's woe" and the "exalted magnificence" to which humanity is destined: "In the lord was shown the sorrow and pity of Adam's woe; and in the lord was shown the exalted magnificence and endless glory to which mankind attains through the power of the Passion and the death of God's much-loved son" (LT 52, par. 4). And for this reason, she continues, "he rejoices greatly in his fall, because of the great exaltation and fullness of bliss that mankind attains, surpassing what we should have if he had not fallen; and so it was to see this surpassing magnificence that my understanding was led into God at the same time that I saw the servant fall" (Ibid.). This vision, breathtaking in Paul, is even more breathtaking in Julian. Julian's profound relativizing of human sin through the comparison with God's grace is comprehensible only if we assume the vantage point of God as Julian's revelations allowed her to do: ". . . only suffering blames and punishes, and our kind Lord comforts and grieves" (LT 51, par. 7).

Julian's conflating of the fall of Adam and the incarnation into one and the same event and her identification of the servant as both Adam and Christ, as the most original and consequential element of the parable, requires some elaboration. Julian took twenty years to come to an understanding of this showing (LT 51, par.6); for us to work out its implications will take some careful reflection. When we first read that the master sends the servant on a mission, which the servant eagerly runs to fulfill only to fall, through no fault of his own—into a slough from which he cannot get out—we do not yet know who the master and servant are. Soon Julian tells us that the servant is Adam, but not only Adam, "for in the servant who represented Adam, as I shall explain, I saw many different properties which could in no way be attributed just to Adam. And so for the moment I was in a state of great bewilderment; for a full understanding of this marvelous parable was not given to me at this time" (LT 51, par. 4). Julian now explains the three stages in which her comprehension unfolded. "The first is the early stage of teaching which I understood from it while it was being shown to me; the second is the inner learning which I have come to understand from it since then; the third is the whole revelation from beginning to end, as set out in this book . . ." (par. 5).

The "properties which could in no way be attributed just to Adam," Julian tells us, are attributed to Christ. But Julian does not tell us so until after she has let us think for several pages that this Adam is the one we read about in Genesis 3. Two differences between Julian's Adam and the Adam of Genesis seem to fly in the face of the traditional interpretation. Genesis presents Adam and Eve as falling, not through eagerness to carry out a mission from God, but as disobeying God's prohibition against eating of the fruit of the tree of the knowledge of good and evil. Julian's Adam falls through no fault of his own; Julian does not even suggest that Adam's eagerness was excessive, a kind of impetuous rushing off before thinking of what he was doing. The Adam and Eve of Genesis, as Genesis describes them and the tradition has interpreted them, commit the originating fault that has brought about the condition we call original sin.

The notion of a faultless fall becomes clearer when Julian tells us that the servant is both Adam and Christ. "In the servant is comprehended the second person of the Trinity, and in the servant is comprehended Adam, that is to say, all men. And therefore when I say 'the Son,' it means the Godhead, which is equal with the Father, and when I say 'the servant,' it means Christ's Humanity, which is truly Adam" (par. 13). We have here not only the Father and the Son but the Holy Ghost "which is the equal love which is in both of them" (Ibid.). Not only is the servant both Adam and Christ, but the fall of Adam is simultaneous with the incarnation of Christ: "Adam fell from life to death into the valley of this wretched world and after that into hell. God's son fell *with Adam* [italics added] into the valley of the Virgin's womb . . . in order to free Adam from guilt in heaven and in earth; and with his great power he fetched him out of hell" (Ibid.). Note that God's son has come to "free Adam from guilt."

For the first time in this parable, Julian has attributed guilt to Adam, which makes us wonder whether, when she spoke of the servant falling into a slough *through no fault of his own*, she might really have been speaking of the servant as Christ and not as Adam. Though Julian had spoken earlier of the servant's eagerness in carrying out the master's mission, she now speaks of human "guilt," but only to say that Christ has taken it on himself so that "our Father neither may nor will assign us any more guilt than he does to his own son, dearly loved Christ" (par. 15). Our suspicion that when Julian spoke of "the fall" she was speaking of the Incarnation is confirmed as we come to the end of the parable. The servant is both strong and weak, strong as the Son of God, weak as Christ and Adam. "The wisdom and goodness in the servant represent God's son. That he was poorly dressed as a labourer and standing near the left-hand side [of the master] represents Christ's humanity and Adam, with all the consequent trouble and weakness; for in this parable our good Lord showed his own son and Adam as but one man. The strength and goodness which we have come from Jesus Christ [as son of God], the weakness and the blindness which we have come from Adam, and these two are represented in the servant" (par.14).

Julian becomes even more explicit in teaching that the mission given to the servant, which the servant eagerly carried out and, through no fault of his own, fell into a slough, is the Father's sending of the Son into the world for the redemption of human beings and not the disobedience of Adam and Eve. And the fall is the Son's fall into our humanity with all its troubles. "Thus the son was the servant before he came to earth, standing ready before the Father, waiting until the time when he would send him to do that glorious deed by which mankind was brought back to heaven . . ." (par. 15). Julian leads us to believe that this is the meaning of the parable: "Therefore what was conveyed was in respect of the Manhood of Christ; for all mankind who shall be saved by Christ's precious Incarnation and blessed Passion, all are Christ's Manhood" (par.16). The phrase "all mankind who shall be saved" is important and we will return to it in discussing Julian's suggestion that *all* people will be saved. Julian repeats the points she has made: "all those under heaven who shall come there shall do so by longing and wishing; and this wish and longing was shown in the servant standing in front of the lord, or to put it differently, in the Son standing in front of the Father in Adam's tunic; for the wish and the craving of all mankind that shall be saved appeared in Jesus; for Jesus is all who shall be saved and all who shall be saved are Jesus" (Ibid.). Not only is the fall of the servant identical with the incarnation of the Son entering into the womb of the Virgin, but the eagerness in carrying out the mission belongs not to Adam and Eve as we know them from Genesis, but to the Son responding to God's determination to send him to earth to free humans from guilt. "[The servant's] leaping up belonged to the Godhead [in the Son] and his running to Christ's manhood; for the Godhead leapt from the Father into the Virgin's womb, falling when he took on our nature; and in this fall he was grievously hurt; the hurt he received was our flesh in which he soon felt deathly pain" (par. 17).

We can summarize the parable in five key points: First, the lord's commission to the servant; second, the servant's eagerness in carrying out the commission; third, the servant's fall and consequent distress, including the inability to see God; fourth, the absence of blame on God's part for the servant's fall; and fifth, the identification of the servant as Adam and Christ and of the servant's fall as Adam's fall and Christ's fall, each in different ways. That the parable does not contain any account of the "sin" of Adam and Eve surprises us since Julian presents it as the story of Adam and the fall. Throughout this study, we have interpreted the story of Adam and Eve according to the tradition that sees in it an account of the origin of sin. The parable is, as Julian calls it, "wonderful," but for us problematic in that it leaves sin out of account.

ORIGINAL SIN IN JULIAN'S REVELATIONS

Given the problematic character of the parable of the lord and the servant with respect to determining an origin of sin, we need to look elsewhere in Julian's writings for some account of the fundamental or originating fault to which every other sin can be reduced. As we have already seen, this originating fault can be viewed temporally, as when we think, following the tradition, of the disobedience of Adam and Eve as being first in time of a long succession of sins. We can also think about original sin in a structural sense as a sin that lies at the root of other sins much as, on the physical level, a defective immune system leaves us vulnerable to opportunistic diseases or anemia can lead to tiredness and depression. By omitting an account of the temporally first sin in the parable of master and servant, where it would most naturally have occurred, Julian forces us to look elsewhere in her texts to see if we can find either a temporal or a structural beginning point of sin, the originating fault through which other sins enter in and flourish.

Chapter 47 of the Long Text, falling between Chapter 45 in which Julian first expresses her struggle to resolve the tension between the Church's judgment about sin and punishment and Chapter 51 that contains the "only answer" she received to satisfy her longing to understand, "a wonderful parable of a lord and a servant, very strikingly shown" (45, par. 3), provides just the sort of account we are looking for. Julian here speaks not of a temporal origin of sin, but a structural one. In statements that hold the opposed perceptions together, each truth undiluted by the presence of its opposite, Julian tells us what she saw: "And from all that I saw it seemed to me that it was necessary for us to see and to acknowledge that we are sinners . . ." (47, par. 2). Our sins, says Julian include both the evil things we do and the good deeds we leave undone. This would seem to merit God's anger but, for Julian, it does not. "And in spite of all this I saw truly that our Lord was never angry and never will be angry, for he is God: goodness, life, truth, love, peace; and his loving kindness does not allow him to be angry, nor does his unity. . . . God is the goodness that cannot be angry" (Ibid.).

In this same Chapter 47, Julian spells out her teaching about original sin. First, Julian tells us what she was looking for based on what she had "already learned" (par. 1), presumably from the teaching of the Church, namely that the mercy of God would consist in the "remission of his anger after our time of sin" (Ibid.). Yet, however much she looked, she "could not see this anywhere in the showing" (Ibid.). What Julian did see was the deepest source of human sin. She saw that humans "are changeable in this life and through frailty and accident we fall into sin" (47, par. 2), that humans are "naturally weak and foolish" and their "will is smothered; and in this world [they suffer] storm and sorrow and woe, and the cause is [their] own blindness" (Ibid.). This blindness seems to be the root of other sins. We do not *see* God; for "if [we] saw God continually, [we] would have no evil feelings, nor any sort of impulse towards the *craving which leads to sin* [italics added]" (Ibid.). The "craving which leads to sin" suggests what the Bible calls "covetousness" (Exod. 20:17; Rom. 6:7–8) and what René Girard calls "mimetic rivalry." But Julian finds something deeper than craving, the blindness that keeps us from seeing God's goodness. We might well say that Adam and Eve were blind before they fell for the serpent's temptation to eat the fruit and become like God. The blindness was a failure to recognize God's goodness to them, a lack of gratitude for their existence that made them susceptible to the enticement the serpent offered.

In Chapter 48, Julian helps us to further understand what she means by "original sin" by extending her presentation of the blindness to God's love that causes sin and the contrariness into which we fall when the vision of God is absent. God is not angry over sins, humans are, and God forgives even that, "for anger is nothing but contrariness and antagonism to peace and love, and it comes from lack of strength—and it is not God who lacks these things but we who lack them . . ." (48, par. 1). What is amazing in all this is the extent of God's mercy and grace, which Julian distinguished from each other: "For I saw the property of mercy and the property of grace, which have two ways of working in one love. Mercy is a pitiful [i.e., pity-filled—see translation by John Julian, *Love's Trinity,* 48, par. 3] property which belongs to motherhood in tender love, and grace is an honourable property which belongs to royal lordship in the same love. . ." (*Revelations,* 48, par. 2). The work of mercy is to protect, tolerate, revive, and heal; the work of grace is to raise, reward, and go infinitely beyond what our love and our effort deserve.

In Chapters 49 and 50, Julian continues her build-up to the parable of the lord and the servant, reaffirming in Chapter 49 that in God no anger exists and that therefore he cannot forgive—"it would be an impossibility" (49, par. 1). Julian seems to imply that anger is what makes forgiveness necessary. Without anger, forgiveness is not necessary, not even possible. And God takes away our anger which proves that he himself must be without anger: "It must needs be that he who wears away and extinguishes our anger and makes us gentle and kind is himself always consistently loving, gentle and kind which is the contrary of anger . . ." (Ibid.). Julian saw "no kind of anger in God, neither for a short time nor for a long one . . ." (Ibid.). In Chapter 50, Julian repeats the question she first posed in Chapter 45 about the opposition between the two truths of which she was equally convinced. First the reality of sin: "For I knew through the universal teaching of Holy Church and through my own experience that the guilt of our sin weighs us down continually, from Adam, the first man, until the time when we come up into heaven . . ." (Ibid.). The reference to her own experience in this formulation does not appear in the earlier statement of Chapter 45, where Julian simply says that "According to this judgement [of the Holy Church] it seemed to me that I had to acknowledge myself a sinner . . ." (45, par. 2). This means that Julian's amazement at God's mercy, the second truth of which she was convinced through her revelations, comes from its contrast not only with the teaching of the Church but with her own experience of sin. "Then this is what amazed me," says Julian, "that I saw our Lord God blaming us no more than if we were as pure and as holy as angels in heaven" (49, par. 1).

At the end of Chapter 50, Julian again expresses her deep anguish, as she had in Chapter 45, at not being able to resolve a contradiction at the very center of her faith. Throughout these six chapters (45–50), Julian has repeated in various ways the contradiction between our sin and God's lack of anger. The tension has become more and more difficult for her to bear. "And between these two contraries my reason was greatly tormented by my blindness, and could not rest for fear that God's blessed presence should pass from my sight and I should be left not knowing how he regards us in our sin . . ." (50, par. 2). Either of two responses would satisfy her: "for either I needed to see in God that all sin was done away with, or else I needed to see in God how he sees it, so that I might truly know how it befits me to see sin and what sort of blame is ours" (Ibid.). "I cried inwardly with all my might," Julian tells us, "beseeching God for help, thinking as follows: 'Ah! Lord Jesus, king of bliss, how can I be helped? Who can show me and tell me what I need to know if I cannot see now in you?'" (Ibid.).

The intensity of Julian's anguish reminds us of Augustine's on the brink of his conversion. "I was in torment," says Augustine, "reproaching myself more bitterly than ever as I twisted and turned in my chain. I hoped that my chain might be broken once for all, because it was only a small thing that held me now. All the same it held me" (*Conf.*, 8, 11, par. 1). But a great difference separates Julian's anguish from Augustine's that makes it more difficult, not easier, to understand. Augustine's was a moral anguish; he longed to be set free from habits of sin that bound him as if in chains. Julian's torment seems metaphysical. By the time we come to this stage in Augustine's life, having followed him through the circuitous path[3] of his struggles, it is easy to appreciate his intense longing to be free. But apart from the cryptic phrase mentioned above, "from my own experience," we have no way of knowing the source of Julian's metaphysical anguish. We can only note that the revelations of God's extraordinary forbearance and mercy seem to have profoundly challenged the way the Church's teaching and her own experience had led her to regard sin. She was trying to come to terms with God's mercy, caught between the guilt and fear of punishment that she had learned and this new, amazing revelation of benevolent love.

Recognition of Julian's struggle is essential if we are to avoid the temptation of seeing only sweetness in her account. Paradoxical as it might seem, her own guilt and fear may have been easier for her to accept, as she says it is for all of us, than the overwhelming graciousness of God, and she knew she was more likely to lose sight of the vision of mercy, as she herself points out, than the sense of guilt. We are more likely to be ignorant of God's love than of our own sufferings caused by sin.: ". . . for many men and women believe that God is almighty and has power to do everything, and that he is all wisdom and knows how to do everything, but that he is all love and is willing to do everything—there they stop" (ST 24, par. 2). The evidence for this lack of confidence lies in the fear that good people experience "when they begin to hate sin and to mend their ways" (Ibid.). Though people take this fear for humility, it is really "foul ignorance and weakness" (Ibid.). "So of all the properties of the Trinity," Julian concludes, "it is God's wish that we should place most reliance on liking and love; for love makes God's power and wisdom very gentle to us; just as through his generosity God forgives our sin when we repent, so he wants us to forget our sin and all our depression and all doubtful fear" (Ibid.).

We have already considered the parable of the lord and the servant, set forth in Chapter 51, which was given to Julian as the "only answer" (45, par. 3) to her insistent questioning. And when, in Chapter 45, Julian first tells us of this "wonderful parable of a lord and a servant" which she promises to recount later, she also recognizes that this story will not completely satisfy her. "And yet," she says, "I still long, and shall until my dying day, through God's grace to understand these two judgements as they apply to me; for all heavenly things and all earthly ones which belong to heaven, are included in these two judgements" (45, par. 3). Julian had asked either "to see in God that all sin was done away with," or "to see in God how he sees it" (50, par. 1). God did not show her that sin had been done away with; he did show her how he regards it, that is, without blame. The heart of the parable, as I have already said, is the identification of Christ and Adam and it is because of this identification that God regards us without attributing guilt: "And thus our good Lord Jesus has taken upon himself all our guilt; and therefore our Father neither may nor will assign more blame to us than he does to his own son, dearly loved Christ" (51, par. 15).

In chapter 13 of ST, when Julian had asked why God had not prevented sin, God had informed her "of all that I needed to know" (ST 13, par. 4), not that she needs no further teaching, "for our Lord, in this revelation, has left me to Holy Church . . ." (Ibid.). Then Julian tells us of God's enigmatic response: "'Sin is befitting.' With this word 'sin' our Lord brought to my mind the whole extent of all that is not good: the shameful scorn and the utter humiliation he bore for us in this life and in his dying, and all the pains and sufferings of all his creatures, both in body and in spirit . . ." (ST 13, par. 5). God showed Julian all this "along with all the pains that ever were and ever shall be; all this was shown in a flash, and quickly changed into comfort; for our good Lord did not want the soul to be afraid of this ugly sight" (Ibid.). And why should we not be afraid of this "ugly sight"? Because sin has no independent reality: "But I did not see sin; for I believe it has no sort of substance nor portion of being, nor could it be recognized were it not for the suffering it causes" (par. 6).

Julian had begun her questioning with the conviction that if sin had never existed, "all would have been well" (13, par. 4). Now she sees that sin has no independent reality and that we are even protected against the suffering it causes by the Passion of our Lord. "He supports us willingly and sweetly, by his words, and says, 'But all shall be well, and all manner of things shall be well.' These words were shown very tenderly, with no suggestion that I or anyone who will be saved was being blamed" (13, par. 6). Julian chooses words carefully. She says that "sin has no sort of substance nor portion of being;" she does not say it has no reality. In saying that sin has no substance, Julian is following a long tradition in Christian theology that denies any independent reality to evil. Augustine firmly teaches that only what is good *exists*. "Therefore, whatever is, is good; and evil, the origin of which I was trying to find, is not a substance, because if it were a substance it would be good" (*Conf.,* VII, 12, par. 2). Augustine applies this teaching to the turning of the will from God that we call sin: "And when I asked myself what wickedness was, I saw that it was not a substance but perversion of the will when it turns aside from you" (VII, 15, par. 2). Thomas Aquinas follows Augustine in denying independent reality to evil: evil is the absence of a quality in an existent that ought to have that quality (Aquinas, *De Malo,* Q. 1, Art 1, "Whether evil is any-thing"). For instance blindness in a human being is a physical evil because sight is an attribute that naturally belongs to humans. In a stone, blindness is not a defect. To attribute an independent existence to evil was the heresy of the Manichees from whom Augustine worked so long to extricate himself. The same confusion about the substantiality of evil surfaced again in the Albigensian heresy that the Church dealt with about two centuries before Julian. Sin is real, but not substantial. Just as sin is real, it has real consequences and the merciful compassion of God alone keeps us from suffering these consequences.

We can summarize Julian's teaching about sin. First, the teaching comes from three sources, the doctrine of the Church, her own experience, and her revelations, and it contains some oppositions that she herself cannot resolve. Second, sin is real and has real consequences. Third, sin is not substantial, i.e., it does not have independent existence. Fourth, the root of sin, the originating sin, is human blindness to God's love. Fifth, God does not blame and is not angry at the sins of "those who will be saved." This last phrase, "those who will be saved," raises a question that we must now explore in some depth. The phrase seems to imply that some will be saved and some not, in which case Julian's teaching seems consistent with Church teaching as she would have known it. But Julian, in some places, suggests that all will be saved. How can we reconcile these two ideas?

"ALL SHALL BE WELL" AND
THE QUESTION OF UNIVERSAL SALVATION

Julian expresses the consequence of Christ's merciful compassion in the famously recurring refrain "All shall be well," which in all its variations, functions as a kind of leitmotiv in Julian's two texts, especially the Long Text. These reassuring words act as an antidote to the anxiety that arises in a faithful soul concerned about the consequences of sin. Even where the refrain does not occur in the context of an explicit mention of sin, it always assumes that context and only makes sense in light of sin and its effects. Some have taken the frequent reiteration of this refrain in the LT as evidence of Julian's belief in universal salvation as if she is saying "all will be well for everyone, believers and unbelievers, good and bad, in spite of everything they have done or not done." Before affirming that conclusion, we need to look carefully at the texts, and particularly at another phrase that recurs regularly, "for all those that shall be saved." This refrain implying that perhaps some will not be saved seems to restrict the scope of "all shall be well;" all shall be well for some, but not for all. However, at least two passages seem to suggest universal salvation.

A passage in Chapter 9 of the LT shows the ambiguity introduced by the phrase "all who shall be saved." Julian begins this chapter by humbly affirming that her visions have not made her a better Christian than those who have not had visions "but only the normal teaching of Holy Church, and who love God better than I do" (LT 9, par. 1). The passage that follows immediately introduces some confusion. I will italicize expressions that introduce a note of ambiguity.

> For if I look solely at myself, I am really nothing; but as one of humankind in general, I am, I hope, in oneness of love *with all my fellow Christians;* for upon this oneness depends the life of *all who shall be saved*; for God is all that is good, as I see it, and God has made all that is made, and God loves all that he has made, and he *who loves all his fellow Christians for God's sake, loves all that is; for in those who shall be saved, all is included: that is to say, all that is made and the Maker of all; for in man is God, and God is in everything* (Ibid.).

The first part of the passage suggests a narrowing of Julian's focus from the phrase "as one of humankind in general" to the more restrictive "oneness of love with all my fellow Christians." The last part of this passage seems to move in the opposite direction, from the restrictive phrase, "those who shall be saved" to the universal, "all is included." In spite of its ambiguity, this passage does open up the possibility that Julian is affirming universal salvation.

Chapters 31 and 32 suggest a Trinitarian work that may well involve the salvation of all people, though some ambiguity still exists even here. Chapter 31 contains Julian's most elaborate expression of the "all will be well" refrain in which she connects various forms of the phrase with the persons and work of the Trinity.

> And thus our good Lord answered all the questions and doubts I could put forward, saying most comfortingly, 'I may make all things well, I can make all things well, and I will make all things well; and you shall see for yourself that all manner of things shall be well.' I take 'I may' for the words of the Father, I take 'I can' for the words of the Son and I take 'I will' for the words of the Holy Ghost; and where he says 'I shall,' I take it for the unity of the Holy Trinity, three persons, one truth; and where he says 'You shall see for yourself,' I understand it as referring to the union with the Holy Trinity of all mankind *who shall be saved* [italics added] (LT 31, par. 1).

The italicized phrase indicates something less than universal salvation, but the passage as a whole expresses a profound theological awareness of the involvement of the Trinity in the work of salvation, at least for those who will be saved.

In Chapter 32, Julian carries forward the image of the Trinity at work in the world for its salvation and takes a significant step beyond where she left us in Chapter 31.

> It appears to me that there is a deed which the Holy Trinity shall do on the last day, and when that deed shall be done and how it shall be done is unknown to all creatures under Christ, and shall be until it has been done. . . . This is the great deed ordained by our Lord God from eternity, treasured up and hidden in his blessed breast, only known to himself, and by this deed he shall make all things well; for just as the Holy Trinity made all things from nothing, so the Holy Trinity shall make all well that is not well (LT 32, par. 2).

And what is the great deed? It is a deed that, as Julian recognizes, profoundly challenges our faith: for ". . . it is part of our faith that many will be damned—like the angels who fell out of heaven from pride, who are now fiends, and men on earth who die outside the faith of Holy Church . . . and also any man who has received Christianity and lives an unchristian life and so dies excluded from the love of God" (par. 3). Given this teaching of the Church, Julian "thought it impossible that all manner of things should be well, as our Lord revealed at this time" (Ibid.). That all should be well seems clearly, from the context, to mean that all shall be saved. The only answer Julian received to her perplexity was that "What is impossible to you is not impossible to me. I shall keep my word in all things and I shall make all things well" (Ibid.).

Just as in the case of the parable of the lord and the servant, we saw Julian maintaining two opposed truths, one the Church's teaching about blame and guilt, the other the content of her revelation that showed no blame of Adam relative to his fall, now we see the opposition between the doctrine that some will be damned and the revelation that all will be made well. The revelation about universal salvation explicitly instructs Julian to hold the opposed truths without knowing how the contradiction might be resolved: "Thus I was taught by the grace of God that I should remain steadfastly in the faith, as I had previously understood, and at the same time that I should firmly believe that all things will be well as our Lord God revealed on the same occasion" (par. 4). How this shall be accomplished "no creature under Christ . . . knows or shall know until it is done" (Ibid.). It seems clear, then, that Julian holds the doctrine of universal salvation, but she holds it as an incomprehensible mystery of God's compassionate love, revealed to her in her showings and not derived from her own reasoning or the teachings of the Church, not from any work she might have read or from her own experience outside the showings.

To properly evaluate Julian's position, we must enter the same space opened up for Julian between these two opposed truths. It may not be a space Julian's readers want to enter, not just because of the Church's traditional teaching, but because of some personal resistance to the possibility that God's justice might be so thoroughly swallowed up by God's compassion. Like Julian, her readers might find themselves suspended between opposed truths and, perhaps, even between conflicting tendencies of their own personalities, their mind's longing for justice on one side and the pull of their heart toward compassion on the other. The divine respect for human choice seems to necessitate God's allowing some to freely reject the offered gift of salvation. That the gift might be given, willy-nilly, to individuals who have steadfastly refused it up to and including the moment of their death suggests a benevolent kind of predestination that renders human choices inconsequential. Such are the thoughts that might occur to those trying to enter into Julian's vision. But then she herself did not understand.

JULIAN'S RELATION TO THE
TRADITION THAT PRECEDED HER

In this chapter, I have noted textual resonances between Julian's *Revelations* and the thought of other authors and works explored in this study. These similarities of thought patterns enable us to use Julian as a summary of what we have already seen. We might be inclined to speculate, as some commentators have, about how various elements of the Christian tradition come to have a place in Julian's thought. Some have concluded that, in spite of her claim that "These revelations were shown to a simple, uneducated creature" (LT 2, par. 1), Julian was in fact highly educated. Colledge and Walsh, for instance, in the introduction to their critical edition of *Showings,* call Julian's claim to be ignorant as "nothing but a well-known, often employed rhetorical device, appealing for benevolence from the reader by dispraising the writer's abilities" (Colledge and Walsh, 19), and that, in fact, Julian had a "profound knowledge and flexible use of the Latin Vulgate text, and she seems to have been familiar with a wide range of the classical spiritual writings that were the foundations of the monastic contemplative tradition" (20). Marion Glasscoe, on the other hand, takes Julian at her word and concludes that Julian's concern is to achieve "a depth of insight into the inner realities of human existence as perceived in Christian terms" (Glasscoe, 223; cited in Bauerschmidt, 205) rather than Christian doctrines about God, sin, and salvation. Bauerschmidt's middle position between these two extremes seems most reasonable: "On the whole I would argue that Glasscoe's presentation of Julian as illiterate in the modern sense is implausible, and Colledge and Walsh's thesis that she was highly educated is unnecessary" (206).

Without being able to resolve the question of Julian's education, we can point to key passages that seem to locate her in the mainstream of Christian tradition. Her identifying the servant in her parable as Adam, for instance, and other references to Adam, suggest a familiarity with the story of Adam and Eve in Genesis. And Julian does, as we have seen, refer specifically to the words of Paul: "Nothing shall separate me from the love of Christ" (Rom. 8:35), and "But every soul, as Saint Paul says, should feel in himself what was in Jesus Christ" (Phil. 2:5, Julian ST 9, par. 2), and Peter, "Lord, save me, I perish" (Matt. 14:30, Julian, ST 10, par. 1). We can, then, safely assume that Julian had some familiarity with Paul and the Gospels. She must have been aware of Paul's identification of Christ as the second Adam, when she took a creative step beyond Paul in identifying Christ as the first Adam. And Julian's references to the superiority of redeemed human condition in comparison to the human condition before the fall (LT 39, par. 2; 51, par. 3) as well as the related caution not to let God's abundant grace tempt us to sin (LT 40, par. 3) seem clearly Pauline.

Certain passages in Julian also echo church Fathers and early medieval scholastics. In the parable of the lord and the servant, pursuing the identity of Christ with Adam and our humanity, Julian describes the glorious clothing worn by the Son as he stands before the Father (the lord of the parable) and concludes with a passage strongly reminiscent of Irenaeus' "God's glory is human being fully alive" (Irenaeus, 4, 20, 5–7), ". . . for it was shown that we are his crown, and that this crown is the Father's joy, the Son's glory, the Holy Ghost's delight . . . (LT 51, par. 15). We have already seen the striking similarity between what Julian's revelations showed her about the insubstantiality of sin and Augustine's declaration that "evil . . . is not a substance" (*Conf.,* VII, 12, par. 2). Aquinas, following Augustine, teaches that "evil of itself is not something, but the privation of some particular good" (*De Malo,* question 1, article 1, Response). Julian's claim that "God is nearer to ourselves than our own soul" (LT 56, par. 2) evokes Augustine's "God is more inward (*interior*) to me than my inmost self (*intimo meo, Conf.,* III, 6, par. 5). For Julian, the indwelling of God in us meant that "it is easier for us to attain certain knowledge of God than to know our own soul; for our soul is so deeply grounded in God, and so eternally treasured, that we cannot attain knowledge of it until we first know God" (par. 2). Finally, and most important, for this study, is Julian's participation, conscious or unconscious, in the renewed emphasis on compassion represented by Hugh of St. Victor (1096–1141) and his followers in the Victorine tradition.

Boyd Taylor Coolman's 2008 *Theological Studies a*rticle, "Hugh of St. Victor on 'Jesus Wept': Compassion as Ideal *Humanitas*," speaks of Hugh's emphasis on compassion in Christ: ". . . it is in fact Hugh's high estimation of compassion as the proper and signature feature of Jesus' humanity that prompts him not only to make Christological sense of Jesus' tears, but also to hold up Jesus as exemplar of such human activity" (Coolman, 532–33). Hugh, as a canon of the order of St. Augustine teaching other canons, "enjoins the feeling of compassion especially on clerics and prelates" (548). He urges them to follow Paul's injunction "to rejoice with those who rejoice and to weep with those who weep" (Rom. 12:15), "and in a striking illustration, he links these two facets of fellow-feeling with the 'breasts of maternal affection' . . ." (549), thus anticipating Julian's striking references to Christ as our mother. "And our Saviour is our true mother," says Julian, "in whom we are eternally born and by whom we shall always be enclosed (LT 57, par. 4). In one of those striking lyrical passages in which Julian ties together the various agents of our salvation, she tells us that Jesus manifests his motherhood by doing good for evil and that the wisdom of his motherhood balances the power and goodness of his fatherhood:

> Thus Jesus Christ who does good for evil is our true mother; we have our being from him where the ground of motherhood begins, with all the sweet protection of love which follows eternally. God is our mother as truly as he is our father; and he showed this in everything and especially in the sweet words where he says, 'It is I,' that is to say, 'It is I: the power and goodness of fatherhood. It is I: the wisdom of motherhood. It is I: the light and the grace which is all blessed

love. It is I: the Trinity. It is I: the unity. I am the sovereign goodness of all manner of things. It is I that make you love. It is I that make you long. It is I: the eternal fulfillment of all true desires' (LT 59, par. 2).

For Julian, motherhood means tender mercy. "But now it is necessary to say a little more about . . . how we are redeemed by the motherhood of mercy and grace . . ." (LT 60, par. 1). Julian plays on the theme of Jesus' motherhood in feeding us: "The mother can give her child her milk to suck, but our dear mother Jesus can feed us with himself, and he does so most generously with the holy sacrament which is the precious food of life itself" (par. 2). In her tenth revelation, Julian was shown that "The mother can lay the child tenderly to her breast, but our tender mother Jesus, he can familiarly lead us into his blessed breast through his sweet open side" (par. 3). Julian does not speak of tender pity only in the context of motherhood. In the parable of the lord and servant she speaks of Jesus as "most comely and handsome, appearing full of tender pity" (LT 51, par. 8).

Coolman observes that the theme of compassion "has vast contemporary currency in diverse discussions of ethical, religious, and political theory," but notes that "these discussions rehearse a summarized history of compassion in Western thought that begins with classical antiquity (especially Aristotle and the Stoics) and then leaps to the early modern period, when, after long neglect (it is implied), the theme emerges prominently in thinkers such as Adam Smith, Rousseau, Kant, Schopenhauer, and Neitzsche" (Coolman, 556). And yet Coolman sees a growing dissatisfaction with the omission of the Christian account of compassion in the middle ages. "Recent scholarship signals an interest in developing a philosophically sophisticated, profoundly Christian 'theology of compassion' that draws deeply from the resources of the Christian tradition" (Ibid.). Hugh of St. Victor and Julian of Norwich would both have contributions toward such a theology of compassion.

CONCLUSION

Julian's elegant prose, both complex and seductive at the same time, has drawn readers into her thought ever since her work was first published in 1670, just three years short of the second anniversary of her revelations. Once inside her imaginative and conceptual world, readers may find themselves wrestling with the power and subtlety of her thought. People inhabiting worlds utterly different from hers in terms of time and range of interest continue to find inspiration in her work. I will mention only two.

Contemporary British theologian and eco-feminist Mary Grey finds in Julian a source of hope in which to ground her own interest in issues of social justice. Grey notes "the apparent clash between the promise that *all will be well*—and the deep-seated problems that affect culture and society today" (Grey 2009, 1). Yet she finds in this visionary who lived the last half of her life in an anchoress' cell a source of inspiration for people committed actively to the work of social transformation. After exploring in some detail the mystical grounding of Dorothy Day and Dorothy Soelle, and mentioning several influential figures grounded in mystical life—Thomas Merton, Jean Vanier, and Ghandi—Grey turns to Julian's prayer for three wounds—contrition, compassion, and longing for God and concludes: "In our contemporary context I understand these as of vital importance for a spirituality of justice" (Grey, 18).

Frederick Bauerschmidt goes beyond Grey's affirming of the mystical life as a source of hope for practitioners of liberation and finds in Julian's vision the roots of a political system. "Julian," Bauerschmidt tells us, "should be read as *one who theologically imagines the political.* This means that my chief concern is not with Julian as a writer of inherent theological and sociological interest, nor as a devotional writer, but with Julian as a resource for thinking about the relationship between theology and social theory and practice" (Bauerschmidt, 3). Following Bauerschmidt through his elaboration of this basic thesis would take us beyond the limits of this chapter. I mention his work to show the scope of inspiration modern thinkers draw from Julian's thought.

I draw three principal conclusions from the short account of Julian's thought contained in this chapter. The first is that her thought unfolds according to the famous definition of theology used by Augustine and Anselm, "faith seeking understanding." By this expression I understand the dynamic quality of faith that pushes it to comprehend what it believes. Anselm says that those who believe and do not try to understand what they believe are lazy. Julian's choice to remain grounded in her faith, the faith of the Church, is a constant feature of her reflections on the revelations she received and is, in fact, reinforced by those revelations. Julian expects her readers to remain grounded in faith as they read her work. She makes it clear, as we have seen, that she intends her book for future readers, but only for those who share deeply enough in the tradition and with enough purity to appreciate what they read. In the last paragraph of the last chapter, Julian prays to almighty God "that this book come into the hands only of those who want to love him faithfully, and to those who are willing to submit themselves to the faith of Holy Church . . . for this revelation is deep theology and great wisdom . . ." (LT 86, par. 4). Julian attributes theological depth and great wisdom, not to herself, but to the revelations she tried so faithfully to record. That readers of her book be grounded in the faith of Holy Church is not just a pious wish on Julian's part, but the condition of possibility, for her readers as it was for her, of understanding these revelations that seem to take Julian and her readers to the outer limits of the faith and beyond.

The second point is that Julian's showings are thoroughly grounded, not only in the attitude of faith, but in the content of that faith as taught by the Church and revealed to her in her showings; that faith is Christological, Trinitarian, and sacramental. The Incarnation of the Son of God for our salvation, his suffering, death, and resurrection, his identification with humanity, and his participation in the life of the Trinity form the core of her thought. And Julian admonishes her readers to take the whole of her revelations: "And beware that you do not take one thing according to your taste and fancy and leave another, for that is what heretics do" (LT 86, par. 4).

Finally, Julian puts her faith, as we have seen, in two convergent but by no means identical sources, the faith of the Church passed down in the tradition and the sixteen revelations she received on those two days in May 1373. Because the two sources of revelation were convergent, the revelations confirming the teaching of the Church, she could accept them without any temptation to reject her faith. But where the revelations stretched beyond the limits of defined faith, as in the showing of universal salvation, she continued to trust those revelations on the basis of God's assurance to her: "What is impossible to you is not impossible to me. I shall keep my word in all things and I shall make all things well" (LT 32, par. 3). For us who read her work, Julian's courage to live in the uncomfortable space between two opposed truths gives us confidence to live in that same space, trusting God even when we do not understand. For us to live in the tension between Julian's showings and traditional church teaching demands a vastly enlarged imagination that can *see* what Julian means by expressions like, "the Lord opened my spiritual eyes and showed me my soul in the middle of my heart" (ST 67, par. 1); an agile intellect comfortable with thinking opposed truths, and, most of all, an expanded heart large enough to entertain as possible the compassion her showings reveal, a compassion that might even lead to the *unthinkable*, universal salvation. The final word is love: "Do you want to know what your Lord meant?" Know well that love was what he meant. Who showed you this? Love. What did he show? Love. Why did he show it to you? For love" (LT 86, par. 2).

NOTES

1. This scriptural quotation is from the New Revised Standard Version Bible: Catholic Edition, copyright © 1989, 1993 National Council of the Churches of Christ in the United States of America. Used by permission. All rights reserved worldwide.

2. This scriptural quotation is from the New Revised Standard Version Bible: Catholic Edition, copyright © 1989, 1993 National Council of the Churches of Christ in the United States of America. Used by permission. All rights reserved worldwide.

3. David Leigh, S. J., in the introduction to his book *Circuitous Journeys: Modern Spiritual Autobiography*, uses Augustine as the prime example of the complex process Leigh calls "circuitous" that typically describes the life journey of spiritually transformed people. We would probably find Julian's journey *circuitous* if we had a full description of it.

Chapter Ten

Shakespeare's *Measure for Measure*
Compassion in the State

Isabella to Angelo: "*. . . go to your bosom, / Knock there, and ask your heart what it doth know / That's like my brother's fault; if it confess / A natural guiltiness such as is his, / Let it not sound a thought upon your tongue / Against my brother's life.*"

—*Measure for Measure* II, ii, 136–41

Julian of Norwich left us with the dialectical tension between the Church's teaching that human beings sin and deserve punishment and the clear teaching of her revelations that God does not impute fault. Love resolves the tension. Shakespeare's *Measure for Measure* presents a different dialectic with a similar solution. The play begins with moral chaos in the city of Vienna, moves toward its dialectical opposite, strict justice, and resolves the tension first through mercy, then through unitive love. Most importantly, for the argument I have been developing in the preceding chapters, *Measure for Measure* dramatizes the intimate connection between awareness of sin (original and actual), in one's self, and the practice of compassion. A brief summary of the story shows the elements of the dialectic at work. A look at various interpretations of what some have considered "a problem play," but which others see as a Christian parable, will help situate the play in the context of the questions being considered in this book. The main characters in the play allow us to see how the dialectic of chaos, justice, mercy, and love unfolds dramatically, and illustrate the central thesis I have been developing—that compassion is the middle term between offense and forgiveness. A comparison of the play's final act with the Truth and Reconciliation Commission's work in South Africa following Nelson Mandela's election, will highlight the elements of restorative justice carried out by the Duke.

THE STORY

The place is Vienna; its ruler, the Duke, has decided to leave the city for a time and turn its governance over to his vice-regent Angelo. The circumstances of the Duke's leaving are important. The city has fallen into moral laxness. In the Duke's words, ". . . Liberty plucks Justice by the nose; The baby beats the nurse, and quite athwart Goes all decorum" (I, iii, 29–31). The Duke picks Angelo to rule in his absence, with the hope that this "man of stricture and firm abstinence" (I, iii, 12), will restore order in the city. The Duke's misleads his noblemen about his destination, leaving them with the impression that he has gone to Hungary to resolve political issues. In fact, he has withdrawn to a nearby Franciscan monastery where he dons a cowl and, disguised as a monk, observes everything that happens in Vienna while he is away and even arranges affairs so that they will turn out according to his intentions. Angelo quickly goes to work, seeing that the brothels are razed as a way of eliminating Vienna's rampant lechery, and punishing violations of the law. A particular case arises to test Angelo's new authority: Claudio, against the law, has gotten his own betrothed pregnant before marriage. Angelo condemns him to death as an example. Lucio informs Claudio's sister, Isabella, a Franciscan novice, of her brother's fate and begs her to intercede, which she does without success. In the course of his interactions with Isabella, Angelo finds himself attracted to her. He agrees to spare her brother if she will sleep with him and instructs her to come back the next evening with her answer.

Isabella informs her brother of Angelo's wicked strategy and explains why she cannot go along even to save her brother's life. The Duke, disguised as a Franciscan friar, overhears the conversation between brother and sister and, coming out of hiding, assures them that Angelo is only testing Isabella's virtue. The Duke suggests a stratagem that will preserve Isabella's virtue and leave Angelo thinking she has given in to his request. At the last moment, Marianna, to whom Angelo was betrothed but whom he has never married because of questions over her dowry, will take the place of Isabella in Angelo's bed. Isabella and Marianna carry out the plan, but Angelo, though he thinks he has slept with Isabella, does not honor the bargain he has made with her and refuses to release Claudio. A second stratagem of substitution, suggested again by the disguised Duke, leaves Angelo thinking that he has executed Claudio when, in fact, another head, the head of someone who has already died, has been presented to him as Claudio's. In the last act of the play, the Duke and Marianna persuade Isabella, even before she knows her brother is actually alive, to pardon Angelo. She does so, reasoning that "A due sincerity governed his deeds, Till he did look on me" (V, 447–450). And Angelo, before he realizes that he has been duped, repents of his insistence on the death of Claudio. Claudio appears alive. The Duke, after professing to condemn the guilty, forgives all. At the end of the play, the Duke asks for the hand of Isabella.

INTERPRETATIONS

In the four hundred years since its first performance at the king's court on the day after Christmas, 1604, *Measure for Measure* has given rise to conflicting interpretations. For many it has seemed a "problem play." Roy Battenhouse lists critics who have found the play, "strange and puzzling," "the despair of commentators" (T. M. Parrott) or have "registered . . . a pained dislike" (Coleridge).[1] "Complaints against the play's subject, its plot, its hero, or its heroine have been heard from critics as eminent as Hazlitt, Sir Arthur Quiller-Couch, and Sir Edmund Chambers" (Battenhouse 1946, 1029). A 1984 article by Marcia Riefer applies a feminist critique to the character of Isabella. Earlier critics have tended to focus on "one implicit question: is she [Isabella] or is she not an exemplar of rectitude?" Riefer turns to what she calls "a more important point, namely that through her [Isabella] one can explore the negative effects of patriarchal attitudes on female characters and on the resolution of comedy itself." [2] According to Riefer, Isabella is uncharacteristically passive and submissive compared to other Shakespearean heroines. Christy Desmet finds the Duke's abdication of power and his "adoption of another identity as friar" problematic.[3]

Once on the trail of problems, it is easy to find them. Why, for instance, does the Duke, having presided over the city's moral decline, suddenly leave town and appoint a man he should have known would apply a rigid standard of morality that the Duke himself does not believe in? Why does he recommend that Marianna sleep with her betrothed Angelo as a substitute for Isabella when this sleeping with one's betrothed before marriage is the very sin that has brought Claudio to the point of execution? But the identifying of problems, as fruitful as it might seem to the deconstructing intelligence, does not bring us closer to the meaning Shakespeare might have intended in writing the play.

Interpreting the play as metaphor might be more useful. Critical analysis can lock the interpreter in the realm of what Hegel called "understanding," as opposed to "reason." Understanding finds antinomies, contradictions, and inconsistencies. Reason reconciles by finding a higher truth that lies under the contradictions. Kierkegaard distinguishes between "ethical" and "spiritual" levels of interpretation. Metaphor opens the door to the spiritual. Roy Battenhouse cites authors who have interpreted *Measure for Measure* in terms of the Christian inspiration evident in the play's title. *Measure for Measure* refers to the Gospel teaching about judgment: "Stop judging, that you may not be judged. For as you judge, so will you be judged, and the measure with which you measure will be measured out to you" (Matt. 7:1–2). Luke's fuller version of this text adds the notion of forgiveness: "Stop judging and you will not be judged. Stop condemning and you will not be condemned. Forgive and you will be forgiven. Give and gifts will be given to you, a good measure, packed together, shaken down, and overflowing will be poured into your lap. For the measure with which you measure will in return be measured out to you" (Lk. 6:37–39).

Several authors look for the "spiritual" meaning of *Measure for Measure* by interpreting it as allegory or parable. Battenhouse finds in *Measure for Measure* "a parable of the Atonement" (Battenhouse 1946, 1053), that is the Christian story of redemption. In this interpretation, the Duke becomes the equivalent of God, who, though "he is the Lord of Men, . . . condescends to become their brother. Acting incognito, he sows within their history the processes whereby they may be reconciled to him in a just and happy kingdom" (1032). Within this overall framework of the doctrine of the Atonement, Battenhouse draws out the Christian meaning of numerous passages in the play. Most important for our purposes are references to original sin, judgment, mercy, and love. We will return to them. G. Wilson Knight, one of the authors to whom Battenhouse refers as a Christian interpreter of the play, points out the "clear relation existing between the play and the Gospels. . . . (Knight 1949, 157). For Knight, as for Battenhouse, the play is dominated by a Christian ethical vision. "The play," says Knight, "tends towards allegory or symbolism" (158). Focusing too literally on the plausibility of individual characters can distract the reader from the overall vision. The play's theme, says Knight, expressed in its title, takes shape in concrete exemplars of judgment and mercy, condemnation, and forgiveness.

More recently, John D. Cox has argued that the medieval morality play can help us understand the meaning of *Measure for Measure.* While acknowledging that this is a thoroughly renaissance play, Cox points out that medieval plays dealing with sexual conduct "raise many of the issues that are also raised in *Measure for Measure,* particularly the necessity to temper justice with mercy, the need for charity and self-examination in judging the faults of others, the problem of slander, the hypocritical abuse of authority, the preferability of forgiveness over harsh punishment, a contrast between the 'old law' and the 'new,' and the nature of true sovereignty" (Cox 1983, 2). Cox does not try to prove that these mystery plays are a source for Shakespeare's play, but points out that medieval religious plays were "a living dramatic tradition in parts of England until the mid-1580s" (2). Seeing them would have made an impression on "an imagination as poetically and theatrically receptive as Shakespeare's" (2).

Without denying the problems that *Measure for Measure* presents, I choose to follow the direction set by these commentators who interpret *Measure for Measure* as a Christian parable. The evidence of Christian inspiration is too overwhelming to neglect. If we take the play as a Christian parable of judgment and mercy, the characters, like the Prodigal son, his father, and his brother of Luke's famous narrative, embody vice and virtue and the dynamic interplay between them.

THREE MAIN CHARACTERS, ANGELO, ISABELLA, AND THE DUKE

Angelo

We begin with Angelo, the "angel," and "fallen angel." This is the man the Duke chooses to rule the city in his absence. The Duke admits that he himself has "for this fourteen years let slip" the city's "strict statutes and most biting laws, The needful bits and curbs to headstrong weeds" (I, iii, 20). Angelo, is possibly the most interesting character in the play, perhaps because evil is often more interesting than good. We look first at this "angel" before his fall, then after. The Duke, in conversation with Friar Thomas, describes his vice-regent: "Lord Angelo is precise, / Stands at a guard with envy, scarce confesses / That his blood flows, or that his appetite / Is more bread than stone . . ." (I, iii, 50–53). That the Duke has his doubts about Angelo's true character is clear from what follows: "Hence we shall see, / If power change purpose, what our seemers be" (I, iii, 53–54). In the eyes of the irreverent wit, Lucio, "Lord Angelo is a man whose blood / Is very snow-broth; one who never feels / The wanton stings and motions of the sense, / But doth rebate and blunt his natural edge / With profits of the mind, study, and fast" (I, iv, 57–61). Angelo's rigidity becomes clear in his condemnation of Claudio. As various characters try to (I, iv, 57–61) dissuade him from his course, he articulates the cold logic that governs his actions. The elder statesman, Escalus, points out to Angelo that he might have erred as Claudio has if his affections had led him and the circumstances been right. Angelo replies, "'Tis one thing to be tempted, Escalus, / Another to fall. I not deny, / The jury, passing on the prisoner's life, / May in the sworn twelve have a thief or two / Guiltier than him they try" (II, I, 17–21). Angelo's sense of justice is, at this point before his fall, impartial. He puts himself on record with Escalus that if he should offend he would expect to be punished (II, 1, 17). In defense of Angelo, but without much feeling, Escalus responds to the Justice's comment that Angelo is "severe" by pointing out, "Mercy is not itself, that oft looks so; / Pardon is still the nurse of second woe. / But yet, poor Claudio! There is no remedy" (II, I, 283–84).

We are still with Angelo before his "fall." He is still "very snow-broth; one who never feels / The wanton stings and motions of the sense . . ." (I, iv, 57–61), one for whom justice is supreme. In the face of Isabella's entreaties, Angelo continues to argue his rationale for condemning Claudio. He appeals to the impartiality of the law: "It is the law not I that condemn your brother. / Were he my kinsman, brother, or my son, / It should be thus with him; he must die tomorrow" (II, ii, 80–82). When Isabella appeals for pity, Angelo identifies justice and pity: "I show it most of all when I show justice, / For then I pity those I do not know, / Which a dismissed offense would after gall; / And do him right that, answering one foul wrong, / Lives not to act another" (II, ii, 100–104). This is the case for law and order, which, after all, the Duke wishes Angelo to restore.

Then, something begins to happen in Angelo. It could be a movement of grace. If grace, it is a grace he turns aside. An opening occurs in him that turns out to pave the way for his fall. From being merely rigid, Angelo becomes evil. Isabella's words have entered his inner sanctum. To himself he says, "She speaks, and 'tis / Such sense that my sense breeds with it" (II, ii, 142), and then bids her farewell. The admission is ambiguous. "My sense breeds" could simply mean that he sees the logic of her argument. But Angelo's subsequent reflection reveals a sensual stirring, a melting of "the snow broth," a waking of "the wanton stings and motions of the sense." To Isabella's parting wish, "Heaven keep your honor safe" Angelo replies, "Amen: / For I am that way going to temptation, / Where prayers cross" (II, ii, 157–58), i.e., where prayers are at cross purposes. Angelo is moving in a dangerous direction away from heaven. When Isabella has left, Angelo enters an extended reflection on what is happening to him, finally goes within himself, becomes a problem for himself, as Augustine professed he was for himself (*Conf.*, X, 16). He is now, at least for a moment, Kierkegaard's "self that relates itself to itself,"[4] and so stands on the threshold of becoming more fully human. The cold judge who has looked only at the law now looks inward to the human heart, his own. "What dost thou, or what art thou, Angelo?" (II, ii, 173).

Angelo's soliloquy begins as a response to Isabella's ritual parting comment, "Save your honor" (II, iii, 161), to which he responds to himself "From thee and from thy virtue!" (162). It is precisely Isabella's virtue that tempts him, yet his desire goes beyond a Platonic admiration: "Dost thou desire her foully for those things / That make her good?" (173–74). Then Angelo acknowledges a connection he has not made before, and will, unfortunately, not make again. Weakness in oneself, he has always argued, should not enter into one's judgments of others when one is entrusted with administration of the law. Now he sees differently, "O, let her brother live: / Thieves for their robbery have authority / When judges steal themselves" (174–76). Angelo closes the soliloquy reflecting on the paradox of his being tempted to sin by virtue: "What is't I dream on? / O cunning enemy, that, to catch a saint, / With saints does bait thy hook! Most dangerous / Is that temptation that doth goad us on / To sin in loving virtue. Never could the strumpet, / With all her double vigor, art and nature, / Once stir my temper; but this virtuous maid / Subdues me quite" (178–185). In the closing line, Angelo acknowledges the profound change that has taken place in him. "Ever till now / When men were fond, I smiled and wond'red how" (185–86). Now his own experience has betrayed his Platonic ideals.

When we next hear Angelo, he is still torn between heavenly and earthly desire: "When I would pray and think, I think and pray / To several subjects: heaven hath my empty words, / Whilst my invention, hearing not my tongue, / Anchors on Isabel; heaven in my mouth, / As if I did but only chew his name, / And in my heart the strong and swelling evil / Of my conception" (II, iv, 1–7). The "swelling evil" prevails. Angelo's experience of temptation, which might have opened him to mercy toward Claudio, impels him instead to make a wicked bargain with Isabella, "Give up your body to such sweet uncleanness / As she that he has stained" (II, iv, 54). At first, Isabella does not understand. Angelo makes his intention clear: "'Redeem thy brother / By yielding up thy body to my will" (163–64). Isabella cannot accept such a proposition, at least not in the form offered. She will go along with the strategem the Duke proposes, to substitute Angelo's betrothed, Marianna, for Isabella herself. But even though Angelo thinks Isabella has fulfilled her half of the bargain, he does not honor his. Angelo's evil multiplies itself. Not only does he try to seduce Isabella, he betrays her even when he thinks she has given in.

In this play, even Angelo is not beyond redemption. Perhaps the opening he has experienced in his attraction to Isabella prepares him for the repentance of the "final judgment" of Act V. For Angelo does repent. Once it becomes clear the Duke has seen everything, Angelo confesses and asks for death: "When I perceive your Grace, like power divine, / Hath looked upon my passes. Then, good prince, / No longer session hold upon my shame, / But let my trial be mine own confession. / Immediate sentence then, and sequent death, / Is all the grace I beg" (V, 372–375). Marianna and Isabella intercede for Angelo, but the Duke remains firm. Finally, before it becomes evident that Claudio is still alive—thanks to the Duke's ruse of substituting another head for Claudio's—Angelo offers full repentance: "I am sorry that such sorrow I procure, / and so deep sticks it in my penitent heard, / That I crave death more willingly than mercy; / 'Tis my deserving, and I do entreat it"

(477–480). Angelo's repentance may be part of his redemption; the Duke's final pardon is another part. The final restoration of Angelo is his marriage to his betrothed, Marianna, who clearly loves him: "I crave no other, nor no better man" (429). The marriage to Marianna is a condition of the Duke's pardon which he seals in his final speech with words of exhortation to Marianna and Angelo, "Joy to you, Marianna. Love her, Angelo; / I have confessed her, and I know her virtue" (529–30). Shakespeare's presentation of redemptive love through marriage may be less psychologically satisfying than his presentation of the reflection occasioned in Angelo by his temptation toward Isabella, but it contains the redemptive solution to the conflicts that have arisen in the play. Here, in the final stage of the play, the symbolic and allegorical takes precedence over the psychological.

Angelo has followed a path from cold virtue untested by temptation, through the stirring of his flesh in sensual attraction, and the fall into a double sin of sexual transgression and betrayal of a promise, to final repentance, pardon, and redemption through love. This is precisely the path laid out by the Hegelian dialectic, from abstract undifferentiated beginning, through negation, to final reconciliation.

Isabella

If Angelo's development unfolds through dialectical stages in his own life, that development also includes a dialectical relation with Isabella. Her pleas for mercy oppose his rigid demand for justice. And, as we have seen, her attractive embodiment of virtue tempts him from his character as "very snow-broth; one who never feels / The wanton stings and motions of the sense . . ." (I, iv, 57–61) and introduces him to the reality of human weakness even in himself. In a way, the two characters Angelo and Isabella are polar opposites, but not entirely. He is administering justice with the impartiality of the head of state; no one has offended him personally. Claudio is not his personal enemy. Angelo makes it clear he would act in the same way with his own kin (II, ii, 80–82). Isabella cannot afford to be so detached; her own brother is condemned. Having noted these qualifications, we can still see in the rationale for mercy enunciated by Isabella the dialectical opposite of Angelo's stern justice.

Like Angelo, Isabella develops as a character in the course of the play. Just as Angelo moves from a detached purity that puts him above temptation into a fall that shows his own capacity for sin and, finally, toward repentance, pardon, and reconciliation, Isabella's development shows marked stages. Isabella's purity has something of the naïve in it. She has chosen chastity as a religious of St. Clare, a choice that puts her outside the normal testing that life in the world provides. She may be holy, at least on the way to holiness; she is not yet fully human. Even the pleas for her brother's life begin in a half-hearted, hesitant way, without the passion we would expect from a sister trying to save a brother from death. She seems torn between condemning the sin her brother has committed and pleading for his life. "There is a vice that most I do abhor, / And most desire should meet the blow of justice; / For which I would not plead but that I must; / For which I must not plead, but that I am / At war 'twixt will and will not" (II, ii, 29–33). Isabella seems torn between wanting to see justice done toward the "vice that most I do abhor" and saving her brother's life. Under Lucio's goading to be more passionate, Isabella warms to her task and speaks with passion for her brother.

What Knight calls Isabella's "ice-cold sanctity" (Knight 1949, 180), and the naïveté that accompanies it, leaves her at first unable to respond appropriately to Angelo. When Angelo proposes his gruesome bargain, Claudio's life in exchange for Isabella's virtue, the aspiring novice does not understand. She responds with pious platitudes, "Sir, believe this: I had rather give my body than my soul" (II, iv, 55). Realizing that she has missed his point, Angelo suggests to Isabella that she is either naïve or crafty: "Your sense pursues not mine; either you are ignorant. / Or seem so, crafty; and that's not good" (II, iv, 74). Finally realizing what Angelo asks of her, Isabella reacts decisively: "Better it were a brother died at once / Than that a sister by redeeming him, Should die forever" (II, iv, 106–108). In a sense, Isabella has "fallen" too, fallen from her untested virtue into the reality of temptation. In a way, she is like Christ, exposed to temptation, but firm in rejecting it. She is becoming human as well as saintly. In the final act, the judgment scene created by the Duke when he abandons his disguise and returns as himself to expose the balance of vice and virtue and effect reconciliation among the injured parties, Isabella manifests the integration of sanctity and humanness in her pardon for Angelo.

I have argued from the beginning of this book that compassion unlocks the door to forgiveness and that, in human beings, consciousness of one's own tendency to sin can make one compassionate. Isabella, in the play's final act, manifests a different kind of sympathy. She recognizes goodness in someone who has shown her only evil. It is important that she pardons even before she knows that her brother is actually alive. In interceding with the Duke for Angelo's life, Isabella shows sympathy for this man who might well have appeared to her as totally evil: "Most bounteous sir, / Look, if it please you, on this man condemned, / As if my brother lived. I partly think / A due sincerity governed his deeds, / Till he did look on me" (V, 447–50). Isabella sees Angelo, not as a devil, but as a human being with a sincere desire for justice, tempted by the weakness of the flesh. But in appealing for mercy toward her brother, Isabella asks Angelo to look, not at some virtue in Claudio that might recommend clemency, but at the weakness in Angelo himself that should make him merciful to another sinner.

Now we turn to the "case" that Isabella makes for mercy. From her first encounter with her brother's judge, Isabella articulates a mature, finely nuanced theology of mercy. Even though she grows personally, becoming more passionate, more human as she goes, Isabella enunciates the Gospel logic of mercy with impressive subtlety and comprehensiveness from the beginning. First, she begs Angelo to condemn her brother's fault, not his person (II, ii, 35). Then Isabella argues that mercy becomes a king and judges more than crowns, swords, "marshall's truncheon, nor the judge's robe" (II, ii, 59–63). She keeps going deeper, into the heart of Christianity, into Angelo's heart. To Angelo's claim that he *could* not pardon Claudio even if he wanted to, Isabella responds, "But might you do't, and do the world not wrong, / If so your heart were touched with that remorse [compassion] / As mine is to him" (II, ii, 53–54). Isabella is trying to take Angelo from his head to his heart. She is aware of the solidarity in sin that Christianity teaches, the mercy of Christ toward sinners that should teach us mercy. "Alas, alas! / Why all the souls that were were forfeit once; / and He that might the vantage best have too / Found out the remedy. How would you be, / If He, which is the top of judgment, should / But judge you as you are? O think on that, / And mercy then will breathe within our lips, / Like man made new" (II, ii, 73–78).

Isabella vainly tries to bring to Angelo's consciousness his own personal share in universal sin and redemption as a motive for mercy: ". . . go to your bosom, / Knock there, and ask your heart what it doth know / That's like my brother's fault; if it confess / A natural guiltiness such as is his, / Let it not sound a thought upon your tongue / Against my brother's life" (II, ii, 136–41). Isabella does not succeed in awakening Angelo's conscience. On the contrary, she awakens his sensual appetite. Such an awakening might have made him more merciful. Instead, as we have seen, it compounds his evil, adding the sins of seduction and betrayal to the weakness of harsh judgment. Isabella's articulation of the Gospel argument for mercy is crucial to an understanding of *Measure for Measure.* So is the Duke's embodiment of mercy in the movement of the play.

The Duke

The Duke's character is complex, godlike in some ways but still human and imperfect. If we treat *Measure for Measure* as a kind of Christian parable, Angelo is the negation of mercy, Isabella is the voice of mercy, and the Duke is the architect of mercy in the form of pardon and reconciliation. Through his omniscient observation and clever stratagems, the Duke brings Angelo to repentance. He guarantees that Angelo's evil intentions will not have their intended effects and brings him, along with all the other characters in the play, to the place of restoration through love, symbolized in the marriage bonds. The development of the Duke's character may at first seem less marked than Angelo's and Isabella's. He functions as a stabilizing force throughout the play. Angelo, once exposed in the final scene, realizes the Duke has exercised a kind of divine scrutiny: "O my dread lord, / I should be guiltier than my guiltiness, / To think I can be undiscernible, / When I perceive your Grace, like pow'r divine, / Hath looked upon my passes" (V, 371–375). But we would be mistaken to overlook the Duke's defects even though Angelo finds in him something "like power divine." If we look behind the Duke's decision to leave town and turn the government over to Angelo, we find a man troubled by the condition of his city and convinced that he cannot restore order by himself. And if we compare this initial troubled stage of the Duke's rule to his confident authority in the final scene, we discover a clear development. And so, though he acts in a kind of god-like way, first behind the scenes as the plot unfolds, then openly in the final act as he uncovers the evil that has taken place secretly and brings about a healing of all the wounds caused by the characters' sins, he is human and therefore capable of development.

The Duke's development as a human being shows us something of the dialectical character of justice and mercy. The Duke's chief imperfection, a defect hard to hide since it is so crucial to the launching of the plot, is a certain acknowledged laxity in enforcing the laws of the city. "We have strict statutes and most biting laws, / the needful bits and curbs to headstrong weeds, / Which for this fourteen years we have let slip . . ." (I, iii, 20–21). The consequence of the Duke's laxity is, as we have seen above, chaos in the city: "And Liberty plucks Justice by the nose; / The baby beats the nurse, and quite athwart / Goes all decorum" (I, iii, 29–31). If moral chaos caused by the Duke's laxity is the first level of the dialectic, the given situation from which the play begins, the Duke's decision to pick the overly-rigid Angelo to put things right might seem merely a failure of judgment. But we can also see Angelo as representing the second stage of the dialectic, the polar opposite of laxity, which is necessary as a first step toward overcoming the city's moral chaos. Angelo's legalism goes in the opposite direction of the Duke's own judgment about how to rule the city but it is a necessary opposite direction if the play is to have its desired outcome. The third stage of the dialectic, represented by the Duke's deepest instincts not yet realized in the opening scenes of the play, consists in the reconciling power of forgiveness and love expressed in the final act. The contradiction between the final act and the opening scenes that set the plot in motion finds its resolution in a dialectal progression from laxity through justice to mercy.

Justice is an antidote to laxity. But mercy is an antidote to the excesses of a justice too strictly applied. Just as justice does not take the place of mercy, mercy does not replace justice. Mercy is not the same as laxity. It goes beyond both laxity and justice. Angelo's claim in answer to Isabella's plea for mercy contains some truth: "I show it [mercy] most when I show justice" (II, ii, 100). His justice shows mercy to those who would be scandalized by letting faults go unpunished (101–102). And he shows mercy to the one condemned by making sure he commits no further faults (103–104). These might seem like weak arguments, but they draw strength from the Duke's admission that chaos has come from his not enforcing the laws. Still the contradiction exists between the Duke's mercy and Angelo's harshness. Perhaps the Duke wants to restore balance in the city by using a means he knows will fail so that he can show how true mercy transcends both laxness and harshness. Mercy has to pass through justice before it can be authentic mercy. And justice has to be complemented by mercy before it becomes true justice. We can imagine the Duke setting this dialectic in motion quite consciously, knowing from the beginning where everything will end up. The defect of this suggestion is that it makes the Duke appear to be above the action of the play rather than a part of it.

Another possibility, one that makes the Duke less omniscient, comes from Daniel Massey, a Shakespearean actor who has played the Duke and written about the experience of entering into the Duke's character. An actor's interpretation adds a valuable perspective because acting requires entering the inner world of the character and bringing it to life. Massey rejects G. Wilson Knight's casting of the Duke as "some sort of Christ figure moving gently through the play dispensing pastoral wisdom" (Massey 2010, 202) in favor of an interpretation that attributes to the Duke "a deep and existential humanity" (202). With this deep humanity in view, Massey explains the dissonance between the opening chaos of the city, brought about by the Duke's lax enforcement of the laws, and the final harmonious resolution of Act V as the manifestation of a character who grows into his true authority and gradually comes to the see the wisdom of mercy in government. The Duke is, according to Massey's interpretation, genuinely troubled by the sorry state of his city and chooses Angelo with the hope of restoring order. This interpretation is appealing because it recognizes that the Duke, like the other principal characters in the play, develops.

But the Duke is not naïve. He recognizes that his choice of Angelo carries some risk. On the one hand, he expects Angelo to model the same combination of qualities that he himself brings. "Hold, therefore, Angelo: / In our remove be thou at full ourself; / Mortality and mercy in Vienna / Live in thy tongue and heart" (I, i, 42–44). On the other hand, the Duke recognizes that

Angelo may not be the solid man of virtue he appears to be. In an important conversation with Friar Thomas at the monastery where he plans to disguise himself as a monk and observe events in the city, the Duke gives us insight about the state of his thinking. He reveals both the dilemma he finds himself in and his doubts about Angelo. After listening to the Duke's plans, Friar Thomas suggests that the Duke could have restored order more effectively himself: "It rested in your Grace / To unloose this tied-up Justice when you pleased, / And it in you more dreadful would have seemed / Than in Angelo" (I, iii, 31–33). "I do fear, too dreadful" responds the Duke, "Sith 'twas my fault to give the people scope, / 'Twould be my tyranny to strike and gall them / For what I bid them do; for we bid this be done / When evil deeds have their permissive pass, / And not the punishment" (34–38). This is the dilemma; a show of authority now would punish the people for a situation the Duke has himself set in motion. Angelo does not share the blame for bringing on the laxity. Therefore he may "in the ambush of my name, strike home, / And yet my nature never in the fight / To do it slander" (41–43). That is the hope: Angelo uncompromised by complicity in the city's moral chaos can bring it to order.

But under the hope lies a doubt that makes the Duke choose to disguise himself as a monk and observe his substitute in action. Angelo, observes the Duke, "scarce confesses / That his blood flows, or that his appetite / Is more to bread than stone. Hence shall we see, / If power change purpose, what our seemers be" (51–54). And the duplicity the Duke sees in Angelo from his monastic observation post confirms his doubts. What is lacking in Angelo is not a sense of justice but the personal virtue that makes the administration of justice credible. A sinful man holding others to account for sins less evil than his own, mocks justice. In a conversation of Act III with the wise Escalus, the Duke makes clear the qualities of one who bears responsibility to exercise judgment. "He who the sword of heaven will bear / Should be as holy as severe. . . . Shame to him whose cruel striking / Kills for faults of his own liking" (III, ii, 264–65; 270–71).

The Duke, then begins with a recognition of his own failure to provide the right balance of justice and mercy. Fearing to suddenly bring down the full force of the law himself, he chooses someone who stands on the side of rectitude with the hope of seeing a better balance achieved in the city's life. But the experiment with Angelo confirms his worst fears about the hypocritical exercise of justice and moves him toward a balance that transcends both his earlier easy going ways and the cruel and inconsistent standard of justice exercised by Angelo. By the end of the play, the Duke enters fully into the exercise of his true authority, conscious of the need for justice but justice tempered by mercy.

The Duke's actions throughout the play reinforce the notion that he recognized the importance of dialectic, not only between justice and mercy but between truth and deception, the simplicity of doves and the cleverness of serpents (Matt. 10:16), outrage at evil deeds and clemency in dealing with them. The Duke's double role through the unfolding of the plot, allows him to take contradictory attitudes to what is happening. As a friar he is both merciful and full of intrigue. In one of the more tender scenes in the play, the disguised Duke visits Juliet, pregnant by Claudio, eliciting from her both repentance for wrong done and a sincere love for the man who wronged her and for herself. *Duke*: Love you the man that wronged you? *Juliet.* Yes, as I love the woman that wronged him" (II, iii, 24–25).[5] Soon after, in Act III, the Duke is proposing to Isabella the ruse by which she may seem to be giving into Angelo, while in fact she is preserving her virginity. Another of the Duke's stratagems is to substitute the head of a man already dead for Claudio's, so that Angelo will think his order has been carried out. In the final act, in a speech that cites the title of the play, the Duke mimics Angelo's harshness, threatening him with the same stern judgment he carried out against Claudio: "The very mercy of the law cries out / Most audible, even from his proper tongue, / 'An Angelo for Claudio, death for death!' / Haste still pays haste, and leisure answers leisure / Like doth quit like, and Measure still for Measure" (V, 410–414). Then the Duke condemns Angelo to death, knowing that he will pardon him, thus reversing the law of retribution to which Angelo subscribes. The Duke pivots between harshness and mercy. But the harshness is feigned, the mercy real.

THE FINAL ACT

Act 5 recapitulates the whole action of the play and brings events to their conclusion. The Duke, returned from his sojourn in the monastery, gathers the characters in the story and delivers final judgment. The action unfolds in four phases. First, the Duke returns to take up where he left off at the beginning of the play, apparently still full of confidence in Angelo, not trusting Isabella who accuses Angelo. Then, in a series of swift movements, comes the revelation of the truth about the characters. The Duke's judgments on the guilty follow, a skillful blend of justice and mercy. Finally, the Duke pardons all and effects reconciliation. A look at each of these stages in turn will help us appreciate the movement of the play as a whole.

First the Duke's return. He seems naïve, greeting Angelo and Escalus warmly with signs of gratitude, "Many and hearty thankings to you both" (V, 4), as if they both deserved praise. The Duke is back at the beginning when he designated Angelo as his regent. But not really. Underneath his cordiality lies knowledge of the truth, which he chooses to draw out bit by bit through the testimony of the players in the drama. The Duke knows now who Angelo is, but chooses not to act. When Angelo observes to the Duke that Isabella "will speak most bitterly and strange" (36), Isabella responds that it is strange but true that Angelo is "forsworn," "a murderer," "an adulterous thief," "an hypocrite," and "a virgin violator" (37–42). The Duke pretends not to believe Isabella's accusations, dismisses her complaint, recommending that she take her case to Angelo (27–28), to which she replies "You bid me seek redemption of the devil" (29). The Duke is unmoved. Probably because he is pretending not to believe, he is all the more harsh with her, ordering her to prison for her impudence. The Duke argues against Isabella's allegations, reasoning that Angelo, had he been guilty, would have had compassion, "would have weighed thy brother by himself" (111). The Duke speaks ironically, of course, knowing that Angelo's sin has not made him compassionate. Then comes Marianna's testimony that Angelo is actually her husband and has, unknown to himself, consummated their marriage. Angelo protests, alleging that behind these women's accusations lurks "some more mightier member / That sets them on" (237–38). The Duke argues against Marianna's impudence in accusing someone "sealed in approbation" (245). The Duke sends for the mysterious "Friar Lodowick," the Duke's other self, to get to the root of things.

Now the revelation of sin that has begun in Marianna's disclosure about her husband, Angelo, becomes generalized. All that has remained hidden up to now comes into the light. The Duke leaves for a while and Friar Lodowick is brought in, wondering where the Duke is: "'Tis he should hear me speak'" (295). Friar Lodowick (the Duke) accuses the Duke of being unjust for turning judgment over to Angelo, the very man who is accused. An angry dialogue ensues between Escalus and the Friar/Duke. Lucio confirms that this is indeed the friar who has put the women up to their accusations and adds that the friar has spoken ill of the Duke himself, calling the Duke "a flesh-monger, a fool, and a coward" (335–336). The friar alleges it was Lucio who said these things, protesting "I love the Duke as I love myself" (343). Finally, in exasperation, Lucio pulls the cowl back from the friar's head revealing the Duke. Now Escalus, Angelo, and Lucio stand revealed. The sins of Angelo have been revealed but not the stratagems by which the Duke has preserved the virginity of Isabella and the life of her brother Claudio. Sin is revealed, not redemption.

Now follows the phase of judgment, which combines both justice and mercy. The Duke pardons Escalus immediately for his rash comments and Isabella for her intemperate accusations of Angelo when the Duke first returned to the city. Now that he stands revealed, Angelo repents before the

Duke: and asks for death: "Then, good prince, / No longer session hold upon my shame, / But let my trial be mine own confession. / Immediate sentence then, and sequent death, / Is all the death I beg" (372–77). To which the Duke responds by sending off Angelo and Marianna to be married. When they return, now married, the Duke makes a double move that combines mercy and justice. First, in an act of mercy, the Duke counsels Isabella: ". . . this new-married man . . . you must pardon / For Marianna's sake" (403). But, though he counsels Isabella to pardon, the Duke himself, in an exercise of justice, holds Angelo accountable for the "double violation, / Of sacred chastity, and of promise-breach . . ." (407–408). He passes sentence on Angelo in language reminiscent of Angelo's own earlier response to Isabella's pleas for pity toward her brother. Angelo had said, "I show it most when I show justice" (II, ii, 100). Now the Duke proclaims "The very mercy of the law cries out / Most audible, even from his proper tongue, / 'An Angelo for Claudio, death for death!' . . . Like doth quit like, and Measure still for Measure" (410–414).

Though the language is similar, Angelo and the Duke actually appeal to a different logic. Angelo was claiming a certain mercy in the impartial exercise of judgment. The Duke's "Measure still for Measure" clearly refers to the Gospel teaching found in Matthew, "Stop judging, that you may not be judged. For as you judge, so will you be judged, and the measure with which you measure will be measured out to you" (Matt. 7:1–2). Matthew asks the question that strikes directly at Angelo's harshness, "Why do you notice the splinter in your brother's eye, but do not perceive the wooden beam in your own eye?" (Matt. 7:3). Isabella and Escalus as well had tried to get Angelo to recognize in himself the same weakness that led Claudio to have relations with Juliet. But even when he fell into temptation, Angelo did not let the sin in himself soften his judgment toward Claudio. Now the Duke is applying the Gospel logic, "as you judge, so you will be judged." The Duke pronounces judgment: "We do condemn thee to the very block / Where Claudio stooped to death, and with like haste. / Away with him" (417–19).

But the Duke's harshness, unlike Angelo's, is a prelude to pardon and reconciliation. He wants Angelo to feel the stern logic of the judgment he has exercised toward Claudio. It is important that Angelo be held accountable. Justice must have its moment, even this passing moment. But the Duke knows a crucial circumstance that will make the act of pardon more plausible. Due to the Duke's own intervention, Claudio has not died. Angelo's harsh judgment has not had its intended consequence. The Duke also knows something else that probably moves him to a reconciling act even before he grants Angelo pardon. Another "sin" lurks in Angelo's background, his dismissal of Marianna simply because she could not produce the dowry she had promised (III, i, 216–227). In a conversation with Isabella, the Duke was suggesting that Marianna take Isabella's place in Angelo's bed to fulfill the bargain he has made with Isabella, to free Claudio if she will sleep with him. The Duke needs to explain to Isabella why it would not be sinful for Marianna to sleep with Angelo; they had in fact been betrothed. When the Duke explains to Isabella that the loss of Marianna's dowry brought an end to her relationship with Angelo, Isabella is amazed: "Can this be so? Did Angelo so leave her?" (III, 1, 228). The Duke replies in words that leave no doubt about his view of Angelo's character: "Left her in her tears, and dried not one of them with his comfort; swallowed his vows whole, pretending in her discoveries of dishonor: in few, bestowed her on her own lamentation, which she yet wears for his sake; and he, a marble to her tears, is washed with them, but relents not" (III, 1, 229–34). In other words, Angelo treated cruelly the woman who loved him because she had lost her dowry.

So now that everything has been revealed and Angelo has repented, asking only "Immediate sentence . . . and sequent death" (V, 376), the Duke responds with an unexpected "sentence" that reveals the core of his sense of justice. Asking Angelo if he was ever "contracted to this woman" (378), and receiving Angelo's affirmative answer, the Duke "sentences" him to marriage: "Go take her hence, and marry her instantly" (380). The notion of marriage as a sentence, implicit in the Duke's command to Angelo, becomes explicit toward the end of Act V when the Duke orders Lucio to marry the woman he has "begot with child" (514). "Marrying a punk, my lord" responds Lucio, "is pressing to death, whipping, and hanging" (525). The sentences pronounced by the Duke on Angelo and Lucio are healing sentences. The Duke's justice is restorative justice not retributive, to use terms from modern criminal justice theory,[6] to which we will return.

The newly completed bond between Angelo and Marianna then becomes the basis of a surprising command made by the Duke to Isabella. At this point, the revelation that Claudio lives has not yet taken place. The Duke expresses his sympathy toward Isabella over the death of her brother and consoles her with pious sentiments about the "better life, past fearing death" (400) that Claudio now enjoys. Then comes the Duke's command: "For this new-married man, approaching here, / Whose salt imagination yet hath wronged / Your well-defended honor, you must pardon / For Marianna's sake" (403–405). This command is all the more surprising in light of what follows immediately, the harshest words we will hear from the Duke.

The Duke's command to Isabella—it *is* a command, "You must pardon"— is followed immediately by a "but. . . ." The "but" is a pivot by which the Duke turns from his command that Isabella pardon Angelo to his own judgment against Angelo. I have already referred in treating of the Duke to the logic of his condemnation here. Angelo must feel the backlash of his own severe judgment. He must understand what "measure for measure" means before he feels the weight of pardon. The weight of pardon is that we must forgive just as we have been forgiven. Isabella appealed to this teaching as she was pleading for her brother, but Angelo was not willing to learn at that moment.

The final phase of Act V consists of reconciliation, effected symbolically through marriage. First Angelo and Marianna marry (V, 380–83). The text is clear about the healing effect of the marriage for Angelo. He has already been married to Marianna by the time that Claudio appears alive, giving assurance of safety to Angelo: "By this Lord Angelo perceives he's safe" (496). Now he can enjoy the restorative power of the marriage. "Methinks I see a quick'ning in his eye," says the Duke. "Well, Angelo, your evil quits you well; Look that you love your wife; her worth, worth yours. I find an apt remission in myself" (497–500). Then the Duke orders Lucio to marry the mother of his child (514–15) and then be whipped for his insolence (514–516). It is clear that for Julio as for Angelo, the real "punishment" is marriage, for the Duke forgives everything else: "Upon my honor, thou shalt marry her. / Thy slanders I forgive; and therewithal / Remit thy other forfeits" (521–23). The Duke next asks Isabella for her hand. She has not really sinned, but as we have seen, some dissonance in her sexual life needs healing. She has gone from the chastity of the convent to the humiliation of an attempted seduction. Now the Duke offers her the fullness of love in marriage. Finally, the Duke, having pardoned Claudio for his sin (492–93), now urges him to marriage: "She, Claudio, that you wronged, look you restore," i.e., marry (528).

A COMEDY THAT COULD HAVE BEEN A TRAGEDY

Measure for Measure began with a chaos in Vienna's sexual mores and ends with the reconciling love of marriage. This comedic ending could easily have been tragic. What keeps the story from ending tragically? I don't mean to address the difference between comedy and tragedy in general but to answer the question about why this play in particular does not turn out tragically, which it could so easily have done. To answer that question, we have to look at how the plot develops. The play begins with an ominous decision by the Duke to put in charge of the dissolute city a man he knew to be rigid. The regrettable situation came, by his own admission, from fourteen years of lax enforcement by the Duke. Rather than address the situation himself, the Duke decides to take a leave of absence from his role as leader and appoint a man of strict self-control and acknowledged integrity. But, as we have seen, the Duke did not entirely trust Angelo, wondering to Friar Thomas whether power might corrupt Angelo (I, iv, 54). The Duke's doubts prove well-founded.

His experiment would have ended tragically if he had not decided to observe events as they unfolded and see at each step along the way that the negative consequences of Angelo's actions did not come to pass. Had the Duke not remained close to the events, observing and intervening, the story would have ended tragically. At least Claudio would have died. Isabella would either have seen her brother die and regretted her inability to act on his behalf or she would have acted, lost her virtue, and lost her brother as well. Angelo would have remained imprisoned in his rigidity; he might have awakened and despaired. Perhaps he would have taken his life. The processes put in motion by the Duke tended in this direction, but the tragedy did not occur.

The Duke took charge in his absence in a way he never did while visibly in charge, as if to reverse the laxness and detachment he had shown during the past fourteen years. He alone, in his monastic retreat, knew all that was happening. He alone could intervene just in time to keep the tragic consequences at bay. He alone had the power of judgment. He could exercise it according to his own understanding. His absentee rule allowed him to rise above his own earlier laxity to show the impotence of justice divorced from mercy and mercy divorced from justice. The Duke resolves to heal the wounds brought about by sexual license, not by rigidly punishing the activity, but by giving sexuality its full expression in marriage. He brings to completion what had been incomplete. Claudio's "sin" is redeemed by his marriage. Angelo's rejection of Marianna that had both left him sexually unsatisfied and confirmed him in cruelty was reversed in his marriage to his betrothed. In spite of his resistance, Lucio takes a step into maturity by marrying the mother of his child. Isabella moves from the protective chastity of the convent to the fullness of married love. And the Duke himself, who has "ever loved the life removed, / And held in idle price to haunt assemblies / Where youth and cost, witless bravery keeps" (I, iii, 7–10), breaks out of his isolation to share his goodness with an equal partner, Isabella. One has the impression that the Duke will no longer live "the life removed." Mercy and the reconciling power of marriage triumph over the detachment of a lax ruler, and the harsh judgment of his substitute.

A LESSON IN GOVERNANCE

Measure for Measure deals not only with virtue and vice, justice and mercy, sin and forgiveness in personal relations, but with these same polarities in administration of the state. The overall good of the state is ultimately reducible to healthy relations among the various groups that constitute it. But the rulers of states have as their principal obligation the preservation of the common good. At the beginning of *Measure for Measure,* Vienna as a whole was afflicted with a moral breakdown. And the reconciliations of the final act restore, we must believe, not only relations between individuals, but the harmonious working of the city as a whole. The play focuses on sexual matters, but rampant sexual license seems to be an expression of the overall chaos in the state where "Liberty plucks justice by the nose" (I, iii, 29). In Act III, the Duke articulates the obligation of those who exercise judgment in the state: They must combine complementary qualities, be "as holy as severe," a model of grace when virtue has broken down around them, "Grace to stand, and virtue go" (III, ii, 265–66). They must have knowledge of their own faults and take their own weakness into account in judging others: "Shame to him whose cruel striking / Kills for faults of his own liking" (270–71). The Duke directs his sketch of the "holy" ruler specifically at Angelo: "Twice treble shame on Angelo, / To weed my vice and let his grow. / O what may man within him hide, / Though angel on the outward side" (272–275).

If Angelo exemplifies the absence of the qualities in one "who the sword of heaven will bear" (264), the Duke exemplifies their presence. The Duke has weaknesses. His *laissez faire* attitude in enforcing the laws has brought about the situation of chaos in the city that requires a solution. As I have mentioned above, the Duke seems a rather detached person. Perhaps his detachment manifests the weak side of virtue. The Duke in acknowledging that he has "ever loved the life removed," adds something we might be inclined to admire: "And held in idle price to haunt assemblies / Where youth and cost, witless bravery keeps" (I, iv, 8–10). But the Duke is also magnanimous. The Duke's greatness lies in the humility that allows him to acknowledge his weakness and seek a solution to the negative consequences it has brought about. The Duke also has a vision of how the city should be ruled and moves towards its realization step by step. First he appoints the over-rigid Angelo to rule in his absence, he then prevents the negative consequences of Angelo's rule and, finally brings about a harmonious resolution of the evils in the city. I referred above to this harmonious resolution as "restorative justice." The term comes from modern criminal justice theory. As often happens, literature anticipates theoretical ideas that come to expression in later developments. A brief exploration of restorative justice in its modern manifestation, anticipated by Shakespeare, can shed light on the conclusion of this Elizabethan play.

RESTORATIVE JUSTICE

Like Shakespeare's *Measure for Measure,* modern restorative justice theory comes from Christian roots. One can find the basic insight expressed in Matthew 18. "If your brother sins against you, go and tell him his fault between you and him alone. If he listens to you, you have won over your brother. If he does not listen, take one or two others along with you, so that every fact may be established on the testimony of two or three witnesses" (Matt. 18:15b–17). Howard Zehr, exploring the implications of biblical teaching, describes the origins of the restorative justice movement. "On May 28, 1974, two young men from Elmira, Ontario, pleaded guilty to vandalizing 22 properties" (Zehr 2005, 158). "No one would have guessed," says Zehr, "that their cases would lead to a movement of international dimensions" (158). It seems that a few days earlier, during a discussion among a small group of Christians about a Christian response to shoplifting, a probation officer remarked, "Wouldn't it be neat for these offenders to meet the victims" (158). The probation officer dropped the idea but others involved with the Elmira case suggested this very approach to the presiding judge of the two men accused in the above case. The judge at first rejected the idea but at the time of sentencing ordered the young men to visit the homes of all but the two victims who had moved (159). "Restitution was negotiated, and within two months repayment had been made" (159). This was the beginning of the "victim-offender reconciliation movement" (VORP) in Canada. The movement began in the United States through a project started in Elkhart, Indiana in 1977–78 (159). "Although approaches and names vary," says Zehr, over a hundred such programs exist in the United States today and several dozen in Canada. One can find examples of restorative justice in the criminal justice systems of New Zealand and Northern Ireland as well.

To highlight the elements of restorative justice in *Measure for Measure,* I turn to the dramatic case of the Truth and Reconciliation Commission (TRC) of South Africa that took place from 1996–1998. This case, like *Measure for Measure,* has to do with justice in the state. Shakespeare's play and Nelson Mandela's post-liberation South Africa are experiments in government. Desmond Tutu, appointed chair of the Commission by Nelson Mandela shortly after his election in 1994, tells the story in his book *No Future Without Forgiveness.* Tutu claims that restorative justice is characteristic of traditional African jurisprudence. "Here the central concern is not retribution or punishment. In the spirit of *ubuntu,* the central concern is the healing of breaches, redressing of imbalances, the restoration of broken relationships, a seeking to rehabilitate both the victim and the perpetrator, who should be given the opportunity to be reintegrated into the community he has injured by his offense"

(Tutu 1999, 54–55). If we look at the relation between Angelo and Marianna, broken by Angelo's cruel rejection of his betrothed when she lost her dowry, we can see an example of restorative justice in the marriage between them ordered by the Duke. Both the victim, Marianna, and the perpetrator, are restored. If we look at the whole of Act V of *Measure for Measure,* we see the "truth" of crimes revealed, restoration of the moral integrity of the state and the reconciliation of broken relationships through the multiple marriages the Duke brings about. Perpetrators and victims meet face to face. Angelo faces Isabella and Claudio. Claudio meets up with Juliet whom, at least in the eyes of the law, he has wronged as she has wronged him. Lucio meets the mother of his child. In each case the truth of injury is followed by reconciliation.

The large-scale TRC effort helps us appreciate Shakespeare's genius in expressing, within the limits of a simpler case, the idea of restorative justice in the state. *Measure for Measure* deals with one kind of decay in state, rampant sexual immorality that grew over a period of fourteen years, and shows the superiority of love over law in restoring integrity. The TRC dealt with a vast system of injustice that had flourished for many years under the regime of racial discrimination. The release of Nelson Mandela from prison in 1990 after twenty-seven years in prison and his subsequent election as president of South Africa under a new constitution that gave freedom to South Africa's black population, presented the nation with a profound challenge. How was the new state to avoid the violent consequences of pent-up rage in a long-oppressed majority and still hold the oppressive minority accountable without turning them into a newly oppressed class?

Nelson Mandela's new government rejected the Nuremburg-type system of justice and chose a new way. Tutu expresses the choice in the title of his second chapter: "Nuremburg or Amnesia? A Third Way" (Tutu 1999, 15–32). "Our country's negotiators rejected the two extremes," Tutu tells us, "and opted for a 'third way,' a compromise between the extreme of Nuremburg trials and blanket amnesty or national amnesia" (30).

> And that third way was granting amnesty to individuals in exchange for a full disclosure relating to the crime for which amnesty was being sought. It was the carrot of possible freedom in exchange for truth and the stick was, for those already in jail, the prospect of lengthy prison sentences and, for those still free, the probability of arrest and prosecution and imprisonment (30).

The law establishing the Commission stated the conditions for amnesty. The TRC would address crimes committed between 1960, the year of the Sharpeville massacre, and 1994, the year of Mandela's inauguration as president. Only political crimes qualified. The applicant had to disclose "all the relevant facts relating to the offense for which amnesty was being sought. The law did not require that the applicant show remorse for crimes committed but, as a matter of fact, Tutu tells us, most applicants did express sorrow. The logic of the process seemed to evoke profound regret from perpetrators once they faced their victims and families of victims and looked at what they had done in the clear light of the pain they had caused.

Another element in the restoration hoped for under the TRC was reparation, paying back something of what they had lost to those who had suffered oppression. This presented a huge challenge because the losses were enormous, incalculable really, and the resources to make amends were limited. South Africa's black population had lost family members, bread-winners, husbands, sons and daughters, parents. Families had been broken up through relocation to bantustans. Whole generations had been denied access to good education. Reparation, says Tutu, was necessary to balance amnesty. According to the rules of amnesty, perpetrators of crimes avoided both criminal prosecution and civil suits against them which meant, in turn that the victims were denied the normal means of redress. So the state was responsible for reparation (58). But the state did not have adequate means and so symbolic gestures in the direction of reparation had to be sufficient. What was important was that the state recognize the principle that some kind of reparation was an integral part of justice for victims.

Measure for Measure illustrates in miniature how forgiveness and restorative justice can work in the state. The tribunal of the last act, under the direction of the Duke, presents truth, reconciliation, and restoration. The truth of Angelo's evil deeds comes out when the Duke's disguise is unmasked. Angelo confesses and repents, and receives pardon, but only after he has agreed to marry Marianna. The fortunes of the women who have been wronged are restored through marriage, Marianna first, then the woman Lucio had made pregnant and afterwards abandoned. The victims and all the parties are reconciled. Both the Truth and Reconciliation Commission and *Measure for Measure* show how compassion, forgiveness, and reconciliation can work in the political realm through the reconciliation between individuals. Nelson Mandela wanted to present a model of how a victorious opposition movement could transcend the usual dialectic of oppressor and oppressed changing places through revolution. The future of the new South Aftrica lay in moving toward reconciliation through an honest confrontation with the truth about crimes committed against the individuals and families that make up the state. Reconciliation took place, or did not take place—attempts were not always successful—instance by instance, through the TRC. Other gestures of reconciliation were important, too. For instance, Mandela surrounded himself with white bodyguards from the former regime as well as black Africans from his own movement.

CONCLUSION

Measure for Measure is about compassion, more specifically, about compassion in the ruler of the state. It is also about the recognition of sin in oneself as a motive for compassion. Isabella's words to Angelo as she pleads for her brother's life, call Angelo to such a recognition: *go to your bosom, / Knock there, and ask your heart what it doth know / That's like my brother's fault; if it confess / A natural guiltiness such as is his, / Let it not sound a thought upon your tongue / Against my brother's life"* (II, ii, 136–41). In his attraction to Isabella, Angelo does come to recognize in himself something like Claudio's fault, but the recognition leads him not to compassion but to a vicious bargain and a betrayal once the terms of the bargain are fulfilled. In the passage just cited, Isabella tries to persuade Angelo that recognizing a "natural guiltiness" in himself like Claudio's, should keep him from harsh judgment. The Duke, real ruler of Vienna, does show compassion, which, in him, seems to come from a magnanimous character that manifests a finely tuned balance between justice and mercy. We might also ask whether his admission of weakness early in the play—"T'was my fault to give the people scope" (I, iii, 35)—might have opened him to compassion for the faults of others. That same compassion would have moved him toward restorative justice as a better way to heal the evils of the state than the harshness of justice.

NOTES

1. Battenhouse, Roy W. 1946. *"Measure for Measure* and Christian Doctrine of the Atonement." *PMLA.* 61:(No. 4):1029–1059.

2. Riefer Poulson, Marcia. "'Instruments of Some More Mightier Member': The Constriction of Female Power in *Measure for Measure,"* originally published in *Shakespeare Quarterly* 1984. 35:157–69, reprinted in the 1988 Signet Classic edition of Shakespeare's *Measure for Measure,* 153–154.

3. Desmet, Christy. 2009. *"Measure for Measure*: A Modern Perspective," published in the Folger Shakespeare Library edition of *Measure for Measure.* New York: Simon and Schuster.

4. In *The Sickness Unto Death*, Kierkegaard defines despair as "the disrelationship in relation which relates itself to itself." *The Sickness Unto Death.* 1954. Translated by Walter Lowrie, New York: Doubleday Anchor. (148). According to Kierkegaard's definition, Angelo has really been in despair up until now in the sense that he had no self-knowledge. Now the possibility of emerging from despair opens to him.

5. Juliet's enlightened self-love might remind us of the concluding lines of the priest's journal in Bernanos' *Diary of a Country Priest,* "Grace is to forget oneself.

But if all pride were dead in us, the grace of all graces would be to love oneself humbly, as any of the suffering members of Jesus Christ."

6. See Howard Zehr's. 2005. *Changing Lenses: A New Focus for Crime and Justice.* Scottsdale PA, Waterloo, Ontario: Heard Press. Chapter 5 is entitled, "Retributive Justice," and chapter 10, "A Restorative Lens."

Chapter Eleven

Detective and Priest

Georges Simenon's
Compassionate Commissioner Maigret

A man was going down from Jerusalem to Jericho, and fell into the hands of robbers. . . . But a Samaritan while traveling came near; and when he saw him, he was moved with pity. He went to him and bandaged the wounds, having poured oil and wine on them.

—Luke 10: 30, 33–34, NRSV[1]

The detective fiction genre seems an unlikely place to seek insight into original sin and compassion. Although the crime world presents abundant examples of human corruption, detective stories tend to maintain a clear distinction between the guilty and the innocent, victimizers and victims, in short, the bad and the good. But the doctrine of original sin claims that all human beings, both the good and the bad, suffer from a radical weakness of will that disposes them to evil deeds, often when they are least conscious of deviating from the right path, and most convinced of their innocence. Simenon's Maigret, though not a religious character, possesses a remarkable sense of the ambiguity of good and evil in human beings. Though he recognizes some of the criminals he deals with as sordid characters (*crapules*), this unpredictable detective sees in others examples of a common human weakness that leads them into compromising situations. Toward this second class of criminals, Maigret shows compassion. And in the self-satisfied observers who wonder if he isn't disgusted with the underworld characters he deals with, Maigret sees hidden vices that no one suspects. This contempt for others is just what Jesus condemned in the Pharisees. And, like Jesus, Maigret is more at home with the manifest sin of criminals than the hidden sin of the self-righteous. The hypocrisy of the Pharisees is, in fact, a manifestation of the blindness to God's love that appears in the writings of Julian of Norwich as the root of "original" sin. For the Pharisees rely on their own fidelity to the commandments, especially the minute ones, rather than on the power of healing grace. In addition to this blindness that characterizes hypocrisy, Maigret notes two other forms of originating sin. In discussing Maigret's conception of his vocation, we will see his notion of a certain displacement he has observed in many people, a missing of one's true purpose in life that will make Maigret want to become "a mender of destinies." I have mentioned in the Introduction to this work Maigret's insight into the universality of fear, and noted that fear could well be a name for original sin: "Everyone is afraid" (*La Patience de Maigret,* 128).

MAIGRET'S DISTINCTIVE TRAITS

What distinguishes the Maigret stories of Georges Simenon (1903–1989)[2] from the detective fiction of authors like Agatha Christie and Arthur Conan Doyle is their attention to the humanity of both the investigator and the investigated. Conan Doyle's Sherlock Holmes and Christie's Poirot are essentially problem solvers, "pure logicians of . . . time and space," as Michel Sirvent calls them (Marivale and Sweeny, 165). Though Maigret can be as meticulous and persistent in his search for clues as other detectives are, he ultimately resolves crimes by entering into the humanity of the criminals he pursues. He is more interested in solving the mystery of broken lives than in finding the perpetrators of crimes. "There are no great feats of ratiocination" in the Maigret stories, "and the problems they present are human as much as they are criminal" (Symons, 150). Commentators have recognized this deeply human character of Simenon's Maigret, but they have not noticed a fundamental paradox: though Maigret is, like his creator, a thoroughly secular man in his personal beliefs, he manifests a profoundly Christian, even priestly character in his approach to solving crimes. An examination of Maigret stories will support my claim by illustrating the sense in which Maigret is priestly, by exploring his virtues, and, above all, by showing the extraordinary compassion that marked his work as detective.

Maigret's Vocation

While never using the term vocation, Simenon takes time in several of his Maigrets to let the reader in on the deeper desire that undergirds Maigret's career as detective (*policier*). At the root of the police career lies a priestly ambition. Chapter V of *La Première Enquête de Maigret (Maigret's First Case)*—not the first of Simenon's Maigrets in spite of its title—bears the title, *La Première Ambition de Maigret, (The First Ambition of Maigret).* It seems that Maigret chose to enter the police because it was closest to the profession (*métier*) he had always desired, a profession that really did not exist. "Even as a young man, in his village, he had always had the impression that a great many people (*des tas de gens*) were not in their rightful place, that they were following a path which was not their own, simply because they didn't know better" (Simenon, *La Première Enquète*, 1948, 90). And he imagined a man "very intelligent and full of understanding (*très intelligent et très compréhensif*) . . . both doctor and priest," someone "who would understand at his first glance the destiny of the other person" (90). People would come to consult such a person as they consult a doctor. He would be in some way a "mender of destinies" (*un raccommodeur de destins*). This person would be a mender of destinies not primarily because of his intelligence—in fact he might not have to be of exceptional intelligence—"mais parce qu'il était capable de vivre la vie de tous les hommes, de se mettre dans la peau de tous les hommes"—"but because he was capable of living the life of all men, of putting himself in the skin of all men" (90). Above all, Maigret puts himself in the skin of those who suffer, who are driven to crime by desperation, or who have lived their whole lives as victims. He has no particular sympathy with the rich or powerful. In his identification with the poor rather than the rich, Maigret shows himself closer to the priestly role of Christ than to the clerics, of whom Simenon may have known some in Liége, who prefer the rich to the poor. If Maigret is priestly, it is according to the model of the compassionate founder of Christianity.

The idea of trying to enter the lives of others, to become part of their world, recurs regularly. In *Maigret et le Client du Samedi* (*Maigret and Saturday's Customer*), Maigret received a strange visitor, Planchon, who is afraid with good reason that Maigret might take him for a fool. But Maigret was not satisfied with the idea that the man was a fool: "*Il cherchait à comprendre davantage; à s'enfoncer dans l'univers ahurissant de Planchon*" ["He was trying to understand better, to enter deeply into Planchon's astounding world"] Simenon 1962, 36). In *Maigret et l'Homme du Banc* (1952), the identification with the victim takes place in two ways. One way is that elements of a victim's or suspect's experience find a resonance in Maigret's own experience. A man assassinated in an alley way is, mysteriously, wearing shoes the color of *caca d'oie,* greenish-yellow—literally the color of goose-dung. He had never worn such shoes at home or work where he was a model of respectability. Maigret, after getting to know more about the man, concludes that the shoes are an expression of independence from his domineering wife during the times the man is away from his family and engaged in criminal activities that provide income after he has lost his job. Maigret, we find out—and this is the key point—"had himself, for years, dreamed of wearing greenish-yellow shoes. It was the style at that time. . . ." (62). He had even bought such a pair of shoes but never wore them after Madame Maigret's mocking question: "You're not going to wear those are you?" (62). A second kind of identification in which Maigret takes on the characteristics of the victim, occurs later in the novel. His wife notices that Maigret does not seem to be himself: "You seem like someone else . . . You are not Maigret" (109). Maigret laughs and realizes that "he has been thinking so much about Louis Thoret [the victim] that he has ended up conducting himself as he imagined Louis would have acted, by taking on the expressions of his face" (109).

The fullest description I have found of this process of entering into the lives of other people, even letting them take up residence in him, *becoming* them in a sense, occurs in *Maigret à New York* (1946). This passage will also be important when we look at the third phase of Maigret's famous "method." Though Maigret is in America, having accompanied a young French man who is worried about his father now living in New York, the author/narrator refers us to Paris and the *Quai des Orfèvres* where Maigret's co-workers would say of him at a certain point in an investigation, "*Ça y est. Le patron est en transes*" ["There it is, the boss is in a trance"] (Simenon 1946, 146). *Le Petit Robert* (1985) gives two meanings for the word *transe*. The first is to be in a state of worried agitation as in *être dans les transes.* The second meaning is closer to the English word "trance," a state of altered consciousness. *En transes,* as opposed to *dans les transes,* designates a kind of exaltation or transport as would be experienced by a depersonalized medium possessed by an alien spirit.

Clearly Maigret's associates were thinking of the second meaning. It may have been said in jest, but it still revealed the truth (Simenon 1946, 147). In a way, Maigret becomes a different person, heavier, having a different way of clenching his pipe between his teeth and of smoking it "in little short puffs widely-spaced" (147). This was "*parce qu'il était entièrement pris par son activité intérieur*" [because he was wholly taken up by his interior activity"] (147). In this altered state, as the characters in the drama "had ceased to be pawns or puppets to become human beings, Maigret put himself in their skin. He worked at (*s'acharnait*) putting himself into their skin" (147). Simenon elaborates further: "What someone like him (*ce qu'un de ses semblables*) had thought, had lived, had suffered—couldn't he think it, relive it, suffer it in turn? Such an individual, at a moment in his life, under definite circumstances, had reacted and [for Maigret] it was a matter of making identical reactions come from the depths of himself (*du fond de soi-même*) by virtue of putting himself in the other's place" (148).[3] It would be hard to find a fuller description of the incarnational character of Maigret's method. We will return to it.

Maigret, then, has conceived his police work in terms of a vocation that enables him to be a mender of destinies by entering into the experience of other people. Unable to complete his medical studies (also mentioned in *Pi-*

eter le Letton, 1931, 127), Maigret had entered the police (Simenon *Première Enquête*, 90–91). As it turns out, Maigret continues to reflect, his entrance into the police may not have been accidental. "Are not detectives (*policiers*) in fact sometimes menders of destinies?" (91). All the previous night, Maigret had continued to live with members of the family where the crime has occurred, people he scarcely knows, yet they fill his thoughts. In *Les Mémoires de Maigret* (*Maigret's Memoirs*), in the midst of complaints that his own reality has been distorted by this young novelist who insists on oversimplifying, caricaturing, and distorting his character, Maigret remarks: "Simenon has spoken of 'a mender of destinies,' and he didn't invent the word, which is truly from me and which I must have let drop one day when we were conversing" (Simenon *Les Memoires,* 1950, 69).

So Maigret, at least at the beginning of his career, seems to think of himself as doctor, detective, and priest, [*médecin, prêtre et policier*] (Simenon *Première Enquête,* 1948, 90–91). I am particularly interested in the emphasis on Maigret's priestly character. It's not just that both detectives and priests can be menders of destinies. A significant number of Maigret stories attest to something priestly about Maigret's way of being a detective. This is not surprising given the presumption early in his life on the part of parents and teachers that Simenon would become a priest. Even though, as we have seen above, Simenon renounced priesthood after his first sexual encounter, he was even after that deeply influenced by a young professor of literature at the Collège St-Servais "who was himself preparing for the priesthood" (Assouline, 13).

Assouline cites a reference to this professor from a letter Simenon wrote to Jean Mambrino in 1951: "He is probably the man who had the greatest influence on me" (13). Patrick Marnham describes Simenon, age 11, at the beginning of the First World War: "At the outbreak of hostilities he was a devout child who sometimes experienced mystical interludes; he was an altar boy, a conformist, and vowed to the priesthood" (Marnham, 38). By the end of the war, says Marnham, "Georges was still only 15, but had lost his faith, abandoned all thoughts of priesthood, left school, started work, lost his first two jobs, and was certain that although he was not yet an adult he was a failure" (38). Out of this dark beginning developed the Simenon who created the extraordinarily sympathetic and priestly character of Maigret.

This priestly connection, which occurs repeatedly, has to do with the role of confessor and sympathetic listener. The same Planchon referred to above, tempted to kill his wife who has taken a lover, comes to Maigret as one would to a priest for confession. "If I still went to church as I did when my mother was still alive, I would no doubt have gone to confession." [*Si je fréquentais encore l'église, comme du vivant de ma mère, je serais sans doute allé me confesser*"] (Simenon 1962, 38). Instead of going to confession to a priest, Planchon comes to Maigret not remembering how he thought of the detective and not even imagining in the beginning that he would have the courage to come find Maigret. "But now that I am here," he says, "I would like to tell everything all at once" ["Je voudrais tout dire à la fois"] (38). Later, Maigret asks Planchon what, had he gone to confession, he thinks the priest would have said. "I suppose he would have tried to turn me from my project . . . [of killing my wife]" (50). "And you would too," Planchon adds.

The conversation continues and it becomes more and more evident that Planchon has come to Maigret not as a detective but as a kind of priest substitute. When Maigret suggests that Planchon might be looking for someone to prevent him from committing the crime, Planchon becomes discouraged, recognizing that such prevention is not possible and fearing now that Maigret has missed the point of the visit. Finally, Maigret draws the inevitable conclusion: "What you have come looking for here is a sort of absolution" ["*ce que vous êtes venu chercher ici, c'est une sorte d'absolution*"] (51). "You need to know that you will be understood, that you are not a monster and that your project is the only solution left you . . ." (51). In another story, *Maigret et le Tueur (Maigret and the Killer,* 1969), Maigret says of his country house at Meung-sur-Loire that it always seemed to him to resemble a priest's house (*une maison de curé*). Maigret is staying there with his wife and tells her he has received a call from the killer of a young man. "To mock you?" she asks, "As a kind of challenge?" (Simenon, *et Le Tueur,* 1969, 152). "No," answers Maigret, "he needed comfort ("*il avait besoin de réconfort*." "And he came to you?" asks Madame Maigret." "He had no one else available," Maigret responds (152*).*

Secular and Christian

The fact that Simenon would inject a priestly quality into Maigret's original conception of his calling (*métier*) and to his way of practicing his profession is ironic. Although both Simenon and his police detective Maigret came from Catholic origins, neither remained committed to their original faith. In *L'Affaire Saint-Fiacre (The Saint Fiacre Affair),* Maigret investigates a crime in the town of St. Fiacre near Moulins, in central France, where he grew up and served Mass in the parish church. Simenon tells us that Maigret always preferred serving the funeral Masses because the prayers were shorter (Simenon 1932, 13). The mature Maigret, however, never gives any sign of a religious commitment or practice. Simenon himself, raised in Liège, Belgium, attended the Jesuit *College St. Louis* and was deeply religious until he learned at age fifteen that his much-loved father, whom he considered a saint, was going to die within a few years. "At that moment, he ceased to be a Believer and the teachings of the Church became a mockery" (Bressler, 28). Another biographer, Pierre Assouline uses the title "Altar Boy" for his first chapter that describes Simenon's life up to age sixteen and tells us that "his family and his teachers had him earmarked for the priesthood" (Assouline, 1992, 12). After his first sexual encounter at age twelve, an event that launched him on a prodigiously active sexual career, "he solemnly informed his teachers and parents that he had decided to renounce the priesthood in favor of—a military career" (12). Still, even after Simenon loses his faith in this "first chapter" of his life, key elements of Christianity appear, probably without any explicit intention, in Simenon's Maigret, especially in his attitude toward his profession and his pursuit of it, both of which show extraordinary human virtues.

In Christian tradition, of course, the primordial paradox is the Incarnation itself, and Christ is the High Priest. Maigret's way of operating too is fundamentally incarnational and in that sense priestly. He solves crimes, as we have seen, by identifying with the objects of his investigation, by "living their lives" and "entering into their skin" (*La Première enquête de Maigret,* 90). Maigret enters into the criminal world, knows its vocabulary, and identifies with both its victims and its perpetrators. In *Les Mémoires de Maigret (Maigret's Memoires),* the real Maigret—as opposed to Simenon's fictional character—speaks of the familial relation the police inspectors had with those they were charged to investigate. Simenon has tried to portray it, says Maigret, without quite succeeding. "The prostitute of the Rue de Clichy and the inspector watching over her both have bad shoes and sore feet from walking miles of pavement. They have endured the same rain and the same freezing wind. Evening and night have for them the same color and both see, almost with the same eye, the underside of the crowd that flows around them" (111–112). Maigret identifies with those who suffer. In this he imitates Christ's compassion, his willingness to take on human suffering, even sin, as well as his incarnation.

Not only does Maigret identify with the people whom society looks on condescendingly as sinners, he recognizes throughout society the universal tendency toward weakness and immoral behavior that Christians call original sin. Respectable (*bien-portants*) people love to look down on criminals, to treat with contempt the immigrants gathered by the thousands in slums, hoping that the police will discover "their dirty secrets, the vices peculiar (*inédits*) to them, and all kinds of sordid behavior (*pouillerie*) that will both justify indignation and provide a source of secret delight" (131). But these respected citizens are not as worthy of respect as they would like us to believe. They too cheat and practice little obscenities (*saletés*) that they carefully camouflage.

These are the same people who ask Maigret, "with a slight trembling of their lips, if he isn't ever disgusted" by the behavior of the people he deals with (131). Maigret contrasts this condescending hypocrisy with the "humility that one scarcely ever finds except among those who have been uprooted from their origins" [*les déracinés*] (133).

One is reminded of the prayers of the Pharisee and the tax collector. The Pharisee prays: "I thank you, God, that I am not grasping, unjust, adulterous like the rest of mankind, and particularly that I am not like this tax collector here. I fast twice a week; I pay tithes on all I get." The tax collector "stood some distance away, not even daring to raise his eyes to heaven; but he beat his breast and said 'God, be merciful to me a sinner.'" And Jesus responded that the tax-collector went home "at rights with God" whereas the Pharisee did not: "For everyone who exalts himself will be humbled, but the man who humbles himself will be exalted" (Lk. 18:9–14). Simenon must have known this text. Whether it influenced his conception of Maigret, we do not know. More clear from his biographers is that Maigret, though he is neither Simenon himself nor Simenon's father, Désiré, "has flaws and virtues borrowed from both" (Assouline, 1997, 92). Another biographer, Fenton Bresler (1983), citing a 1955 radio interview with Simenon, sharpens the connection between Maigret and Simenon's father, Désiré. "When I wanted to create a sympathetic person who understood everything, that is to say Maigret, I gave him without realizing it, certain of my father's characteristics" (Bresler, 68). Bresler adds his own reflection: "Maigret, like Désiré Simenon, loves his fellow men, understands and pities them. He believes they have killed or committed crimes because they are weak or unhappy, because they feel threatened, because they are frightened" (68).

Bresler's words evoke the sentiment expressed by Augustine of Hippo to which I have already referred above (Chapter 4, 109), "Many sins are committed through pride, but not all happen proudly . . . they happen so often by ignorance, by human weakness; many are committed by men weeping and groaning in their distress" (Augustine 1997, 23:241). Maigret's ability to enter into the lives of his characters, victims and suspects, correlates with his sense of universal human weakness and the compassion that follows from that sense. Maigret himself, as we will see, recognizes his own participation in the human weakness that gives rise to the crimes he investigates. What keeps people reading Maigrets is not the intellectual satisfaction of solving a puzzle, but the privilege of seeing the exquisitely tender rapport between the investigator and the investigated, the pursuer and the pursued, the hunter and the hunted. Sometimes we will even see the striking irony of the criminal object of Maigret's investigation pursuing Maigret, desiring to be caught because to be caught is to be known.

THE PARADOXES OF MAIGRET

Within the overarching paradoxes of the Incarnation, the religious manifested in the secular, and the vocation that combines detective and priest, other paradoxical relationships emerge. First is Maigret's famous "method." It comes up in almost every novel. The paradox lies in the fact that although Maigret is famous for his method, he claims not to have a method. The second paradox is that though Maigret's function as a detective is by definition to identify and hunt down criminals—he is the hunter—it often happens that while he looks for the culprit, the culprit is looking for him. A further irony in this dialectic of the hunter and the hunted arises from the fact that Maigret himself, because of his unorthodox methods, sometimes makes himself the object of his superiors' wrath, becoming a suspect in their eyes. Finally, the deepest paradox lies in the mysterious combination of *policier, médecin, et prêtre,* detective, doctor, and priest (Simenon, *La Première Enquête,* 1948, 90) to which I have already referred. I will examine each of these paradoxes.

Maigret's Paradoxical Method

When Simenon refers to Maigret's "method," it is usually to deny that his chief inspector has a method. In an early story, *Le Chien Jaune (The Yellow Dog,* 1931), one of Maigret's inspectors admits that he does not yet understand his boss's methods, but he thinks he is beginning to guess. Maigret looks at the inspector with laughing eyes and responds that in this case: "My method has been precisely not to have one" (*Le Chien Jaune,* 142). An inspector from the city of Groningen where Maigret is investigating a crime asks Maigret what he *thinks.* "That is the question!" answers Maigret. "And there is the difference between the two of us. You think something, you think all kinds of things! While I myself—I believe I don't think anything anymore" (*Un Crime en Hollande* [*A Crime in Holland*], 85). In a 1950 novel, *Maigret et La Vieille Dame (Maigret and the Old Woman),* inspector Castaing, surprised to see the commissaire "sleepy and indecisive," asks Maigret in the middle of their investigation, "What should I do next?" Maigret tells him to do whatever he wants, poke around wherever. Find out what you can. Maybe something will come up (123). Maigret knows that in every investigation this moment comes when he and his colleagues have done all their homework, getting to know the players, asking questions, believing or not believing the responses but being slow to form an opinion. At this stage the characters have pretty clear and simple profiles but remain distant. And then things begin to "come alive" (*grouiller*). The characters become more hazy (*flous*) and at the same time more human, and above all more complicated (*La Vielle Dame,* 124).

Passages like these suggest that Maigret, while protesting that he has no method, does in fact have a method, not a logically rigorous one, but a distinct way of proceeding of which he is very conscious and very much in charge. The method has three stages. The first consists in the normal investigative procedures that any detective would undertake, fingerprint identification, careful examination of the victim's body, looking for traces of blood on clothing, asking questions. Maigret is meticulous about this stage. In one story, *Maigret et Son Mort* (*Maigret's Dead Man*), the victim was wearing a beige raincoat when he was found, but Maigret suspects he was not wearing the coat when he was killed. So Maigret puts the man's clothes, including the raincoat, on a mannequin he has in his headquarters, the famous *PJ* or *Police Judiciare*, to see if the tears made by the knife in the raincoat and those in the suit match. They don't, so Maigret's suspicion, that the victim was not wearing this coat at the time of his death but that the assassins *wanted* the police to believe he was, is confirmed (Simenon, *M. et Son Mort,* 1948, 33–34).

But all this careful, highly professional investigation carried on by a team of collaborators that often crosses national boundaries and involves multiple police jurisdictions, yields only uncertainty and confusion. Thus begins the second stage, the stage of doubt on Maigret's part, sometimes profound discouragement and sluggishness, in which Maigret appears like a lost soul. In England—his visits there always seem to unhinge him—Maigret waits in a bar for a young man he hopes to save from committing a foolish crime. "He felt that everyone was looking at him, that the old gentleman next to him studied him with a critical eye" (Simenon, *Le Revolver de M.,* 1952, 138). "His self confidence was slipping away" (138–139). In the gruesome story of the body without a head (Simenon 1955), Maigret went back to his office and "began to take on the grumpy (*grognon)*, sullen (*maussade*) air that almost always came to him at a certain stage of an investigation" (79), the "certain stage" being what I am calling the second phase of his method. Whereas "just yesterday he was making discoveries, accumulating them without asking where they might lead, he now found himself facing bits of truth that he didn't know how to tie together" (79).

In this second stage, Maigret begins a transition from thinking *about* the characters inhabiting the world of his investigation to letting them enter his world. *Maigret S'Amuse* (*Maigret's Little Joke,* 1956) describes a Maigret who really doesn't know what he is thinking about because his state of consciousness has more to do with *feeling* than with *thinking* (*raisonnement,* 149). He *felt* (*sentait*) the truth close at hand, but he was powerless to take hold of it (*la saisir*). Another example of this movement from confusion through feeling to insight occurs in *Maigret et le Corps sans Tête* (*Maigret and the Headless Body*). For Comeliau, the unsympathetic judge in this case,

Madame Calas was "a broken-down drunk who slept with any one" (*Le Corps Sans Tête,* 1955, 79). For Maigret, she was something other than that; he didn't know exactly what, "and as long as he didn't know, as long as he didn't "feel" (*sentirait*) the truth, he was subject to a vague *malaise*" (79). As Maigret moved from thinking to feeling, the objects of his investigation took on a different character, too: "It was as if the three characters of the drama had taken up life in him" (*Maigret s'Amuse*, 149) and had become no longer abstract entities but real human beings, but unfortunately "incomplete and schematic human beings" (149). At this stage as described in *Maigret à New York* (Maigret in New York) the commissaire "floundered (*pataugait*), did what he had to do, nothing more, gave orders, gathered information on this one and that one, with the air of being interested only moderately in the investigation, sometimes not interested at all" (Simenon 1946, 147). Then, when one least expects it, when Maigret seems discouraged by the complexity of the task, "something clicks"—"*le déclic se produisait*"—(147) and Maigret moves into the state of trance, discussed above, that allows him to enter the lives of the characters. This *déclic* points the way to the third stage of the investigation, a stage dominated by feeling and intuition rather than logical reasoning. "Here as in most cases," the narrator reflects in *Maigret s'Amuse*, "there is not only one solution possible, but at least two." But only one is the right one, only one is the human truth (*la vérité humaine*). One does not arrive at the human truth by "rigorous reasoning or a logical reconstitution of the facts, but by feeling it" (*la sentir*) (149). The French dictionary *Le Petit Robert* (1985) gives as the first meaning of *sentir* "to have the sensation or the perception of (an object, a fact, a quality)." The fifth meaning is "to guess at (*deviner*), to discern (*discerner*)." The second phase of Maigret's method, then, involves a breakdown of thinking, accompanied by confusion, ill-humor, and a lack of self-confidence, a breakdown that opens up the way to feeling or discernment as a way of knowing the truth. Maigret will wait for the revelatory moment that he has been anticipating in the midst of his feelings of discouragement

So we come to the third phase of Maigret's "method," the phase that distinguishes him as a detective different from Michel Sirvent's "pure logicians of time and space" mentioned earlier. The key to grasping this phase is the transition from thinking to feeling, a phase that resembles a certain discernment described by spiritual writers. The notion of a trance, used jokingly but with real meaning, by Maigret's colleagues in *Maigret à New York*, suggests a kind of spiritual—not religious— awareness that disposes the detective to enter into the other person's life and thus resolve the issues involved in the investigation. For Maigret this mode of knowing has a double purpose. First, it enables him to unravel the mystery surrounding the events in a particular story. In the second place, this discerning attitude allows Maigret to carry out his vocation as mender of destinies for those who have somehow lost their way.

Again, *Maigret à New York* provides a striking example. All that I am describing here takes place in that trance-like state that Maigret's colleagues jokingly, but with a significant measure of truth, would often refer to. This mode of knowing that I am comparing to discernment opens Maigret to the existential, human, spiritual truth that lies behind the facts of the case. Little John is a wealthy man who came to America years ago and, after beginning life as an entertainer, has moved into the business of making juke-boxes for restaurants. Little John's son, Jean, has asked Maigret to come with him to New York to see if they can solve the riddle of Little John's changed behavior, formerly tender now detached, toward his son. After being in New York for a while, where he feels intensely uncomfortable, and meeting Little John several times, Maigret makes a startling discovery: ". . . Little John has cold eyes (*les yeux froids*)" (Simenon 1946, 41). Taking this material clue as a starting point, Maigret begins to question what makes John Maura's eyes cold. Later in the story, he can say: "There is something in those cold eyes that resembles anger (*exasperation*), but resembles something else too" (55). To find out what that something else was, Maigret had to *become* Little John (148).

He would not discover the truth by running after it (*courir après*) as his American colleague wanted to do, but by "letting himself be impregnated (*se laisser imprégner*) by the pure and simple truth" (151). Slowly, step-by-step, through a sympathetic recreation of Little John's life, Maigret arrives at the truth about the cold eyes. It seems that Little John had, in a moment of blind jealousy, murdered his lover, the mother of his son whom he thinks his friend may have fathered while Little John was away in France. And now, knowing that his lover's son was also his, Little John lived with the regret at killing the only woman he has ever loved. And, learning this, Maigret knew, as he now told Little John, "the sorrow that gave these eyes their terrible coldness" (183). Little John has paid the price of his crime, not through the system of criminal justice, but through a worse punishment, his own suffering. He had sincerely wished, for one reason only, he tells Maigret, that the whole affair would crack open, *so that he could rest [à me reposer]* (187). Though Simenon does not use here the language of priesthood or mender of destinies, it is clear that his discovery of the mystery behind the cold eyes has given Little John what he has long sought, rest.

Simenon's religious origins may well have opened his eyes to this kind of discernment. His time at a Jesuit high school in Liège would most likely have engaged him in some version of Ignatius of Loyola's *Spiritual Exercises,* where he might well have been introduced to Ignatian discernment. Moreover, some significant residue of the "religious mysticism" that Bresler and Marnham note as a manifestation of the young Simenon's "intense inner life" (Bresler, 21; Marnham, 38) probably remained in the mature Simenon who invested Maigret with his acute intuitive sense. In any case, the practice of Ignatian discernment does shed light on this third phase of Maigret's method and at least provides an analogy to help us understand how Maigret proceeds. Loyola, one of the masters of spiritual discernment, sets out a method for making decisions in harmony with God's will. Maigret, of course, is trying to solve crimes, to determine which is the true solution, not to make decisions according to God's will. But the method is similar. If we look at Ignatius' "Three Times When a Correct and Good Choice of a Way of Life May Be Made" (Ignatius of Loyola 1962, 74), we find in one of these ways a discernment method that clarifies what I have called the third stage of Maigret's method. Ignatius' first time of making a choice occurs when a person is overwhelmed by a personal manifestation of God such that "a devout soul without hesitation, or the possibility of hesitation, follows what has been manifested to it" (74). This kind of immediate certainty, if it occurred, would put an end to any mystery story since all of them depend on lingering uncertainty as an essential ingredient. The third time for making a decision is a "time of tranquility" in which a person can think rationally about his life and come to a sensible decision in conformity with God's will. This parallels the first stage of Maigret's method, the rational investigation of clues, motives, and circumstances.

Ignatius' "second time" offers the comparison we are looking for. It is a time "when much light and understanding are derived through experience of desolations and consolations and discernment of different spirits" (74). The moodiness of the second stage of Maigret's method fits this alternation of "desolations and consolations." The closer Maigret comes to the truth, the more consolation, calmness, and self-assurance replaces ill-humor and doubt. In *Maigret à New York,* the narrator speaks of *"une force tranquille"* (165, 170) that overtakes Maigret as the truth becomes clearer. At times, one can find God's will through reasoning but at other times, when thinking breaks apart, leaving only confusion, doubt, and uncertainty, one is reduced to sorting through the questions that arise from one's feelings and examining one's experience until some insight emerges as a kind of revelation. In this sense, the third phase of Maigret's method can be understood as a kind of discernment. The Commissaire is no longer looking for physical clues that will lead to logical consequences but to human clues. He looks for *"une fissure"*—a cast of characters still missing a crucial person *(Le Charretier de la Providence,* 1931 [*The Crime of Lock* 14], 121); the moment for which he searches, waits, and watches when behind the criminal as playing a role appears the man *(Pieter le Letton,* 1931 [*Peter the Lett*], 57–58). Simeon also speaks of "*la fêlure,*" a kind of moral flaw that reveals the true character of the culprit (*La Tête d'un Homme,* 1931 [A Man's Head], 169). Sometimes "*la fêlure*" consists in a perceptible gap between the words the suspect is saying and reality (*Maigret Hésite* [*Maigret Hesitates*], 169). In *Maigret à New York* the cold eyes of Little John raised Maigret's curiosity. In *Maigret et l'Homme du Banc* (*The Man of the Park Bench,* 1952), Maigret wonders why he has the impression that the woman talking to him is hiding something (Simenon, *L'Homme du Banc,* 1952, 44).

In wondering why he feels that the woman is hiding something, Maigret reflects on his own experience as a way of coming to the truth outside him. Again, Ignatius of Loyola traces the origins of his own teaching about discernment to a similar reflection. In his autobiography, Ignatius describes reactions to two kinds of reading material. When his memory took him back to romantic tales of chivalry that he had always loved to read, he experienced an initial exhilaration that after a time ended in emptiness. But when he read about the lives of Christ and the saints, he experienced a delight that did not diminish. For a long time, Ignatius tells us, he paid no attention to these diverse reactions "until one day his eyes were opened a little and he began to wonder at the difference and to reflect on it, learning from experience that one kind of thoughts left him sad and the other cheerful" (Ignatius of Loyola 1956, 10). He concluded that one sort of thoughts came from the evil spirit, the other from the good spirit. Like Ignatius, Maigret was a man who trusted in the power of his own inner experience to reveal the truth. The similarity is in the method, not in the kind of truth revealed.

Simenon's comment in *Maigret s'Amuse* (1956) on the concluding phase of an investigation illustrates this feature of Maigret's method. The passage in question shows both an objective component, a change of behavior in the suspect, and a subjective change in the investigator himself. "Almost always," comments the invisible narrator, "after a time more or less long, comes a time when the resistance suddenly cracks and the detective (*policier*) has nothing before him but a man in desperation (*aux abois*). For, at this moment, he becomes once again a man, a man who has stolen or killed but, all the same, a man . . ." (Simenon 1956, 176). And this transformation of the suspect corresponds to a change in the investigator. I have already referred to an earlier phase of this investigation when Maigret "sensed (*sentait*) the truth close at hand (*toute proche*) and was powerless (*impuissant*) to grasp it" (149). Now, in a moment of revelation, the power to grasp the truth is given. He has found the truth that eluded him. "He has accomplished his work as a detective (*fait son métier de policier*)" (176). His earlier frustration has given way to a sense that he has done what he can, uncovered the culprit, and can now leave to others to judge. Maigret repeats often that he aims to understand, not to judge. He would not want to be a magistrate or a juror in a trial (*juré dans un procès d'assises*) because he would have to judge. "No, I am certain I would never undertake to judge a human being" (Simenon 1964, 12). Again, "It is not my role to judge" (Simenon, *M. et Le Tuer,* 1969, 167) This resting in the accomplishment of his proper role parallels Ignatius' sense of peace in recognizing that God is leading him to imitate the saints rather than to aim for deeds of chivalry (Ignatius of Loyola 1956, par 8, 10). The contemplation of chivalrous ambitions led Ignatius to desolation, much as technical, but less than human, clues led Maigret to ill humor and frustration. Also Maigret's sense of completion on seeing the suspect revealed before him as a fully human, though imperfect, being corresponds with Ignatius' peace derived from contemplating the path God revealed to him, that of following the saints.

The three phases of Maigret's "method" are related dialectically. The first phase sets the physical, factual, and rational foundation of the investigation. The second phase negates the first phase; it is a coming-to-nothing of all the careful examining, a kind of death. The third phase brings to life the facts that by a revelation emerge for the investigator who is willing to wait. More reasoning or more data collection could not reveal the facts. This third phase, since it relies on Maigret's ability to enter into the lives of others and thus become a *racommadeur de destins,* is precisely the place where the priestly character that the narrator identified with Maigret's original vocation most fully finds expression.

The Paradox of the Hunter and the Hunted

This paradox lies in the third phase of Maigret's method where ordinary investigative procedures no longer help to resolve an investigation. A clear example of this phenomenon occurs in Simenon's *Maigret et le Marchand de Vins* (*Maigret and the Wine Merchant*). Gilbert Pigou, accountant for a wealthy wine merchant, Oscar Chabut, has shot and killed his boss who had mercilessly humiliated him in the presence of another employee and even slapped him across the face, after discovering that the accountant was stealing small sums of money. The accountant stole because his wife spent more than he earned and was constantly after him to bring home more money. Pigou is precisely one of those persons of whom Maigret had always had the impression "that they were not in their rightful place, that they were following a path that was not their own . . ." (*La Première Enquête de Maigret*, 90). Maigret, after a conversation with the wine merchant's secretary, now regards the accountant as a suspect. This all occurs through normal investigative processes.

But now, in the final phase of the investigation, something curious begins to emerge; the suspect is as much interested in Maigret's investigation as

Maigret is in him. He knows more about Maigret's moves than Maigret does about his. "Ever since I began the investigation regarding the death of Oscar Chabut as he was leaving the brothel of Fortuny Street, a man seems to be interested in my every activity. He is intelligent because he seems to anticipate every movement I make" (144). The mysterious observer, it seems, is clever at slipping into a crowd once he knows he has been sighted and Maigret has not yet been able to meet up with him. Maigret is fairly sure, though he has no proof, that this is the culprit. Maigret is both pursuer and pursued.

The man calls Maigret on the telephone but always hangs up when Maigret suggests they should meet. "It was almost a game," comments the author/narrator, "that so far Pigou is winning" (149). Maigret's wife notices in him the discouragement that marks the second phase of his method (151). Maigret's mood continues to deteriorate (154). He understands what is happening without being able to do anything about it; the initiative is in the hands of the suspect, a man who has been humiliated all his life and now has become someone important, keeping at bay the whole police force of Paris. "This," says Maigret,"is why he hesitates between letting himself be caught and continuing to play at cat and mouse" (155). The way the suspect approaches only to draw back reminds Maigret of a squirrel he had played with years before who would get tantalizingly close only to scamper away just as it seemed they might make contact.

Finally, outside Maigret's apartment on the Boulevard Richard-Lenoir, the drama reaches its climactic moment. Gilbert Pigou appears across from the apartment, watching timidly like the squirrel. Asked by Madame Maigret if he thinks the man wants to come see him, Maigret responds: "He is tempted. I think he is afraid to be disappointed. A man like him is very vulnerable. He would like for someone to understand him and at the same time he tells himself it is impossible" (157). Finally, at 2:30 a.m., Pigou knocks at Maigret's door and Madame Maigret lets him in. Hesitant at first, like the squirrel ready to retreat at the first sign of danger, Pigou finally enters. Madame Maigret prepares two grogs. The two men begin to speak. Their dialogue is extraordinary for its human intimacy. "I expected you would come eventually," says Maigret. "Did you see me?" asks Pigou, making a tentative beginning of conversation. Given what we know about Pigou's character and his interest in seeking out Maigret, we can legitimately conclude that his question applies to more than physical seeing. Maigret's answer, which implies a "yes" to Pigou's question, affirms that Maigret did indeed see something beyond the physical form of the man watching his apartment. "I even sensed that you were hesitating. You advanced a step then left for the *Rue du Chemin Vert*" (164). Still more revealing is the response of Pigou: "As for me, I saw your silhouette at the window. Since I wasn't in the light

I didn't know if you were able see me and above all to recognize me" (164). To be seen, to be recognized—Pigou had not experienced this in his entire unfortunate, misdirected life and now before this police officer who has been tracking him down, he begins to hope. He isn't drawn to the police officer as such but to the "mender of destinies," the priest to whom one can confess everything without being judged.

The two men are ill at ease at first, avoiding the inevitable conversation about practical details like prison and trial. They observe each other. Maigret doesn't miss so much as a change of expression on his visitor's face. "In the intimacy of the apartment, a grog within reach of his hand, his pipe in his mouth, [Maigret] had the air of a benevolent older brother to whom one could tell everything" (165). Maigret is looking for Pigou as a criminal but even more as a human being who has lost his way. And Pigou is looking for Maigret, not in his role as detective, but in his role as doctor and priest, mender of destinies.

The Paradox of Maigret as Detective and Priest

If Maigret sometimes plays a priestly role, it is, as I have noted the role of priest as confessor and confidant. This role is not that different from "a benevolent older brother to whom one could tell everything." *Le Revolver de Maigret (Maigret's Revolver)* is even more explicit than *Maigret et le Marchand de Vins* in asserting this priestly role.

The story begins with the phone call from Madame Maigret telling her husband that a young man is in the apartment to see him. Maigret doesn't take the situation seriously and, as he often did, stops for a few minutes at the *Brasserie Dauphine* for a drink with a former colleague. By the time Maigret arrives home, the young man has departed, taking Maigret's revolver with him. Maigret's friend, Dr. Pardon, later tells him of a patient in desperate straits who would like to meet Maigret, Francois Lagrange who turns out to be the father of the boy who had stolen Maigret's revolver. The rest of the story is spent tracking down Francois Lagrange, who, it turns out, has murdered an important official, and pursuing the boy himself who has set out to murder the woman who is blackmailing his father. The father is arrested and Maigret's assistant Janvier goes through his apartment looking for clues. He discovers in a folder several articles on Maigret cut from newspapers. Lagrange has cut out articles that portray Maigret as the defender of the guilty. One of the articles calls Maigret a *bon enfant,* "good natured"; another is entitled, "The humanity of Maigret" (107). Lagrange has underlined the words "indulgence" and "comprehension." Another passage tells the story of a man condemned to death who had refused the ministry of a priest but asked if he could have

a final interview with Maigret (107). This theme of convicted criminals asking for Maigret as a priestly presence at the moment of death recurs in *Les
Memoires de Maigret*: "I could cite several [of these convicted criminals],"
says Maigret, "who have begged me to be present at their execution and have
reserved for me their final regard" (Simenon 1950, 151). All these articles
that Lagrange had saved explain why he wanted to meet Maigret.

Toward the end of the story, Maigret—in England where he has followed
the son Alain Lagrange, intent on killing the woman who was the real culprit—
finally enters the hotel room where he knows Alain is hiding. With exquisite
patience and a delicacy that perfectly exemplifies the characteristics described
in the collected newspaper stories of Francois Lagrange, Maigret waits. Here
Maigret is both detective and priest. He knows the young man is armed and
at the end of his wits, capable of doing anything. Maigret has an interest as a
detective in getting the young man to surrender the gun before he becomes a
criminal himself. But he uses a method supplied by his humanity rather than his
police training. He identifies with the young man: "At your age," says Maigret,
"in your condition, I might have done the same thing" (153). Maigret even
admits it was his fault; if he hadn't stopped for a drink he would have arrived
home before the young man left.

When the young man finally comes out from under the bed, he asks Maigret "Why are you doing all this?" "All what?" Maigret responds. "You know
what I mean," Alain replies. "Maybe," Maigret goes on, "it's because I was a
young man too. And because I had a father" (158). Later in the same chapter
Maigret becomes more explicit: "I lost my mother when I was very young
and my father raised me" (163). Maigret's ability to enter into the deepest
experience of those he is tracking, which leads often enough to the apprehen-
sion of the guilty person, in this case prevents a crime and puts on the right
path a young man who has lost his way.

Maigret's Virtues

The preceding review of the paradoxes of Maigret has revealed a set of
related virtues, humility, the ability to enter into the lives other people, a
determination to understand and not to judge, and, above all, compassion.
These are human virtues and Christian virtues. They are precisely the human
virtues Christ encouraged in the Gospels. Specifically, they are the attitudes
and habits Jesus taught in the famous Sermon on the Mount (Matt. 5–7),
including the beatitudes, and the Sermon on the Plain that includes Jesus'
admonition, "Stop judging and you will not be judged. Stop condemning and
you will not be condemned. Forgive and you will be forgiven" (Lk. 6:37).
One of Simenon's biographers, Lucille Becker, after noting in Simenon's

work "the repeated references to the Catholic atmosphere of his youth," comments on Simenon's and Maigret's refusal to judge others and its connection to Church teaching: "The maxim, '*comprendre sans juger* (to understand without judging), at the heart of Simenon's philosophy of life—expressed as Maigret's moral code—might seem to reflect the Church's understanding of and compassion for the sinner" (Becker, 8). Here, too, we find a paradox. The man who best embodied these virtues and served as a model for Maigret was Simenon's father, Désiré, the less religious but probably more Christian of his parents. Simenon's overtly religious mother, the one who saw that he served as an altar boy and attended Catholic schools, was notably lacking in compassion, particularly toward her husband. Her decision to take student boarders into the Simenon home as a way of supplementing her husband's meager earnings, effectively reduced Désiré to the status of an inmate whose needs became secondary to those of the paying boarders and awakened a deep resentment in Georges Simenon against his mother, even though he profited from the presence of the foreign students in the Simenon home, learned their language, and used them as the basis of characters in his novels (Bresler, 18–20; Assouline, 10–11). Henriette continued to complain to her husband about turning down a better job in another city and for not buying an insurance policy even though he was an insurance salesman. As it turned out, the insurance company had refused to sell a policy to Simenon's father because of his precarious health, a fact he hid from his wife. But instead of understanding she judged—that trait so foreign to both Simenon and Maigret—and harbored resentment.

If we want to uncover the roots of Maigret's virtues in the life of his creator, we need also to look beyond the model he found in his father and consider Simenon's early religious life. We have seen that he suddenly abandoned religion at the age of fifteen after learning that his beloved father was terminally ill. Simenon's discovery of sex at the age of twelve and his need, once awakened, for an active sexual life added motivation to renounce the Church whose strict sexual morality presented the young Simenon with an impossible burden. But Simenon did not, by his own admission, abandon certain aspects of the faith he had so fervently followed up until the age of fifteen. For he was not just an altar boy because his mother wanted it; he entered into the life represented by serving at the altar. Even when the Friar Superior of the *Institut St. André*, Bresler tells us, where Simenon was a student, forced him to lie about an incident he and his brother were involved in, "he remained firmly a believer, bending low before the Cross" (Bresler, 21). Simenon, again according to Bresler, had an intense interior life of which religious mysticism was a manifestation (21). Given a common characteristic of Simenon and Maigret, their "aptitude for living the lives of others and for immersing themselves in a milieu" (Assouline, 93), it is reasonable to suppose that the young Simenon entered deeply into the religious atmosphere of his first fifteen years.

And so we have an author, Simenon, and his principal fictional creation, Maigret, who, while not outwardly religious, manifest deeply Christian sensibilities. Augustine himself in the fifth century anticipated this distinction. In opposing the Donatists who demanded heroic adherence to the Christian faith, condemning those who had handed over the holy books to avoid persecution, Augustine affirmed a truth that seems to apply to Simenon. The Donatists had a rigid criterion for membership in the Church, perfect fidelity. For Augustine, it was not so easy to determine who was *inside* the Church and who was *outside.* "For in that unspeakable foreknowledge of God, many who seem to be without are actually within [the Church], and many who seem to be within, yet really are without" (Augustine 1979, IV. 27–38, 477, col. 2). Simenon's mother may have seemed to be squarely in the Church but her lack of compassion sets her outside. Simenon and, our principal concern here, Maigret, may seem to be outside, but their compassion brings them within the sphere of the Gospels' central teachings.

In chapter six (168–170) we considered the short treatise of Hugh of St. Victor (1096–1141) on the four wills of Christ in which he develops the idea of compassion as ideal humanity.[4] The Church had long since defined that Christ had both a divine and a human will. Hugh subdivided the human will into a rational will (*voluntas secundum rationem*), the will of the flesh, *(voluntas secundum carnem)*, and the will of tender pity (*voluntas secundum pietatem*). The rational will is that by which Christ followed the Father's plan for him, the will of the flesh is the resistance Christ instinctively felt at the thought of undergoing the passion, and the will of compassion or tender pity is Jesus' capacity to enter into the sufferings of other people. After Hugh has elaborated on this quality of compassion in Jesus, he promotes the idea of compassion as constituting the ideal of humanity for everyone. Maigret embodies the ideal. We have seen this compassion worked out in some detail in Maigret's attitude toward Little John in *Maigret à New York,* Pigou in *Maigret et le Marchand de Vins,* and Alain Lagrange in *Le Revolver de Maigret.* Maigret's compassion appears in some way in all of the novels discussed here. Compassion is a priestly quality, not as necessarily pertaining to the clergy but to that deeper sort of priesthood that belongs to all Christians, making them, ideally if not in fact, children of a merciful God following Jesus' admonition: "Be merciful, just as your Father is merciful" (Lk. 6:36). Compassion characterizes people of other religions, too, and many non-religious people—like Maigret—who come to it through the mysterious workings of their own inner lives. It sums up what is most appealing about Simenon's Maigret.

CONCLUSION

I have developed a view of Simenon's Maigret based on interconnected paradoxes that suggest Christian roots even though they appear in a secular guise. The first paradox is the Incarnation itself, which lies at the core of Christianity, reflected in Maigret's habit of entering the lives of those who inhabit the world he investigates. Another, related, paradox appears in Maigret's conception of his *vocation* as a detective, a vocation that is explicitly priestly.[5] Maigret is detective, "mender of destinies, and priest." He is all three at once—this is the paradox. Simenon develops this paradoxical vocation using further paradoxes: a method that is not a method, the hunter who is being hunted, and the policeman who is also a priest. I have argued that underneath all these particular paradoxes, lies another, the presence of Christian traits in a hero who does not profess Christianity, an unbelieving hero created by an author who stopped believing in God at age fifteen. One does not need to be a Christian to manifest the qualities that Simenon attributes to his hero, but the fact that both the author Simenon and his character Maigret began life as devout Christians in Catholic Belgium and France, suggests that perhaps a residue of their early piety might be traceable in Maigret's character and methodology. Simenon did recognize the profound effect of his early Christian education, "That education marks you for life, even if you stopped believing [as I have] all you were taught long ago" (Simenon 1970, vol. I, 125–6, cited in Becker 1999, 8).

Maigret's encounters with criminals makes one think at times of Jesus' encounters with sinners in the Gospel. Over and over again, the Pharisees accuse Jesus of eating and drinking with sinners. Just as Jesus regarded with contempt the righteousness of the religious establishment of his time, Maigret separates himself definitively from the judges and investigators whose work is motivated by a desire to protect privilege rather than a concern to find the truth, especially the deep human truth of people whose live have strayed from righteous paths.

René Girard's criterion for separating great literature from merely good literature is whether the author can see his characters from the perspective of their common humanity without raising his heros, alter egos, to a place of superiority over other humans. Girard came to this insight, as a kind of intellectual conversion, when he was working on the last chapter of his first book,

Deceit, Desire, and the Novel. He noticed that some great novelists moved from an earlier conception of their work to a later understanding. The first draft was "an attempt at self-justification" (Williams, 284) either focusing on "a wicked hero, who is really the writer's scapegoat, his mimetic rival" or "a knight in shining armor, with whom the writer identifies" (284). This first project fails somehow and the author realizes that "The self-justification he had intended in his distinction between good and evil will not stand self-examination. The novelist comes to realize that he has been the puppet of his own devil. He and his enemy are truly indistinguishable" (284). This realization is "shattering to the vanity and pride of the writer" (284). This experience, which Girard calls "an existential downfall," is often enough "written symbolically, as illness or death, in the conclusion" (284).

Whether Simenon moved from an earlier, more superficial conception of his work as a writer to a more profound understanding as described by Girard, I do not know. Perhaps a comparison of Simenon's 190 pre-Maigret novels, written under a variety of pseudonyms, with the Maigrets he wrote under his own name and his later even more serious novels, the so-called *roman durs* or hard novels, might provide some clues. Even as a student in the Jesuit high school in Liége, Simenon would sign his essays "Georges Sim," saying that only when he had written something worthy of his real name would he sign it (Bresler, 26). This suggests that Simenon himself saw in the post-1930 Maigrets, published under his own name, a form of literature significantly elevated above the earlier pseudonymous writings.[6] What that superiority consisted in could be the subject of another essay.

Whatever the history of his development as an author, it is evident that, in his character Maigret, Simenon has achieved a deeply human character who understands that he is no better and no worse than the people he is charged to investigate; therefore, he is able to enter their lives as a mender of destinies, detective, and priest at the same time.

NOTES

1. This scriptural quotation is from the New Revised Standard Version Bible: Catholic Edition, copyright © 1989, 1993 National Council of the Churches of Christ in the United States of America. Used by permission. All rights reserved worldwide.

2. Georges Simenon (1903–1989) was probably the most prolific author of the twentieth century. The exact number of his works is difficult to ascertain. According to one of his biographers, he wrote 573 works (Becker 1999, viii), among them the famous Maigret series. Becker lists 77 Maigrets in her bibliography, Patrick Marnham lists 76, but Jean Forest has published the names, characters, and plots of 107 Maigrets. Becker lists 114 *romans durs,* hard or serious novels, the category

that first won Simenon recognition as a serious novelist. Before the Maigrets and the *romans durs,* Simenon's career began with a series of 190 "potboilers" under various synonyms that earned him a large amount of money and prepared him for the more serious Maigrets most of which were published under his own name.

3. Michel Lemoine in his article "The method of investigation according to Maigret : A methodical absence of method? (http://www.trussel.com/maig/lemoine.htm) notes that this process of identification, though not present in all Maigrets is present in a significant number. In addition to the novels I have cited, Lemoine adds the following: M. Gallet, décédé [The Death of M. Gallet, Maigret Stonewalled], Un Crime en Hollande [A Crime in Holland], Le Port des brumes [Death of a Harbor Master], Le Fou de Bergerac [The Madman of Bergerac], Liberty-Bar, Cécile est morte [Maigret and the Spinster], La Maison du juge [Maigret in Exile], Signé Picpus [To Any Lengths, Maigret and the Fortuneteller], L'Inspecteur Cadavre [Maigret's Rival], Maigret et la Grande Perche [Maigret and the Burglar's Wife] or Maigret à Vichy [Maigret Takes the Waters, Maigret in Vichy], and Félicie est là [Maigret and the Toy Village] (1944) an investigation that drags Maigret to Orgeval and during which he has many opportunities to get into the skin of the victim, Jules Lapie, known as Peg-Leg: "Once on being asked to comment on Maigret's methods by a visiting criminologist, the Chief Commissioner of the Police Judiciare replied with an enigmatic smile: 'Maigret? How can I put it? He settles into a case as if it were a pair of comfortable slippers'" G. SIMENON, Félicie est là, t. XI, 314–316, 374 et 382. [Maigret and the Toy Village, Harvest/HBJ Ch. 2, 21–23; Ch. 5, 87; Ch.6, 96]

4. See the article "Hugh of St. Victor on 'Jesus Wept,'" by Boyd Taylor Coolman in *Theological Studies*, September 2008, 69 (No. 3)528–556.

5. Many mystery stories feature detectives who are actually ordained priests or ministers. One can find a list on the website, "Clerical Detectives and some other crime fiction, selected by Philip Gorsset": http://homepage.ntlworld.com/philipg /detectives/contents.html. Some of these stories are written by priests, come feature a priest or minister as the central character. The list is extensive, One of the best known is Chesterton's Father Brown; see G. K. Chesterton, *The Father Brown Omnibus,* Dodd Mead and Company, New York, 1943. To see how their priesthood influences the method of these detectives and to compare these influences with the priestly dimension of Maigret's method would be an interesting study.

6. Lucille Becker comments on Simenon's stature as a writer. Until the 1970s, after he had actually stopped writing novels, Simenon was, according to Becker "dismissed as an author of detective novels, a genre relegated to the status of paraliterature" (Becker, vii). Even though he had written more *roman durs* ("hard" or serious novels) than Maigrets, Simenon's fame rested more on the Maigrets, which had been translated into multiple languages and become the subject of about forty films. In 2003, the critical evaluation of Simenon's work changed when his home town of Liége in Belgium celebrated the centenary of his birth, an event which enabled him to take his place among the great writers of the modern era. "In May of 2003," says Becker, "Georges Simenon took his place in the pantheon of letters, alongside distinguished writers like Hemingway, Montaigne, Dostoevsky, and Proust, with the publication of 21 of his novels in two volumes of Gallimard's prestigious collection,

Bibliotheque de la Pleiade" (vii). Five of the 21 were Maigrets. So it seems that Simenon's Maigrets form part of the basis on which his reputation as a great writer rests. In Maigret, Simenon has created a character comparable to Victor Hugo's Jean Valjean or Balzac's Pere Goriot.

Conclusion

What conclusions emerge from this study that begins with the story of Adam and Eve in the Hebrew Testament and ends with the detective stories of George Simenon in the twentieth century? We have explored an alternative to a common way—perhaps the usual way—of assessing the relation between good and evil. So the emergent conclusions have to be set over against that alternative. The normal response to evil done against us is to blame, to judge, and to seek retribution or even vengeance. Self-blame and self-punishment offer an alternative response. The possibility of forgiveness also exists, of the other or of oneself. But forgiveness does not come easily to human beings. And so we need to look for the condition of the possibility of forgiveness. The chapters leading up to this conclusion have tried to establish that compassion is the condition that opens up the possibility of forgiveness and that the personal consciousness of a common vulnerability of the will, "original sin"—a vulnerability that each of us shares—can help move people toward compassion. Having stated the default response to evil and the alternative, we will need to review the alternative way chosen here to see if it is trustworthy. We will be a little like engineers testing the reliability of a highway or bridge or airplane we have built. Or like a painter standing back from a painting to see if it expresses the original inspiration. Augustine did something similar in the Reviews or *Retractrationes*, formulated at the end of his long writing career to set each work in its place and evaluate it. It is not a matter of verifying a proof but of reviewing a result to see if it meets expectations. Our review will involve a recapitulation of the three stages through which the study has progressed, a look at the alternative viewpoints offered by each of the texts examined, and a review of the hermeneutical principles that have been at work. We will then be in a position to see if it all comes together in a coherent view that can be expressed in a few conclusions.

Before beginning, we need to recall an important distinction implicit in the choice of texts that make up this study. The chapters of this book trace an outer and an inner journey. The outer journey consists in the written texts that set forth biblical narratives, theoretical arguments, and literary formulations. We find these texts in written forms that we can read and interpret. Sometimes we find references to texts that have been lost in their outward forms—like the *Hortensius* of Cicero that had such a profound effect in the development of Augustine of Hippo. And then we regret the loss of the outer form that we could enter ourselves. We have in these cases to satisfy ourselves with the inner transformation that someone like Augustine has recorded in his own writings. The inner journey refers to the consciousness that gives rise to written texts and to the transformation that occurs in those who read the texts. Without the inner dimensions the texts remain just words on a page. Some prior inner experience of what we are reading, some curiosity arising from that experience, and some consequent openness to what the author writes about conditions our appreciation of a serious work. Rudolf Otto puts the potential reader on the spot in the first pages of his work, *The Idea of the Holy*. If the notion "religious experience" suggests nothing recognizable in your own life, then don't waste your time reading this book. If we do have some idea of the subject matter from our own experience, then we can enter in and allow the text to expand, correct, confirm, and even transform what we already know.

This study has progressed through three phases. We began with the archetypal images, symbols, and narratives—mythical and historical—that have grounded the Christian tradition and given rise to various forms of commentary, reflection, and theory through which the tradition has developed. This first phase has included the Adamic Myth, a comparison of that myth with other myths of the origin and end of evil, a study of that myth as it appears in the book of Genesis where we now have access to it, and in the New Testament where it has been revived to serve as source of Christian thought and literature. Then, following Paul Ricoeur's hermeneutic principle, "the symbol gives rise to thought." We have considered theoretical reflections that interpret and give rational coherence to the generating symbols. This second phase includes the elaboration of the notion of original sin by Augustine of Hippo, medieval, Reformation, and modern formulations of Augustine's theories, the anthropological theory of René Girard, a summary chapter elaborating the connection between original sin and compassion. The third phase, inspired by a corollary hermeneutical principle according to which theory once formulated tends to clothe itself again in images, symbols, and narrative, has explored selected works of literature in the western canon, the medieval epic of Perceval, the mystically inspired narratives of Julian of Norwich, Shakespeare's *Measure for Measure*, and the twentieth century Maigret stories of Georges Simenon.

In addition to the hermeneutical theory, "the symbol gives rise to thought," and its corollary, "thought once formulated moves to clothe itself again in image, symbol, and narrative," several other fundamental principles of interpretation have been at work in the chapters of this work. Their significance is described in detail in the introduction. The first principle, at work in the early theological reflections of the Christian Church, contains a double truth. The first truth, explicitly formulated in the New Testament is that only God can forgive sin (Mk 2:7b). The second truth, formulated by Gregory of Nazianzen in his dispute with Apollinarius, affirms that Jesus healed human nature by taking it on as his own, "For that which he has not assumed he has not healed" (Nazianzen, 1978, 441).

How has this double principle been illustrated in the preceding chapters? Some examples will suffice to indicate the answer. The first of the two truths expressing this principle occur throughout the texts from the Hebrew Bible, the New Testament, the writings of the Fathers of the Church, including Augustine and throughout the literature examined in the principal authors treated in this study. Pelagius and his followers resisted the truth. Their resistance provoked the protracted dispute with Augustine that gave rise to his clear formulation of the doctrine of original sin. For the Pelagians, human failings were not radical enough to require a special salvific intervention by the Creator of human nature. In the act of creation itself, they maintained, God has given us everything we need to live a life of virtue. The second truth included in this principle that only God can save, belongs particularly to the New Covenant of Christianity. In this dispensation, the Incarnation of the Word of God in the humanity of Jesus of Nazareth is the foundation of human healing. Jesus Christ entered so deeply into our humanity that he even endured death on a cross. By rising, he overcame the sting of death and opened up the possibility of life for his followers. Interestingly, these two truths, only God saves and God only saves what he has taken on, play a role in the secular Commissaire Maigret of George Simenon. Maigret sometimes appears as a kind of "God the Father" (*La Pipe de Maigret*, for instance, 183). Even more striking is Maigret's entry into the lives of both victims and criminals. He becomes one of them, takes on their characteristics., and in this way solves crimes and sometimes becomes a "mender of destinies." "He had to become Little John" (see *Maigret à New York*, 148).

The second principle of interpretation at work in the preceding pages is Augustine's circular description of his own theological method, "I believe in order to understand; I understand in order to believe more fully" (Sermon 43, 7,9). This study has proceeded from a theological viewpoint, from a position of faith seeking understanding with the hope that understanding will deepen faith. Most of the authors included have begun in faith with the hope of deepening faith through understanding. I do not know if Shakespeare was a believer. He lived in a culture still pregnant with Christian themes and symbols. Certainly his *Measure for Measure* provides dramatic depth for a common set of Christian beliefs. Simenon clearly did not write from the perspective of faith. His character Maigret, also not a believer, has a particular value precisely because he manifested some of the deepest traits of Christian faith without a personal grounding in the tradition. Simenon seems to write these detective stories out of a deep humanity that coincides with most profound teachings of Christianity. Readers of this book may or may not begin from faith. The texts and themes might well appeal to believers and unbelievers because of their humanity and might serve as a corrective for certain superficial convictions about the nature of Christian faith.

The third principle, that liberating truths are revealed to the heart through conversion, finds ample manifestation in the chapters through which this exploration has progressed. The writings of Paul and Augustine focus on conversion. Perceval seems to experience the kind of transformation associated with conversion. Julian of Norwich speaks of extraordinary revelations that give evidence of special divine interventions. Even Angelo of *Measure for Measure* seems to melt before the incisive but gentle intervention of the Duke. Angelo confesses and awaits his sentence and the death that will follow; "That is all the grace I beg" (*Measure for Measure*, 5.1, 370–375). To speak of religious or moral conversion in the Maigret stories seems a stretch. But a character like Little John who has killed the only woman he ever loved out of jealousy, experiences a lightness of spirit after Maigret discovers the secret of John's eyes, "the pain that gave them their terrible coldness" (*Maigret in New York*, 183). And when Little John discovers the son that he thought he had lost he, redeems, in a very real sense, the "lost time" of which Proust wrote so eloquently. "Maigret may not have been an agent of conversion; he was a mender of destinies."

The fourth principle, that truth is revealed historically, underlies the choice of texts from the first chapters of the book of Genesis, the Middle Ages, the Renaissance, and the twenty-first century.

It will be helpful to review the contribution each part of the study has made to the whole beginning with the Adam and Eve narrative of Genesis and ending with Maigret before drawing a limited number of conclusions to be drawn from this study.

The Jahwist editor who placed the mythical account of Adam and Eve at the beginning of the Hebrew Bible must have had a sense of the incongruity of human life and wondered how it came about. How does it happen, for instance, that human beings are ashamed of their nakedness? Or why do people find it so hard to cultivate the earth and why is the earth so often stingy with its products? Why do men lord it over women and why do women continue to be attracted to men? And why do women endure agony to have their children? Why do humans find it so difficult maintain terms of intimacy with God who created them? The Jahwist took none of this for granted, as if it had always been and must always be. As if these difficulties and contradictions belonged to the essence of being human. The story of Adam and Eve, placed at the beginning of the Bible, gives an account of the origins of shame and hardship and struggle in the human being's relations with self, with other humans, and with God. The story also gives an account of the human situation before the rebel couple decided to take things into their own hands. "The man and his wife were both naked, yet they felt no shame" (Gen. 2:25). By implication, all the other hardships and distortions in human life did not trouble the first couple before their act of disobedience. God's surprise, for instance, at not seeing Adam and Eve "at the breezy time of the day" as he walked about in the garden suggests that usually they would have joined him. When they did not, God knew that they had eaten the forbidden fruit. The reduced condition came about partly as the intrinsic result of their acts, partly as divine punishment.

The Jahwist must also have had a sense of a divine compassion as counterpoint to the punishment divinely inflicted. For he includes God's tender gesture of making leather garments for the naked couple, the first manifestation of God's compassion. Seeing that they were ashamed by their nakedness, God personally clothed them. And God seems to indicate some kind of salvific intent in his declaration of the eternal enmity between serpent and the woman and her offspring. So the archetypal story of Adam and Eve sets in motion the dialectic of sin, and punishment, and compassion, and forgiveness.

In the chapters that have preceded, we have explored this dialectic as it has continued to develop in biblical narratives, theoretical speculations, and literary expressions. Sometimes we have seen variations on the story of Adam and Eve itself. Though the Hebrew Testament does not pursue the story of Adam and Eve significantly in its long history, the New Testament, especially the writings of Paul, revives the story and makes it central to the Christian faith. Paul accounts for both the condition that has come from the disobedience and the remedy in the compassionate grace and goodness of Jesus Christ. Paul enlarges the story by making of Christ the second Adam who reverses the consequences of the first Adam's disobedience. Augustine of Hippo in the fourth and fifth centuries picks up Paul's version of the story and develops an extensive theoretical elaboration, including the doctrine of original sin. Augustine's elaboration, like Paul's, entails a dialectic of punishment and compassion. Julian of Norwich received a series of sixteen mystical revelations that included a very original retelling of the story. For her the fall was the result of an accident not a punishment for disobedience. The consequence of the fall was that Adam could not get himself out of the ditch. Julian's vision involves a mystical identification of Adam's fall into the ditch and Jesus' descent into the womb of the Virgin Mary in such a way that the fall entailed its own reversal from the beginning.

Some chapters have focused more on the dialectics of sin and compassion, without direct reference to the story of Adam and Eve. The medieval story of Perceval, for instance, considers the consequences of the hero's failure to show compassion to his mother as he was leaving home. Had Perceval opened his heart through compassion, he would have been able to heal the wounded Fisher King and restore the kingdom to health. Shakespeare's play, *Measure for Measure*, shows the disruptive results of Angelo's rigid, unforgiving attitude during his interim rule of the city during the Duke's absence and the healing brought about by the compassionate Duke. George Simenon's compassionate detective, Maigret, employs compassion as a way of solving crimes. By entering into the lives of victims and perpetrators, he solves crimes and even becomes a "mender of destinies."

As a way of drawing these diverse accounts together, it will help to examine how each of them regards the wound under which humanity labors and the nature of the healing available. In the Genesis version of the myth of Adam and Eve, the wounds, as we have seen, are shame about nakedness, hardship in cultivating the earth and childbearing, and disruption of relationships. The healing comes through God's compassion and the promise of salvation in the future. For Paul, the wound afflicts the human will, which seems impotent to choose the good that it longs for and avoid the evil that it abhors. Healing comes about through the gracious intervention of Jesus Christ. "Who will save me from this body of death?" Paul asks and responds, "Thanks be to God through Jesus Christ our Lord. . . . Hence, now there is no condemnation for those who are in Christ Jesus" (Rom. 7:24b-8:1).

As we move into the realm of theory, we meet Augustine who continued Paul's focus on the servile will, describing in the *Confessions* his own struggle to avoid the evil habits that held him down like a chains and to choose the freedom he longed for, then systematically elaborating a theological anthropology of sin and grace. And for Augustine, as for Paul, redemption came through submission of the will to the grace of Christ. Chapter five examines classical and modern thinkers who have continued to explore the notion of original sin in their historical contexts. Chapter six elaborates in a systematic way the relations between compassion and forgiveness, focusing on the four intimacies wounded through sin and their restoration through the inner healing brought about by grace. Chapter seven presents René Girard's systematic elaboration of mimetic rivalry or covetousness and its consequences in the life of society.

Moving into the realm of literature, we considered the medieval poem, *Perceval*, which describes a twofold wound. First we see Perceval's wound, a mysterious inhibition about asking questions that would have led to the healing of the Fisher King and his kingdom. If he had but asked the questions about the dish containing a single host and the lance that bled carried before him in the Fisher King's palace, Perceval would have healed the king. But Perceval couldn't bring himself to ask, even though he was curious about what he saw. And the wound that would have been healed through his questions was the crippled condition of the Fisher King. Some interpret the King's crippled condition as a wound to his sexuality, which would be consistent with the story in Genesis and with Augustine's interpretation of it. Whatever the interpretation, the wound was curable through the posing of the saving questions about lance and grail. Julian of Norwich symbolizes the wound as Adam's inability to turn and see his master who could have rescued him from the ditch into which he had fallen. Julian generalizes Adam's inability to see his master as a human condition of despair about salvation, a chronic inability to access what is available for us in the loving mercy of God. And healing comes through that very mercy, which for Julian, accomplishes even the salvation of the most unrepentant sinner.

Shakespeare's *Measure for Measure*, locates the wound in the harshness of judgment that Jesus warns against in the Gospel of Matthew. "Stop judging, that you may not be judged. For as you judge, so will you be judged, and the measure by which you measure will be measured out to you" (Matt. 7:1–2). Angelo, the interim ruler of the city in the Duke's absence, presents a type of the harsh judge who is himself afflicted with the very vice against which his righteous judgment is directed. This tendency toward judgment lies in wait as a constant temptation for religious and morally upright people. The healing antidote, of course, is mercy, illustrated in Shakespeare's *Measure for Measure* in the wise and compassionate Duke who not only exposes Angelo's hypocrisy, but brings about a reconciliation of all the characters in the play.

Georges Simenon, probably the most secular of the authors we have considered, discerns, through the eyes of his character, Maigret—also a basically secular man—a variety of weaknesses afflicting the human condition. Maigret notes that many human beings never find their proper place in life, follow a path foreign to them. They are lost. And Maigret's vocation, as he saw it, was to be policeman, doctor, and priest who could see at first glance the destiny of the other person. He would be a mender of destinies. But not everyone is lost. Maigret saw a more universal weakness afflicting human beings, fear in its multiple forms, fear of water, of fire, of darkness, of making bad choices, of failing to take hold of our lives, of being betrayed. Maigret imagines these as "the notes of a muffled and tragic symphony: the hidden fears that one drags behind one, sharp fears that make one cry out in pain, fears that one dismisses once they have passed, fear of accidents, of sickness, of the police, of people, what they will say and the looks they give you as they pass (*The Patience of Maigret*, 128). And Maigret's healing method was to enter into the places in his characters where fear resides, in all the many forms it takes and in the consequences to which it gives rise, and let these cracks, or fissures, or weaknesses lead to the solution of crimes.

All these different ways of naming original sin have a certain validity. The important thing is to uncover and identify quite concretely the way original sin operates in ourselves as individuals and in our society. We might call this original sin fear (Simenon), anxiety (Kierkegaard), mimetic rivalry (Girard), alienation from the self (Proust), lack of confidence in God (Julian of Norwich), separation of mind and heart (Augustine), selfishness (Domning), discrimination based on male domination (feminist theologians), or any other kind of oppressive condition. Original sin under its many names manifests itself as a kind of polymorphous perversity, appearing in different guises but always working against the full development of human beings and their world.

All of these wounds can be taken as manifestations of the condition traditionally call original sin. What is important is that we come to recognize that all of us are afflicted. We are like the prototypical detective, Oedipus, King of Thebes, who set out to find the cause of the plague ravaging his city and found that it was he himself. We look for the speck in our neighbor's eye blinded by the beam in our own (Matt. 7:3–5). Throughout the preceding pages, I have argued that a conviction that original sin afflicts all human beings, including ourselves, tends to open us up to compassion for the weaknesses in others. And compassion tends to open us to forgiveness.

The question we spontaneously ask when we see evil done, especially to ourselves: "How could he (she, they) have done this?" inclines us to be unforgiving. If we can come to understand that they did what they did precisely because *they are like us*, we are more likely to be both sympathetic and forgiving. If we think of ourselves as needing to attend to the consequences of original sin in ourselves—whatever they might be concretely—before we set out to right the wrongs done around us and to us, we are more likely to end up as agents of reconciliation than perpetrators of division. Oedipus, having recognized his crimes and suffered exile, becomes a "defense . . . a bulwark stronger than many shields" (*Oedipus at Colonus*, 1724–25) for the city of his final rest, Athens. If we can accept that we belong to "a universal democracy of sinners" (Prudentius, cited in Jacobs 82), and are consequently divided selves, we open ourselves to healing and, once healed, to being healers ourselves. Following the prophetic advice of the Dutch Jewess Etty Hillesum, who died at Auschwitz, we are well-advised to try to destroy in ourselves what we think should be destroyed in the other (Hillesum 1996, 199).

But what about those who already begin life with a sense of inferiority? Those whom Suchocki and other feminists describe as "hiding," or Georges Bernanos near the end of his novel, The *Diary of a Country Priest*, describes as hating themselves? "It is easier than one thinks to hate (hair) oneself" (Bernanos 1936, 316).[1] Such people sometimes end up constructing grandiose imaginary structures to live in, as was the case for Xavier Marton in Simenon's *Maigret's Scrupules* (Simenon 1957) who grew up as a ward of an uncaring state and, as an adult, found his place in an imaginary world of electric trains. Some simply lead lives of quiet desperation. Are we to say to them that they should first destroy in themselves what they think should be destroyed in the other? That they should look for the beam in their own eye and forget about the speck in the others' eyes? And if we give the obvious answer, "no," does that limit the scope of compassion? I would say rather that compassion is wider in scope than we might have thought. It includes not only the other, but the self. The people of whom I have been speaking are more likely to be unfair in judging themselves than in judging others.

When Bernanos spoke of those who hate themselves, he included the formula for how, under the guidance of grace, we should love ourselves: "It is easier than one thinks to hate oneself. Grace is to forget oneself. But, if all pride were dead in us, the grace of all graces would be to love oneself humbly, as any of the suffering members of Jesus Christ" (Bernanos 1936, 316). Entering into such a life of grace requires conversion. Once we have entered the path of conversion, recognizing, through grace, the affliction common to all human beings, we can afford to be compassionate. And being compassionate, we can move bit by bit, again through grace and our own efforts, toward forgiveness, of others and of ourselves.

NOTE

1. I have cited this passage already at the end of the second chapter of this present work. That chapter elaborates the thought of Paul Ricoeur who cites the passage from Bernanos as the "warrant" for his book, *Oneself as Another*. See reference at the end of chapter one.

Bibliography

Alison, James. *The Joy of Being Wrong: Original Sin Through Easter Eyes*. New York: Herder and Herder, 1998.

Alszegy, Soltan and Maurice Flick. A personalistic view of original sin. *Theology Digest* 15 (1967):190–196.

———. An Evolutionary View of Original Sin. *Theology Digest*. 15 (1967):197–202.

———. Il peccato originale in prospettiva evoluzionistica, *Gregorianum*. 47 (1966):201–225.

———. Il peccato originali in prospettiva personalistica, *Gregorianum*. 46 (1965):705–732.

Anselm. *Basic Writings*.Translated by S. N. Deane. Chicago: Open Court Publishing Company, 1968.

Aristotle. *Metaphysics*. Translated by W. D. Ross in *Great Books of the Western World*. Chicago: Encyclopedia Brittanica, 1952.

Aquinas, Thomas. De Malo, [On Evil] from *Quaestiones Disputatae,* vol. 2. Turin and Rome: Marietti, 1949.

Augustine. *Answer to Julian*. 421. Translated by Roland Teske, S. J. *The Works of St. Augustine, a Translation for the 21st Century*. Part I, Books, vol. 24. Hyde Park, New York: New City Press, 1998.

———. *Answer to the Letter of Mani Known as The Foundation,* 396. Translated by Roland Teske. *The Works of St. Augustine, a Translation for the 21st Century*. Part I, Books, vol. 19. Hyde Park, New York: New City Press, 2006.

———. *Answer to the Two Letters of Pelagius,* 420–421. Translated by Roland Teske, S. J., *The Works of St. Augustine: A Translation for the 21st Century*. Part I, Books, vol. 24. Hyde Park, New York: New City Press, 1998.

———. *The City of God Against the Pagans*. 413–426. Translated by R. W. Dyson. Cambridge and New York: Cambridge University Press, 1998.

———. *Confessions*. Latin/English., Translation by William Watts. London: William Heinemann. Cambridge: Harvard University Press, 1950.

————. *The Confessions,* 397–400. Translated by R. S. Pine-Coffin. London: Penguin Books, 1961.

————. *The Deeds of Pelagius.* 417. Translated by Roland Teske, S. J. *The Works of St. Augustine: A Translation for the 21st Century.* Part I, Books, Vol. 23. Hyde Park, New York: New City Press, 1997.

————. *Interpretation of Psalm 118* (119), 421–22. Translated by Maria Boulding, O.S.B. *The Works of St. Augustine: A Translation for the 21st Century.* Part III, Books, Vol. 19. Hyde Park, New York: New City Press, 2003.

————. *The Grace of Christ and Original Sin,* 418. Translated by Roland Teske, S. J. *The Works of St. Augustine: A Translation for the 21st Century.* Part I, Books, Vol. 23. Hyde Park, New York: New City Press, 1997.

————. *Letter 10 (to Nebridius),* between 388 and 391. *The Works of St. Augustine, a Translation for the 21st Century.* Translated by Roland Teske. Part II, Letters, Vol. 1. Hyde Park, New York: New City Press, 2001.

————. *On Baptism Against the Donatists* (400–401 AD) from *A Select Library of the Niceneand Post-Nicene Fathers of the Christian Church,* Vol. IV, St. Augustine, The Writings Against the Manichaeans and Against the Donatists. Edited by Philip Schaff. Grand Rapids, Michigan: Eerdmans, 1979.

————. *On Christian Teaching,* 396–97. Translated with introduction, R. P. H. Green. New York, New York: Oxford University Press, 1997.

————. *On Marriage and Desire* 419–21. Translated by Roland Teske, S. J., *The Works ofAugustine: A Translation for the 21st Century,* Part I, Books, Vol. 24, Hyde Park: New City Press, 1998.

————. *On Nature and Grace* (*De Natura et Gratia*), *The Works of Saint Augustine: Translation for the 21. Century.* Translated by Roland J. Teske, S. J. Hyde Park, New York: New City Press, 1997.

————. *On the Gift of Perseverance,* 419–20. Translated by John A. Mourant and William Collinge. *Saint Augustine: Four Anti-Pelagian Writings. The Fathers of the Church, a New Translation.* Washington, D.C.: Catholic University of America Press, 1992.

————. *On the Harmony of the Evangelists,* 400. Edinburgh, 1873. Translated by The Rev. William Findlay, M. A., and The Rev. S. D. F. Salmond, M. A. Edinburgh: T & T Clark, 400 AD.

————. *On True Religion,* 389. Translated by Louis O. Mink, Philadelphia: Westminster Press, 1953.

————. *The Punishment and Forgiveness of Sins and the Baptism of Little Ones,* 412. Translated by Roland J. Teske, S. J. *The Works of St. Augustine: A Translation for the 21st Century,* Part I, Books, Vol. 19. Hyde Park: New City Press, 1997.

————. *Retractations,* 426–27. Translated by Sister Mary Inez Brogan, R. S. M., Ph.D. *The Fathers of the Church,* Vol. 60. Washington, D.C.: The Catholic University of America Press, 1968.

————. Sermon 26, 417. Translated by Edmund Hill, O.P. *The Works of St. Augustine: A Translation for the 21st Century,* Part III, Sermons, Vol. II, 20–50. Brooklyn, New York: New City Press, 1990.

———. *Sermons III/5.*, Translation and notes by Edmund Hill, O. P. from *The Works of Saint Augustine: A Translation for the 21st Century.* New Rochelle, New York: New City Press, 1992.

———. *The Spirit and the Letter,* 412. Translated by Roland Teske, S. J. *The Works of St. Augustine: A Translation for the 21st Century.* Part I, Books, Vol. 23. Hyde Park, New York: New City Press, 1997.

———. *To Simplician on Various Questions,* 396. Translated by J. H. S. Burleigh, *Augustine's Earlier Writings,* Philadelphia: The Westminster Press, 1943.

———. *The Trinity,* 399–419. Translated by Edmund Hill, O. P. *The Works of St. Augustine: A Translation for the 21st Century.* Part I, Books, Vol. 5, Hyde Park, New York: New City Press, 1991.

———. *Unfinished Work in Answer to Julian,* 429–430. Translated by Roland Teske, S. J., *The Works of St. Augustine: A Translation for the 21st Century.* Part I, Books, Vol. 25. Hyde Park, New York: New City Press, 1999.

Battenhouse, Roy W. 1946. "Measure for Measure and Christian Doctrine of the Atonement." *PMLA.* 61:(No. 4):1029–1059.

Bauckham, R. Revelation. *The Oxford Bible Commentary.* Edited by John Barton and John Muddiman. New York, Oxford University Press, 2001.

Bauerschmidt, Frederick Christian. *Julian of Norwich and the Mystical Body Politic of Christ.* Notre Dame: University of Notre Dame Press, 1999.

Becker, Lucille F. *Georges Simenon: Maigrets and the Romans Durs.* New York: Twane Publishers, 1999.

Bernanos, G. *Journal d'un Cure de Campagne.* Paris: Librarie de Plon.

———. *The Diary of a Country Priest.* Translation by Pamela Morris. New York: Carroll and Graf Publishers, 1936.

Bettenson, Henry. *Documents of the Christian Church.* Second edition. London: Oxford University Press, 1963.

Blocher, Henri. *Original Sin: Illuminating the Riddle.* Grand Rapids: William Eerdmans, 1997.

Bresler, Fenton. *The Mysteries of George Simenon: A Biography.* New York: Stein and Day Publishers, 1983.

Brooks, Cleanth. *Critical Essays on T. S. Eliot's* The Wasteland. Edited by Lois Cuddy and David Hirsch. Boston: G. K. Hall & Co., 1991.

Brown, P. *Augustine of Hippo: A Biography.* Berkeley and Los Angeles: University of California Press, 1967. [reprinted 2000]

Burleigh, J. H. S. *Augustine: Earlier Writings.* Philadelphia, The Westminster Press, 1953.

Burns, J. Patout. *The Development of Augustine's Doctrine of Operative Grace.* Paris: Etudes Augustiniennes, 1980, and 2011.

Byrne, B. *Romans,* Sacra Pagina Series. vol. 6. Collegeville, Minnesota: The Liturgical Press, 1996.

Chrétien de Troyes. *Perceval: The Story of the Grail.* Translated by Burton Raffel. New Haven: Yale University Press, 1999.

Clifford, Richard. Psalms, *The Collegeville Bible Commentary.* Collegeville, Minnesota: Liturgical Press, 1989.

Cline, Ruth Harwood. Introduction to *Perceval* or *the Story of the Grail*. Translated by Ruth Harwood Cline. Athens, Georgia: The University of Georgia Press, 1985.

Clines, David. *The Theme of the Pentateuch*. Sheffield, England: Sheffield Academic Press, 2001.

Collins, Adela Yarbro. Revelation, *New Jerusalem Bible Commentary*, 996–1016. Edited by Raymond E. Brown, S. S., Joseph A. Fitzmyer, S. J., Roland E. Murphy, O. Carm. Englewood Cliffs, New Jersey: Prentice Hall, 1990.

Coolman, B. Hugh of St. Victor on 'Jesus Wept': Compassion as Ideal Humanitas, *Theological Studies*, 69 (2008):528–556.

Cover, Robin C. Sin, Sinners (OT), *Anchor Bible Dictionary*. 6:31–40. New York: Doubleday, 1992.

Cox, John D. The Medieval Background of *Measure for Measure*. *Modern Philology*. 81 (1983):1–13.

Dahood, Mitchell. *Psalms, II, The Anchor Bible*. Garden City, New York: Doubleday, 1966.

Denziger, H. J. D. Prepared by Adolf Schönmetzer. *Enchiridion Symbolorum Definitionum et Declarationum de rebus fidei et morum*. New York: Herder, 1963.

Desmet, Christy. 2009. "*Measure for Measure*: A Modern Perspective," published in the Folger Shakespeare Library edition of *Measure for Measure*. New York: Simon and Schuster.

Domning, Daryl P. *Original Selfishness: Original Sin and Evil in the Light of Evolution*. Burlington, Vermont: Ashgate Publishing Company, 2006.

Dover, Kenneth J. Fathers, Sons, and Forgiveness. *Illinois Classical Studies*, 16 (1991):173–82.

Dubarle, A. M. *The Biblical Doctrine of Original Sin*. Translated by E. M. Stewart, New York: Herder and Herder, 1967.

Duffy, Eamon. *The Stripping of the Altars: Traditional Religion in England c.1400–c.1580*. New Haven: Yale University Press, 1992.

Eliot, T. S. *The Complete Poems and Plays*. New York: Harcourt Brace, 1952.

Ely, P. The Adamic Myth in the Christian Idea of Salvation: An Exploration. *URAM Journal*, 28 (2005):127–48.

———. Forgiveness in Christianity. *Ultimate Reality and Meaning*, 27 (2004):108–26.

———. Revisiting Paul Ricoeur on the Symbolism of Evil: A Theological Retrieval. *URAM Journal*, 24 (no. 1):40–64. Toronto: University of Toronto Press, 2001.

Endo, S. *Deep River*. New York: New Directions, 1994.

Epiphanius, Bishop of Cyprus. *Patrologiae Graecae*, vol. 43. Turnholti, Belgium: Typographi Brepols Editores Pontificii, 1959.

Evans, R. *Pelagius: Inquiries and Reappraisals*. New York: The Seabury Press, 1968.

Farley, W. *Tragic Vision and Divine Compassion: A Contemporary Theodicy*. Louisville: Westminster/John Knox Press, 1990.

Fishbane, Michael. *Text and Texture: Close Readings of Selected Biblical Texts*. New York: Schocken Books, 1979.

Fitzgerald, F. Scott. *Crack-Up*. New York: New Directions, 1993.

Flick, Maurice. Original Sin and Evolution, Part I, The Problem. The Tablet, September 10 (1966), 1008–1010.

———. Original Sin and Evolution, Part II, The Solution. *The Tablet*, September 17 (1966), 1039–1041.

Forest, Jean. *Les Archives Maigret.* Montreal: Les Presses de l'Universite de Montreal, 1994

Forster, E. M. *Aspects of the Novel.* Hammondsworth: Penguin, 1962.

Fowler, David. *Prowess and Charity in the Perceval of Chrétien de Troyes.* Seattle: University of Washington Press, 1959.

Franklin, E. Luke, *The Oxford Bible Commentary.* Edited by John Barton and John Muddiman. New York: Oxford University Press, 2001.

Frappier, Jean. *Chrétien de Troyes et le Mythe du Graal.,* Paris: Société d'Enseignement Supérieur, 1979.

Frend, W. H. C. *The Donatist Church: A Movement of Protest in Roman North Africa.* London: Oxford at the Clarendon Press, 1971.

Friedman, Richard Elliott. *The Disappearance of God.* Boston: Little, Brown and Company, 1995.

Girard, R. *Des choses caches depuis la fondation du monde,* Paris: Editions Grasset et Fasquelle, 1978.

———. *Deceit, Desire, and the Novel.* Baltimore: Johns Hopkins, 1966.

———. *I See Satan Fall Like Lightning.* New York: Orbis, Novalis, Gracewing, 2001.

———. *Je vois Satan tomber comme l'éclair.* Paris: Editions Grasset et Fasquelle, 1999.

———. *Mensonge romantique et vérité Romanesque.* Paris: Editions Bernard Grasset. 1961.

———. *Oedipus Unbound.* Edited by Mark Anspach. Stanford: Stanford University, 2004.

———. Proust: *A Collection of Critical Essays.* Edited by René Girard. Westport Connecticut: Greenwood Press, 1962.

———. *Quand ces choses commenceront . . . Entretiens avec Michel Treguer,* Paris: Arlea, 1994

———. *Things Hidden Since the Foundation of the World,* London: Athlone Press and Stanford: Stanford University, 1987.

———. *Violence and the Sacred.* Baltimore: Johns Hopkins University, 1977.

———. *La violence et le sacre.* Paris: Editions Bernard Grasset, 1972.

Green, J. *Moira.* Paris: Librairie Plon, 1950.

Greenblatt, S. *The Rise and Fall of Adam and Eve.* New York, London: W. W. Norton and Company, 2017.

Gregory of Nazianzen. To Cledonius the Priest Against Apollinarius. *The Nicene and Post-Nicene Fathers.* Second Series. 7 (1978.): 439–443.

Grey, Mary. 'And All Shall Be Well'—Julian's Theology of Hope in an Age of Violence. 29th Annual Julian Lecture. Published by the Friends of Julian Norwich, 2009.

Hahn, Lewis Edwin. *The Philosophy of Paul Ricoeur.* Chicago: Open Court Press, 1995.

Heidigger, Martin. *Introduction to Metaphysics.* New Haven, Connecticut: Yale University, 2000.

Heim, S. Mark. *Saved from Sacrifice: A Theology of the Cross.* Grand Rapids: Eerdmans, 2006.

Herion, Gary. Wrath of God, *Anchor Bible Dictionary.* 6 (1992):991. New York: Doubleday.

Hillers, Delbert R. *Covenant: The History of a Biblical Idea.* Baltimore: John Hopkins, 1982. (originally published, 1969).

Hillesum, Etty. *An Interrupted Life.* New York: Henry Holt and Company, 1981.

Hilton, Walter. *The Scale of Perfection.* Translated from Middle English with an introduction and notes by John P. H. Clark and Rosemary Dorward. Preface by Janel Mueller. New York and Mahwah: Paulist Press, 1991.

Hugh of St. Victor. On the Four Wills of Christ (*De Quatuor Voluntatibus in Christo Libellus*). J. P. Migne, *Patrologiae,* 176 (1996):841–46.

Ignatius of Loyola. *Spiritual Exercises.* Translated by Louis J. Puhl, S. J. Westminister, Maryland: Newman Press,1960

———. *St. Ignatius' Own Story as Told to Luis Gonzalez de Camara.* Translated by William J. Young, S. J. Chicago: Loyola University Press, 1956

Ilibagiza, Immaculée. *Left to Tell.* New York: Hay House, 2006.

Irenaeus of Lyon . *Five Books of S. Irenaeus Against Heresies,* translated by The Rev. John Keble, M. A., Oxford. James Parker and Co.; Rivingtons, London, Oxford, and Cambridge, 1872.

Jacobs, A. *Original Sin: A Cultural History.* New York: Harper Collins Publishers, 2008.

Jantzen, Grace. M. *Julian of Norwich: Mystic and Theologian.* Mahwah: Paulist Press, 1988.

John Paul II. Message of his Holiness, Pope John Paul II for the Celebration of the World Day of Peace. 1 January, 2002. Vatican Website.

———. Message to the Pontifical Academy of Sciences, October 22, 1996. Vatican Website.

Johnson, Elizabeth. *She Who Is: The Mystery of God in Feminist Theological Discourse.* New York: Crossroad Press, 1996.

Johnson, Robert A. *He: Understanding Masculine Psychology.* New York: Harper and Row, 1974.

Leigh, David. *Circuitous Journeys: Modern Spiritual Autobiography.* New York: Fordham University Press.

Lutheran World Federation and Roman Catholic Church. *Joint Declaration on the Doctrine of Justification.*Grand Rapids, Michigan: Eerdmans, 1999. see also [http://www.vatican.va/roman_curia/pontifical_councils/chrstuni/documents/rc_pc_chrstuni]

Jackson, Russell and Robert Smallwood (eds.). *Further Essays in Shakespearean Performance with the Royal Shakespeare Company.* Cambridge: Cambridge University Press, 1989.

Jones, L. Gregory. *Embodying Forgiveness: A Theological Analysis.* Grand Rapids, Michigan: William Eerdman, 1995.

Julian, John. *Love's Trinity: A Companion to Julian of Norwich.* Collegeville: Liturgical Press, 2009 (translation of and commentary on the Long Text).

Julian of Norwich. *Julian of Norwich: Revelations of Divine Love.* Translated by Elizabeth Spearing. London: Penguin, 1998.

Julian of Norwich. *Showings.* Translated and introduced by Edmund Colledge, O. S. A. and James Walsh, S. J. Preface by Jean Leclerq, O. S. B. Mahwah, New Jersey: Paulist Press.

Kasper, Walter Cardinal. *Mercy: The Essence of the Gospel and the Key to Christian Life.* Mahwah: Paulist Press, 2013.

Karris, R. The Gospel According to Luke, *The New Jerome Biblical Commentary.* 675–721. Englewood Cliffs, New Jersey: Prentice Hall, 1990.

Kierkegaard, S. *The Concept of Anxiety.* Translated by Reidar Thomte in collaboration with Albert B. Anderson. Princeton, New Jersey: Princeton University Press, 1980.

———. *The Sickness Unto Death.* 1954. Translated by Walter Lowrie, New York: Doubleday Anchor. (148)

Knight, G. Wilson. *Measure for Measure* and the Gospels. *The Wheel of Fire.* 4th Edition, London: Methuen and Co., 1949 [New York: Signet. Reprinted in the 1964 Signet edition of *Measure for Measure,* 157–185].

Kolb, Robert, and Timothy Wengert, eds. *The Book of Concord.* Minneapolis: Fortress Press, 2000.

Kselman, John and Michael Barre. Psalms, *The New Jerome Biblical Commentary.* Englewood Cliffs, New Jersey: Prentice Hall, 1990.

Lancel, S. *St. Augustine.* Translated by Antonia Nevill. London: SCM Press, 2002.

Le Petit, Robert. *Dictionnaire Alphabetique & Analogique de la Langue Francaise* (no. 1) Paris, 1985.

Lonergan, B. *Method in Theology.* New York: Herder and Herder, 1974.

———. *Method in Theology.* New York: Herder and Herder, 1972.

———. *De Verbo Incarnato.* Rome: Gregorian University, 1961 [Original 1960; second edition: 1961, text unchanged].

Markus, Robert A. *Conversion and Disenchantment in Augustine's Spiritual Career.* The Saint Augustine Lecture (1984). Villanova, Pennsylvania: Villanova University Press, 1989.

Marnham, Patrick. *The Man Who Wasn't Maigret.* New York: Farrar, Straus, Giroux, 1992.

Massey, Daniel. The Duke in *Measure for Measure,* reprinted in the Norton Critical Edition of *Measure for Measure,* 200–16, from *Players of Shakespeare 2, 2010.*

May, Gerald. *Addiction and Grace: Love and Spirituality in the Healing of Addictions.* San Francisco: Harper, 1998.

———. *Addiction and Grace: Love and Spirituality in the Healing of Addictions.* New York: Harper Collins. 1991. (Harper One).

———. *Addiction and Grace: Love and Spirituality in the Healing of Addictions.* San Francisco: Harper, 1988.

McClory, R. Parish Turns Murder to Grace. *National Catholic Reporter*, November 7, 1997.

McGilchrist, I. *The Master and his Emissary: The Divided Brain and the Making of the Western World.* New Haven: Yale University Press, 2009.

Mendenhall, George and Gary Herion. Covenant. *Anchor Bible Dictionary.* 3 (1992):1179–1202. New York: Doubleday.

Merivale, Patricia and Susan Elizabeth Sweeny, eds. *Detecting Texts: The Metaphysical Detective Story from Poe to Postmodernism.* Philadelphia: University of Pennsylvania Press, 1999.

Murdoch, Brian. *Adam's Grace: Fall and Redemption in Medieval Literature.* Cambridge, England: D. S. Brewer, 2000.

Muscadine, Charles. The Emergence of the Psychological Allegory in Old French Romance. Publications of the Modern Language Association of America. 68 (1953):1160–82.

Neuner, J. and J. Depuis. *The Christian Faith: Doctrinal Documents of the Catholic Church.* New York: Alba House, 1990.

———. *The Christian Faith in the Doctrinal Developments of the Church.* New York: Alba House, 1982.

New American Bible. Revised Edition. Washington, D.C: Confraternity of Christian Doctrine, 2010, 1991, 1986, 1970.

Newman, Cardinal John Henry. *An Essay on the Development of Christian Doctrine.* Garden City, New York: Image Books, 1960.

———. *Apologia Pro Vita Sua: Being a History of his Religious Opinions.* London: Longmans Green and Company, 1924.

New Revised Standard Version Bible: Catholic Edition. National Council of the Churches of Christ in the United States of America, 1989, 1993.

Nickelsburg, G. The Son of Man, *The Anchor Bible Dictionary*, volume 6. 1992.

Noth, Martin. *A History of Pentateuchal Traditions.* Translated with an introduction by Bernhard W. Anderson, Englewood Cliffs, New Jersey: Prentice Hall, 1972.

Nussbaum, Martha. Equity and Mercy. *Philosophy and Public Affairs.* 22 (1993):83–125.

Olschki, Leonardo. *The Grail Castle and its Mysteries.* Translated by J. S. Scott. Edited by Eugène Vandever. Manchester, England: Manchester University Press, 1966.

O'Meara, John. Introduction to The City of God. New York: Penguin Books, 1984 [translated by Henry Bettenson, 1972].

Pagels, E. *Adam and Eve, and the Serpent.* New York: Vintage Books, 1988.

———. The Politics of Paradise: Augustine's Exegesis of Genesis 1–3 versus that of John Chrysostom, *Harvard Theological Review,* 78(1985):1–2.

Piscitelli, E. Paul Ricoeur's Philosophy of Religious Symbol: A Critique and Dialectical Transposition. *Ultimate Reality and Meaning* 3 (1980): 275–313.

Pope Francis. *The Name of God is Mercy.* With A. Tornelli. New York: Random House, 2016.

Proust, Marcel. *Du Coté de chez Swann.* Vol I of *À la Recherche du Temps Perdu.* Paris: Gallimard, 1988.

————. *In Search of Lost Time.* Paris: Grasset. 1912–1927.

————. Letter of Proust to Henry Gheon. 1914. Published at the end of Proust, 1988, *Du Coté dechez Swann.*

————. *Le Temps Retrouvé.* Paris: Gallimard, 1989.

Quasten, J. *Patrology,Vol. 3, The Golden Age of Greek Patristic Literature from the Council of Nicea to the Council of Chalcedon.* Utrecht: Spectrum Publishers, 1960.

Reuther, Rosemary Radford. *Gaia and God: An Ecofeminist Theology of Earth Healing.* San Francisco: HarperSanFrancisco, 1992.

————. *Sexism and God: Toward a Feminist Theology.* Boston: Beacon Press, 1983.

Ricoeur, P. *The Conflict of Interpretations: Essays in Hermeneutics.* Evanston: Northwestern University Press, 1974.

————. *Fallible Man.* Chicago: Henry Regnery, 1965.

————. *Freedom and Nature: The Voluntary and the Involuntary.* Evanston: Northwestern University Press, 1966.

————. *Freud and Philosophy: An Essay on Interpretation.* New Haven: Yale University Press, 1970.

————. *Lectures on Ideology and Utopia.* Edited and Introduced by G. H. Taylor. New York: Columbia University Press, 1986.

————. *Oneself as Another.* Chicago: University of Chicago Press, 1992.

————. *The Rule of Metaphor.* Toronto: University of Toronto Press, 1978.

————. *The Symbolism of Evil.* Translated by Emerson Buchanan. Boston: Beacon Press, 1967.

————. *The Symbolism of Evil.* New York-Evanston-London: Harper and Row, 1967.

————. *Time and Narrative. Volume I.* Chicago: University of Chicago Press, 1984.

————. *Time and Narrative. Volume II.* Chicago: University of Chicago Press, 1985.

————. *Time and Narrative. Volume III.* Chicago: University of Chicago Press, 1988.

Riefer Poulson, Marcia. "'Instruments of Some More Mightier Member': The Constriction of Female Power in *Measure for Measure*," originally published in *Shakespeare Quarterly* 1984. 35:157–69, reprinted in the 1988 Signet Classic edition of Shakespeare's *Measure for Measure*, 153–154.

Sanders, E. P. Sin, Sinners, The New Testament, *The Anchor Bible Dictionary.* New York: Doubleday, 1992.

Schimmel, S. *Wounds Not Healed by Time: The Power of Repentance and Forgiveness.* Oxford: Oxford University Press, 2002.

Schoonenberg, Piet, S. J. *Man and Sin.* Translated by Joseph Donceel, S. J. South Bend: University of Notre Dame Press, 1965.

Schussler-Fiorenza, Elizabeth. *Bread not Stone: The Challenge of Feminist Biblical Interpretation.* Boston: Beacon Press, 1984.

Shakespeare, W. *Measure for Measure.* ed., S. Nagarajan. New York, Signet. 1988.

Shogren, Gary S. Forgiveness in the New Testament. *The Anchor Bible Dictionary.* Vol. 2. New York: Doubleday, 1992.

Simenon, Georges. *L'Affaire Saint-Fiacre.* Paris: Fayard, 1932.

————. *Le Charretier de la Providence* Paris: Fayard, 1931.

————. *Le Chien Jaune.* Paris: Presses Pocket, 1931.

————. *Un Crime en Hollande,* Paris : Presses Pocket, 1931.

————. *Maigret à New York.* Paris: Presses de la Cité, 1946.

————. *Maigret et le Client du Samedi.* Paris: Presses de la Cité, 1962.

————. *Maigret et le Corps Sans Tête.* Paris: Presses de la Cité, 1955.

————. *Maigret et l'Homme sur Banc.* Paris: Presses de la Cité, 1952.

————. *Maigret et la Vielle Dame.* Paris: Presses de la Cité, 1950.

————. *Maigret et le Marchand de Vins.* Paris: Presses de la Cité, 1969.

————. *Maigret et le Tueur.* Paris: Presses de la Cité, 1969.

————. *Maigret et son Mort.* Paris: Presses de la Cité, 1948.

————. *Maigret Hésite.* Paris: Presses de la Cité, 1968.

————. *Maigret S'Amuse.* Paris: Presses de la Cité, 1956.

————. *Maigret se Defend.* Paris: Presses de la Cité, 1964.

————. *Les Mémoires de Maigret.* Paris: Presses de la Cité, 1950.

————. *La Patience de Maigret.* Paris: Presses de la Cité, 1965.

————. *Pieter le Letton.* Paris: Fayard, 1931.

————. *La Première Enquête de Maigret,* U. G. E. Poche. Paris: Presses de la Cité, 1948.

————. *Quand J'étais Vieux.* Paris: Presses de la Cité, 1970.

————. *Le Revolver de Maigret.* Paris: Presses de la Cité, 1952.

————. *Les Scrupules de Maigret.* Paris: Presses de la Cité. Paris, 1957.

————. *La Tête d'un Homme.* Paris: Fayard, 1931.

Sophocles. *The Three Theban Plays: Antigone, Oedipus the King, Oedipus at Colonus.* Translated by Robert Fagles. New York: Penguin Classics, 1984.

Spearing, A. C. Introduction, *Julian of Norwich: Revelations of Divine Love.* London: Penguin, 1998.

Stöger. A. The Gospel According to Luke, *New Testament for Spiritual Reading,* vol. 5, Edited by John L. McKenzie, S. J., New York, New York: Crossroad Publishing, 1981.

Suchocki, Marjorie Hewitt. *The Fall to Violence: Original Sin in Relational Theology.* New York: Continuum, 1995.

Symons, Julian. *Mortal Consequences.* New York: Schoken Books, 1972.

Teske, Roland, S.J., General Introduction to *Answer to the Pelagians IV: To the Monks of Hadrumetum and Provence,* The Works of Saint Augustine: A Translation for the 21st Century. Vol. 26. New York: New City Press, 1999.

————. Introduction to Augustine's The Punishment and Forgiveness of Sins and the Baptism of Little Ones, *The Works of Saint Augustine: A Translation for the 21st Century.* Vol. 23. New York: New City Press, 1997.

Thrall, W. F., and A. Hibbard. *A Handbook to Literature.* New York: Odyssey, 1960.

Topel, J., *Children of a Compassionate God.* Collegeville, Minnesota: Liturgical Press, 2001.

Tutu, Desmond. *No Future without Forgiveness.* New York: Doubleday, 1999.

Voiss, J. *Rethinking Christian Forgiveness: Theological, Philosophical, and Psychological Explorations,* Collegeville: MN: A Michael Glazier Book Published by Liturgical Press, 2015.

Von Rad, Gerhard. *Genesis, A Commentary.* Translated by John H. Marks. Philadelphia: The Westminster Press, 1961.

Watson, Nicholas. The Composition of Julian of Norwich's *Revelation of Divine Love, Speculum,* 68(1993):637–83.

Westerman, Claus. *Arten der Erzahlung in der Genesis.* Munich: Chr. Kaiser, 1961.

Weston, Jessie L. *From Ritual to Romance.* Cambridge, England: Cambridge University Press, 1920.

Wiesenthal, S. *The Sunflower: On the Possibilities and Limits of Forgiveness.* New York: Schoken Books, 1997.

Wilken, R. L. *The Spirit of Early Christian Thought: Seeking the Face of God.* New Haven: Yale University Press, 2003.

Wiley, Tatha. *Original Sin: Origins, Developments, Contemporary Meanings.* New York: Paulist Press, 2002.

Williams, James G. *The Girard Reader.* Epilogue: The Anthropology of the Cross: A Conversation with René Girard. New York: Herder and Herder, 2007.

———. *The Girard Reader.* New York: Crossroads Publishing, 1996.

Worthington, Everett. The Forgiveness Teacher's Toughest Test of Pyramid of Forgiveness, *Spirituality and Health.* 1(2) (1900): 30–31 [Cited in Schimmel 2002, 100.]

Zehr, Howard. *Changing Lenses: A New Focus for Crime and Justice.* Scottsdale, Pennsylvania: Herald Press, 2005.

Index

Abraham, 36, 38, 62, 65–66, 72–74, 85, 92, 93, 100, 180; as model for justification by faith, 55, 86–87

Adam and Eve, 1, 5, 8, 55, 73, 78, 108, 307, 310, 311, 312; in the context of covenant, 61; creation-uncreation theme, 64–66; in primeval history, 58–59, 61, 62, 81; sin-speech-mitigation-punishment theme, 61–64; spread of sin, spread of grace theme, 64

Adamic Myth, 15, 16, 17, 34–42, 52, 165, 166, 167, 308; as covenant, 66, 72; not historical, 35; in Paul, 36; in Paul's Letter to the Romans, 85–92; primacy of among Ricoeur's four myths, 46; related to Christian forgiveness, 51

Alison, James, 5, 7

Alszeghy and Flick: personalism and evolution, 153–56

Aquinas, 19, 147–49, 156, 160–61, 164, 253; original sin according to Aristotle's four causes, 142–44; original sin, final cause of 144, 163; original sin, material, formal, efficient causes of, 143, 158, 163

Augustine, 78, 107–37, 225, 262, 290, 308, 309, 311–13, 314;

Adam and Eve, 130, 131, 139; addiction, 133–34; the Church, 128, 130; City of God, 18, 116–18, 130–31; compassion, 107, 109, 118, 119, 120–22, 124, 126–28, 134; Confessions, 120; contemplation, 119, 122; conversion of, 118, 119, 122, 123, 129, 132, 134, 173, 245; on conversion, 126, 310; counsel of compassion, 120; delight, importance of, 132–33; doctor of grace, 107; Donatists, 123, 125–28; evil, 124, 125; on forgiveness, 114, 128, 129; free will, 117–18, 124; on freedom, 130, 131, 135; on grace, 18, 107, 108, 109, 110, 112, 113, 114, 115, 117, 118, 119, 121, 122, 126, 128, 129, 131, 132, 136n2, 136n6; grace in relation to the law, 129; interiority, 135; Julian of Eclanum, 119, 123, 125; logic of grace, 122–23; Manichees, 118, 119, 123, 124, 125, 130, 132, 135; memory, 135; Monica, 134; original sin, 107, 109, 117, 118, 128, 131, 139; original sin as origination, 122, 133; original sin as separation of thought and feeling, 132; Pelagians, 109, 114, 115–16, 118, 123–24,